PRAISE FOR *CONSUMER BEHAVIOUR*

"Jean-Eric Pelet's *Consumer Behaviour* offers an essential insight into how digitalization is reshaping consumer psychology and decision-making. As an expert in the field, I can attest to the book's clarity and relevance, making it an indispensable resource for both scholars and practitioners."
Said Ettis, Assistant Professor, University of Jeddah College of Business, Kingdom of Saudi Arabia

"Jean-Eric Pelet has written a game-changing textbook that combines rigorous academic theory with practical case studies. *Consumer Behaviour* is a valuable tool for students and professionals eager to excel in today's digital economy."
Basma Taieb, Associate Professor, EMLV - École de Management Léonard de Vinci, France

"This textbook is a testament to Jean-Eric Pelet's expertise in digital consumer behaviour. His ability to demystify complex concepts with real-world examples makes this book an essential guide for understanding today's competitive landscape."
Rami Alkhudary, Assistant Professor, Université Paris-Panthéon-Assas, France

"Jean-Eric Pelet's textbook provides a profound understanding of how technology and consumer behaviour intersect. It's a comprehensive and engaging resource that will resonate with students and professionals alike."
Erhard Lick, Associate Professor, ESCE International Business School, France

"With *Consumer Behaviour*, Jean-Eric Pelet has delivered an exceptional textbook that reflects his deep knowledge of the field. This is an invaluable resource for those who aim to excel in the digital marketplace."
Mathias Naudin, Université Paris Cité, France

"Jean-Eric Pelet's latest book is an outstanding contribution to the study of consumer behaviour. Combining theory with practical insights, it is an indispensable tool for navigating the challenges of digital marketing."
Stéphane Fauvy, Associate Professor, ESSCA School of Management, France

"Jean-Eric Pelet's *Consumer Behaviour* is an outstanding resource for understanding how digitalization is reshaping consumer psychology. It's a must-read for anyone serious about excelling in this dynamic field."
Gilles Trigano, IAE de Nantes, France

"This book is a comprehensive and insightful exploration of digital consumer behaviour. Jean-Eric Pelet's ability to integrate theory with practice makes it a valuable resource for academics and practitioners alike."
Nic Terblanche, Emeritus Professor and Research Fellow, Department of Business Management, Stellenbosch University, South Africa

"Jean-Eric Pelet has written a textbook that sets a new standard in the field of consumer behaviour. His engaging and insightful approach makes it a cornerstone for anyone seeking to understand the digital consumer."
Dr Maria Mercanti-Guérin, Senior Lecturer, IAE De Paris, France

Consumer Behaviour

Understanding consumers
in a digital landscape

Jean-Eric Pelet

Publisher's note

Every possible effort has been made to ensure that the information contained in this book is accurate at the time of going to press, and the publishers and authors cannot accept responsibility for any errors or omissions, however caused. No responsibility for loss or damage occasioned to any person acting, or refraining from action, as a result of the material in this publication can be accepted by the editor, the publisher or the author.

First published in Great Britain and the United States in 2025 by Kogan Page Limited

All rights reserved. No part of this publication may be reproduced, stored or transmitted by any means without prior written permission from Kogan Page, except as permitted under applicable copyright laws.

Kogan Page
Kogan Page Ltd, 2nd Floor, 45 Gee Street, London EC1V 3RS, United Kingdom
Kogan Page Inc, 8 W 38th Street, Suite 90, New York, NY 10018, USA
www.koganpage.com

EU Representative (GPSR)
Authorised Rep Compliance Ltd, Ground Floor, 71 Lower Baggot Street, Dublin D02 P593, Ireland
www.arccompliance.com

Kogan Page books are printed on paper from sustainable forests.

© Jean-Eric Pelet, 2025

The moral rights of the author have been asserted.

All trademarks, service marks, and company names are the property of their respective owners.

ISBNs

Hardback	978 1 3986 1864 0
Paperback	978 1 3986 1861 9
Ebook	978 1 3986 1862 6

British Library Cataloguing-in-Publication Data

A CIP record for this book is available from the British Library.

Library of Congress Cataloging-in-Publication Data

2025931359

Typeset by Integra Software Services, Pondicherry
Print production managed by Jellyfish
Printed and bound by CPI Group (UK) Ltd, Croydon, CR0 4YY

CONTENTS

Outline ix
Foreword xii
Preface xiv

Introduction 1

1   **Understanding consumer behaviour in the digital age** 11
Introduction 13
The evolution of consumer behaviour 13
Sensory stimulation through connected objects 16
Navigating the IoT landscape in the service industry 17
Sensory marketing and human–computer interaction 23
Augmented reality: a 'still in progress' technology 23
Print media: crafting narratives in ink 26
The impact of technology on consumer behaviour 30
E-commerce and online shopping: a new way to consume 33
The influence of social media on consumer decision making 34
Conclusion 35
Summary 35
Key terms 36
Key learning points 37

2   **The new era of consumer needs and motivations** 38
Introduction 39
Changing consumer needs in the digital world 40
Shifts in consumer demographics 42
Evolution of the World Wide Web: from Web 1.0 to Web3 43
The impact of digital technology on consumer needs 46
The influence of personalization on consumer motivations 47
User experience in m-commerce 56
The role of sustainability in consumer decision-making 57
Conclusion 60
Key terms 60
Key learning points 61

3   Psychological and social dynamics in digital consumer behaviour 62

Introduction 64
The power of online reviews and ratings 64
Exploring virtual reality and augmented reality in consumer perception 68
Consumer reception and adoption of VR/AR 78
Prospects of VR/AR in retail 78
The dynamics of influencer marketing in shaping consumer perceptions 79
Conclusion 82
Key terms 82
Key learning points 83

4   The science of digital learning and memory 84

Introduction 86
The role of artificial intelligence in personalized learning 87
Creative and cultural industries in the era of AI 87
How AI customizes consumer learning experiences 89
Enhancing consumer memory through gamification 94
Understanding the impact of personalized recommendations on consumer behaviour 98
Personalization and privacy concerns 100
Conclusion 101
Key terms 102
Key learning points 102

5   Building brand loyalty in the digital age 104

Introduction 106
The power of brand advocacy and user-generated content 106
Leveraging social media for building brand communities 112
Strategies for creating emotional connections with consumers 118
Measuring emotional connection 122
Conclusion 124
Key terms 124
Key learning points 125

6   The digital consumer decision-making process 126

Introduction 128
The influence of big data on consumer decision-making 128
Consumer behaviour and emerging technologies 134

Understanding the role of chatbots and virtual assistants in consumer decision-making 141
Blockchain and consumer trust 144
The impact of user experience design 145
Consumer behaviour and sustainable innovation: a transformative approach 149
Conclusion 151
Key terms 152
Key learning points 152

7   Advancing consumer experiences in the digital world 154
Introduction 155
The role of augmented reality in retail experiences 156
Strategies for creating seamless omnichannel experiences 163
Voice commerce 167
Conclusion 172
Key terms 173
Key learning points 173

8   The power of online communities and social influence 175
Introduction 177
The impact of online communities on consumer behaviour 177
The multidevice consumer journey 186
The psychology of social influence in consumer decision-making 187
Effective social media strategies for increasing engagement 196
Conclusion 198
Key terms 199
Key learning points 200

9   Ethical considerations in the digital consumer landscape 202
Introduction 204
Addressing privacy and data security concerns in the digital world 204
Digitization of route management 212
How brands can address privacy concerns 216
Promoting ethical marketing practices in the age of personalization 219
The role of corporate social responsibility in influencing consumer behaviour 224
Conclusion 226
Key terms 227
Key learning points 227

10 The future of consumer behaviour in the digital era 229
Introduction 230
Emerging technologies and their impact on consumer behaviour 231
Quantum computing and consumer behaviour: a new frontier 238
The rise of voice commerce and Internet of Things in consumer decision-making 240
Anticipating and adapting to changing consumer behaviour trends 245
Conclusion 255
Key terms 256
Key learning points 257

References 258
Glossary 301
Index 318

OUTLINE

The landscape of consumer behaviour is undergoing a profound transformation in the digital age, where individuals navigate a vast array of digital channels and engage with products, services and content through the prism of the internet, mobile applications and various digital platforms. This paradigm shift has given rise to a discernible consumer segment – the digital consumer – characterized by distinctive behaviours, preferences and consumption patterns intricately shaped by the digital environment.

In the realm of digital marketing, the relentless evolution of consumer behaviour, coupled with technological advancements, necessitates a contemporary re-evaluation of established frameworks. While the foundational principles of the traditional marketing mix, encapsulated in the 4Ps – Product, Price, Place and Promotion – remain pertinent, their application in the dynamic digital landscape demands nuanced adaptation (Knight and Vorster, 2023).

This book embarks on a scholarly exploration to elucidate the revitalization of the 4Ps within the context of digital marketing. Through a meticulous examination of consumer behaviour, technological trends and marketing strategies, each chapter delves into multifaceted aspects of the digital consumer journey, offering profound insights and pragmatic approaches.

Unveiling the digital learning mind: AI, gamification and personalization

The foundational chapter (Chapter 1) initiates an exploration into the evolution of consumer behaviour from the traditional pre-digital age to the contemporary digital era. Subdivided into sections, it meticulously dissects traditional consumer behaviour, the transformative impact of the digital revolution and the nuanced aspects of the modern consumer's behaviour shaped by technology, including the role of the internet, mobile devices and the influence of social media on decision-making processes.

In Chapter 2, the focus shifts to the evolving landscape of consumer needs and motivations in the digital realm. The chapter examines changing demographics, the profound influence of digital technology on consumer needs and emerging trends in the era of e-commerce. Further, the chapter delves into the intricate relationship between personalization and consumer motivations, drawing insights from data analytics, and explores the growing influence of sustainability on shaping consumer decisions.

The third chapter delves into the intricate psychological and social dynamics that underpin digital consumer behaviour. Divided into sections, it scrutinizes the influential role of online reviews and ratings, investigating their impact on consumer purchase decisions. The chapter then extends its exploration into the realm of virtual reality and augmented reality, elucidating their role in shaping consumer perception. It concludes with a comprehensive examination of influencer marketing, addressing its ascent, impact and ethical considerations.

Chapter 4 takes a scholarly dive into the science of digital learning and memory. The sections within this chapter dissect the role of artificial intelligence in personalized learning, highlighting how AI customizes consumer learning experiences and its impact on information retention. Further, it explores the gamification of learning experiences, drawing insights from successful case studies, and probes the impact of personalized recommendations on consumer behaviour, addressing concerns related to privacy.

Chapter 5 is dedicated to elucidating strategies for building brand loyalty amidst the digital consumer landscape. Sectioned content explores the power of brand advocacy and user-generated content, emphasizing the importance of engagement. It further delves into leveraging social media to foster brand communities, dissecting the role of social media in community engagement and offering case studies of successful brand communities. The chapter concludes by unravelling strategies for creating emotional connections with consumers, underscoring the significance of emotional branding.

The sixth chapter rigorously examines the digital consumer decision-making process, with sections dedicated to the influence of big data on consumer decisions, the role of chatbots and virtual assistants, and the impact of user experience design. Each section carefully dissects emerging trends and technologies, providing a comprehensive understanding of their effects on consumer behaviour and ethical considerations.

Chapter 7 envisions the future of consumer experiences in the digital realm. Sections delve into the role of augmented reality in retail experiences, strategies for creating seamless omnichannel experiences, and the evolution of voice commerce. Each subsection provides an in-depth analysis, incorporating case studies and predictions for the future.

The eighth chapter is dedicated to exploring the power of online communities and social influence. Sections define online communities and their influence, unravel the psychology of social influence in the digital age and offer effective strategies for brands to leverage social influence. The comprehensive examination extends to strategies for increasing engagement through social influence.

In Chapter 9, ethical considerations take centre stage. Subsections address privacy and data security concerns, delve into ethical marketing practices in the age of personalization and explore the role of corporate social responsibility in influencing consumer behaviour. Case studies are presented to illustrate the consequences of data security breaches and the lessons learned.

The concluding chapter (Chapter 10) peers into the future of consumer behaviour in the digital era. Sections provide an overview of emerging technologies and their impact on consumer behaviour, including AI, machine learning and blockchain. The chapter further explores the rise of voice commerce and the Internet of Things, predicting future trends and offering strategies for anticipating and adapting to changes in consumer behaviour.

Collectively, these ten chapters constitute a comprehensive academic inquiry into the multifaceted dimensions of digital consumer behaviour, providing readers with a rich tapestry of insights, theories and practical applications in the ever-evolving digital landscape.

Keywords that are defined in the Glossary appear in **bold** in the text.

This book serves as a valuable resource for academics, researchers, marketers and professionals seeking to navigate the complex terrain of digital consumer behaviour, offering a nuanced perspective on the multifaceted interplay between consumers, technology and marketing strategies. As we embark on this academic journey, we invite readers to delve into the depths of consumer behaviour in the digital era, exploring its nuances and implications for the future.

Reference

Knight, H. & Vorster, L. (2023). *Digital Marketing in Practice: Design, implement and measure effective campaigns*. Kogan Page.

FOREWORD

In an era where technology is reshaping every aspect of our lives, understanding consumer behaviour has become more complex yet more essential than ever. My name is Bonnie Canziani. I am a professor and researcher with a long-standing focus on consumer behaviour, hospitality management and digital marketing. Throughout my career, I have witnessed firsthand how the integration of technology with consumer experiences has transformed industries, particularly in sectors like hospitality, wine tourism and e-commerce. This background gives me a unique perspective on why this book, *Consumer Behaviour*, by Jean-Eric Pelet, is both timely and essential reading for marketers, business leaders and scholars alike.

I first met Jean-Eric Pelet during our mutual presentation of research related to consumer behaviour in the wine industry. From the start, I was struck by not only Jean-Eric's deep understanding of the psychological nuances that drive consumer decision-making but also his mastery of digital interfaces and design elements that can make or break the online user experience. His passion for dissecting how colour schemes, website design and user interfaces affect consumer trust and behaviour was truly inspiring. Over time, it became clear that his insights extended beyond theoretical research and had real-world implications for improving digital consumer experiences. His expertise in applying these concepts to real-world scenarios has earned him acclaim in both academic and business communities.

Working with Jean-Eric, I have come to appreciate his unique ability to blend academic rigour with practical applications. His academic research has been published in numerous international journals and his insights have helped businesses around the world understand the complexities of consumer engagement in the digital era. This book, *Consumer Behaviour*, takes the reader on a journey through the complexities of how modern technologies – ranging from social media and AI to virtual and augmented reality – are reshaping the ways in which consumers interact with brands. Whether you are a marketing professional or a business leader, you will find valuable insights in Jean-Eric's exploration of how emerging technologies are influencing everything from purchase decisions to brand loyalty.

Jean-Eric is the perfect author for this book because of his deep-rooted knowledge of digital marketing, e-commerce and user experience design. His years of research in these areas, combined with his forward-thinking approach to technology, make him an authoritative figure in understanding how digital trends impact consumer behaviour. The book is packed with real-world examples, practical strategies and examples that show how companies can harness these technologies to stay ahead of consumer trends. At the same time, and my favourite aspect, this book addresses the moral responsibilities businesses face in this new age – how to balance personalization with privacy, how to foster loyalty in a world where consumers have endless options, and how to build trust in a time when ethical considerations such as sustainability and corporate social responsibility are no longer optional but demanded.

As you dive into *Consumer Behaviour*, you will find yourself equipped with the tools to better understand your customers and anticipate their needs in an increasingly digital world. This book offers actionable strategies and fresh perspectives that can help any organization stay competitive in today's fast-paced, tech-driven marketplace. I am honoured to write this foreword and confident that this book will leave a lasting impact on how you approach consumer behaviour in the digital age.

Bonnie Canziani
Professor Emerita and Researcher in Consumer Behaviour, Digital Marketing and Hospitality Management

PREFACE

The future of consumer behaviour in the digital era

In this book, we explore the evolving landscape of consumer behaviour in the digital age. As technology continues to advance, consumer preferences and purchasing habits are shifting dramatically. This analysis delves into the key trends shaping the future of consumer behaviour, including the impact of social media, personalization and the rise of e-commerce, while also considering the implications for businesses and marketers.

Introduction

The digital era has transformed the way consumers interact with brands and make purchasing decisions. With the proliferation of smartphones, social media and online shopping platforms, consumers are more informed and empowered than ever before. Understanding these changes is crucial for businesses aiming to thrive in this competitive environment.

Key trends influencing consumer behaviour

1. The rise of e-commerce

E-commerce has seen exponential growth, particularly accelerated by the Covid-19 pandemic. Consumers are increasingly opting for online shopping due to its convenience and the wide variety of options available. Businesses must adapt their strategies to enhance the online shopping experience, focusing on user-friendly interfaces and efficient delivery systems.

2. Personalization

Consumers now expect personalized experiences tailored to their preferences and behaviours. Data analytics and AI technologies enable brands to offer customized recommendations, targeted advertisements and personalized communication. This trend not only enhances customer satisfaction, it also fosters brand loyalty.

3. Social media influence

Social media platforms play a pivotal role in shaping consumer opinions and behaviours. Influencer marketing has become a powerful tool for brands to reach their target audiences. Consumers often rely on social proof from peers and influencers when making purchasing decisions, making it essential for brands to cultivate a strong social media presence.

4. Sustainability and ethical consumption

Today's consumers are increasingly conscious of the environmental and social impact of their purchases. Brands that prioritize sustainability and ethical practices are more likely to attract and retain customers. Transparency in sourcing and production processes is becoming a key factor in consumer decision-making.

5. Mobile shopping

With the rise of mobile technology, consumers are increasingly using their smartphones to shop. Mobile-optimized websites and apps are essential for capturing this audience. Features such as mobile payment options and location-based services enhance the shopping experience and drive sales.

Implications for businesses

To succeed in the digital era, businesses must adapt to these evolving consumer behaviours. This includes investing in technology to enhance the online shopping experience, leveraging data for personalization and maintaining an active presence on social media. Additionally, companies should prioritize sustainability and ethical practices to align with consumer values.

Conclusion

The future of consumer behaviour in the digital era will be characterized by rapid change and increased expectations. Businesses that embrace these trends and adapt their strategies accordingly will be well positioned to thrive in this dynamic landscape. By understanding and responding to the evolving needs of consumers, brands can build lasting relationships and drive growth in the years to come.

Introduction

> **CHAPTER OUTLINE**
>
> Introduction to digital consumer behaviour.
>
> Revitalizing the marketing mix for digital consumers.
>
> Planning a digital marketing strategy.
>
> Strategic planning in digital marketing.
>
> Categorization of business models in the digital economy.

A digital consumer refers to an individual who engages in the consumption of goods, services or content primarily through digital channels, such as the internet, mobile applications and digital platforms. This consumer segment exhibits distinctive behaviours, preferences and consumption patterns shaped by the digital environment, including online shopping, social media interaction and reliance on digital technologies for information acquisition and decision-making processes.

Revitalizing the 4Ps: adapting traditional marketing principles for the digital landscape

In the realm of digital marketing, the evolution of consumer behaviour and technological advancements necessitates a contemporary re-evaluation of the traditional marketing mix framework. The foundational principles of the 4Ps – Product, Price, Place and Promotion – remain relevant, yet their application in the digital landscape requires nuanced adaptation (Knight and Vorster, 2023). This adaptation is essential to effectively engage with and capitalize on the opportunities presented by the digital consumer base. Drawing from scholarly insights, let's elucidate how the 4Ps can be revitalized within the context of digital marketing:

- Product: Tailoring digital products or services to meet the specific needs of online consumers, incorporating features and online user experience considerations. For instance, as suggested by Liang and Turban (2011), digital products may need to emphasize factors such as usability, interactivity and customization to enhance consumer satisfaction and engagement in online environments.

- Price: Implementing dynamic pricing strategies based on real-time data, consumer preferences and online market conditions. Research by Ratchford et al. (2003) highlights the importance of leveraging digital data and analytics to adjust pricing strategies dynamically, maximizing profitability and competitiveness in online markets.
- Place (distribution): Utilizing efficient digital distribution channels such as websites, online marketplaces, social media platforms and mobile applications to reach consumers effectively. According to Chaffey et al. (2019), digital distribution channels offer unparallelled reach and accessibility, enabling businesses to expand their market reach and facilitate seamless transactions in the digital space.
- Promotion: Implementing targeted digital marketing campaigns, including content marketing, search engine optimization (SEO), search engine advertising (SEA), social media marketing and influencer marketing, to increase brand visibility and drive online consumer engagement. Research by De Vries et al. (2012) underscores the effectiveness of personalized and contextually relevant digital promotions in capturing consumer attention and fostering brand loyalty in the digital age.

REFLECTIVE QUESTION

How can businesses effectively balance the integration of traditional marketing principles with emerging digital tools to create a seamless and engaging experience for digital consumers? What challenges might arise in maintaining this balance?

FURTHER DISCUSSION

In light of the digital implications, understanding the nuances of digital consumer behaviour becomes paramount for businesses aiming to thrive in the digital marketplace. By recognizing the distinctive behaviours, preferences and consumption patterns of digital consumers, organizations can strategically tailor their marketing efforts to effectively engage with this segment. Moreover, embracing technological advancements and leveraging digital tools and analytics enable businesses to optimize their marketing mix strategies, ensuring relevance, competitiveness and resonance with the digital consumer base. Ultimately, the adaptation of traditional marketing principles for the digital landscape not only facilitates enhanced consumer experiences but also unlocks opportunities for sustainable growth and success in an increasingly digital-centric world.

Planning a digital marketing strategy

Overview of benefits

Crafting a comprehensive digital marketing strategy offers numerous advantages in navigating the dynamic landscape of digital consumer behaviour. By strategically planning your approach, you position your brand to not only enhance its visibility and engagement but also cultivate enduring relationships with your digital audience. Here's a brief outline of the overarching benefits:

- Consumer-centric approach: Tailoring your strategy to the needs, preferences and experiences of digital consumers ensures relevance and resonance, driving sustained engagement and loyalty.
- Informed decision-making: Conducting thorough consumer research and analysis provides invaluable insights, empowering informed decision-making and targeted marketing efforts.
- Clear objectives and goals: Setting clear, measurable objectives allows for focused efforts aimed at specific outcomes, be it improving user experience, boosting conversions or broadening market reach.
- Personalized targeting: Segmenting your audience and crafting detailed buyer personas enable personalized and precisely targeted marketing initiatives, maximizing relevance and effectiveness.
- Content excellence: A well-defined content strategy spanning various formats and channels enables the delivery of informative, engaging and valuable content to digital consumers, fostering trust and credibility.
- Enhanced user experience: Prioritizing user experience across digital touchpoints ensures seamless navigation, intuitive design and swift loading times, enhancing user satisfaction and engagement.
- Multichannel integration: Implementing an integrated multichannel marketing approach enables reaching digital consumers across diverse platforms and devices, providing consistent and unified brand experiences.
- Data-driven optimization: Leveraging data analytics and performance metrics facilitates monitoring of effectiveness, identification of improvement areas and optimization for maximal impact.
- Agility and adaptability: Continuous evaluation and refinement foster agility and adaptability, allowing swift responses to evolving consumer behaviours, market trends and technological shifts, ensuring ongoing relevance and efficacy.

In essence, a meticulously crafted digital marketing strategy not only amplifies brand visibility and engagement but also fosters meaningful interactions, nurturing enduring connections with your digital audience.

Planning the strategy

Planning a digital marketing strategy with the aim of targeting the digital consumer involves a comprehensive approach that prioritizes consumer needs, preferences, and experiences. In order to do so, a structured framework for developing such a strategy is necessary:

- Consumer research and analysis, as a starter. Begin by conducting thorough research to understand the digital consumer landscape. Utilize market research, data analytics and consumer insights to identify key demographics, behaviours, pain points and preferences of your target audience (Hollensen, 2020). This foundation will inform the rest of your strategy.
- Set clear objectives to follow. Define specific and measurable goals aligned with assisting digital consumers. Whether it's improving **user experience**, enhancing product **accessibility** or providing valuable content, ensure your objectives are tailored to address consumer needs and add value to their digital interactions (Chaffey and Smith, 2022).
- Segmentation and targeting. Segment your audience based on relevant criteria such as demographics, psychographics and online behaviour. Develop detailed **buyer personas** to represent different segments of your target audience, allowing for more personalized and targeted marketing efforts (Ryan, 2020).
- Content strategy and creation. Develop a content strategy that focuses on delivering informative, engaging and valuable content to digital consumers. Leverage various content formats and channels, including scenes on metaverses, blogs, videos, social media and email marketing, to provide relevant information, address consumer concerns and build trust and credibility (Strauss and Frost, 2020).
- Optimized **User Experience (UX)** and **Customer Experience (CX)**. Prioritize user experience across all digital touchpoints to ensure seamless navigation, intuitive design and fast loading times. Conduct usability testing, analyse user feedback and continuously optimize website and app interfaces to enhance user satisfaction and engagement (Chaffey et al., 2019).
- **Multichannel integration**, to appear everywhere. Implement an integrated multichannel marketing approach to reach digital consumers across various platforms and devices. Coordinate messaging, branding and promotions across channels such as social media, search engines, email and mobile apps to provide consistent and cohesive brand experiences (Chaffey and Smith, 2022).
- Data-driven optimization is mandatory. Utilize data analytics and performance metrics to monitor the effectiveness of your digital marketing efforts. Measure key performance indicators (KPIs) such as website traffic, conversion rates and

customer engagement metrics and use these insights to refine and optimize your strategy over time (Hollensen, 2020).
- Continuous evaluation and improvement. Regularly evaluate the performance of your digital marketing initiatives and iterate based on insights and feedback. Stay agile and adaptive, responding to changing consumer behaviours, market trends and technological advancements to ensure your strategy remains effective and relevant (Smith and Chaffey, 2021).

Strategic planning: definition

Strategic planning is a systematic and iterative process undertaken by organizations to establish long-term objectives, formulate strategies, allocate resources and make decisions that guide the organization toward achieving its mission and vision. It involves the analysis of internal and external environments, identification of strengths, weaknesses, opportunities and threats (SWOT analysis), setting clear goals and priorities and developing action plans to achieve desired outcomes. Strategic planning serves as a framework for aligning organizational activities, fostering coordination and collaboration across departments and facilitating adaptive responses to changing internal and external conditions in pursuit of sustainable competitive advantage and organizational success.

Strategic planning plays a crucial role in understanding digital consumer behaviour within an academic context for several reasons:

- It ensures alignment between business objectives and efforts to understand digital consumer behaviour.
  - Establishing clear goals and objectives allows organizations to direct research and analysis toward gaining insights directly relevant to their strategic priorities (Chaffey and Smith, 2022).
- It helps focus research efforts by identifying specific questions or areas of enquiry relevant to strategic objectives.
  - Digital consumer behaviour encompasses various aspects such as online browsing habits, purchasing preferences and engagement patterns (Hollensen, 2020).
- It enables effective allocation of resources by prioritizing research initiatives likely to yield actionable insights for informing marketing strategies and tactics.
  - Understanding digital consumer behaviour often requires investment in resources such as market research, data analytics tools and expertise (Ryan, 2020).

- It informs strategic decision-making processes across marketing aspects like product development, pricing strategies, distribution channels and promotional activities.
    - Strategy planning ensures decision-makers have access to timely and relevant consumer insights (Frost and Strauss, 2016).
- It helps organizations stay ahead in the competitive digital landscape by continuously monitoring and analysing digital consumer behaviour.
    - Anticipating needs and preferences provides a competitive advantage (Chaffey and Smith, 2022).
- It fosters adaptability by providing a framework for ongoing monitoring, analysis and adjustment in response to evolving consumer behaviour patterns.
    - Digital consumer behaviour is subject to rapid and continuous change due to technological advancements and market dynamics (Smith and Chaffey, 2021).
- It includes considerations of ethical guidelines and best practices to ensure research and analysis are conducted ethically and responsibly.
    - Ethical considerations involve data privacy, consumer consent and responsible use of consumer data (Hollensen, 2020).

In conclusion, strategic planning is essential for understanding digital consumer behaviour as it provides a structured approach to research, resource allocation, decision-making and adaptation in the dynamic digital landscape. By systematically planning their approach, organizations can gain valuable insights informing effective marketing strategies and fostering competitive advantage in the digital marketplace.

Categorization of business models

In a digital context, business models refer to the framework through which a company generates revenue and sustains profitability in the digital economy. Several common business models have emerged in the digital realm:

- E-commerce: Selling products or services directly to consumers through online platforms or digital marketplaces.
- Subscription-based: Offering access to products, services or content in exchange for a recurring subscription fee, providing ongoing value and convenience to customers.
- Freemium: Providing basic features or services for free while offering premium or advanced features for a fee, allowing customers to upgrade based on their needs or preferences.

- Advertising-based: Generating revenue through displaying advertisements to users, leveraging user data and engagement metrics to attract advertisers and monetize digital content or platforms.
- Affiliate marketing: Earning commissions by promoting and selling third-party products or services through affiliate links or referral programmes, leveraging digital channels such as websites, blogs and social media.
- SaaS (software as a service): Delivering software applications or solutions over the internet on a subscription basis, providing customers with access to software functionality without the need for up-front investment in hardware or infrastructure.
- Marketplace/Platform: Facilitating transactions between buyers and sellers or connecting service providers with customers, charging fees or commissions for transactions conducted on the platform.
- Live streaming commerce (LSC) or social commerce: Integrating social media platforms and online commerce to facilitate consumer engagement, product discovery and purchase transactions within a social context.

LIVE SHOPPING DYNAMICS AND ADOPTION FACTORS

While live shopping has gained immense popularity in China, it remains relatively unknown in France. This paradox prompts an exploration into the phenomenon and an inquiry into the perceptions of French consumers. The section aims to understand the extent to which live shopping sessions converge or differ in terms of entertainment, social interaction, flow and value provided compared with traditional e-commerce practices. The primary goal is to identify the determinants influencing the adoption of live shopping.

This emerging form of purchasing eliminates the frictions of the buying process, such as travelling during specified time slots, creating a more appealing journey for the consumer and presenting new opportunities for brands to generate interest among consumers. Introduced as early as 2012 in China, live streaming commerce has experienced unprecedented growth in this country since 2017 (FEVAD, 2022). Globally, LSC generated approximately $728 billion in revenue in 2022. With an expected compound annual growth rate (CAGR) of 31.6 per cent between 2023 and 2030, revenues in this segment are projected to reach around $6.2 trillion by 2030 (Statista, 2022). Although already highly popular in markets like China, LSC remains relatively modest elsewhere. In 2021, $37 billion of goods and services were purchased through LSC channels. By 2025, this figure was expected to reach nearly $80 billion, accounting for 5 per cent of total e-commerce in the United States

(Statista, 2023). Globally, the LSC market was projected to exceed $2 trillion by 2025. Due to policy differences, cultural contexts and consumer purchasing habits in each country, LSC struggles to gain traction and expand in Europe, with limited awareness and a narrow range of products sold via live streaming (Li and Nabec, 2023). In France, the share of LSC remains low due to cultural differences with the country of its origin, China. Thus, usage remains relatively rare, with approximately 14 per cent of the French population familiar with this sales method (Gaillard, 2023).

In China, the tradition of orality favours this type of sale, with the seller acting as a market vendor during an LSC session. On a technical level, there is a significant difference between the two countries. In China, there is a ubiquitous social network to which every consumer is constantly connected, WeChat. While WeChat provides access to numerous websites or e-commerce applications, in France consumers use computers (not connected to millions of mini-programs like WeChat) and their phones to shop online. For the past 40 years, since they began purchasing via Minitel and then through traditional e-commerce, they have tended to asynchronously order the products they want rather than waiting for the seller to discuss a product and decide whether to buy it or not. This disparity is significant and helps explain the vast difference in LSC session purchases between France and China. Live streaming shopping made its debut in the French market in 2020 during the Covid-19 pandemic. 70 per cent of European consumers were interested in LSC, with 67 per cent in France, boasting a conversion rate ten times higher than traditional e-commerce (FEVAD, 2022).

Social commerce encompasses various activities, including:

- social media marketing
- influencer collaborations
- user-generated content
- social shopping features
- peer recommendations

Key components of social commerce include:

- Social shopping platforms: Dedicated online platforms or features within existing social media platforms that enable users to browse, discover and purchase products directly within the social environment.
- User-generated content: Consumer-generated reviews, ratings, photos and videos shared on social media platforms, influencing purchasing decisions and providing social proof to other users.

- Influencer marketing: Collaboration with social media influencers or content creators to promote products or brands to their followers, leveraging their influence and credibility to drive engagement and sales.
- Social recommendations: Personalized product recommendations based on social connections, past purchases and browsing behaviour, enhancing relevance and facilitating discovery.
- Social sharing and virality: Integration of social sharing features that enable users to share product recommendations, purchases and experiences with their social networks, amplifying reach and engagement.
- Social customer service: Provision of customer support and assistance through social media channels, allowing for real-time communication and problem resolution to enhance the overall shopping experience.

Overall, social commerce represents a convergence of social media and e-commerce, harnessing the power of social networks to drive consumer engagement, brand visibility and online sales in the digital marketplace.

The intention to purchase in e-commerce

Table 0.1 presents various forms of e-commerce along with their respective time factors, site opportunities and their impact on purchase intention. Each form represents distinct strategies and platforms utilized by businesses to engage with digital consumers and drive purchasing behaviour in online environments.

Table 0.1 Various forms of e-commerce

E-commerce forms	Time factor	Site opportunities	Impact on purchase intention
Social commerce or s-commerce	Synchronous	Social networks (X, Meta, LinkedIn, Instagram, Pinterest, etc.)	Reinforces customer engagement and brand awareness, can generate impulse purchases through recommendations and user reviews.
Live streaming commerce	Synchronous	Live streaming platforms (Twitch, YouTube Live, etc.)	Creates a sense of urgency and exclusivity, allows customers to ask questions in real-time and see products in action.

(continued)

Table 0.1 (Continued)

E-commerce forms	Time factor	Site opportunities	Impact on purchase intention
Online catalogues	Asynchronous	Online shopping websites (Amazon, Cdiscount, etc.)	Offers a wide variety of products and brands, allows customers to compare prices and product features before purchasing.
Marketplaces	Asynchronous	Online selling platforms (Temu, Etsy, eBay, etc.)	Enables third-party sellers to sell their products on a single platform, offers a wide variety of products and brands, can enhance customer trust through seller reviews and ratings.
Brand websites	Asynchronous	Brand-specific online sales websites (Nike, Zara, etc.)	Reinforces brand awareness and customer loyalty, offers personalized shopping experience, and may provide exclusive offers.
Mobile applications	Asynchronous	Online shopping apps (Amazon, Wish, etc.)	Provides convenient and personalized shopping experience, allows customers to receive push notifications for special offers and promotions.

1 | Understanding consumer behaviour in the digital age

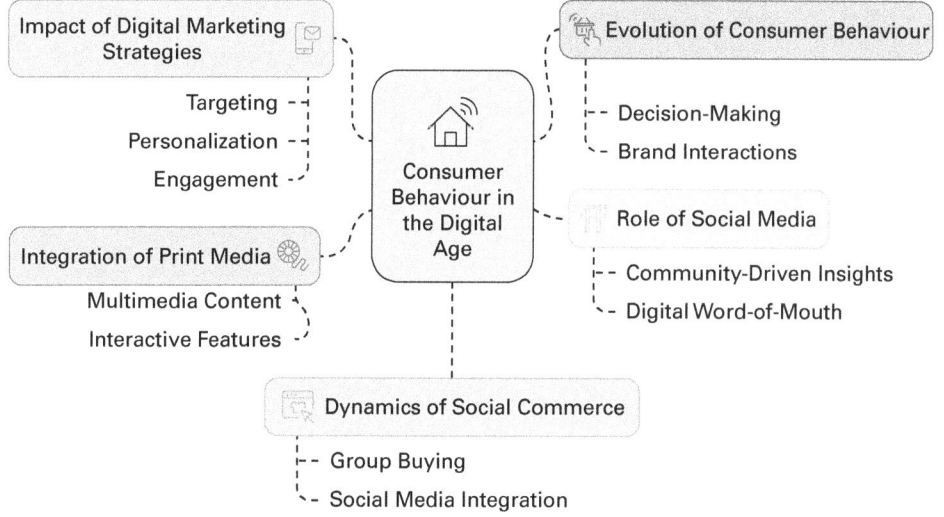

LEARNING OBJECTIVES

By the end of this chapter, you should be able to:

- Analyse the evolution of consumer behaviour: Understand the shift from traditional to digital consumer behaviour and its implications for decision-making and brand interactions.
- Evaluate the impact of digital marketing strategies: Assess how digital marketing enhances targeting, personalization and engagement compared with traditional marketing methods.

- Explore the role of social media in shaping consumer decisions: Examine how social media platforms influence consumer behaviour through community-driven insights and digital word-of-mouth.
- Assess the integration of print media in the digital age: Analyse how print media can be revitalized through digital enhancements such as multimedia content and interactive features.
- Understand the dynamics of social commerce: Evaluate the success of platforms like Pinduoduo in leveraging social commerce strategies, including group buying and social media integration.

CHAPTER OUTLINE

- Importance of understanding consumer behaviour in the digital age
- Historical context of consumer behaviour

Traditional consumer behaviour:

- The digital revolution
- The mobile revolution
- The rise of Web3 and beyond
- Impact of technology on marketing and consumer engagement

Enhanced targeting and personalization:

- Real-time data and insights
- Global reach and cost-efficiency
- Interactivity and omnichannel experiences
- Social media's influence on consumer decision-making

Transition from individual to collective consciousness:

- Role of social media in shaping consumer preferences
- The emergence of the 'consumer-actor'
- Integration of print media in the digital age

Transformations through digital platforms:

- Examples of enhanced print media: digital magazines, AR experiences, digital catalogs
- Case study: Pinduoduo and social commerce

> Overview of Pinduoduo's group buying model:
>
> - Integration with social media platforms
> - Insights into social commerce success in China
> - Key learnings and implications

Introduction

In the rapidly evolving landscape of consumer behaviour, understanding the shift from traditional practices to modern digital paradigms is crucial. This chapter aims to explore how technological advancements have reshaped consumer interactions and marketing strategies. From the slow, deliberate decision-making processes of the pre-digital era to the instantaneous, data-driven choices of today, the transformation is profound. The chapter will delve into how digital and mobile technologies have revolutionized consumer behaviour, highlighting the influence of social media, the integration of print media with digital platforms and the emergence of innovative e-commerce models such as social commerce. By examining these developments, we aim to provide a comprehensive overview of the current consumer landscape and offer insights into how brands can adapt to thrive in this dynamic environment.

This chapter delves into the evolution of consumer behaviour, exploring shifts from traditional teleshopping to interactive models like live streaming commerce. It analyses factors driving this evolution and the role of technology in shaping modern consumer interactions. Through case studies, it offers insights into the dynamic landscape of consumer behaviour and its implications for businesses and society.

Consumption has assumed unprecedented importance, attracting considerable attention due to its dynamic evolution. This chapter endeavours to emphasize the relevance of contemporary consumption within the spheres of political and economic discourse. Beyond the confines of an economic crisis, our current milieu is characterized by an information crisis, thereby engendering the formulation of novel reference points. The resulting metamorphoses create a conducive environment for endeavours to reintroduce enchantment and the emergence of novel mythologies. Appreciating the consumer, with an understanding of their biases and emotions, becomes imperative for comprehending the contemporary citizen within the paradigm of informational flux.

The evolution of consumer behaviour

The marketing landscape is undergoing a significant shift, moving beyond the traditional presentation of products in catalogues to a dynamic and interactive experience known as live shopping or live commerce. This trend has become commonplace in advertising and e-commerce, especially in China with platforms like Taobao and in the United States with Amazon. The concept is now making its debut in the French market, exemplified by Sephora's live shopping platform.

The pre-digital age: traditional consumer behaviour towards the social shopper

In the era preceding the digital revolution, consumer behaviour was predominantly shaped by traditional channels such as brick-and-mortar stores, print media and word-of-mouth recommendations. This epoch, characterized by a lack of digital connectivity, witnessed consumers navigating a landscape dominated by these traditional avenues. Brands relied on physical presence and personal connections to build trust with customers and the decision-making process was often slower, influenced by direct product interactions and geographical constraints. Television advertisements served as a primary means of shaping consumer behaviour, with communication flowing unidirectionally from the brand to the customer.

However, this paradigm shifted with the advent of digital technologies. Today, consumers engage in bidirectional interactions through live streaming sessions and social commerce platforms, marking a departure from the traditional teleshopping model. This transformation has been driven by factors such as real-time engagement and the increasing role of technology in shaping consumer choices. This chapter explores the evolution of consumer behaviour from traditional channels to modern interactive models, shedding light on the bidirectional communication inherent in contemporary marketing strategies.

Brick-and-mortar stores: the embodiment of consumer experience

Brick-and-mortar stores were the epicentres of commerce, serving as tangible hubs where consumers engaged with products through tactile experiences. The ambiance, layout and in-store interactions played pivotal roles in shaping purchasing decisions. The physicality of these spaces not only facilitated transactions but also served as a platform for cultivating brand loyalty through sensory engagement.

In the hotel industry, the use of sensorial cues is also becoming important since using robots to welcome guests has not proved palatable, if we look at what happened in Japan a few years ago, for example, with the integration of robotics and smart devices in Japanese hotels for enhanced guest experience. Social and service robots have become increasingly prevalent in our society, offering potential benefits such as companionship, enhanced communication and cost reduction, particularly in labour-shortage industries like hospitality. Robots are viewed as the emerging labour force in the hospitality sector, providing continuous service to customers without breaks. However, the introduction of service robots also impacts the customer service experience (Pinillos et al., 2016). The first robot-staffed hotel was launched in Japan in 2015, drawing attention to the concept of human-less hotel services. Previous research on robots has primarily focused on their usability, productivity improvement, employee perceptions and overall attitudes towards them (de Graaf and Ben Allouch, 2013). However, customer attitudes toward robots' appearance and their interaction with service robots have been overlooked. Given that customer attitudes towards robotic staff may influence further robot adoption in the hospitality industry, this study aims to address this research gap by examining visitors' and hotel guests' attitudes and behaviours towards robot staff at Henn-na Hotel Tokyo Hamamatsucho (https://group.hennnahotel.com/).

The behavioural observation conducted aimed to investigate customers' actions and reactions towards the hotel's robotic staff. Except for hotel guests who conducted the check-in process at the reception counter, most visitors maintained a distance of at least one metre from the reception counter. Many paused at the entrance, surveying their surroundings before approaching the reception counter. Upon reaching the counter, they either remained at the entrance or moved to the stanchion to observe the robots. This observation suggested that visitors displayed hesitation upon encountering the robot staff for the first time. According to Duronto et al. (2005), individuals in Asian cultures tend to experience anxiety and avoidance when encountering strangers. Consequently, when encountering an android for the first time, people may perceive them as unfamiliar individuals, leading to initial hesitation. Younger generations demonstrated greater proficiency in interacting with robots, attempting verbal or physical interaction. Upon entering the hotel, most observers verbally complimented the robots. Some attempted verbal interaction with the robots, but as these humanoid robots lacked voice recognition systems, they did not respond to greetings. Consequently, customers displayed disappointment when their greetings went unanswered. The role of robots in the hotel remains largely at a presentation level, lacking comprehensive interactive capabilities and their appearances are not yet perfected, potentially triggering the Uncanny Valley effect (Seyama and Nagayama, 2007).

The hospitality landscape in Japan was witnessing a transformative shift with the incorporation of cutting-edge technology, particularly robots and smart devices, in some newly established hotels. This innovative approach aimed to provide a warm and accommodating reception to guests, especially those who might not be proficient in the local language. A leading travel agency inaugurated a 'smart hotel' in Hamamatsucho, central Tokyo, showcasing humanoid robots proficient in greeting guests in English, Chinese, Korean, or Japanese at the front desk. These humanoid robots extended their functionality to encompass cleaning duties as well. The utilization of such technology was strategically aligned with addressing Japan's ongoing labour shortage, as articulated by hotel officials. In another hotel situated in

Akihabara, central Tokyo, guests were empowered to control various aspects of their room environment through the use of smartphones or smart speakers. This encompassed managing lighting, air conditioning and curtains, enhancing the overall guest experience through seamless and intuitive technological interfaces. The integration of humanoid robots at the reception and the incorporation of smart devices for room control not only cater to the diverse linguistic needs of guests but also align with the broader objective of mitigating the challenges posed by Japan's labour shortage. This innovative approach signifies a proactive response to the evolving demands of the hospitality industry and exemplifies the growing synergy between technological advancements and guest-centric services in Japanese hotels.

We must consider that such progress has already been tackled by the Japanese hospitality industry.

Sensory stimulation through connected objects

Pelet et al.'s 2021 study suggests that touch, smell, hearing, sight and taste, stimulated by connected objects in hotels, positively influence the emotional value, affective experience and overall well-being of customers within a physical space (e.g. hotel room, lobby, restaurant). Upscale hotels typically deploy two types of technologies: those enhancing hotel efficiency and process quality, such as apps capturing customer preferences during reservations, and those improving the digital experience, encompassing the perception and personal interaction with the provided digital service during a guest's stay. This includes factors such as the ambiance of the hotel room in terms of music and lighting. It is the latter application, combined with the implementation of a sensory marketing strategy, that piques our interest. Managers of 4–5-star hotels, interviewed as part of this study, expressed a generally favourable disposition towards the use and provision of connected objects. They recognized the potential to enhance the customer experience, acknowledging the current challenge faced by hoteliers to differentiate and pleasantly surprise clients. For some managers, connected objects were deemed indispensable, representing the future, especially concerning room amenities like connected bulbs, speakers and other intelligent devices. These objects provide a means of differentiation and offer opportunities for a unique customer experience.

While the study suggests that the five senses can be effectively stimulated by connected objects, a detailed analysis reveals variations in impact among the senses and differences in perception between genders. For instance, the online survey of 357 clients from 4–5-star hotels indicates that the affective experience is positively influenced by touch, hearing and sight, while the state of well-being is positively impacted by smell and taste. Moreover, the impact of one stimulus can be amplified by another. For instance, virtual reality experiences (visual stimulation) can be intensified with the diffusion of scents. Our results also confirm neuroscientific findings that suggest a connection between smell, taste and memory in the brain, emphasizing the efficacy of senses in influencing customer mood, satisfaction and loyalty.

The survey results further reveal that smell has a stronger impact on well-being among women, aligning with existing research showing that women are more sensitive to and adept at categorizing odours. Managers can therefore apply scents through connected objects with lower intensities or even different scents directed towards a female clientele compared with male clients. Prestigious hotels possess a plethora of tools to create surprising, captivating and personalized multisensory experiences for their clients. This involves the establishment of unique and original environments in various hotel spaces using connected objects. For example, gamification mechanisms can lead to increased customer engagement, as observed in hotels offering dedicated gaming rooms with highly immersive atmospheres. While clients and hoteliers currently prioritize safety and precaution, the upscale hospitality industry has a significant opportunity to engage new niche markets and provide intense and unforgettable moments of happiness to clients in the current sombre context.

The international hotel industry has undergone a profound transformation, driven by the development and integration of novel technologies and the pervasive influence of information communication technology (ICT). This study examines the transformative effects of these advancements, with a focus on the escalating demand for online interactions by guests through digital touchpoints, reshaping their experiences (Nadkarni et al., 2020). State-of-the-art, high-tech services have emerged as essential prerequisites for ensuring customer satisfaction and enhancing the overall performance of hotels (Melián-González and Bulchand-Gidumal, 2016). This trend is anticipated to gain further prominence in the future (Gonzalez et al., 2019; Sigala, 2020).

Navigating the IoT landscape in the service industry

The rapid growth of the Internet of Things (IoT) and smart devices has had a significant impact across various sectors, including healthcare, smart cities and smart homes (Stankov et al., 2019). For instance, the global smart home market is expected to exceed US$141 billion by 2023 (Statista, 2020). This surge in IoT technology is not just reshaping industries, it's also transforming how businesses understand and respond to consumer behaviour.

IoT allows businesses to gain a deeper understanding of consumer needs and behaviours by tracking interactions across multiple platforms and devices (Gupta et al., 2020). For companies, particularly in the service industry, incorporating smart devices into their offerings is crucial. This strategic integration prepares them for future consumer interactions with IoT and offers a competitive advantage.

As Ives et al. (2016, p. 281) point out, 'the IoT is firmly rooted in tangible objects with their "mind" in the cloud', enabling real-time interactions between devices and users. For marketers, the challenge is to understand not just how individual devices function but also how these devices shape consumer experiences (Hoffman and Novak, 2018). For example, technology-driven strategies like gamification can significantly enhance customer engagement (Xu et al., 2017).

The digital transformation of consumer experiences extends to sensory marketing, where businesses create multi-sensory experiences that influence customer behaviour. Traditionally, this was known as 'atmospherics' (Kotler, 1973) and later expanded to 'servicescape' (Bitner, 1992). While these concepts have long been applied in physical settings, there's growing interest in understanding how IoT and human–computer interaction (HCI) can create similar experiences in digital spaces (Obrist et al., 2017).

The study by Pelet et al. (2021) addresses this emerging area by exploring how IoT devices in upscale hotels engage the five senses to influence guest emotions, experiences, and well-being, which in turn affects their behaviour. The researchers also examine how gender might moderate the effects of these IoT-driven sensory stimuli. The findings are intended to help managers in the hotel industry and beyond develop effective multi-sensory marketing strategies that resonate with today's digitally savvy consumers.

The following analysis shows how hotels can perform in this direction when using IOT.

KEY TERM: RESPONSIVE

Responsive architecture is an evolving field of architectural practice and research. Responsive architectures are those that measure actual environmental conditions (via sensors) to enable buildings to adapt their form, shape, colour or character responsively (via actuators).

Sight

Strengths

Responsive hotels may allow adjusting lights through IoT, depending on the amount of natural light. Voice commands may replace switches to turn on/off, e.g. the light or music, or to open/close shutters. Visual footprints may be applied to open the safe-deposit box in the room.

Weaknesses

Guests may become confused due to the absence of switches.

Opportunities

The use of voice commands may look reassuring for guests who want to avoid touching surfaces for various reasons, such as Covid-19.

Threats

Voice command technology is not useful for guests who are deaf-mute.

Managerial implications

The guest room may be equipped with both voice command technology and visually appealing switches to cater to guests who are not familiar with this new technology.

In the guest room, through the use of a concierge tablet connected to a screen mounted on the wall, the guest may choose a specific landscape, e.g. a beach or mountain scenery. The resulting ambiance may be enhanced through congruent auditory cues (the sound of sea waves, wind, etc.). IoT devices may automatically detect the guest's mood and propose a selection of 'ambient sceneries' to the guest.

Hearing

Strengths

On arrival at the hotel, the guest's voice is reliably recorded for automatic voice recognition purposes during their stay at the hotel. Speakers in the guest room, like OK Google, may be used to replace the phone when contacting hotel staff to place an order or ask for information, for example.

Weaknesses

If there is more than one guest in the room, the speaker may encounter difficulties in differentiating between voices. If the voice is not recognized correctly, the guest may get into a negative mood and hence may show avoidance behaviour.

Opportunities

Guests may use speakers in the guest room to benefit from purchasing products sold in the country where the hotel is located and vendors in this country only deliver domestically.

Threats

Speakers in the guest room may raise concerns about the protection of the guests' private data, since speakers may be hacked.

Managerial implications

IoT may automatically recognize the guest's mood and propose, accordingly, a playlist of music titles which they can choose from the concierge tablet in their guest room.

Smell

Strengths

Carpets, towels, shutters and bed linen may diffuse fragrances and change the fragrance automatically with each new guest.

On arrival at the hotel, the guest can choose a perfume category, like floral, citrus, or oceanic. Their preference may serve as the basis for the creation of their personalized scent. The diffusion of this scent may be triggered through face recognition. In the ballroom (at a business event, wedding, etc.), depending on the number of people present, IoT may adapt the temperature and air conditioning to avoid bad odours.

Weaknesses

The presence of a large variety of odours may prevent the guest from distinguishing different scents. In public spaces (the lobby, elevators, hallways, etc.) the presence of different guests may lead to an olfactory overload. Hence, the optimal stimulation level needs to be determined.

Opportunities

Hotels may pursue a co-branding strategy together with luxury perfume houses, with their products being diffused through IoT devices in the hotel room.

Threats

Guests with allergies may react negatively to olfactory stimuli.

Managerial implications

Different mood scents may emanate from diffusers in different areas of the hotel. Such diffusers may be automatically recharged and may adapt scent type and intensity through the use of IoT, according to any changes in temperature, climate or other variables, which a computer may analyse in real time.

Touch

Strengths

Switches with a surface that gives the guest a pleasant feeling when turning on the light, opening/closing the curtains, etc., may be used. The same material may be used on smart switches and other surfaces, such as remote controls, to create a coherent tactile experience.

Weaknesses

Surfaces need to be regularly disinfected due to the recent Covid-19 pandemic and for general hygiene.

Opportunities

Mobile integration (with the guest's permission) provides data, which helps the hotel to remember the guest's tactile preferences. Hotels may opt for speakers or any other Bluetooth systems that allow the guest to pair their private phone to these devices in order to ensure their privacy. To turn this on, guests must touch the speakers.

Threats

Guests would have to touch the switches. With GDPR (General Data Protection Regulation), guests may be reluctant to access any data from any system.

Managerial implications

Tactile/haptic experiences may be personalized through the use of IoT. When guests are identified through face recognition, surfaces to be touched may be adapted to the guests' tactile preferences. Examples of such surfaces would be the touch pad in the elevator on which the guest selects their floor, handrails, or couches and chairs in the guest room.

Taste

Strengths

Hotels may offer tastings of local food specialties (cheese, bacon, truffles, etc.) and wines. They may give guests directions for how to get to local producers. For this purpose, maps and location-based services or beacon aerials in the proximity of the hotel may be applied.

Weaknesses

Fewer guests may visit the hotel restaurant if they discover competing restaurants in the vicinity through this location system, based on AI and IoT.

Opportunities

The hotel may establish business partnerships with vendors of locally produced food specialties and wines near the hotel.

Threats

The cooperation with vendor brands of locally produced food specialties and wines may not match the image of the upscale hotel. The guests' perception of security and comfort may be jeopardized through employing too many sensors (RFID, WIFI, Bluetooth, beacon aerials).

Managerial implications

The guest, provided with the necessary equipment in their room, may experience a virtual reality or augmented reality visit to the restaurant which also allows them to view the meals virtually. Information on the ingredients, nutritional values or any potential allergens may augment their virtual experience.

EXPLORING THE INTEGRATION OF IOT IN UPSCALE HOTELS

Exploring the integration of IoT in upscale hotels reveals a transformative shift in consumer experiences within the hospitality sector. Upscale hotels are increasingly using IoT technologies to enhance guest satisfaction, streamline operations and create personalized environments. These establishments employ interconnected devices and sensors to offer smart room controls, allowing guests to adjust lighting, temperature and entertainment systems according to their preferences. IoT integration extends beyond individual rooms, encompassing automated check-in processes, keyless entry systems and intelligent maintenance protocols. The implementation of IoT in upscale hotels not only caters to the evolving expectations of tech-savvy consumers but also enables data-driven insights into guest behaviours and preferences. This wealth of information allows hotels to tailor their services more effectively, potentially increasing guest loyalty and driving repeat business.

As the adoption of IoT in hospitality continues to grow, it is reshaping consumer perceptions of luxury accommodations and setting new standards for personalized, efficient and immersive hotel experiences.

Selecting upscale hotels for IoT integration

We chose upscale hotels for our study due to their greater financial capacity for integrating IoT devices, with dominant global upscale hotel chains showing a high propensity for adopting such technology. Our article is organized as follows: providing an overview of ICT, particularly IoT, in the hotel industry; establishing connections between sensory marketing and HCI, focusing on sensory-enabling technologies (SETs); introducing our research model and hypotheses; presenting findings from exploratory (Study 1) and confirmatory (Study 2) phases; discussing results and implications; outlining paper limitations; and suggesting future research directions.

The role of IoT in enhancing guest experiences

The use of information communication technology in hotels spans support-centred technologies for back-stage processes (e.g. property management systems) and customer-centred technologies integral to the service experience (e.g. in-room entertainment) (Murphy and Rottet, 2009). IoT has revolutionized the hospitality industry by integrating connected devices into the overall guest experience, fostering multi-sensory encounters and influencing guest emotions and outcomes (Lemon and Verhoef, 2016).

The concept of effective IoT in hotels

Pieroni et al. (2015) introduced the concept of effective IoT, where smart devices possess artificial 'feeling' and personality, enabling emotional exchanges within a networked domain. Interconnected smart devices, like beacon technology, facilitate object-to-object and object-to-human exchanges, with implications for monitoring and improving the overall affective state of a hotel. IoT can personalize services based on guests' mood states, utilizing wearables and environmental sensors to enhance the guest experience (Grewal et al., 2020).

Sensory marketing and human–computer interaction

In the realm of sensory marketing, creating multi-sensory experiences in 'service-scapes' has been fundamental (Hultén, 2015; Krishna, 2013). Sensory marketing engages consumers' senses, influencing their perception, judgement and behaviour (Krishna, 2013). The connection between sensory marketing and HCI is bolstered by SETs, such as smartphones, touch screens, virtual reality, augmented reality and digital interfaces generating taste and smell stimuli (Petit et al., 2019). The integration of SETs in upscale hotels holds promise for creating IoT-enabled multi-sensory guest experiences.

Augmented reality: a 'still in progress' technology

Over the course of time, the retail sector has undergone significant transformations propelled by the rise of digitalization and online platforms (Verhoef et al., 2015).

This swift evolution is largely attributed to advancements in new technologies (Grewal et al., 2017). Among these technological innovations, augmented reality (AR) has emerged as a notable force, holding substantial promise in enhancing retail experiences.

The utilization of virtual reality (VR) and augmented reality (AR) headsets remains exceedingly marginal to date, with little indication of significant change in the near future. According to estimates from Statista Market Insights, approximately 120 million individuals currently have access to a VR or AR headset worldwide. Even if the global user base of VR/AR equipment is projected to double in the coming years, Statista analysts estimate that it will likely remain below 250 million individuals by 2027, representing a minute fraction of the global population.

The anticipated growth of AR technology and associated devices is rooted in their versatile applications across diverse sectors, including aerospace, defence, commerce, consumer electronics, industry and the medical field.

ACTIVITY 1

Analysing consumer behaviour evolution

Objective: To understand the transformation from traditional to digital consumer behaviour.

Instructions: Divide students into small groups and assign each group a different era of consumer behaviour (Traditional, Digital Revolution, Mobile Revolution, Web3). Ask each group to create a brief presentation on their assigned era, highlighting key changes in consumer behaviour, technology impacts and marketing strategies. Each group will present their findings, followed by a class discussion comparing the different eras.

ANALYSIS OF APPLE VISION PRO'S MARKETING STRATEGY

The text analyses Apple's marketing campaign for its augmented reality headset, the Apple Vision Pro. This strategy leverages an ostensibly spontaneous video depicting a man working in the subway with the headset, projecting an image of the future within the banal setting of the present. In reality, this video, posted on social media by influencers such as Nikias Molina, is meticulously crafted to generate buzz and shape collective imagination. Although the video appears discrete and candid, it is designed to look authentic, creating a striking contrast between futuristic technology and an everyday environment.

The analysis reveals that these content creators, though not officially paid by Apple, play a crucial role in the brand's marketing strategy. Apple relies on a decentralized ecosystem of influencers who naturally promote its products, thereby amplifying their visibility and normalization. The impact was further heightened as the video quickly amassed millions of views and sparked debates about the social implications of this technology.

While the campaign has generated criticism and ridicule, it serves to gradually familiarize the public with this innovation, drawing a parallel with the introduction of smartphones. The text highlights the risks of too radical a change, citing the example of Google Glass, and how Apple anticipates these reactions by initially targeting influencers and developers before broader public adoption.

This marketing strategy aims to normalize the Apple Vision Pro by playing on apparent authenticity and the appeal of novelty, while preparing the ground for its integration into daily life despite initial challenges and resistance.

SOURCE Magazine presented by Sonia Devillers (France, 2023, 11mn). Production: Arte France Développement. The video can be found here: https://urls.fr/2GMWk0

At its essence, AR involves the real-time overlay of virtual images onto the physical world, computed by software (Yaoyuneyong et al., 2016). The widespread adoption of smartphones ensures that consumers have convenient access to AR technology through various applications. Notably, several companies spanning different sectors, such as Converse, Sephora, IBM, IKEA and Tissot, have already embraced AR technology. This adoption empowers consumers to visualize products before making a purchase, thereby streamlining the decision-making process. Beyond its utilitarian value, AR provides an engaging and interactive experience, enabling consumers to virtually experience products ranging from clothing to furniture.

However, despite the evident applications and adoption of AR in the retail domain, the conceptualization of AR in this context remains a work in progress and scholarly research on the subject is relatively scarce. The evolving nature of AR in retail necessitates further exploration and academic inquiry to comprehensively understand its implications, potential and evolving role in shaping consumer behaviour and retail dynamics. Snapchat utilizes AR through a feature known as 'Lenses'.

Sensory marketing and luxury

Like many sectors, the luxury industry has been significantly impacted by the health crisis. Consequently, new strategies had to be deployed to present the various luxury collections to clients. According to Chandon and Valette-Florence (2016), there are different types of luxury consumers whose needs must be analysed to ensure that Snapchat Lenses are as effective and appealing as possible to future consumers.

Artificial intelligence and augmented reality have provided golden opportunities for a sector like luxury to maintain connections with its audience and keep consumers engaged. Due to the pandemic, in-store customer consumption was significantly affected. As a result, more consumers have been transitioning from physical stores to online shopping (Pantelimon et al., 2020).

With physical boutiques no longer serving the same functions, they are reinventing themselves, and brands are seeking to offer new methods to their clients. Today, we talk about Luxury 4.0, which stems from Industry 4.0. According to Scholz and Duffy (2018), sensory experiences build relationships with brands. They disrupt industrial production and reshape how customers search, interact and purchase by offering a new playful method. This is now referred to as augmented reality. AR is a new interactive technology that 'can overlay virtual 3D models of real products in the real world, such as human bodies or objects, and users can manipulate these virtual 3D models by rotating, moving and enlarging them' (Poushneh and Vasquez-Parraga, 2017).

By leveraging new technologies, brands are now able to collect information from multiple touchpoints and analyse consumer behaviour to offer more precise and personalized services. Indeed, companies increasingly claim to be 'customer centric', meaning they place the customer at the heart of their organization and decision-making processes. Thus, one of the major challenges in this drive for change is integrating the customer into their digital transformation.

While luxury has historically relied on images of rarity and exclusivity, the internet has been built on principles of easy access, dissemination and abundance. The apparent opposition between inclusivity and accessibility in luxury has long hindered the digitization of the industry. However, luxury brands have the capacity to harness digital technology because the industry has always prioritized consumer experience, and digital technology has significantly adapted and refocused this concept of experience.

Print media: crafting narratives in ink

Print media has long been recognized as a powerful tool for shaping consumer perceptions and influencing behaviour. Through newspapers, magazines and catalogues, print media has provided a platform for advertisements, articles and reviews to sway consumer choices. The printed word, with its tangible presence, has held a unique influence over readers, allowing brands to carefully craft their image and narrative. In today's digital age, the convergence of print media with digital platforms opens up new avenues for engagement and interaction. One example is the use of QR codes, which serve as a bridge between the physical and digital realms.

QR codes

QR codes, short for quick response codes, function as a conduit linking physical objects or environments with digital content or information, facilitating seamless interaction between the physical and digital realms. Developed in the 1990s by Denso Wave, a subsidiary of Toyota, QR codes consist of black squares arranged on a white background in a square grid pattern. These codes encode data such as text, URLs, or other information, which can be decoded using a smartphone or a dedicated QR code reader application. The versatility of QR codes lies in their ability to bridge the gap between offline and online experiences, enabling users to access digital content or perform actions simply by scanning the code with their mobile device.

In academic contexts, QR codes find diverse applications, ranging from enhancing learning materials by providing supplementary digital resources to facilitating efficient data collection in research projects. Furthermore, QR codes serve as an effective marketing tool, enabling businesses to engage consumers with interactive content, promotions, or product information. The widespread adoption of QR codes underscores their utility as a bridge between the physical world and the digital landscape, offering opportunities for enhanced connectivity, information dissemination and user engagement across various domains.

Bridging physical and digital realms: the role and applications of QR codes

The utility of QR codes extends across diverse domains, including marketing, education, healthcare and retail, where they are leveraged to enhance user engagement, deliver targeted content and streamline processes. In marketing, for example, QR codes embedded within printed materials can seamlessly link readers to digital content, such as interactive flipbooks. These flipbooks, similar to the example of Flipbook, enable the conversion of static PDFs into dynamic, engaging publications with realistic flipping page effects. Additionally, other digital platforms, such as online magazines and interactive websites, offer further opportunities for enhancing the traditional print experience with interactive elements, multimedia content and social sharing features. These advancements highlight the evolving nature of print media and its integration with digital technology to create immersive and interactive storytelling experiences for consumers.

Additional examples of how print media can be transformed and enhanced on digital platforms exist, such as:

- Digital magazines: Many print magazines now offer digital editions that replicate the look and feel of their print counterparts while adding interactive features. Digital magazines may include embedded videos, audio clips, slideshows and clickable links to provide a richer and more engaging reading experience. Examples include Zinio (https://www.zinio.com/), Magzter (https://www.magzter.com/) and Readly (https://gb.readly.com/).

- Interactive websites: Brands and publishers often create companion websites for their print publications, offering additional content, behind-the-scenes insights and interactive features. These websites may include exclusive articles, photo galleries, interactive quizzes and forums for reader engagement.
- AR experiences: AR technology can enhance print media by overlaying digital content onto physical pages when viewed through a smartphone or tablet. Readers can use AR apps to unlock hidden animations, 3D models, interactive games and product demonstrations embedded within print materials.
- Digital catalogues: Retailers and brands can create immersive digital catalogues that mimic the browsing experience of a print catalogue while offering additional features such as search functionality, product videos, customer reviews and one-click purchasing options. Digital catalogues enable customers to shop directly from the digital publication, enhancing convenience and interactivity.
- Social media integration: Print media can leverage social media platforms to extend reach and engagement. Publishers may encourage readers to share articles, photos and quotes from print publications on social media channels, fostering community interaction and increasing brand visibility. Social media platforms also provide opportunities for live streaming events, interactive Q&A sessions and real-time updates related to print content.

These examples demonstrate how print media can be reimagined and extended on digital platforms to create more dynamic, interactive and immersive experiences for readers. Moreover, to enhance the integration of information in a flexible and accessible manner, the ePUB format can also be developed to maximize its attractiveness by utilizing Sigil (https://sigil-ebook.com/) software, for example (Darmaji et al., 2020). Learning outcomes encompass various domains, including the cognitive domain (Asrial et al., 2020). These outcomes reflect the skills acquired upon completion of learning activities and signify the process through which individuals strive to induce relatively permanent changes in behaviour (Darmaji et al., 2019).

In educational contexts, learning objectives are typically established by instructors and successful students are those who attain these objectives. Learning outcomes, such as cognitive, affective and psychomotor changes in student behaviour following learning activities, play a pivotal role in gauging learning progress and informing instructional strategies (Maison et al., 2020). Modules serve as essential resources in tailored learning, designed to meet student needs by systematically organizing learning materials according to students' knowledge levels and age in a comprehensible language, facilitating independent learning with minimal or no teacher guidance (Darmaji et al., 2019).

Word-of-mouth recommendations: the ripple effect of trust

In an era predating the viral nature of online reviews, word-of-mouth recommendations were the social currency driving consumer decisions. Personal interactions, familial advice and community discussions were powerful determinants of trust. A satisfied customer's endorsement reverberated within local circles, establishing a brand's reputation through authentic, interpersonal connections. This is always true, not necessarily in any culture, but in China it works very well, as we will see with the example of Pinduoduo.

Online group buying (OGB) represents a dynamic business model wherein consumers can access discounted prices by aggregating their orders with those of others, thereby benefiting from volume-based discounts (Yu et al., 2022). Three distinct group-buying models have been delineated by Cheng and Huang (2013): customer-initiated transactions, merchant-initiated transactions and independent third-party-initiated transactions. This paper centres on third-party online selling platforms, which are external software developed separately to the main website provider. Specifically, the focus is on Pinduoduo as the website provider and the WeChat social media platform as the externally developed software.

In China, Pinduoduo stands as a prominent third-party group-buying platform (Statista, 2022), offering a range of products, including fresh produce and seafood. Operating on a 'farm to the fridge' model, Pinduoduo enables consumers to pre-order food-related items directly from farmers (Chen et al., 2022). Through the integrated social media platform WeChat, consumers can communicate group offers or participate in team purchases. The group-buying prices offered by Pinduoduo entail discounted rates on bulk orders, fostering opportunities for consumers to enjoy cost savings. Leveraging social media-supported OGB has helped Pinduoduo gain a competitive edge within a relatively short time frame.

The OGB business model has garnered significant attention from researchers in the fields of information systems and operations management (Aral et al., 2013; Cheng and Huang, 2013; Kuan et al., 2014; Potdar et al., 2018; Ha and Stoel, 2009; Sun et al., 2021). Notably, discounted pricing, electronic word of mouth (e-WOM), website quality, reputation and trust have been identified as crucial determinants of OGB behaviour. However, there exists a research gap concerning group-buying intentions utilizing third-party OGB platforms such as Pinduoduo, which this paper aims to address (Wang, 2017).

As highlighted by Kumar et al. (2019, p. 179), the management of user engagement and interaction becomes intricate in the transformation of e-commerce platforms into social e-commerce platforms. Consequently, this study directs its focus towards the antecedents of consumer engagement and trust in a third-party OGB platform, thereby influencing group buying intentions. Two primary research questions are addressed:

1 What factors (e-tail quality, price perception and e-WOM) drive customer engagement and trust in the OGB third-party platform?

2   What is the relative importance of consumer engagement with and trust in the OGB platform in elucidating group buying intention?

To investigate customer engagement and trust towards the OGB third-party platform, leading to group-buying intentions, this study integrates features of both the Technology Acceptance Model (TAM) and uses and gratifications (U&G) theory. Prior research has successfully employed TAM to comprehend online shopping acceptance, while U&G theory has elucidated individuals' media usage motivations and gratifications. The present study extends this by examining how perceived gratifications, such as discounted prices and e-WOM, influence OGB intentions within the framework of the U&G theory and TAM model.

Slower decision-making and geographical constraints

The pace of decision-making in the pre-digital age was measured and deliberate. Consumers lacked the instantaneous access to information that characterizes the modern era, leading to thorough contemplation before committing to a purchase. Geographical constraints further shaped choices, limiting options to what was available within one's immediate surroundings.

Brands as anchors of trust: physical presence and personal connections

Trust, a cornerstone of consumer relationships, was cultivated through a brand's physical presence and personal connections. A store's welcoming atmosphere, knowledgeable staff and consistent quality created a foundation of reliability. Consumers formed enduring bonds with brands they could touch, feel and interact with on a personal level.

In delving into the annals of traditional consumer behaviour, we uncover a rich tapestry of experiences that laid the groundwork for the seismic shifts to come. The digital revolution, with its promise of connectivity and information at the fingertips, waited on the horizon, poised to reshape the very fabric of how consumers engage with the marketplace.

The impact of technology on consumer behaviour

In the realm of digital marketing, several key benefits emerge, each contributing to the shaping of the digital consumer profile. These benefits encompass a spectrum of advantages conferred by digital marketing strategies and platforms, ultimately influencing consumer behaviour and preferences in the digital landscape. Below are key benefits elucidated within our context.

Enhanced targeting and personalization

Digital marketing offers unparalleled capabilities for precise audience targeting and personalized messaging based on demographic, psychographic and behavioural data (Smith and Chaffey, 2022). Through techniques such as data analytics, machine learning and customer relationship management (CRM) systems, marketers can tailor content and offers to individual consumer preferences, fostering deeper engagement and loyalty.

Real-time data and insights

Digital marketing channels provide immediate access to real-time data and performance metrics, enabling marketers to monitor campaign effectiveness, consumer interactions and market trends in granular detail (Hollensen, 2020). This wealth of actionable insights facilitates agile decision-making and optimization, empowering marketers to adapt strategies swiftly to changing market dynamics and consumer behaviours.

Global reach and accessibility

Digital marketing transcends geographical boundaries, offering businesses the ability to reach a global audience with minimal barriers to entry (Ryan, 2020). With the proliferation of internet connectivity and mobile devices, brands can engage with consumers across diverse markets, driving brand awareness and market penetration on a global scale.

Cost-efficiency and ROI

Compared with traditional marketing channels, digital marketing often presents a more cost-effective alternative, offering greater flexibility and scalability for businesses of all sizes (Chaffey, 2016). The ability to precisely target audiences, optimize campaigns in real-time and track performance metrics allows marketers to maximize return on investment (ROI) and allocate resources efficiently.

Interactivity and engagement

Digital marketing platforms foster interactive and immersive brand experiences, enabling two-way communication and engagement between brands and consumers (Frost and Strauss, 2016). Social media, content marketing and user-generated content (UGC) encourage active participation and dialogue, fostering brand advocacy and community building among digital consumers.

Integration and omnichannel experience

Digital marketing facilitates seamless integration across multiple channels and touchpoints, enabling brands to deliver consistent messaging and experiences throughout the consumer journey (Bansal, 2016). By orchestrating omnichannel marketing strategies, marketers can enhance brand visibility, drive cross-channel engagement and optimize conversion pathways for digital consumers.

Overall, the key benefits of digital marketing encompass a spectrum of advantages, ranging from enhanced targeting and personalization to global reach, cost-efficiency, interactivity and integration. These benefits collectively contribute to shaping the digital consumer profile, influencing behaviours, preferences and interactions within the digital ecosystem.

The role of the internet and mobile devices

The interface of a website holds paramount significance for success in e-commerce, exerting a profound influence on customer interactions and behaviour (Pelet and Papadopoulou, 2012). Extensive research in information systems has emphasized not only the perceived quality but also the technical characteristics of websites as pivotal determinants of online consumer behaviour (Torkzadeh and Dhillon, 2002; Singh et al., 2005). In the realm of mobile commerce (m-commerce) website design, Cyr et al. (2006) contend that attributes such as colour, shape, font type, music and animation play pivotal roles. Correspondingly, Ingraham and Bradburn (2003) identified three crucial attributes – colour (foreground-background contrast), layout (e.g. line spacing) and typefaces (size and font) – essential for developing a highly usable web page.

A visually aesthetic website interface has demonstrated the potential to enhance task performance, positively influence usability (Cyr et al., 2006; Moshagen et al., 2009; Choi and Lee, 2012) and even elevate consumer impulsiveness (Chopdar and Balakrishnan, 2020).

In the context of mobile commerce, Sarkar et al. (2020) disclosed that design attributes of interfaces can enhance perceived usefulness, customization and ease of use, consequently reinforcing customers' trust in m-commerce. The exploration of ease of use and its impact on users' behavioural intentions has been a focal point in the domain of HCI (Murray and Häuble, 2011; Morris and Turner, 2001; Venkatesh et al., 2003). Despite this, a noticeable dearth of research exists regarding the role of ease of use in m-commerce (Visinescu et al., 2015).

E-commerce and online shopping: a new way to consume

The early 1990s witnessed the inception of the World Wide Web (WWW) by Tim Berners-Lee, revolutionizing information dissemination and access on a global scale (Berners-Lee, 1989). This period saw the development of foundational web technologies and the release of pioneering web browsers such as NCSA Mosaic and Netscape Navigator, democratizing internet usage and enabling mass adoption (Cerf, 2012). Afterwards, the 'dot-com bubble' (late 1990s) marked a period of unprecedented growth and speculation in internet-based businesses. Companies invested heavily in online ventures, fuelled by optimistic projections of internet commerce. However, this speculative fervour led to the eventual collapse of overvalued dot-com companies by the early 2000s (Krueger and LePlastrier, 2009). Then, the Web 2.0 era (2000s) rose. The early 2000s witnessed the transition to Web 2.0, characterized by the evolution of static web pages to dynamic, interactive platforms enabling UGC and social interaction (O'Reilly, 2005). Notable examples included the emergence of Wikipedia, YouTube and social networking sites such as MySpace and later Facebook (Meta nowadays), which transformed the web into a participatory and collaborative medium (Kaplan and Haenlein, 2010). The mobile revolution came during the 2010s, driven by the widespread adoption of smartphones and mobile internet access. The introduction of the iPhone in 2007 revolutionized the mobile landscape, catalyzing the development of mobile apps and responsive web design (RWD) to accommodate varying screen sizes and user experiences (Campbell, 2013). It marked a significant milestone in the history of smartphones, introducing a touch screen interface, a revolutionary design and various innovative features that have since become standard in the mobile industry. The 2010s witnessed the ascendancy of social media platforms such as Facebook, Twitter and Instagram, reshaping online communication, content sharing and digital advertising (Boyd and Ellison, 2007). Concurrently, e-commerce experienced exponential growth, propelled by platforms like Amazon, Alibaba and eBay, redefining consumer behaviour and retail dynamics (Hausman et al., 2010).

The emergence of Web3 and beyond (2020s) shows, in our current decade, what is witnessing. It is characterized by decentralized technologies such as blockchain, artificial intelligence and the Internet of Things. Concepts such as the metaverse, decentralized finance (DeFi) and the semantic web are shaping the future trajectory of the internet, promising new paradigms of connectivity, privacy and digital interaction (Shadbolt et al., 2006).

The influence of social media on consumer decision making

The digital revolution, coupled with the rise of social and community networks and communication between objects and humans, profoundly alters how consumers perceive things. They now have access to a multitude of real-time information on a global scale. Grouped in networks, they can compare and gather information on a vast scale before making a purchase. This profound transformation occurs in the collaborative context of the 'Uberization' of the environment, where internet users prefer to rely on the community rather than professionals for their service purchases whenever possible. Faced with the proliferation of these new digital sphere purchase possibilities, the brain gradually transforms its personal consciousness into collective awareness.

This media revolution compels retailers to adapt and promptly respond to the demands of a consumer who, with a strong desire for interactivity, becomes a 'consumer-actor'. Accompanied by the emergence of big data, traditional marketing and communication are forced to quickly transform and employ techniques such as e-marketing, m-marketing, e-communication and 'one to one' (or 'mass customization'). New approaches like 'permission marketing', 'desire marketing' and 'inbound marketing' are emerging. Recently established professions, such as webmasters, community managers and social network officers, are employed by retailers to develop strategies, policies and digital and community actions tailored to the new behaviours, perceptions and expectations of the brains of 'neuro-consumer-actors'. All of this occurs in an environment where individual brains are gradually becoming collective.

ACTIVITY 2

Social media influence debate

Objective: To evaluate the role of social media in shaping consumer decisions.

Instructions: Organize a debate on the statement: 'Social media has more influence on consumer decision-making than traditional advertising.'

Assign half of the students to argue in favour of the statement and the other half against it. Allow each side to present their arguments and evidence, followed by a Q&A session where students can challenge each other's points.

> **ACTIVITY 3**
>
> Case study analysis of Pinduoduo
>
> **Objective**: To understand the dynamics of social commerce through a practical example.
>
> **Instructions**: Provide students with a brief case study on Pinduoduo, including its group-buying model and social media integration.
>
> Ask students to analyse how Pinduoduo's strategies reflect the concepts discussed in the chapter.
>
> Have students write a short report or engage in a class discussion on what other companies can learn from Pinduoduo's approach.

Conclusion

As we conclude our exploration of consumer behaviour in the digital age, it is evident that the landscape has undergone a remarkable transformation. The transition from traditional to digital and mobile consumer behaviours highlights a shift towards greater immediacy, connectivity and personalization. The rise of social media and the integration of digital enhancements into print media illustrate the increasingly interactive nature of consumer engagement. The case study of Pinduoduo underscores the significant impact of social commerce in leveraging group buying and social media to drive consumer trust and engagement. Moving forward, brands must navigate this evolving terrain with strategies that embrace these technological advancements and cater to the ever-changing expectations of the digital consumer. The insights gained from this chapter will serve as a foundation for understanding how to effectively engage with today's informed, empowered and interconnected consumers.

Summary

- This chapter delves into the profound impact of digital transformation on consumer behaviour, tracing the journey from traditional shopping habits to the highly connected and data-driven landscape of modern e-commerce. The evolution of consumer behaviour is explored through the lens of historical developments in technology, from the early days of the World Wide Web to the current advancements in Web3, mobile commerce and social media.

- The chapter emphasizes how digital marketing has revolutionized the way brands engage with consumers, offering unprecedented levels of personalization, global reach and real-time data analysis. The role of social media in shaping collective consumer consciousness is also discussed, highlighting the transition from individual decision-making to community-driven purchasing behaviours.
- Additionally, the chapter covers the integration of print media into the digital domain, showcasing how traditional formats can be enhanced through multimedia and interactive content. A case study on Pinduoduo provides practical insights into the dynamics of social commerce, particularly within the Chinese market, where group buying and social media integration have proven to be highly effective.
- Overall, the chapter provides a comprehensive overview of the key factors influencing modern consumer behaviour and the strategies brands must adopt to thrive in this ever-evolving digital landscape.

KEY TERMS

Digital marketing: Strategies and practices used to promote products or services through digital channels, including social media, search engines and email.

Social commerce: E-commerce practices that leverage social media platforms to facilitate buying and selling activities.

Print media: Traditional media formats such as newspapers and magazines, which can be enhanced through digital integration.

Augmented reality (AR): Technology that overlays digital content onto the physical world through devices like smartphones or tablets.

e-WOM (electronic word-of-mouth): Online consumer reviews and recommendations that influence purchasing decisions.

Web 2.0: The evolution of the internet characterized by user-generated content and interactive web applications.

Mobile commerce (m-commerce): The buying and selling of goods and services through mobile devices.

Group buying: A purchasing model where consumers buy products in bulk through collective orders to receive discounts.

Omnichannel experience: A seamless consumer experience across various channels, including online and offline touchpoints.

Technology acceptance model (TAM): A theoretical model that explains how users come to accept and use new technologies.

KEY LEARNING POINTS

Traditional vs. digital consumer behaviour:

- Traditional consumer behaviour was characterized by slow, deliberate decision-making, driven largely by personal interactions, geographical constraints and trust built through physical presence.
- The digital revolution introduced rapid access to information, transforming consumers into more informed, engaged and empowered actors in the marketplace.

Impact of technology on marketing and consumer engagement:

- Digital marketing enables enhanced targeting, personalization and real-time engagement, offering a more cost-efficient and scalable approach than traditional marketing.
- Website design, especially in mobile commerce, plays a crucial role in shaping consumer behaviour, influencing usability, trust and even impulsiveness.

Social media's role in consumer decision-making:

- Social media has shifted consumer behaviour from individual to collective consciousness, where community influence and digital word-of-mouth (e-WOM) play pivotal roles in decision-making.
- The rise of the 'consumer-actor' reflects a demand for interactivity and personalization, forcing brands to adapt their strategies to meet these evolving expectations.

Integration of print media with digital platforms:

- Print media can be revitalized through multimedia integration, social media engagement and the development of interactive digital catalogues, enhancing consumer experience and accessibility.
- The shift from physical to digital books has profound implications for education, enabling more dynamic and flexible learning opportunities.

Case study of Pinduoduo and social commerce:

- Pinduoduo's success in China illustrates the power of social commerce, particularly in leveraging group buying and social media integration to drive consumer engagement and trust.
- The platform's model highlights the importance of understanding local consumer behaviours and adapting digital strategies accordingly.

2 | The new era of consumer needs and motivations

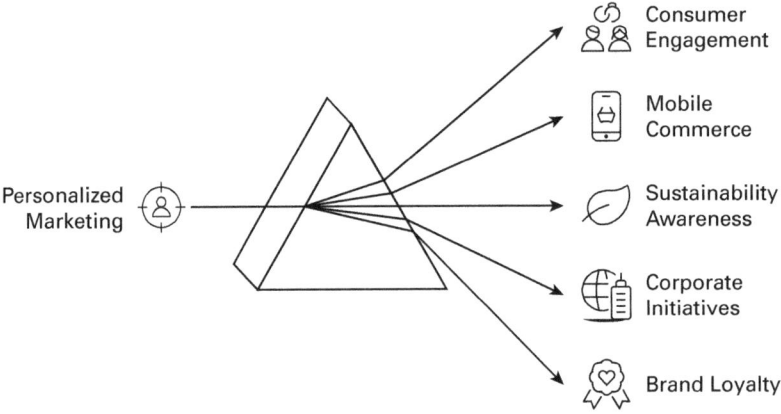

LEARNING OBJECTIVES

By the end of this chapter, you should be able to:

- Understand the role of personalization: Explain how personalized marketing strategies enhance consumer engagement and influence purchase decisions by tailoring content to individual preferences.
- Analyse the impact of mobile commerce: Assess how personalization in mobile commerce (m-commerce) improves user experience and conversion rates, considering the significance of interface design, usability and aesthetics.
- Evaluate the influence of sustainability: Identify how increasing consumer awareness of environmental issues affects purchasing behaviour and the importance of integrating sustainability into business strategies.

- Explore corporate sustainability initiatives: Describe how corporate sustainability efforts and effective communication of these practices impact consumer perceptions, loyalty and competitive advantage.
- Apply key concepts in real-world scenarios: Utilize the concepts of personalization and sustainability to analyse case studies and develop strategies for enhancing consumer engagement and fostering brand loyalty.

CHAPTER OUTLINE

Personalization and consumer engagement:

- Definition and significance
- The relationship between personalization and engagement
- Case studies and examples

The impact of personalization on purchase decisions:

- Enhancing relevance and decision-making
- Building trust and perceived value
- Personalization in mobile commerce

Sustainability in consumer decision-making:

- Increasing consumer awareness
- The influence of sustainability on purchase decisions
- Corporate sustainability initiatives and consumer perceptions

Introduction

In the evolving landscape of modern marketing, personalization has emerged as a cornerstone of effective customer engagement and business success. The ability to tailor content, offers and experiences to individual consumer preferences has become a critical factor in driving brand loyalty and increasing conversion rates. This chapter delves into the multifaceted role of personalization in marketing, exploring how it enhances consumer engagement and influences purchasing decisions. Furthermore, it examines the growing importance of sustainability in shaping consumer behaviour and the impact of corporate sustainability initiatives on consumer perceptions. By understanding these dynamics, businesses can better align their strategies with evolving consumer expectations and market trends.

Changing consumer needs in the digital world

As mentioned in Chapter 1, live streaming commerce entered the French market in 2020 during the Covid-19 pandemic. 70 per cent of European consumers were interested in live streaming commerce, with 67 per cent in France, boasting a conversion rate 10 times higher than traditional e-commerce (FEVAD, 2022). The emergence of live streaming commerce has influenced and reshaped consumer preferences. In their work, Taieb and Pelet (2024) have investigated factors such as real-time interaction, personalized services and immersive experiences, which contribute to a transformation in the way consumers make purchasing decisions.

With the integration of LSC or 'social commerce' into the realm of e-commerce, a new offering emerges for customers, aimed at providing them with an enriched shopping experience based on reality within an interactive cyber-physical environment (Sun et al., 2019). Consumers, facing their computer or phone screens, explore products and conduct transactions via social networks or content creation platforms, all within an application or website. In this format, which involves both gamification of product purchases and a powerful social element with other live users, LSC sellers often establish a relationship with their customers by engaging in discussions during product presentations. The website or application displays a seller presenting products on one part of the screen, a chat for asking questions in another part and the catalogue displaying information and the price of the presented product in a third part when using a computer.

All this information is displayed on the screen when using a phone. This emerging form of shopping eliminates the frictions of the buying process, such as having to move during a specific time slot, creating a more engaging journey for the consumer and presenting new opportunities for brands to capture consumer interest.

> **SEPHORA'S LIVE SHOPPING INITIATIVE**
>
> Sephora, positioning itself as a 'prestige omni-retail leader', has introduced a Sephora Live Shopping page, inviting visitors to experience the magic of the store from the comfort of their homes. This live shopping feature allows visitors to engage directly with beauty advisors, utilizing real-time video presentations to showcase products and interact with potential buyers. The platform enables consumers to express opinions and post real-time comments, making it particularly effective for introducing and selling experiential products such as clothing and cosmetics.

The integration of social interaction in live streaming commerce

When we delve into the multifaceted aspects of LSC, exploring how it goes beyond traditional e-commerce by integrating social interactions into the shopping experience, we aim at elucidating the impact of social elements, user-generated content and real-time engagement on contemporary consumer decision-making processes.

On one hand, this real-time interaction helps reduce uncertainty about the quality of products and increases consumer confidence (Lee and Turban, 2001; Li et al., 2012). Additionally, consumers can experience an immersive state like flow due to the interactive nature of perceived features of live streaming, allowing interaction with the seller or other viewers using text and emojis, offering a form of playability as defined by Hoffman and Novak, where 'irrelevant thoughts and perceptions are eliminated and the consumer's attention is fully focused on the interaction' (1996). This interaction with sellers enhances the emotional engagement of the user, leading to a sense of immersion (Kim et al., 2016).

Some researchers emphasize that establishing consumer trust in the live buying process is a crucial foundation for transaction completion (Luo et al., 2022; Zuo et Xiao, 2021). Trust transfer in the LSC domain relies on effective bidirectional communication between streamers and consumers (Zhang et al., 2022). This dimension highlights the importance of interactive exchanges where consumers receive comprehensive product information through questions and comments, both from streamers and from other consumers, significantly influencing their trust in promoted products (Sharma et al., 2019; Zhang et al., 2022). Others argue that the success of online sellers depends on their ability to foster this flow state among their customers (Hsu et al., 2012; Gao and Bai, 2014; Zhang et al., 2014).

Exploring the world of Roblox: a hub for user-generated content and creativity

This section highlights how user-generated content and interactive platforms influence consumer behaviour and engagement in the digital age.

Games offer a diverse range of experiences for players on the Roblox platform, from life simulation and pet collection to first-person shooters and adventure games. The games are developed using the Roblox engine. This platform provides a unique experience where users can unleash their creativity by designing and playing a wide variety of games, including platformers, racers and RPGs. Unlike Minecraft, which is a game itself, Roblox offers a platform with a simple but powerful **Lua scripting language** for game creation. Users can easily create their own 'experiences' on Roblox by following tutorials and utilizing the free Roblox Studio app on their PC with an internet connection.

Shifts in consumer demographics

The phases of web evolution, from Web 1.0 to Web3, are not directly correlated with age. Instead, they represent distinct stages in the development and transformation of internet technologies and practices. While certain age demographics may exhibit preferences or behaviours associated with specific phases (e.g. younger generations being more inclined towards interactive Web 2.0 platforms), the categorization of phases primarily pertains to technological advancements, user interaction paradigms and underlying principles of internet architecture. Indeed, many adults keep playing virtual games and easily go on to Roblox for example, which is a platform known as a metaverse.

Launched in 2006, Roblox has grown into a diverse ecosystem with millions of user-generated games spanning various genres, from role-playing and simulation to action and adventure. One of the key features of Roblox is its user-friendly game creation tools, which enable players to design their own virtual worlds and experiences using Roblox Studio. This aspect has contributed to its appeal to a wide range of age groups, from children and teenagers to adults.

There are many reasons why adults use Roblox extensively, including creative expression, as Roblox provides a creative outlet for adults to express themselves through game development. Whether they have a background in programming, art or game design, adults can leverage Roblox Studio to bring their ideas to life and share them with a global community. In this aspect, the community engagement is extremely important as Roblox fosters a vibrant and diverse community of players and developers. Adults may join Roblox to connect with like-minded individuals, collaborate on projects and participate in social events within the platform. It provides users with entrepreneurial opportunities as Roblox offers monetization options for developers through the sale of virtual items, game passes and developer products. Adult developers may see Roblox as a potential source of income or a platform to showcase their skills and portfolio to a large audience.

The parental involvement is also important as many adults, particularly parents, use Roblox to engage with their children in a shared virtual environment. By playing Roblox games together, adults can ensure a safe and enjoyable gaming experience. Nostalgia and entertainment are also present on Roblox. Whether revisiting childhood favourites or discovering new experiences, Roblox offers a vast library of games catering to diverse interests and preferences. But overall, the flexibility, creativity and social aspects of Roblox appeal to adults seeking immersive gaming experiences, creative outlets, entrepreneurial opportunities or ways to connect with others in a virtual space.

Evolution of the World Wide Web: from Web 1.0 to Web3

Web 1.0 is characterized by static web pages and limited user interactivity, focusing on basic information retrieval. Timothy John Berners-Lee proposed this initial phase, featuring a structured graph and link organization to facilitate simple user tasks (Goel et al., 2022).

Web 2.0 marked a shift to dynamic content creation, social networking and user-generated content, significantly enhancing user interaction and engagement.

Web3 emphasizes decentralization, semantic understanding and user empowerment. This evolution has profoundly influenced communication, information interaction and commercial activities, driven by advancements in technology, changes in user behaviour and improvements in internet infrastructure.

Each phase of the Web reflects a progression in online interaction, from the rudimentary tasks of Web 1.0 to the more sophisticated and interactive experiences of Web 2.0 and Web3.

The subsequent phase, denoted as Web 2.0, emerged from brainstorming sessions and introduced innovative technologies such as the document object model, asynchronous JavaScript and XML, Cascading Style Sheets and JavaScript Object Notation. These advancements facilitated the generation and dissemination of diverse content types on the internet, thereby underscoring the significance of interactivity within Web 2.0 design. The proliferation of social media platforms, music and video-sharing websites and e-commerce platforms has significantly influenced the creative inclinations of younger demographics. Nonetheless, concerns have arisen regarding data collection practices by Web 2.0 platforms, which often prioritize maximizing revenue, fostering uncertainties regarding the utilization and privacy of user information.

With the advent of Web 2.0, consumer behaviour underwent significant transformation driven by the introduction of interactive technologies and platforms. The proliferation of social media, multimedia sharing websites and e-commerce platforms empowered users to engage in more dynamic online experiences such as with **User-Generated Content** websites, like TripAdvisor. This shift in consumer behaviour towards increased interactivity can be attributed to the expanded possibilities for content creation, social interaction and commercial transactions afforded by Web 2.0 technologies.

The onset of the Web3 epoch, alternatively termed the semantic web or the decentralized Web, is currently unfolding (Gan et al., 2023). This conceptual framework envisions an increasingly intelligent, decentralized and user-centric internet architecture. A comprehensive inquiry into Web3 delineates its foundational principles, potential technological innovations, prevailing trends and foreseeable consequences. Central to the ethos of Web3 is the empowerment of individuals through user-generated content and authority, granting them agency over the visibility of information on both user interfaces and platforms.

The emergence of Web3 heralds another shift in consumer demographics, characterized by a focus on decentralization, user empowerment and data sovereignty.

Understanding decentralization: forms, benefits and applications

Decentralization refers to the distribution of power, authority and decision-making away from a central authority or governing body in an organization. There are different forms of **Decentralization**, including political, administrative, fiscal and market **Decentralization**:

- Political **Decentralization**: Aims to give citizens or their elected representatives more power in public decision-making, supporting democratization and better-informed decisions.
- Administrative **Decentralization**: Involves redistributing authority, responsibility and financial resources for providing public services among different levels of government or entities.
- Fiscal **Decentralization**: Focuses on financial responsibility, ensuring that local governments have adequate revenues to carry out decentralized functions effectively.
- Market **Decentralization**: Involves privatization and deregulation, allowing functions previously managed by the government to be carried out by businesses or non-government organizations.

Decentralization offers various benefits such as quick decision-making, executive development, managerial skill enhancement, relieving top management, facilitating growth, better control, effective communication and improved data reconciliation. However, it also has potential disadvantages, such as inefficiency for standardized services and loss of control over financial resources by the central government.

In the context of blockchain technology, **Decentralization** refers to the transfer of control and decision-making from a centralized entity to a distributed network. Table 2.1 is a two-column table summarizing the good and bad aspects of decentralization in blockchain.

Table 2.1 The key advantages and disadvantages of decentralization in blockchain technology

Aspect	Good	Bad
Trustless environment	- Reduces the risk of fraud and manipulation. - Trust is placed in technology rather than human intermediaries.	- Difficult to resolve disputes or reverse fraudulent transactions - Relies on the robustness of the blockchain protocol.
Improves data reconciliation	- Ensures all participants have access to the same updated and verified data. - Reduces data discrepancies between parties.	- Consensus process can be resource-intensive and slow compared to centralized systems.
Reduces points of weakness	- Lowers the risk of a single point of failure. - Makes the system more resilient to attacks and failures.	- Managing a decentralized network can introduce new challenges, such as synchronization and increased attack surface.
Optimizes resource distribution	- Utilizes resources more efficiently by distributing tasks across the network. - Potentially lowers costs for participants.	- Can lead to inefficiencies like duplication of efforts and increased energy consumption, especially in proof-of-work systems.
Enhances security	- Provides strong security guarantees through decentralization and cryptographic techniques. - Hard for malicious actors to alter the blockchain.	- Not immune to attacks, such as 51% attacks. - New types of attacks are continuously being discovered.

Consumers in this phase are increasingly conscious of privacy and data security concerns, prompted by the pervasive data collection practices of Web 2.0 platforms. As a result, consumers seek greater control over their online identities and information, gravitating towards decentralized platforms that prioritize user autonomy and transparency. Examples might include Mastodon, which is a social media platform aimed at giving more freedom to users, compared with X (previously Twitter), knowing that they are designed to give the same content.

Blockchain technology, synonymous with decentralized governance models, epitomizes the underlying infrastructure of Web3.0, facilitating transparency and resilience. Ethereum co-founder Gavin Wood contends that the dominance of centralized services perpetuates corporate monopolies, heralding a paradigm shift in the forthcoming era. Consequently, the forthcoming transition is poised to reshape the landscape of Web 2.0 (Gan et al., 2023), accentuating shifts in consumer demographics and societal dynamics.

ACTIVITY 1

Case study analysis

Objective: Apply chapter concepts to real-world scenarios.

Instructions: Divide the class into small groups and give each group a case study involving a company's personalization and/or sustainability strategies.

Ask each group to analyse how the company's approaches impact consumer engagement, purchase decisions and brand loyalty.

Have each group present their findings and recommendations for improving the company's strategies based on the chapter's concepts.

The impact of digital technology on consumer needs

The impact of digital technology on consumer needs is a multifaceted topic that has garnered significant attention in academic literature. In the realm of consumer behaviour, the integration of digital technology has revolutionized how consumers interact with products and services. Digital advancements have led to a shift in consumer expectations, preferences and behaviours. For instance, the convenience of online shopping platforms has altered traditional shopping patterns, with consumers now valuing speed, personalization and seamless experiences. Digital tools have empowered consumers, enabling them to make more informed decisions, access a wider range of products and engage with brands on a deeper level (Arnold et al., 2024; Bartosik-Purgat and Filimon, 2022). Moreover, businesses adapt their strategies to meet the evolving needs of digital consumers (Youssef and Mansour, 2024).

The impact of digital technology on consumer needs is a dynamic area of study that continues to shape the landscape of consumer behaviour. By examining insights from leading academic journals and books in this field, researchers can gain a comprehensive understanding of how digital advancements influence consumer preferences and expectations in today's digital era.

Consumer needs in the era of e-commerce

The evolution of e-commerce, from static web pages (Web 1.0) to social media helping catalogues (Web 2.0) to live streaming commerce – also called social shopping – and shopping on the metaverse (Web3), has significantly influenced consumer behaviour in the digital era, reshaping how individuals interact with businesses and make purchasing decisions. Initially met with scepticism due to security concerns, e-commerce platforms have now gained trust through improved security measures, offering consumers a more reliable online shopping experience.

The impact of e-commerce on consumer behaviour is profound, with notable advancements such as personalization, targeted marketing and the rise of online shopping platforms transforming the way consumers shop and engage with brands. The convenience, accessibility and personalized experiences offered by e-commerce have revolutionized the retail landscape, leading to increased competition among businesses striving to meet the evolving needs of digital consumers.

Understanding consumer behaviour in the digital age is crucial for businesses to thrive and succeed. With the empowerment of consumers through access to vast product information online and the ability to engage directly with businesses via social media platforms, businesses must adapt their strategies to cater to informed and demanding consumers.

The influence of personalization on consumer motivations

Personalization plays a crucial role in shaping consumer motivations in the digital age, influencing their purchasing decisions and interactions with brands. Research indicates that personalized advertisements enhance consumers' perception of relevance, leading to increased engagement and purchase intent (Pelet and Ettis, 2022). The customization of shopping experiences based on individual preferences and behaviours has become a key strategy for businesses to connect with consumers on a deeper level and foster loyalty (Pelet and Taieb, 2023). Studies highlight that personalization in e-commerce is highly valued by consumers, with a significant percentage expressing a preference for brands that offer tailored recommendations and experiences.

Moreover, the benefits of personalization in e-commerce are extensive, ranging from increased customer satisfaction and loyalty to improved conversions and reduced cart abandonment rates. Personalization not only enhances the overall shopping experience for consumers but also provides businesses with valuable insights into customer behaviour, enabling them to tailor their marketing strategies effectively.

The ability to deliver personalized experiences gives businesses a competitive edge by differentiating them from competitors and fostering stronger relationships with customers.

The role of data analytics in personalization

Data analytics plays a pivotal role in driving personalization strategies in the realm of customer experiences and marketing campaigns. By harnessing data analytics tools and techniques, businesses can create tailored and targeted experiences that resonate with individual customers, ultimately fostering trust and long-lasting relationships. The integration of predictive analytics and machine learning enables businesses to delve deep into customer data, allowing for the customization of marketing campaigns based on precise insights derived from data analysis. Website analytics further contributes to personalization efforts by providing valuable information on user behaviour and preferences, guiding businesses in optimizing their online platforms to better meet customer needs.

> **WHY IS PERSONALIZATION SO IMPORTANT FOR THE CONSUMER? IS IT BECAUSE WE LIVE IN AN ERA WHERE CUSTOMERS EXPECT US TO UNDERSTAND THEIR WANTS AND NEEDS?**
>
> The influence of personalization on consumer motivations is profound, driving increased engagement, loyalty and sales in the e-commerce landscape. By leveraging personalization strategies informed by consumer data and preferences, businesses can create meaningful connections with customers, ultimately leading to enhanced brand image and customer satisfaction. Understanding the motivation behind personalization is paramount in today's rapidly evolving e-commerce landscape. A staggering acceleration in e-commerce growth can be observed, with consumers exploring myriad stores, websites and brands within a compressed time frame. This surge in consumer activity has prompted retailers to intensify their investments in research, development and technological advancements, notably in artificial intelligence adoption.
>
> The convergence of heightened consumer expectations and escalating market competition, coupled with technological advancements, underscores the critical importance of personalized and seamless purchasing experiences. From the customer's standpoint, empirical evidence shows a strong preference for personalization. The majority of consumers are inclined to patronize brands offering tailored recommendations. All in all, it indicates a significant preference for personalized interactions among frequent shoppers. The repercussions of neglecting

personalization are palpable. Brands risk alienating consumers and jeopardizing their market position. A substantial portion of consumers unwilling to engage with non-personalized platforms signals a potential loss of revenue and customer loyalty. However, the mere implementation of personalization strategies is insufficient. Poorly executed or intrusive personalization efforts can backfire, driving consumers away from brands.

Presently, while brands acknowledge the imperative of personalization, many grapple with implementation challenges. We can elucidate the struggle faced by retailers in effectively identifying website visitors, hampering their personalization capabilities. Despite recognizing personalization's centrality, a considerable gap persists between retailers' aspirations and their operational realities. The pivotal role of data emerges as a fundamental pillar in enhancing personalization efforts. Access to comprehensive datasets, particularly first-party or zero-party data, enables retailers to discern consumer preferences, interests and behaviours in real-time. However, prevailing challenges, such as deciphering consumer intent and distinguishing between browsers and buyers, underscore the pressing need for innovative solutions.

Collaborative endeavours between retailers and technology partners exemplify proactive measures to address personalization challenges. Implementing real-time customer identification and data capture technologies empowers retailers to deliver tailored communications based on individual browsing behaviours. Such initiatives not only augment customer experiences but also bolster retailers' revenue streams and marketing efficacy. Looking ahead, the trajectory of personalization hinges on several key considerations. Embracing first-party data acquisition, recognizing the value of customer retention and swiftly adapting to evolving technological landscapes emerge as imperative strategies for brands navigating the personalized commerce landscape. As the industry grapples with impending changes, a proactive stance towards personalization underscores its enduring significance in shaping future consumer engagements and brand success.

Moreover, the synergy between AI and data analytics is reshaping personalization strategies, enhancing the overall customer experience and driving customer loyalty. Through hyper-personalization fuelled by data, AI and automation, companies can deliver custom experiences that cater to individual preferences and behaviours, thereby increasing engagement and satisfaction. The strategic utilization of data analytics not only empowers businesses to personalize their interactions with customers but also enables them to stay ahead in a competitive market by delivering tailored solutions that align with evolving consumer expectations.

In the contemporary milieu of e-commerce, personalized marketing assumes heightened importance across businesses of all dimensions. As consumers increasingly expect personalized interactions, enterprises failing to embrace personalized marketing strategies risk ceding market share to competitors who adeptly cater to consumer expectations. Thus, personalized marketing has metamorphosed into an indispensable tool for businesses striving to remain competitive and relevant in an ever-evolving marketplace. Data serves as the linchpin in enabling personalized marketing campaigns, furnishing insights into customer behaviour, interests and preferences. These insights, gleaned from data analytics, empower companies to curate targeted content that resonates with individual customers' unique needs and inclinations. Through data, companies can decipher customer demographics, discern behavioural patterns and even anticipate future consumer behaviour through predictive analytics. This enables the creation of personalized marketing campaigns that anticipate and cater to consumers' evolving needs and preferences, thereby driving engagement and loyalty.

MORE ON THE ROLE OF DATA IN PERSONALIZED MARKETING CAMPAIGNS

In the contemporary landscape of marketing, personalized campaigns have evolved into a standard practice, with businesses across diverse scales leveraging data analytics to craft bespoke experiences for their clientele. Such campaigns, ranging from tailored product recommendations to targeted advertisements, harness data to deliver content that is not only relevant and engaging but also notably efficacious. However, an inquiry into the mechanisms through which data facilitates personalized marketing campaigns, as well as an examination of the ethical considerations inherent in the utilization of customer data, is imperative. At its core, personalized marketing entails tailoring messages, products and experiences to the individual preferences and needs of customers, in contrast to disseminating generic content to a broad audience. Leveraging customer data, personalized marketing campaigns curate targeted and pertinent content, directly addressing a customer's proclivities, behaviours and purchase history. The significance of personalized marketing lies in its potential to significantly enhance the efficacy of marketing endeavours. By employing data to generate targeted content, enterprises can furnish customers with more immersive and tailored experiences, thereby fostering heightened customer loyalty, elevated conversion rates and enhanced return on investment. Moreover, personalized marketing enables businesses to forge deeper connections with their clientele, signalling an understanding of their requirements and preferences.

Personalized marketing campaigns hinge on various types of data to craft targeted and relevant content that aligns with individual customer proclivities. These encompass demographic data, shedding light on customers' age, gender, location and income, thereby facilitating segmentation and tailored messaging. Behavioural data elucidates customers' past interactions, purchase history and browsing behaviour, offering insights into their interests and preferences. Psychographic data delves into customers' personality traits, values and beliefs, enabling the creation of messaging that resonates with their intrinsic motivations. Contextual data, encompassing factors such as location and device usage, facilitates the delivery of timely and relevant marketing messages. Finally, predictive data leverages machine learning algorithms to anticipate future customer behaviour based on historical trends, enabling proactive and personalized marketing initiatives.

Companies employ myriad methodologies to collect and analyse customer data for personalized marketing campaigns. These range from online tracking mechanisms such as cookies to customer surveys, social media monitoring and loyalty programmes. Subsequently, companies utilize data mining, predictive analytics and customer segmentation techniques to glean actionable insights from collected data, thereby informing the creation of targeted and personalized marketing campaigns. Successful personalized marketing campaigns driven by data serve as exemplars of the efficacy of leveraging customer data to create immersive and engaging experiences. Prominent examples include Amazon's personalized product recommendations, Netflix's tailored content suggestions and Spotify's curated playlists. These campaigns underscore the transformative potential of personalized marketing in driving consumer engagement, loyalty and brand affinity.

However, amidst the plethora of opportunities presented by data-driven personalized marketing, several challenges and ethical considerations loom large. Foremost among these is the imperative to uphold customer privacy and data protection regulations, ensuring transparent data collection practices and safeguarding against data breaches. Additionally, concerns regarding data quality, customer consent and discrimination underscore the need for responsible and ethical data utilization practices. As such, companies must adopt a principled approach to collecting and using customer data, balancing the imperatives of personalized marketing with respect for consumer privacy and rights.

The effective utilization of data lies at the heart of personalized marketing campaigns, facilitating the creation of tailored and immersive experiences that resonate with individual customer needs and preferences. By leveraging customer data judiciously, companies can enhance engagement, foster loyalty and drive business growth. However, navigating the complex terrain of data-driven personalized marketing necessitates a nuanced understanding of ethical considerations and regulatory frameworks, ensuring that consumer trust and privacy remain paramount. As technology continues to evolve, personalized marketing will undoubtedly remain a cornerstone of contemporary marketing strategies, heralding a future characterized by enhanced consumer engagement, loyalty and brand affinity (Ettis et al., 2023).

Personalization and consumer engagement

Personalization and consumer engagement represent critical components of contemporary marketing strategies, profoundly shaping interactions between businesses and their clientele. Personalization, in this context, pertains to the customization of marketing efforts and offerings to cater to individual preferences, needs and behaviours of consumers, as we have seen already. It involves leveraging data analytics, artificial intelligence and machine learning algorithms to deliver tailored experiences across various touchpoints, such as websites, emails, advertisements, social media platforms, and live streaming commerce platforms. Through personalized marketing initiatives, companies endeavour to forge deeper connections with consumers by offering relevant content, product recommendations and promotional offers that resonate with their interests and aspirations.

Consumer engagement, meanwhile, refers to the degree of involvement, interaction and emotional connection that individuals exhibit towards a brand or its offerings. It encompasses a spectrum of activities, including but not limited to browsing products, participating in discussions, providing feedback and making purchases. Effective consumer engagement strategies aim to foster meaningful relationships with customers, cultivate brand loyalty and drive long-term value. By actively involving consumers in brand experiences and decision-making processes, companies can nurture trust, advocacy and loyalty, thereby fortifying their competitive position in the marketplace. This is what happens with McDonald's, as we observed already with WeChat, the main social media used in China.

Smart e-commerce systems (SESs) present a promising avenue for businesses to seamlessly incorporate elements of social media entertainment, interaction and advertisement into their e-commerce endeavours. By harnessing enhanced operational efficiencies, these SESs integrate social exchange mechanisms alongside payment functionalities, thereby facilitating intelligent business transactions. Such integration exemplifies features observed in WeChat, the widely popular Chinese social media platform. WeChat boasts a feature known as 'moments', akin to Facebook's timeline, enabling users to engage in communication with friends while sharing everyday moments and preferred content. Research indicates that the dynamic interactions among users within online spaces, including the exchange of social media 'moments', yield enjoyment and consequential behavioural effects (Kao et al., 2019).

Web-drama clips represent a notable subset of content shared among users on WeChat, emerging as a potent platform for online advertising (Kang, 2020). Chinese users leverage various social media platforms such as Weibo, Renren and WeChat to express their fondness for web-drama content. The act of sharing web-drama content, including brands featured within the shows, on WeChat moments is supported by Lawler's affect theory of social exchange (Lawler, 2001). This theoretical framework posits that sharing information or content induces positive emotions among individuals (Chen et al., 2019; Lawler, 2010; Lawler and Yoon, 1993, 1996, 1998; Lawler et al., 2000, 2006), subsequently extending the positive emotional response to the associated brand (Price and Collett, 2012).

Consequently, the emotional engagement and attachment viewers experience with web-drama content transition into the social media realm when shared within a close-knit circle. This spillover effect from web-drama engagement to the advertised brand is evident in mini-film advertising (Karpinska-Krakowiak and Eisend, 2019). Thus, when users share digital content from web-dramas about a brand, a sense of enjoyment and playfulness is fostered among individuals, resembling a real-life sensation termed 'ticklish moment'. These moments extend beyond the scope of web-drama content and may encompass implicit advertising embedded within the show, fostering a sense of entertainment and leisure within a trusted community (Karjaluoto et al., 2016).

Social media-embedded word-of-mouth (WOM) notably influences consumers' purchasing decisions (Hubbard, 2020). Wu et al. (2020) suggest that brand mentions within web-drama content evoke a positive advertising effect. The combined impact of brand affection and WOM through WeChat 'ticklish moments' influences expenditures on the advertised brand. This study underscores that the interplay between brand affinity and spending mediated via 'ticklish moments' is prevalent within WeChat. Such social exchange on social media platforms mirrors dynamic relationships that are enjoyable and elicit behavioural outcomes, such as increased spending on favoured brands (Kao et al., 2019).

The nexus between personalization and consumer engagement lies in their symbiotic relationship, wherein personalized marketing initiatives serve as catalysts for enhancing consumer engagement levels. Personalized experiences engender a sense of relevance, exclusivity and individuality, compelling consumers to actively engage with brands and their offerings. When tailored content and recommendations align closely with consumer preferences and needs, individuals are more likely to invest time, attention and resources in exploring and interacting with brand offerings. Consequently, heightened consumer engagement manifests in increased brand awareness, affinity and advocacy, driving positive business outcomes such as higher conversion rates, repeat purchases and customer lifetime value.

To summarize, these points encapsulate the essence of the relationship between personalization and consumer engagement, highlighting the importance of individualized experiences and meaningful interactions in driving business success:

- Symbiotic relationship: Personalization and consumer engagement are interconnected, with personalized marketing initiatives acting as catalysts for enhancing consumer engagement levels.
- Sense of relevance: Personalized experiences create a sense of relevance, exclusivity and individuality, compelling consumers to actively engage with brands and their offerings.

- Alignment with preferences: When tailored content and recommendations align closely with consumer preferences and needs, individuals are more likely to invest time, attention and resources in exploring and interacting with brand offerings.
- Increased engagement: Heightened consumer engagement results in increased brand awareness, affinity and advocacy.
- Positive business outcomes: Enhanced engagement drives positive business outcomes such as higher conversion rates, repeat purchases and increased customer lifetime value.
- Paradigm shift: The convergence of personalization and consumer engagement represents a paradigm shift in contemporary marketing strategies.
- Prioritizing individualized experiences: Businesses must prioritize individualized experiences and meaningful interactions with their target audience.
- Data-driven personalization: Embracing data-driven personalization strategies is crucial.
- Authentic engagement: Fostering authentic consumer engagement helps cultivate enduring relationships with customers.
- Brand loyalty: Personalized and engaging experiences foster brand loyalty.
- Sustained growth: Companies can achieve sustained growth and competitiveness by prioritizing personalization and engagement in an increasingly dynamic and competitive marketplace.

The impact of personalization on consumer purchase decisions

Personalization plays a crucial role in shaping consumer purchase decisions, significantly influencing how individuals engage with brands and ultimately make buying choices. One of the primary ways personalization impacts purchasing behaviour is by increasing the relevance of product recommendations and marketing messages. When consumers receive tailored suggestions that align closely with their preferences and needs, they are more likely to consider these products, leading to higher purchase intent.

Moreover, personalized experiences enhance the decision-making process by reducing the cognitive load on consumers. By presenting options that are specifically curated for them, brands simplify the shopping journey, making it easier for consumers to arrive at a decision. This streamlined experience can result in increased conversion rates, as consumers feel more confident in their choices.

The overall customer experience is also improved through personalization. Engaging and relevant interactions foster a sense of satisfaction, which can lead to not only immediate purchases but also long-term customer loyalty. When consumers perceive that a brand understands their individual needs, they are more likely to develop a deeper affinity for that brand, further influencing their purchasing decisions.

Additionally, personalized marketing can create a greater perceived value in the offerings presented to consumers. When individuals receive tailored offers or product suggestions, they often feel that these recommendations are more valuable, which increases their willingness to make a purchase. This effect is particularly pronounced when personalized recommendations trigger impulse buying, as consumers may be drawn to products that resonate with their interests at the right moment.

Trust is another critical factor influenced by personalization. Effective personalization builds a sense of trust between the consumer and the brand, fostering a connection that positively impacts purchase decisions. When consumers feel understood and valued, they are more likely to engage with the brand and make purchases.

Personalization also reduces the time consumers spend searching for products. By providing relevant options upfront, brands can facilitate quicker purchase decisions, enhancing the overall efficiency of the shopping experience. Furthermore, personalized recommendations can create opportunities for cross-selling and upselling, introducing consumers to complementary or higher-value products that they may not have considered otherwise, thereby increasing the average order value.

However, it is essential to recognize that the effectiveness of personalization can vary based on several factors, including the level of personalization, consumer privacy concerns and the perceived intrusiveness of the personalized content. Striking the right balance between personalization and privacy is crucial for maximizing the positive impact of personalization on consumer purchase decisions.

Personalization significantly influences consumer purchase decisions by enhancing relevance, simplifying decision-making, improving customer experiences and fostering trust and loyalty. By leveraging data-driven strategies to personalize interactions, brands can effectively guide consumers through their purchasing journeys, ultimately driving better business outcomes.

Personalization in mobile commerce has become a powerful driver of consumer purchase decisions, transforming the way users interact with digital platforms. As consumers increasingly seek tailored experiences, m-commerce applications have evolved to deliver personalized content, offers and recommendations that align closely with individual preferences and behaviours. This shift towards customization not only enhances user engagement but also significantly boosts conversion rates by fostering a deeper connection between the consumer and the brand. The growing body of research underscores the importance of this trend, highlighting how personalized interfaces and user experiences are crucial for optimizing satisfaction and driving purchasing behaviour in the fast-evolving landscape of m-commerce. The work Pelet and Taieb (2022) have conducted highlights this shift.

User experience in m-commerce

The increasing prevalence of mobile devices has transformed the landscape of e-commerce, prompting extensive research into factors influencing user experience (UX) in mobile commerce. This literature review examines key themes, including the importance of interface design, usability, aesthetics and their effects on consumer behaviour and satisfaction in m-commerce contexts.

Interface design and usability

Interface design is critical in shaping the user experience in m-commerce. Several studies have highlighted that usability, which includes ease of navigation, intuitive layout and accessibility, is a primary determinant of user satisfaction and engagement (Li et al., 2020; Pao et al., 2011). For example, Patel et al. (2020) found that high interface quality in mobile shopping apps significantly boosts purchase intentions, underscoring the importance of a well-designed user interface (UI) in facilitating positive user interactions.

Ease of use, a key component of usability, is often measured by the efficiency and effectiveness with which users can complete tasks on an app. According to Murray and Häuble (2011), ease of use can significantly shape users' interface preferences, further emphasizing the role of intuitive design in enhancing user experience.

Aesthetics and visual design

The aesthetic appeal of a mobile application, including colour schemes, layout and visual complexity, also plays a significant role in influencing user perceptions and behaviour. Studies have shown that visual aesthetics can affect users' initial impressions, emotional responses and long-term satisfaction with a digital product (Lavie and Tractinsky, 2004; Lindgaard et al., 2006). For instance, Seckler et al. (2015) demonstrated that both the structure and colour of a website could significantly impact its perceived visual aesthetics, influencing user engagement and satisfaction.

Moreover, Tractinsky et al. (2006) found that users form consistent aesthetic judgements within milliseconds of viewing a web page, highlighting the critical role of first impressions in m-commerce. The concept of perceptual fluency, where users perceive aesthetically pleasing interfaces as more usable, further underscores the interconnectedness of aesthetics and usability (Reber and Schwarz, 1999).

User satisfaction and trust

User satisfaction in m-commerce is influenced by a combination of usability, aesthetics and perceived trustworthiness of the platform. Trust in mobile applications is a critical factor that affects users' willingness to engage in transactions. Mukherjee and Nath (2007) re-examined the commitment–trust theory in online retailing, concluding that electronic trust is a significant predictor of customer loyalty and satisfaction.

Stewart and Jürjens (2018) explored the relationship between data security and consumer trust in fintech applications, finding that users are more likely to trust and engage with platforms that prioritize data protection. This relationship is crucial in m-commerce, where users are often required to share personal and financial information.

The impact of visual complexity

The perceived visual complexity of mobile online shops can affect user satisfaction and purchase behaviour. Sohn et al. (2017) examined this aspect and found that a balance between simplicity and sufficient detail is essential to maintain user interest without overwhelming them. Overly complex designs can lead to cognitive overload, reducing user satisfaction and increasing the likelihood of abandonment.

Personalization and user engagement

Personalization in m-commerce, facilitated by smart technologies, has been shown to enhance user engagement by offering tailored experiences. Song et al. (2019) discussed the integration of smart e-commerce systems, which utilize data analytics to provide personalized recommendations, thereby improving user satisfaction and increasing conversion rates.

Parker and Wang (2016) further explored the role of hedonic and utilitarian motivations in m-commerce, concluding that personalized content and interactive features significantly enhance user engagement and satisfaction. This aligns with the findings of Tsai et al. (2017), who highlighted the importance of precise positioning and targeted marketing in mobile commerce, particularly in the context of the IoT.

The literature underscores the importance of well-designed interfaces, aesthetic appeal and trustworthiness in shaping user experience in mobile e-commerce. As m-commerce continues to evolve, future research should focus on the integration of emerging technologies, such as AI and IoT, to further enhance personalization and user engagement.

The role of sustainability in consumer decision-making

Consumer awareness about sustainability issues

Consumer awareness regarding sustainability issues has significantly increased in recent years, driven by growing concerns about environmental degradation, climate change and resource depletion. This heightened awareness is reflected in the way consumers prioritize sustainability in their purchasing decisions. Studies indicate that consumers are becoming more informed about the environmental and social impacts of their consumption choices, leading them to seek out products and services that align with their values of sustainability (Toukabri and Mohamed Youssef, 2023). Educational initiatives, media coverage and the efforts of environmental organizations have played crucial roles in raising awareness. Consumers are now more likely to consider the ecological footprint of their purchases, including factors such as carbon emissions, water usage and waste generation. This shift in consumer consciousness is not limited to a specific demographic; it spans across various age groups, with younger generations like Generation Z showing a particularly strong inclination towards sustainable consumption (Djafarova and Foots, 2022; Rustam et al., 2020).

ACTIVITY 2

Personalization strategy workshop

Objective: Develop personalized marketing strategies based on consumer behaviour insights.

Instructions: Provide a brief overview of a hypothetical company and its target market.

In groups, students will create a personalized marketing plan for the company, including content recommendations, mobile commerce enhancements and privacy considerations.

Each group will present their plan, highlighting how it aligns with the principles of personalization and addresses consumer privacy and engagement.

The influence of sustainability on purchase decisions

Sustainability has become a key determinant in consumer purchase decisions, influencing not only what products consumers buy but also which brands they support. Research shows that consumers who are aware of environmental and social issues are more likely to prioritize products that demonstrate a commitment to sustainability (Bulut et al., 2022). This trend is evident across various sectors, including fashion, food and electronics, where eco-friendly products are gaining market share, and even in education.

The influence of sustainability on purchase decisions can be attributed to several psychological and social factors. Firstly, the concept of social proof plays a significant role; consumers are influenced by the behaviours and opinions of others, particularly when it comes to adopting sustainable practices. Secondly, cognitive biases such as the availability heuristic make consumers more likely to choose products that are prominently marketed as sustainable. Furthermore, the perceived value of sustainable products, which includes both intrinsic and extrinsic benefits, enhances their attractiveness. Consumers often associate sustainable products with higher quality, better health outcomes and a sense of contributing to a greater good (D'Souza et al., 2006).

Corporate sustainability initiatives and consumer perceptions

Corporate sustainability initiatives are increasingly shaping consumer perceptions and, consequently, their purchasing behaviours. Companies that actively promote their sustainability efforts tend to build stronger relationships with their customers, who value transparency and ethical practices. These initiatives can range from reducing carbon footprints and using renewable energy to implementing fair trade practices and ensuring ethical sourcing of materials (Clarasight, 2023). Consumers are particularly responsive to brands that integrate sustainability into their core business strategies rather than treating it as an afterthought. Effective communication of these initiatives is crucial; consumers need to be informed about the specific actions companies are taking to reduce their environmental impact. Certifications and labels, such as those from the Forest Stewardship Council (FSC) or the Rainforest Alliance, serve as important indicators of a company's commitment to sustainability and help build trust with consumers (Bullshark Digital, 2023). Furthermore, the alignment of corporate sustainability initiatives with consumer values can lead to increased brand loyalty and advocacy. When consumers perceive that a brand shares their commitment to sustainability, they are more likely to engage in repeat purchases and recommend the brand to others. This alignment also provides a competitive advantage, as businesses that prioritize sustainability can differentiate themselves in the marketplace and attract a growing segment of environmentally conscious consumers (Sánchez and Vega, 2018).

In conclusion, sustainability plays a pivotal role in consumer decision-making processes. Increased awareness of sustainability issues, the influence of sustainable practices on purchase decisions and the impact of corporate sustainability initiatives collectively drive consumers towards more eco-friendly choices. As businesses and policymakers continue to emphasize sustainability, understanding these dynamics will be crucial for fostering a more sustainable and responsible marketplace.

> **ACTIVITY 3**
>
> Sustainability debate
>
> **Objective**: Discuss the impact of sustainability on consumer behaviour and corporate practices.
>
> **Instructions**: Organize a debate on the topic: 'Does integrating sustainability into business strategies lead to increased consumer loyalty and competitive advantage?'
>
> Assign roles to students to argue for and against the proposition, using evidence and examples from the chapter.
>
> Facilitate a discussion after the debate, summarizing key points and insights about the role of sustainability in consumer decision-making.

Conclusion

This chapter explores the transformative role of personalization in modern marketing, highlighting its impact on consumer engagement and purchase decisions. By tailoring content and recommendations to individual preferences, businesses can enhance relevance, simplify decision-making and build trust with consumers. The chapter also addresses the growing importance of sustainability in consumer decision-making, emphasizing that awareness of environmental issues and corporate sustainability initiatives significantly influence purchasing behaviour. Effective personalization and sustainability practices not only improve customer satisfaction but also provide a competitive edge in a rapidly evolving marketplace. Looking ahead, businesses must continue to adapt to these trends to stay relevant and successful in meeting consumer expectations.

> **KEY TERMS**
>
> Personalization: Tailoring marketing content and recommendations to individual consumer preferences and behaviours.
>
> Mobile commerce (m-commerce): The use of mobile devices to conduct commercial transactions and interactions.
>
> Engagement: The level of interaction and involvement a consumer has with a brand or its marketing efforts.
>
> Conversion rate: The percentage of users who take a desired action, such as making a purchase, as a result of marketing efforts.

Sustainability: Practices and strategies that aim to reduce environmental impact and promote long-term ecological balance.

Social proof: The influence of others' behaviours and opinions on an individual's decision-making process.

Corporate social responsibility (CSR): A company's commitment to ethical practices and sustainability in its operations and interactions with stakeholders.

Data privacy: The protection of personal information collected from consumers and ensuring it is used transparently and responsibly.

Consumer loyalty: The ongoing preference and repeat purchasing behaviour of consumers towards a specific brand.

Digital sobriety: The principle of using digital technologies in a mindful and sustainable manner to minimize environmental impact.

KEY LEARNING POINTS

Effective implementation of personalization:

- Personalization strategies, when implemented effectively, can significantly enhance customer engagement and satisfaction. However, businesses must navigate challenges related to data privacy and quality to maximize the benefits of personalization.

Balancing personalization with privacy:

- While personalization can drive positive business outcomes, it is essential to balance tailored experiences with consumer privacy concerns. Companies must ensure that their data practices are transparent and respectful to maintain trust and avoid negative repercussions.

The role of sustainability in shaping consumer choices:

- Increasing consumer awareness of sustainability issues is influencing purchasing decisions. Businesses that integrate sustainability into their core strategies and communicate their efforts effectively can build stronger relationships with customers and differentiate themselves in the marketplace.

Corporate sustainability initiatives and consumer perceptions:

- Companies that actively promote their sustainability efforts and align them with consumer values tend to gain a competitive advantage. Effective communication and transparency about sustainability practices are crucial for building trust and driving consumer loyalty.

3 | Psychological and social dynamics in digital consumer behaviour

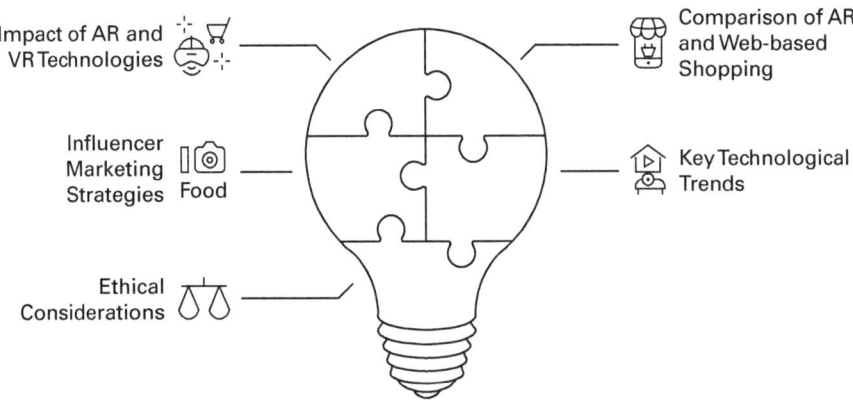

Analysing Consumer Behavior and Retail Strategies

- Impact of AR and VR Technologies
- Influencer Marketing Strategies Food
- Ethical Considerations
- Comparison of AR and Web-based Shopping
- Key Technological Trends

LEARNING OBJECTIVES

By the end of this chapter, you should be able to:

- Analyse the impact of AR and VR technologies: Evaluate how augmented reality and virtual reality enhance consumer decision-making, engagement and satisfaction in the retail sector.

- Compare AR and web-based shopping modes: Distinguish between the user experiences and purchase intentions associated with AR versus traditional web-based shopping platforms.
- Assess influencer marketing strategies: Understand how influencer marketing shapes consumer perceptions and behaviours and identify key metrics to measure its effectiveness.
- Identify key technological trends: Recognize current and future trends in VR/AR and their potential impact on consumer behaviour and retail strategies.
- Evaluate ethical considerations: Discuss the ethical implications of influencer marketing, including transparency and credibility and their impact on consumer trust.

CHAPTER OUTLINE

The power of online reviews and ratings:

- The influence of reviews on purchase decisions
- The role of social proof in consumer decision-making
- How reviews shape perceptions of product quality and credibility
- Understanding the psychology behind ratings
- Cognitive biases influencing ratings interpretation (e.g. anchoring effect, availability heuristic)
- The impact of high and low ratings on consumer behaviour
- Managing negative reviews and ratings
- Strategies for responding to and mitigating the impact of negative feedback
- Leveraging negative reviews for product or service improvement

Exploring virtual reality and augmented reality in consumer perception:

- The role of VR/AR in shopping experiences
- Overview of VR and AR technologies
- Case studies: IKEA's AR app and other examples of VR/AR in retail
- Key mechanisms influencing purchase intentions
- How VR and AR enhance decision-making, engagement and confidence

- Impact of AR on consumer behaviour
- Effects on decision-making, engagement and return rates
- Comparative analysis with traditional online shopping methods

The dynamics of influencer marketing in shaping consumer perceptions:

- The rise of influencer marketing
- Evolution and significance of influencer marketing in the digital age
- Measuring the impact of influencer marketing
- Metrics and methodologies for assessing the effectiveness of influencer campaigns
- The ethics and credibility of influencer marketing
- Ethical considerations and maintaining credibility in influencer partnerships

Introduction

In the digital era, understanding consumer behaviour has become increasingly complex due to the rapid evolution of technology and the proliferation of online platforms. This chapter delves into the psychological and social dynamics that shape digital consumer behaviour, focusing on the power of online reviews and ratings, as well as the impact of emerging technologies like virtual reality and augmented reality. Online reviews and ratings have become critical factors influencing purchasing decisions, leveraging social proof to guide consumer choices. Simultaneously, VR and AR technologies are transforming shopping experiences, offering immersive and interactive ways to engage with products. By exploring these elements, this chapter aims to provide insights into how psychological factors and technological advancements influence consumer behaviour in the digital marketplace.

The power of online reviews and ratings

Olivier Ertzscheid's work (2024) on social networking sites delves into the complex dynamics of online social interactions, focusing on how these platforms have evolved from simple communication tools into influential agents of social change. The text suggests a deep engagement with theories of uses and gratifications, which have been foundational in understanding why individuals engage with various media, particularly in the digital age. Ertzscheid's exploration into social networking sites reveals a profound understanding of how these platforms have reshaped social interactions, identity construction and community building in the digital era. Drawing on the uses and gratifications theory, Ertzscheid illustrates that social networking sites cater to a diverse array of user needs, ranging from the fundamental human desire for connection and belonging to more complex motivations such as self-expression, status seeking and information sharing.

Ertzscheid's analysis likely underscores the transition from traditional media to digital platforms, where users are not mere consumers of content but active participants in the creation and dissemination of information. This shift has empowered users to construct and curate their digital identities, influencing how they are perceived both online and offline. Furthermore, the social cognitive aspects of these interactions highlight how online behaviours are shaped by a combination of individual predispositions and the digital environments in which they operate.

Moreover, Ertzscheid examines the implications of these developments for social structures, considering both the positive aspects of increased connectivity and the potential challenges, such as the reinforcement of echo chambers and the erosion of privacy. His work might emphasize the need for a critical understanding of the role that these platforms play in shaping public discourse and cultural norms in the 21st century.

Olivier Ertzscheid's contributions to the discourse on social networking sites offer valuable insights into the ways in which digital platforms have become integral to modern social life. By integrating theoretical perspectives with empirical research, his work provides a comprehensive framework for understanding the evolving landscape of online interactions and their broader societal impact.

The influence of reviews on purchase decisions

Online reviews have emerged as a critical factor influencing consumer purchase decisions. In the digital age, consumers often rely on the experiences and opinions of others to guide their own purchasing behaviour. Reviews provide valuable insights into product quality, functionality and overall satisfaction, which can significantly impact a consumer's decision-making process. Positive reviews can enhance a product's credibility and attractiveness, leading to increased sales and customer trust. Conversely, negative reviews can deter potential buyers, highlighting the importance of managing online feedback effectively. The psychological underpinnings of this phenomenon are rooted in social proof, where individuals look to the behaviour and opinions of others to make informed decisions, particularly in uncertain situations.

Understanding the psychology behind ratings

Ratings, often presented in the form of stars or numerical scores, play a pivotal role in shaping consumer perceptions and behaviours. The psychology behind ratings is multifaceted, involving cognitive biases and heuristics that simplify decision-making. For instance, the anchoring effect can cause consumers to rely heavily on initial ratings they encounter, influencing their overall judgement of a product. Additionally, the availability heuristic suggests that consumers are more likely to be influenced by recent and easily accessible ratings. High ratings can create a perception of quality and reliability, encouraging consumers to proceed with a purchase. Meanwhile, low ratings can raise doubts and lead to hesitation. Understanding these psychological dynamics enables marketers to strategically present ratings to maximize positive consumer responses.

White and Ronfeldt (2024) examine standardized observation systems, which aim to reliably measure specific conceptualizations of teaching quality while managing rater error through mechanisms such as certification, calibration, validation and double-scoring. These mechanisms are intended not only to ensure high-quality scoring but also to generate the empirical evidence necessary to support the inference that the scores accurately represent the intended construct. Previous efforts to substantiate this inference have generally assumed that rater error can be accurately estimated from a limited number of scoring occasions. However, White and Ronfeldt empirically test this assumption using two datasets from the Measures of Effective Teaching project. Their results reveal that rater error is highly complex and challenging to measure precisely from only a few scoring instances. The authors suggest that current rater monitoring and control mechanisms may not be sufficient to measure rater error with the precision required to distinguish between levels of teaching quality typically observed. The study concludes with a discussion of the implications for supporting the scoring inference, including recommendations for enhancing rater monitoring and control mechanisms.

Managing negative reviews and ratings

Negative reviews and ratings pose a significant challenge for businesses, but they also offer opportunities for improvement and engagement. Effective management of negative feedback involves several key strategies. First, timely and empathetic responses to negative reviews can demonstrate a commitment to customer satisfaction and transparency, potentially mitigating the adverse impact. Addressing specific issues raised in reviews and offering solutions or compensation can turn dissatisfied customers into loyal advocates. Moreover, analysing negative feedback provides valuable insights into product or service shortcomings, guiding future enhancements. From a psychological perspective, demonstrating responsiveness and a willingness to improve can build trust and credibility, essential components for fostering long-term customer relationships.

The interplay between online reviews, ratings and consumer psychology underscores the importance of these elements in digital consumer behaviour. By harnessing the power of reviews and ratings, businesses can influence purchase decisions, enhance customer satisfaction and drive sustained growth in the competitive digital marketplace.

ANALYSING AND PROPOSING A HOTEL WEBSITE SERVICE QUALITY RANKING METHOD

The study conducted by Van Huy and Thai Thinh (2024) aims to analyse and propose a hotel website service quality ranking method, identifying priority factors for improving website service quality. This research is based on data collected from tourists at four-star hotels in Vietnam and employs an integrated methodology, including the gap-score scale, ratio-score scale and **Entropy method**, to establish a website service quality ranking index in the hotel industry.

The integrated methodology used in this study combines several analytical tools to assess and rank the service quality of hotel websites. The gap-score scale measures the difference between customer expectations and perceptions, while the ratio-score scale quantifies the relative importance of various service quality dimensions. The Entropy method is then applied to determine the weight of each factor, ensuring an objective and comprehensive evaluation.

The study identifies four primary factors that directly improve the quality of hotel website services: website design, website functionality, interactivity and information quality. These factors are crucial in enhancing user experience and satisfaction, ultimately influencing customer loyalty and retention:

- Website design: Aesthetic appeal and user-friendly navigation are essential for attracting and retaining visitors.
- Website functionality: Efficient and reliable website performance, including fast loading times and seamless transactions, is critical for user satisfaction.
- Interactivity: Features that enable user engagement, such as live chat support and interactive booking tools, enhance the overall user experience.
- Information quality: Accurate, comprehensive and up-to-date information about hotel services, amenities and local attractions is vital for meeting customer needs and expectations.

The findings of this study have significant implications for hotel management and website development. By focusing on the identified priority factors, hotels can improve their website service quality, leading to increased customer satisfaction and competitive advantage. The study underscores the importance of continuous monitoring and enhancement of website features to meet evolving consumer expectations and technological advancements.

The research by Van Huy and Thai Thinh (2024) provides a robust framework for evaluating and improving hotel website service quality. By leveraging the proposed ranking method, hotels can systematically identify areas for improvement and implement targeted strategies to enhance their online presence and customer engagement.

Exploring virtual reality and augmented reality in consumer perception

The role of VR/AR in shopping experiences

Virtual reality and augmented reality are reshaping the shopping experience by offering immersive and interactive environments. AR allows consumers to overlay digital information onto their real-world surroundings, enhancing their ability to visualize products in their intended context. For example, IKEA's AR app lets users place virtual furniture in their homes, which has increased sales by 30 per cent by reducing the uncertainty associated with online purchases.

Augmented reality for remote product testing

AR is a transformative technology that overlays virtual images onto the real world, enhancing the way consumers interact with products remotely. AR allows users to experience a blend of physical and digital environments, offering a unique method for product testing and consumer engagement. Iconic examples include Pokémon Go, where players interact with virtual creatures in real-world settings, and Google Translate, which translates text in real-time using a smartphone camera.

It is challenging to discuss augmented reality without referencing Nintendo's Pokémon Go application. Launched in 2016, Pokémon Go was a groundbreaking success, enabling users to capture Pokémon by viewing the real world through their smartphones, augmented with virtual images. This innovative game reached a peak of approximately 65 million users, marking a significant milestone in augmented reality gaming (Horizon IQ, 2024). Its popularity was evident as it led to numerous teenagers and young adults exploring their neighbourhoods, engrossed in their mobile devices.

The core functionality of AR relies on integrating virtual 2D or 3D images with real-world environments, viewable through devices such as smartphones, tablets, computers or specialized headsets like Microsoft's HoloLens. Implementing AR requires essential components: a camera for capturing the real environment, an operating system to process the AR content and a display to present the augmented images. This setup allows users to interact with virtual elements seamlessly integrated into their physical surroundings, impacting not only visual perception but also auditory and tactile experiences through binaural sound and haptic feedback.

REVOLUTIONIZING BUILDING PROJECTS WITH THE HELP OF AR

AR technologies have rapidly advanced and are transforming the fields of architecture and construction. By overlaying digital information onto the physical world, AR provides architects, engineers and construction professionals with powerful tools to visualize, design and collaborate more effectively.

In architecture, AR allows for immersive visualization of building designs before construction begins. Architects can superimpose 3D models onto existing environments, enabling clients and stakeholders to experience a virtual walkthrough of a building or space as if it were already built. This enhances communication and decision-making, as design concepts are more easily understood and modifications can be made in real-time. AR also assists in the design process itself, enabling architects to test different design elements, materials and lighting conditions in a simulated environment.

In construction, AR is revolutionizing how projects are managed and executed. AR-enabled devices can guide workers through complex tasks by displaying instructions, measurements and safety information directly in their field of view. This reduces errors and increases efficiency on-site. For instance, AR can be used to compare the ongoing construction against the digital plans, highlighting discrepancies and ensuring that the project stays on track. It also facilitates remote collaboration, allowing experts from different locations to view and interact with the same augmented environment, providing real-time guidance and troubleshooting.

Moreover, AR technologies are being integrated with building information modelling (BIM) systems, creating a powerful synergy that enhances project accuracy and coordination. By visualizing BIM data through AR, construction teams can better understand the spatial relationships and construction sequences, leading to improved project outcomes.

AR technologies are reshaping the architecture and construction industries by providing innovative solutions for visualization, design, project management and

> collaboration. As these technologies continue to evolve, their impact on how buildings are designed and constructed will only grow, leading to more efficient, accurate and creative outcomes.
>
> As explained by Souza (2024), AR is revolutionizing the architecture and construction industries by integrating virtual elements with real-world environments. As consumers live in buildings which shape their behaviour, it is interesting to see how AR also plays a role in this regard. Unlike virtual reality, which creates entirely separate digital spaces, AR enhances the existing physical space, enabling more efficient and accurate project execution. This technology benefits all members of the construction team, from engineers and architects to project managers and service providers, by reducing errors and optimizing resource use.
>
> AR applications in construction allow for a more precise visualization of projects, incorporating all layers of materials and installations that are often complex to interpret through traditional drawings. By using 3D plans and virtual model holograms, AR facilitates a comprehensive understanding of the project, even allowing users to see through walls to understand technical installations. This capability significantly reduces the potential for errors and guides the construction of complex geometries.

AR's ability to enhance product testing is significant. It enables businesses to create realistic and interactive prototypes, facilitating rapid iteration and feedback collection without the need for physical prototypes. This approach not only saves time and resources but also allows for personalized and immersive consumer experiences. As noted by industry experts, AR can simulate various scenarios and user interactions, providing valuable insights into product performance and consumer preferences (LinkedIn, 2023).

Moreover, AR's potential extends beyond visual enhancements. It can influence auditory perceptions by providing immersive sound experiences and tactile feedback through haptic devices. This multidimensional interaction offers a comprehensive testing environment that virtual reality, which immerses users in entirely fictional settings, cannot provide. As Alain Goudey emphasizes, AR's integration into product testing represents a significant advancement in consumer engagement and product innovation, aligning with the growing demand for interactive and personalized experiences in the digital age.

Augmented reality offers a powerful tool for remote product testing, enabling businesses to innovate and engage with consumers in unprecedented ways. By bridging the gap between the physical and digital worlds, AR not only enhances the consumer experience but also drives product development and market success.

Augmented reality in retail

In contemporary, diverse and all-encompassing settings, consumers are inundated with information regarding various products and services. Retailers must address numerous concerns such as high return rates, webrooming, cart abandonment in online purchases and overall customer satisfaction. Engaging customers by providing personalized information and value is crucial for retailers as it not only differentiates them from competitors but also fosters strong customer engagement. The primary challenge of online shopping lies in the inability to experience and physically interact with products, which distinguishes it from the tactile engagement available in physical stores. Technology plays a pivotal role in bridging this gap, helping retailers reach their target audience and enabling consumers to make more informed decisions.

AR technology serves as a bridge between online and offline purchasing by delivering a sense of direct shopping. AR is a highly interactive, advanced and spatially aware implementation, where digital objects such as videos or 3D models are overlaid onto the real-world view, giving the impression of their physical presence. This technology allows customers to virtually test products in any physical environment, whether it be furniture, clothes, cosmetics or sunglasses. The 'test before you purchase' experience offered by AR holds great potential for retailers to improve online conversion rates and decrease return rates. Companies like IKEA and ASOS are experimenting with AR and VR to simplify customer decision-making, which in turn increases customer engagement and shopping intent.

According to Ebrahimabad et al. (2024), due to its growing popularity, extensive research has been devoted to understanding the distinctions between AR-based shopping and other online shopping methods. Studies by Baek et al. (2018), Javornik (2016) and Verhagen et al. (2014) provide compelling evidence supporting the superiority of the AR experience over other online purchasing approaches.

Key mechanisms influencing purchase intentions

Verhagen et al. (2014) identify three key mechanisms influenced by AR technology: local presence, product tangibility and product likability. These elements collectively enhance consumers' purchase intentions. Conversely, Javornik (2016) highlights perceived augmentation, interactivity and flow as critical mechanisms impacting purchase intentions. Baek et al. (2018), Hilken et al. (2017) and Yim et al. (2017) propose alternative mechanisms, such as spatial presence, self-brand connections and effective communication advantages through higher levels of novelty, immersion, enjoyment and usefulness. This leads to more favourable attitudes towards the medium and increased purchase intentions compared with web-based product presentations. Poushneh (2018) asserts that AR contributes to increased user satisfaction and willingness to make a purchase.

Despite the extensive research, there remains a gap in understanding the impact of AR technology on both user experience and online purchase intention, specifically comparing the use of AR with traditional websites. Addressing this gap, research typically tests hypotheses related to both modes and employs multi-group analysis to compare outcomes. Notably, the impact of AR technology on shopping behaviour in developing countries remains underexplored. Economic conditions, regulatory environments and market imperfections in these countries present unique challenges and opportunities for technology adoption.

The integration of AR in online shopping offers the potential to significantly enhance user experience and online purchase intentions by improving information presentation and reducing cognitive load. The utilization of AR technology can reshape how information about online products is conveyed, providing consumers with a more immersive and informed shopping experience. As such, AR stands as a promising tool to bridge the gap between the online and offline shopping experiences, driving higher engagement and satisfaction among consumers.

IKEA'S AR APP

IKEA's AR app, known as IKEA Place, was launched in 2017. The app allows users to place virtual furniture in their homes using their smartphones or tablets. Key features include:

- True-to-scale models: Ensures that the virtual furniture fits perfectly in the intended space
- Ease of use: Simple interface allowing users to drag and drop items
- Extensive catalogue: Includes a wide range of IKEA products
- Sharing capabilities: Users can share their designs with friends and family for feedback.

In their study, Ebrahimabad et al. (2024) investigate the potential of AR to enhance user experience and online purchase intentions compared with traditional web-based shopping. AR allows users to place virtual products in their physical environment, providing a tangible visualization before purchase. The research aims to compare AR and web-based shopping modes by examining six key attributes – interactivity, information, enjoyment, novelty, vividness and intrusiveness – and their impact on user experience and purchase intention.

To achieve this, the authors developed two electronic questionnaires targeting different user groups: 204 participants using the IKEA website (web-based mode) and 206 participants using the IKEA Place app (AR mode). The data were analysed

> using structural equation modelling and multi-group analysis to evaluate the comparative outcomes.
>
> The findings reveal that in the AR mode, interactivity and novelty positively and significantly impact user experience and purchase intention, while intrusiveness negatively impacts these factors. This study, conducted in a developing country, provides insights into how emerging technologies like AR can be adopted in different contexts, highlighting new aspects of shopping behaviour and habits.
>
> The results have significant implications for retailers, offering practical guidance on implementing AR technology to enhance user experience and boost online purchase intentions, particularly in developing countries.
>
> The authors' findings consist largely of three parts:
>
> 1. The mode of purchasing plays a moderating role in the impact of six underlying mechanisms, named AR attributes, on user experience and online purchase intention.
> 2. A comparison between two modes (AR versus web-based) assessing the positive or negative, as well as significant impact of AR attributes on user experience and online purchase intention.
> 3. Consideration that the research was conducted in a developing country.

The theoretical foundation of this research is rooted in cognitive load theory. Due to the infancy of research on AR, especially in a developing country, the cognitive load theory provides a useful theoretical foundation. According to Fan et al. (2020), cognitive load theory suggests that people have finite cognitive capacities and an excess of cognitive burden, often resulting from information overload, can have adverse effects on consumers. In the context of online shopping, customers encounter difficulties in mentally visualizing products in their personal spaces, leading to an increased cognitive load (Scholz and Duffy, 2018). Zhao et al. (2017) illustrated that the incorporation of AR and VR in online shopping has varying effects on the cognitive load of consumers. This, in turn, minimizes cognitive load, facilitating smoother information processing and user engagement with the system, ultimately elevating the overall user experience (Fan et al., 2020).

Interactivity refers to how technology facilitates user interaction with content (Steuer et al., 1995). It has been shown to increase product knowledge (Li et al., 2002), user engagement (Ko et al., 2005) and purchase intention (Fortin and Dholakia, 2005) while decreasing consumers' cognitive load (Zhao et al., 2019). Ebrahimabad et al. (2024)'s study supports the idea that the interactivity provided by AR technology has a positive and significant impact on both user experience and online purchase intention. Additionally, their study found that when people used the IKEA website for online shopping, they did not perceive interactivity. As discussed by Hoffman and Novak (2018), in the context of online shopping, user experience is influenced by interactions with smart objects. This implies that the level of interactivity in AR mode plays a significant role in users' preference over the web-based mode for online shopping.

AR can enhance consumers' processing of product information by offering virtual representations of how products may appear in reality. Consequently, this approach aligns the information users interact with more closely with their own physical environment, reducing reliance on imagination (Fan et al., 2020). In line with prior research by Smink et al. (2019) and Verhagen et al. (2014), which assert that AR provides the most direct interaction with products, aiming to deliver a comprehensive and informative experience, Ebrahimabad et al. (2024)'s study supports the idea that the information provided by AR technology enhances both user experience and online purchase intention. In their study, they observed that individuals using the IKEA website expressed satisfaction with the information provided. However, when it came to the AR mode, they did not perceive a substantial increase in information. This observation can be attributed to the fact that when consumers decide to purchase an armchair, they often seek to physically touch and feel the fabric to assess its quality. Additionally, they may be uncertain about the precise colour of the armchair. Consequently, the information presented on both the website and the app remains consistent.

Numerous research studies consistently demonstrate that enhancing the vividness and interactivity of online shopping experiences contributes to the generation of enjoyment (Yim et al., 2017; Van Noort et al., 2012; Kim and Forsythe, 2008). These vivid and interactive encounters, whether occurring through mobile applications, websites or purchasing platforms, not only enhance the sensory aspect but also lead to a more engaging and pleasurable shopping experience. While Ebrahimabad et al. (2024) had anticipated that AR would augment enjoyment compared with the web-based mode, their study indicates that AR did not significantly heighten the level of enjoyment.

As discussed by Etminani-Ghasrodashti and Hamidi (2020), individuals' perceptions and attitudes towards shopping play a crucial role in determining their shopping preferences and frequency. Various motivations underlie individuals' decision-making processes when making purchases. For example, as pointed out by Lee et al. (2017), some people find enjoyment in traditional in-store shopping experiences, while others choose online shopping for its time-saving convenience. In their study, the reported level of enjoyment remained relatively consistent both on the website and in the AR app. Given the challenges associated with internet access in developing countries, there exists a noteworthy disparity in how people engage in online shopping. Ebrahimabad et al. (2024) attribute these challenges to the overall experience of enjoyment during online shopping. Using the AR app requires a high-speed internet connection; otherwise, virtual furniture cannot be placed in the studied environment. Sometimes, it takes a long time to position an armchair in the house using the AR application, or there may be issues with the presentation, resulting in incomplete visuals. All these challenges are attributed to the internet and impact enjoyment during online shopping, as users become tired and confused.

In this context, novelty, referring to the unique and exceptional content generated by AR, has a positive and significant impact on user experience and online purchase intention. Aligned with the findings of Javornik (2016) and Preece et al. (2015), Ebrahimabad et al. (2024) propose that novelty provides individuals with the opportunity to visualize how a piece of furniture, enriched with highly personalized and innovative content, would integrate into their actual living space. However, in the context of their study, it appears that AR did not significantly heighten the level of novelty. Ebrahimabad et al. (2024) attribute this to the fact that there is less familiarity with AR technology in developing countries, where people may not comprehend the term 'novelty' because AR technology itself is new and understanding novelty in content requires more information and time.

Vividness, within the technological realm, refers to its capability to construct an environment that is perceptually rich and heightened (Steuer et al., 1995). As noted by Flavián et al. (2017) and Griffith and Gray (2002), vividness is often associated with the quality of visualizing products and their aesthetic appeal. Initially, Ebrahimabad et al. (2024) anticipated that AR would provide more vividness compared with the web-based mode. However, no significant distinction was observed between the two conditions. This lack of distinction again can be attributed to the challenges associated with internet accessibility in non-Western countries, which impeded AR from delivering a vivid and explicit encounter. In line with Keller and Block (1997), Jiang and Benbasat (2007) and Nisbett and Ross (1980), a visually captivating presentation of products is inclined to influence customers' cognitive processing and facilitate a more thorough assessment of product-related information. However, as the quality of devices and internet connectivity assumes a pivotal role in the provision of vividness, Ebrahimabad et al. (2024) realized that consumers may not possess a clear understanding of the concept of vividness.

With regard to intrusiveness, the introduction of AR increased the level of intrusiveness compared with the web-based mode. This outcome contradicted Ebrahimabad et al. (2024)'s initial expectations, as they anticipated, in line with Smink et al. (2019), whose study showed that intrusiveness did not have negative impacts on consumer reactions (brand attitude, purchase intention and willingness to share personal data), that in Ebrahimabad et al. (2024)'s study it would not adversely affect both user experience and online purchase intention. This observation can be attributed to the complex interplay of various factors influencing online purchasing behaviour, particularly in non-Western countries. Numerous studies have developed theories and models concerning how individuals adopt and accept advanced technologies.

Among these, the Technology Acceptance Model (TAM) (Davis et al., 1989; Davis, 1989) is noteworthy as it addresses issues related to the adoption and acceptance of technology. Our study draws a conclusion regarding intrusiveness and its negative impact on both dependent variables based on this theory. TAM relies on two primary factors: perceived usefulness (PU) and perceived ease of use (PEOU), alongside attitude. Perceived ease of use relates to the extent to which an individual believes that utilizing a specific system would require minimal effort, while perceived usefulness relates to the extent to which an individual believes that using a particular system would enhance their job performance. In light of this, Ebrahimabad et al. (2024) found that limitations in accessing international online shopping platforms may lead to less familiarity with technology adoption among individuals in developing countries and they find it difficult to use. Consequently, they reported a higher level of intrusiveness in AR mode compared with the web-based mode.

Their second finding, regarding the comparison of the two modes, highlights a noteworthy discovery: AR attributes exert a considerably stronger influence on enhancing user experience and online purchase intention. This phenomenon stems from AR applications' unique capability to empower users by visualizing products within their immediate physical surroundings. The multi-group analysis further illustrates that the impact of interactivity on user experience and online purchase intention with AR technology is more positive and significant compared with its impact via traditional web-based platforms (Davis, 1989; Davis et al., 1989). In AR mode, interactivity provides consumers with opportunities to explore diverse product designs and visualize how well they integrate into their living spaces – a feature not available in conventional web-based e-commerce (Steuer et al., 1995).

Furthermore, the multi-group analysis shows that the impact of novelty in AR mode on user experience is positive and significant compared with the web-based mode. These results confirm that the novelty of the content presented through AR plays a pivotal role in shaping the user experience and stimulating consumers' information processing.

ACTIVITY 1

AR vs. web-based shopping comparison

Objective: To understand the differences in user experience between AR and web-based shopping modes.
  Instructions: Divide students into small groups.
  Assign each group a case study (e.g. IKEA's AR app vs. a traditional e-commerce website).

> Have each group create a presentation comparing user experiences, interactivity and purchase intentions based on the case study.
> Each group should present their findings and discuss how AR and web-based modes impact consumer behaviour.
> **Discussion**: Discuss which attributes (e.g. interactivity, vividness) are more effective in enhancing user experience and why.

Impact of AR on consumer behaviour

AR technology significantly impacts consumer behaviour in various ways:

- Enhanced decision-making: Consumers can make more informed decisions by visualizing how products will look and fit in their homes.
- Increased engagement: AR apps create an interactive and engaging shopping experience, increasing the time consumers spend on the app.
- Reduced return rates: By allowing consumers to see how products fit and look in their spaces before purchasing, AR helps in reducing the likelihood of returns.
- Boosted confidence: The ability to visualize products in context boosts consumer confidence, leading to higher conversion rates.

Challenges

- Technical limitations: Ensuring the AR models are accurate and realistic can be technically challenging.
- User adoption: Not all consumers are quick to adopt new technologies.
- Cost: Developing and maintaining an AR app can be expensive.

Opportunities

- Personalization: AR can offer personalized shopping experiences tailored to individual preferences and home layouts.
- Future integration: Combining AR with other technologies, like AI, can further enhance the consumer experience.

Conclusion

These technologies address several challenges in online shopping, such as the inability to try on products like clothing and accessories. AR can provide a try-on experience that helps consumers make more informed decisions, thereby reducing return rates and increasing satisfaction. VR, meanwhile, creates entirely immersive environments where users can explore virtual stores and interact with products in a simulated space, enhancing the overall shopping experience.

Consumer reception and adoption of VR/AR

The adoption of VR and AR technologies by consumers has been a topic of growing interest in recent years. These technologies offer immersive experiences that enhance consumer engagement and satisfaction, particularly in sectors like retail and e-commerce. Consumer readiness plays a crucial role in the adoption of AR, as it significantly influences user reception and the intention to reuse AR-based applications (Voicu et al., 2023). The sense of immersion, product presence and perceived realism are key factors that drive consumer acceptance and satisfaction with AR apps (Daassi and Debbabi, 2022). Despite the potential of VR/AR, the adoption has been relatively slow due to technological limitations, such as the need for high-resolution images and minimal latency to provide a truly immersive experience (Sia Partners, 2023).

Prospects of VR/AR in retail

The future of VR/AR in retail looks promising, as these technologies continue to evolve and integrate into the consumer shopping experience. VR and AR offer unique opportunities for retailers to create engaging and personalized shopping environments that can differentiate them from competitors. For instance, VR can be used to create immersive store experiences, allowing consumers to explore products in a virtual space, while AR can enhance the in-store experience by overlaying digital information onto physical products (Queuche, 2023). The rise of VR/AR technologies is also expected to transform marketing strategies, enabling brands to connect with consumers on a deeper level through interactive and memorable experiences (Laraba and Derradji, 2024). As consumers increasingly seek personalized and engaging shopping experiences, the demand for VR/AR applications in retail is likely to grow. Retailers that leverage these technologies effectively can enhance brand loyalty and drive sales by offering unique value propositions that resonate with modern consumers (Queuche, 2023). Furthermore, the continuous development of VR/AR technologies, coupled with the increasing acceptance among consumers, suggests a bright future for these technologies in retail. As the cost of VR/AR equipment decreases and the technology becomes more user-friendly, it is anticipated that more retailers will adopt these tools to enhance customer experiences and streamline operations (Laraba and Derradji, 2024).

> ### ACTIVITY 3
>
> AR/VR future trends brainstorming
>
> **Objective**: To predict developments in AR/VR technologies and their potential impact on retail.
> **Instructions**: Ask students to brainstorm and list potential future applications of AR and VR in retail.
> Have them consider technological advancements, consumer preferences and market trends.
> Each group presents their predictions and discusses how these trends could shape consumer behaviour and retail strategies.
> **Discussion**: Reflect on how emerging technologies might change the retail landscape and what opportunities or challenges might arise.

The dynamics of influencer marketing in shaping consumer perceptions

Influencer marketing has emerged as a pivotal strategy within the digital marketing landscape, significantly shaping consumer perceptions and behaviours. By leveraging the reach and credibility of influencers, brands can effectively engage with target audiences, build trust and drive purchasing decisions. Influencers, who often have dedicated followings on social media platforms, act as intermediaries between brands and consumers, providing authentic and relatable content that resonates with their audience (Schiffman and Kanuk, 2010; Arnould and Thompson, 2005).

The rise of influencer marketing

The rise of influencer marketing can be attributed to the increasing popularity of social media platforms and the shift in consumer trust from traditional advertising to peer recommendations. Influencers, ranging from celebrities to micro-influencers, have gained prominence due to their ability to connect with audiences on a personal level. This form of marketing allows brands to tap into niche markets and engage with consumers through authentic storytelling and personalized content. The democratization of content creation and the accessibility of social media have enabled influencers to build substantial followings, making them valuable partners for brands seeking to enhance their visibility and credibility (Sheth, 2020; Kim et al., 2011).

Measuring the impact of influencer marketing

Measuring the impact of influencer marketing involves evaluating various metrics such as engagement rates, reach and conversion rates. Brands often use KPIs to assess the effectiveness of influencer campaigns, including likes, shares, comments and click-through rates. Additionally, advanced analytics tools can track the ROI by analysing sales data and customer acquisition costs attributed to influencer partnerships. Understanding the impact of influencer marketing is crucial for optimizing strategies and ensuring that campaigns align with brand objectives and target audience preferences (Sweeney and Soutar, 2001; Chunmei and Weijun, 2017).

UNDERSTANDING INFLUENCERS IN CONSUMER BEHAVIOUR

Influencers play a pivotal role in shaping consumer behaviour by leveraging their persuasive power to guide the opinions and actions of their followers. As outlined by Gallic and Marrone (2023), influencers are seen as opinion leaders who engage their communities through expertise and passion in specific domains such as travel, food, lifestyle and sports. Their influence is rooted in a psychological process where individuals adopt viewpoints seemingly spontaneously, influenced by the authority and credibility of the influencer.

Influencers operate within a framework of authority, where their attractiveness increases with audience size, relevance of content and endorsements from fans and reputable brands. This authority model is akin to principles found in search engine optimization, where visibility and engagement are key metrics of success.

Types of influencers

Gallic and Marrone (2023) categorize influencers into three main types based on community size, influence degree and specialization:

1 Stars: These are widely recognized public figures who captivate audiences with aspirational content, generating significant engagement. Examples include celebrities like soccer player Antoine Griezmann and swimmer Léon Marchand.

2 Specialized influencers: With communities exceeding 10,000 followers, these individuals are experts in specific fields, sharing trends and insights that resonate with followers who share similar interests. They are valued for their relatability and expertise.

3 Micro-influencers: With smaller, niche communities, these influencers are accessible and engage deeply with their audience. Their proximity and authenticity make them attractive to brands seeking dynamic and genuine connections.

The role of influencers in modern marketing

In the digital age, brands have shifted from traditional advertising to more interactive and transparent marketing strategies. Influencers facilitate this transition by enabling brands to engage in multidirectional dialogues with consumers. However, Gallic and Marrone (2023) caution that brands often focus on short-term gains rather than building long-term relationships with influencers.

Influencers are trusted experts within their communities, embodying honesty, competence and benevolence. Their recommendations are perceived as more reliable than traditional advertising, significantly impacting consumer decisions. As independent entities, influencers create user-generated content that resonates with audiences, amplifying brand messages without appearing overly promotional.

Influencers and consumer purchase behaviour

Influencers impact consumer behaviour throughout the purchase journey, from inspiration to post-purchase recommendations. Their ability to create authentic and relatable content fosters trust and engagement, guiding consumers in their decision-making processes. As Gallic and Marrone (2023) highlight, the sale of experiential products, such as travel, is particularly influenced by influencers who share authentic experiences and recommendations.

Influencers have transformed the marketing landscape by bridging the gap between brands and consumers. Their ability to engage and inspire trust makes them invaluable partners in modern marketing strategies, as they help brands build credibility and foster long-term consumer relationships.

The ethics and credibility of influencer marketing

The ethics and credibility of influencer marketing have become increasingly important as the industry grows. Transparency is a key concern, as consumers expect influencers to disclose sponsored content and maintain authenticity in their endorsements. Regulatory bodies, such as the Federal Trade Commission (FTC) in the United States, have established guidelines to ensure that influencer marketing practices are ethical and transparent. Additionally, the credibility of influencers is vital, as consumers are more likely to trust recommendations from influencers who align with their values and demonstrate genuine enthusiasm for the products they promote. Brands must carefully select influencers whose values and audience align with their own to maintain credibility and foster long-term relationships with consumers (Lewis and Potter, 2013; Hu et al., 2015).

> **ACTIVITY 2**
>
> Influencer marketing role play
>
> **Objective**: To explore the dynamics of influencer marketing and its impact on consumer perceptions.
>
> **Instructions**: Assign students roles as influencers, brand managers or consumers.
>
> Each group develops a short campaign proposal incorporating influencer marketing strategies.
>
> Role-play interactions between influencers and brands and between influencers and consumers.
>
> Discuss the ethical considerations and effectiveness of the proposed campaigns.
>
> **Discussion**: Evaluate how different types of influencers (stars, specialized, micro) can impact consumer trust and brand loyalty.

Conclusion

Chapter 3 explores the interplay between psychological dynamics and technological advancements in shaping digital consumer behaviour. It begins with an examination of how online reviews and ratings influence purchasing decisions through the lens of social proof and cognitive biases. The chapter then transitions to the impact of emerging technologies such as virtual reality and augmented reality, highlighting their role in enhancing the shopping experience and consumer decision-making. Case studies, including IKEA's AR app, demonstrate how these technologies can drive engagement and reduce return rates. Finally, the chapter addresses the growing significance of influencer marketing, discussing its impact on consumer perceptions and the importance of ethical considerations in these digital endorsements. Understanding these elements equips businesses with the knowledge to effectively navigate the digital marketplace and engage with consumers in a meaningful way.

> **KEY TERMS**
>
> Augmented reality (AR): Technology that overlays digital content onto the real world, enhancing user interaction with physical surroundings.
>
> Virtual reality (VR): Immersive technology that creates a fully digital environment, allowing users to experience virtual spaces and objects as if they were real.

Cognitive load theory: A psychological framework suggesting that excessive cognitive demands can impair information processing and decision-making.

Interactivity: The extent to which users can engage with digital content and influence their experience, often enhancing engagement and knowledge.

Intrusiveness: The degree to which a technology disrupts the user's experience, potentially leading to negative reactions and decreased satisfaction.

Novelty: The quality of being new and unique, which can enhance user engagement and interest in digital content.

Vividness: The capacity of a technology to create a rich and detailed sensory experience, impacting the perception of product information.

Influencer marketing: A strategy where brands leverage individuals with significant social media followings to promote products and influence consumer behaviour.

Social proof: The psychological phenomenon where individuals look to others' behaviours and opinions to guide their own decisions, often seen in online reviews and ratings.

Technology Acceptance Model (TAM): A model that explains how users come to accept and use new technologies based on perceived usefulness and ease of use.

KEY LEARNING POINTS

Influence of social proof:
- Online reviews and ratings act as forms of social proof, heavily influencing consumer decisions by providing insights into product quality and satisfaction.

Psychological mechanisms behind ratings:
- Cognitive biases, such as the anchoring effect and availability heuristic, play a significant role in how consumers interpret and respond to ratings.

Effective management of negative feedback:
- Proactive and empathetic responses to negative reviews can mitigate their impact and provide valuable feedback for improvement.

Impact of VR and AR on shopping:
- VR and AR enhance consumer engagement by providing immersive and interactive experiences, improving decision-making and reducing return rates.

Influencer marketing dynamics:
- Influencer marketing leverages social media personalities to shape consumer perceptions, with effectiveness measured through specific metrics and considerations of ethical practices.

4 | The science of digital learning and memory

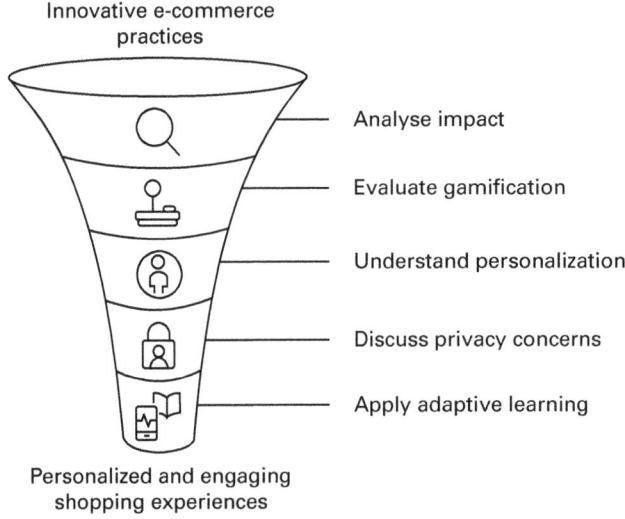

Enhancing e-commerce practices

Innovative e-commerce practices
— Analyse impact
— Evaluate gamification
— Understand personalization
— Discuss privacy concerns
— Apply adaptive learning

Personalized and engaging shopping experiences

LEARNING OUTCOMES

By the end of this chapter, you should be able to:

- Analyse the impact of Pinduoduo's innovative e-commerce practices: Understand how Pinduoduo's business model, including gamification and team buying, has revolutionized consumer engagement and agricultural support in China.
- Evaluate the role of gamification in consumer behaviour: Assess how gamification strategies, such as rewards and badges, influence consumer engagement and impulse buying, particularly during major shopping events like the Double Eleven festival.

- Understand the significance of personalized recommendations: Explain how personalized recommendation systems leverage consumer data to enhance shopping experiences and influence purchase decisions.
- Discuss privacy concerns related to personalization: Identify and articulate the privacy issues associated with data collection for personalized recommendations and strategies to address these concerns.
- Apply adaptive learning principles to e-commerce: Explore how adaptive learning systems and emerging technologies, such as AI and wearable devices, can be integrated into e-commerce to create more personalized and engaging shopping experiences.

CHAPTER OUTLINE

The evolution of e-commerce:

- Historical development and growth of e-commerce
- Major players and innovations in the industry

Pinduoduo: A case study in e-commerce innovation:

- Introduction to Pinduoduo and its founder, Colin Huang
- Business model and strategies (e.g. team buying, gamification)
- Impact on rural agriculture and the Chinese e-commerce landscape

Gamification and consumer engagement:

- Definition and principles of gamification
- Examples of gamification in e-commerce (e.g. McDonald's 'World of Goods')
- Impact on consumer behaviour and impulse buying

Personalized recommendations and consumer behaviour:

- Mechanisms and technologies behind personalized recommendations
- Effect of personalization on purchase decisions
- Privacy concerns and balancing personalization with consumer trust

Adaptive learning systems and e-commerce personalization:

- Insights from adaptive learning systems and their application to e-commerce
- Role of wearable technologies and real-time data

- Measurement and assessment challenges in personalization
- Future directions (e.g. AI, VR)

Conclusion:

- Summary of key findings
- Implications for businesses and consumers
- Future trends in e-commerce consumer behaviour

Introduction

In the rapidly evolving world of e-commerce, understanding consumer behaviour has become paramount for businesses seeking to thrive in a competitive marketplace. The digital revolution has transformed how consumers interact with brands, shifting the focus from traditional shopping experiences to dynamic, online environments. This chapter delves into the intricate dynamics of consumer behaviour within the e-commerce sector, exploring pivotal innovations and strategies that have reshaped the landscape.

Central to this discussion is the remarkable rise of Pinduoduo, a Chinese e-commerce giant that has redefined online shopping through its unique business model and technological advancements.

By examining Pinduoduo's impact on both consumer behaviour and the agricultural sector, this chapter illustrates how innovative practices can drive engagement and address broader societal challenges.

The concept of gamification, which incorporates game-like elements into non-game contexts, has emerged as a powerful tool for enhancing consumer engagement. The chapter explores how gamification strategies, exemplified by initiatives like McDonald's 'World of Goods', foster deeper connections with consumers and stimulate impulse buying.

Moreover, the advent of personalized recommendations has revolutionized online shopping by tailoring suggestions to individual preferences. However, this personalization raises significant privacy concerns, highlighting the need for a balance between personalized experiences and data protection.

Finally, insights from adaptive learning systems offer valuable perspectives on e-commerce personalization. By leveraging user data and emerging technologies, businesses can create highly tailored shopping experiences that drive customer satisfaction and loyalty.

The role of artificial intelligence in personalized learning

Artificial intelligence is revolutionizing the field of personalized learning by enabling the creation of adaptive and customized educational experiences that cater to individual consumer needs. AI technologies such as intelligent systems, machine learning algorithms and natural language processing tools can analyse vast amounts of data on preferences and behaviour to provide tailored content and support. This personalization helps students learn at their own pace and in ways that best suit their learning styles, thereby enhancing engagement and improving outcomes (Chen et al., 2020).

Moreover, AI-powered systems facilitate independent learning by providing people with a wide range of resources tailored to their current knowledge level and interests. For instance, recommendation algorithms, similar to those used by online platforms like Netflix or Amazon, can suggest relevant articles or videos, past interactions with the system (Zawacki-Richter et al., 2019). This personalized approach not only helps maintain motivation but also encourages exploration beyond.

Despite these benefits, the integration of AI in personalized learning raises several ethical and practical challenges. Concerns about data privacy, algorithmic bias and the potential over-reliance on technology must be addressed to ensure that AI tools are used responsibly and effectively (Luckin, 2017).).

Creative and cultural industries in the era of AI

Research on artificial intelligence in marketing has received particular attention in recent years (Choura, 2024), with calls encouraging a more in-depth exploration of the role of AI in different areas of marketing (Kumar et al., 2019; Davenport et al., 2020). The work carried out in this area has focused on identifying the promises, but also the risks and challenges associated with AI and proposing forward-looking reflections on the evolution of AI and its implications for research and practice in marketing (Sabouk and Sidmou, 2019; Vlačić et al., 2021). In this regard, the role of AI has been studied in the context of business-to-business (B2B) marketing (Kumar et al., 2020), but has also received significant attention in the context of online sales, with several studies on social interaction and virtual agents (Syam and Sharma, 2018; Dwivedi et al., 2019; Sin and Munteanu, 2020; Sun and Botev, 2021), bringing a social and personalized dimension to business–consumer exchanges in a virtual context (Schmidt et al., 2019). The technology has thus disrupted the sales sector by reinforcing the possibilities for interaction between the company and the consumer via intelligent and interactive interfaces and platforms (Rauschnabel and Ro, 2016; Ponsignon and Derbaix, 2020; Jafari-Sadeghi et al., 2021).

In the creative and cultural industries, the use of artificial intelligence is growing rapidly at different levels of the creation, distribution and consumption process of cultural products. The technology has also significantly contributed to a paradigm shift for culture, which has evolved from a logic of scarcity to one of abundance, placing an entire sector facing the challenges of digitization (Alexandre et al., 2022). Digital technologies have led to a significant reduction in the fixed costs of production, distribution and advertising of cultural goods. This has resulted in strong enthusiasm for this sector of activity and therefore a very strong creation of products easily accessible to consumers. Since the beginning of the 2000s, the number of new songs, new films, new television shows and new books has more than doubled (Waldfogel 2017), thus improving individual and collective well-being (Aguiar and Waldfogel, 2018). However, cultural products are closely linked to the arts and are characterized by their uniqueness as creations of artists. While the notions of 'artistic creation' and 'cultural product' are often used interchangeably, it is appropriate to distinguish between them (Assassi, 2003). The cultural product initially finds its origin in the idea and creation of an artist, then evolves in a process of transformation in the context of production and distribution activities, thus giving it this commercial dimension.

AI has also been associated with human creativity and artistic practice, raising an ethical issue in relation to human creative capacity and thought (Anantrasirichai and Bull, 2022). The literature on the subject has also focused on issues related to copyright, the industrial organization of culture and the economic implications of artificial intelligence that complements, or even perhaps replaces, human creativity in terms of cultural participation (Peukert, 2019). Although AI may be endowed with increasingly important capacities in terms of idea generation, the maturity of generative AI remains limited with regard to the sense of intuition, personal inspiration and the affective aspect (Sabouk and Sidmou, 2019). If the machine's reactivity is based on algorithms capable of calculating the probabilities of reaction to programmed situations, it is now possible to develop the machine's creativity and improvisational capacities based on the creative processes observed in nature (Heudin and Kyrou, 2020; Zlatoff and Ribaupierre, 2023).

Other studies have focused on the study of AI applications in the fields of culture and the arts, such as music (Briot and Pachet, 2020; Ariani et al., 2023), theatre (Zlatoff and Ribaupierre, 2023), cinema (Halmaoui, 2022; Jacques, 2023) and literature (Brunet et al., 2021; Chen et al., 2023). Among the applications of AI in this sector, it is possible to mention the use of AI in musical composition, in the generation of text, video and visual content, as well as in theatre with the use of robots improvising actor games.

How AI customizes consumer learning experiences

AI plays a significant role in customizing consumer learning experiences in the digital realm through several key mechanisms.

Personalized content delivery

AI algorithms analyse individual user data, including browsing history, content engagement and purchase behaviour, to tailor the learning content presented to each consumer. This personalization ensures that consumers receive information most relevant to their interests and needs, enhancing the efficiency and effectiveness of their learning process. Here is an application in the e-learning industry, where key aspects of AI-driven personalization in learning highlight the types of user data analysed, the goals of personalization, the benefits of such approaches and the various applications in the educational landscape.

Adaptive learning paths

AI-powered systems can dynamically adjust the difficulty and progression of learning materials based on a consumer's performance and comprehension levels. This adaptive approach allows for a more optimized learning experience, challenging learners appropriately without overwhelming or underwhelming them. Table 4.1 shows an application of the latter in the e-learning.

Intelligent recommender systems

By leveraging machine learning algorithms, AI can provide personalized recommendations for products, services, or content that align with a consumer's learning objectives and preferences. These recommendations are continuously refined based on user interactions and feedback, improving the relevance and usefulness of suggested materials over time. This is mainly the way Pinduoduo works (see 'Empowering farmers with an e-commerce platform' please).

Table 4.1 How AI algorithms personalize learning content based on individual user data

Aspect	User data types	Personalization goals	Benefits	Applications
Data analysis	Browsing history	Identify user preferences	Faster progress through materials	E-learning platforms
	Content engagement (e.g., clicks, likes)	Predict learning needs	Higher engagement with content	MOOCs (Massive Open Online Courses)
	Purchase behaviour	Tailor content recommendations	Improved retention of information	Adaptive learning systems
	Learning progress and performance	Present relevant content	Better overall learning outcomes	Educational apps and games

Natural language processing for enhanced interaction

AI-powered chatbots and virtual assistants utilize natural language processing (NLP) to engage in more intuitive and context-aware interactions with consumers. This technology enables more natural and personalized communication, facilitating better understanding and addressing of consumer queries or concerns related to their learning journey.

A zoom on **Natural Language Processing** (NLP)

In the context of modern education, learners face an unprecedented challenge of information overload. The proliferation of digital resources and learning materials has created an environment where students often struggle to identify and extract relevant, high-quality information that aligns with their specific learning objectives. This abundance of data can lead to inefficiencies in exploratory search, potentially hindering the learning process.

However, recent advancements in artificial intelligence, particularly in the field of deep learning and the development of **large language models (LLMs)** such as ChatGPT, have opened new avenues for enhancing exploratory search strategies in education. These technological innovations offer promising solutions to the challenges posed by information overload.

Natural Language Processing NLP, a branch of artificial intelligence focused on facilitating human–computer interaction through natural language, has emerged as a key technology in this domain. Research by Shaari and Hamzah (2016) has demonstrated that certain exploratory learning strategies can establish a philosophical connection between NLP and pedagogical approaches.

Early NLP models faced limitations in comprehending complex language structures. While the combination of information retrieval and NLP theoretically provided a robust foundation for exploratory search, there was a disconnect in their focus areas. Information retrieval emphasized macro-level structural understanding, whereas NLP concentrated on micro-level language structure and comprehension (Manning, 2016). This discrepancy led to challenges in semantic understanding during exploratory searches utilizing NLP.

The shift from statistical language models to neural language models marked a significant step toward overcoming these challenges. In 2003, Bengio et al. introduced the neural network language model based on deep learning technology, paving the way for more sophisticated text comprehension capabilities.

Deep learning technology, through its ability to train multilayer network structures, can capture more nuanced abstract semantics of text and images. This enhanced capability allows for better interpretation of user search intents and more effective extraction of relevant content from vast information repositories. Consequently, this approach helps mitigate the issue of information overload, thereby improving the efficiency and effectiveness of exploratory search in educational contexts.

Predictive analytics for anticipatory learning

AI systems can analyse large datasets to predict future consumer behaviours and preferences. This predictive capability allows for the proactive delivery of learning content or experiences that consumers are likely to find valuable, even before they explicitly express interest.

AI algorithms can process vast amounts of user data, including past behaviours, engagement patterns and demographic information, to identify trends and patterns that may not be apparent through traditional analysis methods. By leveraging machine learning techniques, AI systems can create sophisticated models that forecast future consumer behaviours with a high degree of accuracy. These models continuously improve as they process more data over time. The predictive capabilities of AI enable the anticipation of user needs and interests, allowing for the proactive delivery of relevant learning content or experiences. This approach can significantly enhance the efficiency and effectiveness of the learning process. AI systems can tailor content and experiences to individual users based on their predicted preferences, effectively providing mass personalization that would be impractical or impossible to achieve manually. By predicting a learner's future needs and potential areas of difficulty, AI can dynamically adjust learning pathways to optimize the educational experience for each individual. There are some similarities between e-learning and e-commerce.

Both domains use AI to tailor experiences to individual users. In e-commerce, this involves personalizing product recommendations and marketing messages, while in education, it means customizing learning content and pathways. AI systems in both fields analyse user data to predict future behaviours or needs. E-commerce platforms predict purchase intentions, while educational systems forecast learning challenges. Both systems adapt in real-time based on user interactions. E-commerce sites modify product displays and offers, while educational platforms adjust lesson difficulty and content. Both rely heavily on collecting and analysing large datasets to inform decision-making and improve user experiences. Predictive AI can help determine the optimal timing, format and delivery method for educational content, maximizing user engagement and retention. This is something that is expected in the student's timetable in order to help them to organize more effectively. By predicting potential challenges or disengagement, AI systems can trigger early interventions to support learners before issues become significant.

While predictive AI offers numerous benefits, it also raises important ethical questions regarding data privacy, consent and the potential for algorithmic bias in educational contexts. It's important to note that predictive models are not infallible and may struggle with novel situations or rapid changes in user behaviour. Educators and system designers must be aware of these limitations. The most effective implementations of predictive AI in education typically combine algorithmic predictions with human expertise to ensure appropriate interpretation and application of insights.

Table 4.2 compares the key differences between AI applications in e-learning and e-commerce.

The distinct characteristics and applications of AI in e-learning and e-commerce highlight some unique challenges and approaches in each domain.

Sentiment analysis for emotional intelligence

By employing sentiment analysis tools, AI can gauge consumer reactions and emotional responses to different learning materials or experiences. This emotional intelligence enables the system to adjust content delivery or interaction styles to better resonate with individual consumers, potentially improving engagement and retention.

Behavioural analytics for continuous optimization

AI continuously monitors and analyses consumer behaviour within digital platforms, identifying patterns and trends that can inform the ongoing refinement of learning experiences. This data-driven approach allows for real-time adjustments to content, interface design, or interaction models to optimize the consumer learning journey.

Table 4.2 Key differences between AI applications in e-learning and e-commerce

Aspect	E-learning	E-commerce
Primary goal	Optimize learning outcomes and knowledge retention	Drive sales and increase customer loyalty
Data analyzed	Learning progress, assessment results, engagement metrics	Purchase history, browsing behaviour, demographic data
Prediction focus	Future learning needs, potential areas of difficulty	Purchase intentions, product preferences
Personalization	Customized learning pathways, adaptive content difficulty	Tailored product recommendations, personalized marketing
Ethical considerations	Higher scrutiny due to working with students and long-term impact on education	Focus on data privacy and fair marketing practices
Feedback mechanisms	Structured (tests, assignments, quizzes)	Indirect (purchases, click-through rates, reviews)
Timeframe	Long-term learning trajectories and outcomes	Short-term predictions and immediate conversions
User agency	AI system plays a significant role in shaping the learning experience	Users have more immediate control over choices
Complexity of predictions	Higher, involving cognitive processes and skill development	Lower, primarily based on consumer behaviour patterns
Adaptation speed	Gradual, based on learning progress	Rapid, often in real-time based on user actions
Success metrics	Knowledge acquisition, skill development, course completion rates	Sales figures, conversion rates, customer lifetime value
Regulatory environment	Subject to educational standards and policies	Governed by consumer protection and e-commerce regulations

By leveraging these AI-powered techniques, digital platforms can create highly customized learning experiences that adapt to individual consumer needs, preferences and behaviours. This level of personalization not only enhances the efficiency of consumer learning but also potentially increases engagement, satisfaction and long-term retention of information.

It's important to note that while AI offers significant benefits in customizing consumer learning experiences, ethical considerations regarding data privacy and algorithmic bias must be carefully addressed to ensure fair and responsible implementation of these technologies.

Enhancing consumer memory through gamification

REAL-WORLD EXAMPLE	Pinduoduo – revolutionizing e-commerce and agriculture

Introduction

Pinduoduo, founded in 2015 by entrepreneur Colin Huang, has quickly established itself as an e-commerce giant in China. This case study examines how Pinduoduo used innovative practices to boost its business model and impact rural agriculture in China, highlighting its strategies for managing interactions with customers and prospects.

Practices and strategies

'Team buying' business model: Pinduoduo has revolutionized the concept of group selling by offering substantial discounts when consumers buy as a team. This approach boosted virality and user engagement.

Strategic partnership with WeChat: By partnering with WeChat, Pinduoduo was able to capitalize on the power of social sharing to attract new users and drive the growth of its platform.

Gamification: Through interactive games such as Duo Duo Orchard, Pinduoduo fostered user engagement and encouraged repeat purchases.

Duo Duo Farm Program: Pinduoduo launched this program to empower farmers by providing them with e-commerce knowledge and marketing resources, while using AI to optimize planting decisions.

Technologies used

E-commerce platform: Pinduoduo has developed a robust and user-friendly platform, facilitating online transactions for millions of users.

AI: AI has been used to predict consumer demand and optimize farmers' planting decisions, thereby improving the efficiency of the process.

Livestreaming: Faced with the challenges posed by the Covid-19 pandemic, Pinduoduo quickly adopted livestreaming to connect farmers with consumers, thereby facilitating the sale of agricultural products.

Analysis of interactions with customers and prospects

Promotion via social sharing: Pinduoduo capitalized on the power of word of mouth by encouraging users to share deals with friends and family.

Engagement through gamification: Interactive games created an entertaining experience for users, enticing them to return to the platform regularly.

Training and support for farmers: Pinduoduo offered online training to farmers to help them better use the platform and optimize their agricultural activity.

Conclusion

Pinduoduo demonstrated how innovation and technology can be harnessed for e-commerce and agriculture, creating value for consumers and farmers. Its ability to understand and respond to changing market needs makes it a key player in China's e-commerce landscape.

Gamification and consumer engagement

Gamification, the application of game-design elements in non-game contexts, has emerged as a powerful strategy to enhance consumer engagement. By incorporating elements such as points, badges, leaderboards and challenges into marketing and customer interaction strategies, businesses can create more engaging and rewarding experiences for consumers. This approach taps into the intrinsic motivations of consumers, such as the desire for achievement, competition and social interaction, thereby fostering deeper emotional connections with brands.

The effectiveness of gamification in consumer engagement lies in its ability to transform mundane or routine interactions into dynamic and interactive experiences. For instance, loyalty programmes that incorporate gamified elements can motivate consumers to participate more actively, increasing brand loyalty and encouraging repeat purchases. Moreover, gamification can facilitate learning about products and services, making the consumer journey more informative and enjoyable.

Furthermore, gamification can enhance social interaction among consumers by encouraging them to share achievements and compete with peers, thereby expanding brand reach through word-of-mouth and social media. As consumers become more engaged, they are more likely to provide valuable feedback and insights, enabling businesses to refine their offerings and improve customer satisfaction.

Gamification represents a significant opportunity for businesses to enhance consumer engagement by creating interactive and rewarding experiences. By leveraging the principles of game design, companies can foster stronger emotional connections with consumers, driving loyalty and advocacy in an increasingly competitive marketplace.

Gamification as a tool for differentiation

In today's information-saturated world, where individuals are constantly exposed to news about economic downturns, political crises, ecological issues and health threats, entertainment has become a necessary escape. This need for diversion extends beyond traditional gaming, presenting an opportunity for businesses to differentiate themselves through gamification. Gamification involves integrating game-like elements into various domains, including education, healthcare and human resources, to enhance engagement and interaction.

A notable example of gamification in a corporate setting is McDonald's 'World of Goods', launched in 2014 to familiarize employees with the brand. This initiative featured engaging quizzes about the company, accessible via an online gaming platform on the intranet. Participants earned points for correct answers, with the potential to win prizes valued up to $50. Such gamified experiences not only educate but also motivate participants through rewards and competition, embodying the principles of gamification that drive consumer engagement.

The strategic use of gamification in business settings leverages intrinsic and extrinsic motivators to foster consumer loyalty and interaction. By incorporating elements like points, leaderboards and rewards, companies can create engaging experiences that resonate with consumers' desires for achievement and recognition. This approach not only enhances consumer satisfaction but also provides valuable insights into consumer behaviour and preferences.

Gamification serves as a powerful tool for businesses seeking to stand out in a crowded marketplace. By transforming serious domains into interactive and enjoyable experiences, companies can engage consumers more effectively, driving loyalty and fostering long-term relationships. As the demand for interactive and personalized experiences grows, gamification will continue to play a crucial role in shaping consumer behaviour and brand differentiation.

ACTIVITY

Gamification strategy

Objective: Develop a gamification strategy for an e-commerce platform.
  Instructions: In pairs, choose an e-commerce product or service and consider how gamification could be applied to enhance user engagement.
  Consider elements such as rewards, leaderboards and interactive features.
  Present your gamification strategy to the class, explaining how it will improve user experience and drive sales.

Gamification and impulse buying in e-commerce

The Double Eleven festival, also known as Singles' Day (光棍节), is the world's largest online shopping event, held annually on November 11th. Started in the 1990s by Chinese university students as an anti-Valentine's Day for singles, the date (11/11) was chosen because the numbers represent 'bare sticks', a Chinese slang term for single men.

In 2009, Alibaba's e-commerce platforms, particularly Taobao and Tmall, transformed Singles' Day into a massive shopping festival. It now surpasses other global shopping events like Black Friday and Cyber Monday in terms of sales. During Double Eleven, consumers enjoy significant discounts and promotions and brands compete to offer the best deals, making it a highly anticipated event for both shoppers and retailers.

> **Taobao**: Launched in 2003, Taobao is a consumer-to-consumer (C2C) platform, similar to eBay, where individual sellers and small businesses can list their products for sale. It offers a vast range of goods, from everyday items to unique, niche products. Taobao is known for its affordability and the sheer variety of items available, making it one of the most popular online shopping destinations in China.
>
> **Tmall**: Established in 2008 as a spin-off from Taobao, Tmall (short for Taobao Mall) is a business-to-consumer (B2C) platform. It caters to larger brands and official retailers, offering a more premium shopping experience compared with Taobao. Tmall hosts official stores for global and domestic brands, ensuring authenticity and higher quality, often appealing to consumers seeking trusted products from well-known brands.
>
> Both platforms are integral to Alibaba's dominance in the Chinese e-commerce market. In 2018, for instance, Taobao and Tmall reported a staggering transaction volume of 10 billion RMB (1,397,980,000 USD) within just two minutes of the festival's commencement, illustrating the power of impulse purchases during this promotional period.

Gamification has become a crucial strategy employed by platforms like Taobao and Tmall to enhance consumer engagement and stimulate impulse buying. The introduction of gamified systems during the Double Eleven festival, which includes mechanisms such as rewards and badge upgrades, serves to create an enjoyable shopping atmosphere that encourages consumers to participate actively. These gamification elements not only provide hedonic enjoyment but also foster social interactions, as consumers are incentivized to share links and invite friends to join the experience.

Research indicates that gamification can significantly influence consumer behaviour, particularly in the context of impulse buying. While previous studies have primarily focused on traditional marketing strategies, a study by Zhang et al. (2021) has used the Double Eleven festival as a focus to show that the integration of gamification into e-commerce presents a novel approach to understanding and enhancing impulse buying behaviour. Understanding how different groups respond to gamification in online shopping contexts is essential for developing tailored marketing strategies that resonate with diverse consumer segments.

The interplay between gamification and impulse buying during events like the Double Eleven festival highlights the evolving landscape of e-commerce. By leveraging game-like elements, businesses can create engaging and interactive shopping experiences that not only drive sales but also foster deeper connections with consumers.

Understanding the impact of personalized recommendations on consumer behaviour

Personalized recommendations have become a pivotal aspect of consumer interaction in digital marketplaces, significantly shaping purchasing behaviours and consumer experiences. By leveraging data-driven insights, these systems tailor suggestions to individual preferences, enhancing the relevance and appeal of products offered to consumers.

How personalized recommendations work

Personalized recommendation systems utilize sophisticated algorithms to analyse consumer data, including browsing history, purchase patterns and demographic information. This analysis enables the generation of tailored product suggestions that align closely with individual consumer interests. By integrating **machine learning techniques**, these systems continuously refine their recommendations, improving accuracy and relevance over time. Such personalized interactions enhance the consumer experience by reducing the effort required to find desirable products and increasing the likelihood of discovering new items that meet consumer needs.

The effect of personalization on purchase decisions

The impact of personalized recommendations on purchase decisions is profound as they significantly influence consumer behaviour by presenting products that align with individual preferences. This tailored approach not only increases conversion rates but also enhances customer satisfaction and loyalty. Consumers are more likely to engage with brands that provide personalized experiences, as these interactions make them feel understood and valued. Studies have shown that personalized recommendations can lead to higher sales and foster long-term customer relationships by creating a more engaging and relevant shopping experience.

Enhancing e-commerce personalization through insights from adaptive learning systems

1. The shift toward personalization

Recent advances in adaptive and personalized learning systems highlight a growing trend toward personalization in various domains, including education and e-commerce. Just as personalized learning technologies have transformed educational practices by tailoring content to individual needs and preferences, similar strategies can enhance e-commerce experiences. Research emphasizes the importance of integrating user data and context to create adaptive systems that respond to individual characteristics and behaviours (Borthwick et al., 2015; Hong et al., 2009).

2. Understanding user needs and context

In the realm of adaptive learning, systems utilize a variety of data sources, such as user profiles and contextual information, to personalize learning experiences (Lin et al., 2013; Huang and Chiu, 2015). Translating these practices to e-commerce involves leveraging customer data – such as browsing history, purchase behaviour and contextual cues – to tailor product recommendations, marketing messages and user interfaces. This approach not only enhances user satisfaction but also drives engagement and conversion rates (Wang and Liao, 2011).

3. The role of wearable technologies

The emerging trend of wearable technologies in personalized learning, as discussed by Borthwick et al. (2015), can also be applied to e-commerce. Wearable devices can provide real-time data on user behaviour and preferences, allowing e-commerce platforms to offer more dynamic and context-aware personalization. For example, wearable tech can track physical activities or environmental factors that influence shopping habits, enabling businesses to deliver highly relevant offers and recommendations (Greenwald et al., 2017).

4. Addressing measurement and assessment challenges

One key takeaway from adaptive learning systems is the challenge of measuring and assessing complex user interactions and outcomes (Mavroudi et al., 2016). In e-commerce, similar challenges arise in evaluating the effectiveness of personalization strategies. Businesses must develop sophisticated metrics and analytics tools to assess how personalized experiences impact customer behaviour and satisfaction. This includes tracking engagement with personalized content, conversion rates and overall customer satisfaction (Wu et al., 2012).

5. Integrating theoretical frameworks

Theoretical frameworks such as Bruner's spiral organization (1966) and constructivist principles inform adaptive learning systems by emphasizing the need for structured and sequenced content. Applying these principles to e-commerce means designing personalization strategies that guide users through a coherent and engaging journey. For instance, e-commerce platforms can use data-driven insights to present users with a personalized shopping path, ensuring that content and offers are aligned with their evolving interests and needs (Tsai et al., 2012).

6. Future directions

Looking ahead, the integration of advanced technologies such as AI and VR in both education and e-commerce presents new opportunities for personalization. AI can enhance recommendation algorithms and predictive analytics, while VR can create immersive shopping experiences that cater to individual preferences (Shi and Weninger, 2017; Lin and Lan, 2015). As these technologies evolve, they will further refine personalization strategies, making e-commerce experiences more intuitive and engaging.

Conclusion

Incorporating insights from adaptive learning systems into e-commerce personalization strategies can lead to more effective and tailored customer experiences. By leveraging user data, embracing emerging technologies and addressing measurement challenges, e-commerce platforms can create highly personalized environments that drive user satisfaction and business success. The continued development of these strategies will be crucial in meeting the evolving demands of consumers in an increasingly digital marketplace.

Personalization and privacy concerns

Despite the benefits, personalized recommendations raise important privacy concerns. The extensive collection and analysis of personal data necessary for personalization can lead to apprehensions about data security and privacy breaches. Consumers may worry about how their information is stored, used and shared, particularly with third parties. To address these concerns, companies must implement robust data protection measures and maintain transparency about their data practices. By offering consumers control over their data and communicating clearly about how it is used, businesses can build trust and enhance the effectiveness of personalized recommendations.

Personalized recommendations play a crucial role in shaping consumer behaviour by providing tailored shopping experiences that drive engagement and sales. However, balancing personalization with privacy is essential to maintain consumer trust and ensure the long-term success of these strategies.

> **ACTIVITY 3**
>
> Privacy debate
>
> **Objective**: Debate privacy concerns in personalized e-commerce.
> **Instructions**: Organize a debate on the tradeoffs between personalized recommendations and consumer privacy.
> Assign roles (e.g. privacy advocates, data-driven marketers) and prepare arguments.
> Conduct the debate, encouraging participants to consider both the benefits and challenges of personalization in e-commerce.

Conclusion

This chapter has provided a comprehensive overview of the multifaceted nature of consumer behaviour in the e-commerce realm, emphasizing the importance of innovation and personalization in shaping modern shopping experiences. Through the lens of Pinduoduo's success and the application of gamification and personalized recommendations, it is evident that understanding and responding to consumer needs are crucial for maintaining a competitive edge.

The integration of adaptive learning principles and emerging technologies, such as AI and wearable devices, promises to further refine e-commerce strategies, offering increasingly personalized and engaging experiences. However, as businesses continue to innovate, they must also navigate the challenges of privacy and data security to build and sustain consumer trust.

Looking ahead, the evolution of e-commerce will likely be marked by continued advancements in technology and an ever-deepening understanding of consumer behaviour. By staying attuned to these trends and leveraging insights from both academic research and practical applications, businesses can drive growth and enhance the overall consumer experience in the digital age.

KEY TERMS

Gamification: The use of game-design elements and principles in non-game contexts to enhance user engagement and motivation.

Team buying: A business model where consumers receive discounts by purchasing items in groups, fostering social interaction and virality.

Personalized recommendations: Tailored product suggestions based on consumer data such as browsing history and purchase patterns.

Impulse buying: Spontaneous, unplanned purchasing behaviour driven by emotional or situational factors rather than premeditated decision-making.

Adaptive learning systems: Technologies that customize learning experiences based on individual needs and behaviours, applicable to e-commerce for personalized shopping experiences.

Privacy concerns: Issues related to the collection, storage and use of personal data, which can impact consumer trust and security.

Artificial intelligence (AI): Technologies that simulate human intelligence processes to analyse data and make predictions or recommendations.

Wearable technologies: Devices that monitor physical activities and environmental factors to provide real-time data, influencing personalization in e-commerce.

Double Eleven festival: Also known as Singles' Day, it is the world's largest online shopping event, characterized by massive sales and impulse buying.

E-commerce personalization: Customizing the online shopping experience by tailoring content, recommendations and interactions based on individual consumer data.

KEY LEARNING POINTS

Gamification in e-commerce:
- The use of game-like elements to enhance consumer engagement, drive impulse buying and create a more enjoyable shopping experience.

Personalized recommendations:
- The role of data-driven insights in tailoring product suggestions, enhancing consumer experiences and influencing purchase decisions.

Impulse buying:

- Exploration of the emotional and situational factors that lead to unplanned purchasing behaviours in an online context.

Adaptive learning systems:

- Leveraging adaptive technologies that respond to individual user needs and preferences to enhance e-commerce personalization.

Privacy concerns:

- Balancing the benefits of personalized experiences with the need to address consumer apprehensions regarding data security and privacy.

Artificial intelligence:

- Utilizing AI to improve recommendation algorithms, enhance predictive analytics and create dynamic shopping experiences.

Wearable technologies:

- The potential of wearable devices to provide real-time data on consumer behaviour, influencing personalization strategies in e-commerce.

5 | Building brand loyalty in the digital age

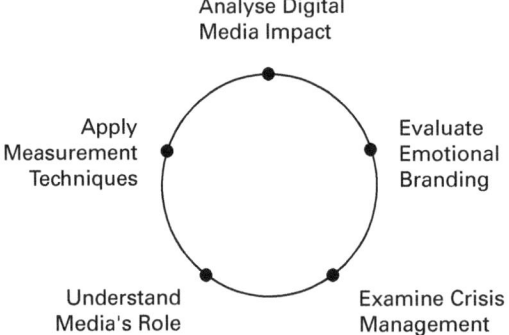

Continuous Brand-Consumer Interaction Improvement

- Analyse Digital Media Impact
- Evaluate Emotional Branding
- Examine Crisis Management
- Understand Media's Role
- Apply Measurement Techniques

LEARNING OBJECTIVES

By the end of this chapter, you should be able to:

- Analyse the impact of digital media: Understand how social media and digital platforms influence consumer behaviour and brand interactions.
- Evaluate emotional branding strategies: Assess the effectiveness of emotional branding techniques and their impact on consumer loyalty and engagement.
- Understand the role of media in consumer behaviour: Identify how media content, including web-dramas, influences consumer attitudes and purchasing decisions.
- Apply measurement techniques: Utilize various methods to measure emotional connections and consumer engagement with brands.

CHAPTER OUTLINE

The digital age and its impact on consumer behaviour:

- Psychological influences
- Sociocultural factors
- Economic determinants
- Technological advancements

The role of digital media in shaping consumer behaviour:

- Social media influence
- E-commerce and online purchasing patterns
- The impact of user-generated content and peer reviews
- Viral marketing and influencer culture

Emotional branding and consumer loyalty:

- The psychological foundations of emotional branding
- Strategies for emotional engagement
- Measuring emotional connections in the digital age
- Case studies: Impact of emotional branding on consumer loyalty

Emerging trends in consumer behaviour:

- The rise of social commerce
- The influence of web-dramas and media on consumer actions
- Advances in neuromarketing and emotion tracking
- Personalized marketing and its impact on consumer engagement

Measuring and analysing consumer behaviour:

- Traditional vs. advanced measurement techniques
- The role of KPIs in assessing consumer engagement
- Challenges in interpreting emotional data
- Future directions in consumer behaviour research

Introduction

In the rapidly evolving landscape of modern commerce, understanding consumer behaviour has become more critical than ever. As digital media, social platforms and technological advancements continue to reshape how consumers interact with brands, the study of consumer behaviour offers invaluable insights into the motivations, preferences and decision-making processes that drive purchasing patterns. This chapter delves into the multifaceted nature of consumer behaviour, exploring its theoretical foundations, the impact of digital media, the role of emotional branding and the importance of effective crisis management.

By examining contemporary case studies, including the complex dynamics of social media influence and the implications of public controversies on brand perception, this chapter provides a comprehensive overview of the factors that shape consumer behaviour in the digital age. Whether you are a student, researcher, or marketing professional, the insights presented in the chapter will equip you with the knowledge to navigate the increasingly complex landscape of consumer behaviour and apply this understanding to real-world scenarios.

In the digital age, building brand loyalty requires innovative strategies that leverage the power of brand advocacy, user-generated content and social media to foster deep connections with consumers.

The power of brand advocacy and user-generated content

Brand advocacy and user-generated content (UGC) are crucial in shaping consumer perceptions and enhancing brand loyalty. Encouraging brand advocacy involves engaging consumers in meaningful ways, prompting them to become vocal supporters of the brand. This can be achieved through interactive campaigns and personalized experiences that resonate with consumers' values and interests.

In the modern consumer landscape, brand advocacy and UGC have emerged as pivotal elements shaping brand perception and consumer behaviour. This dynamic interplay between consumers and brands underscores a shift towards more interactive and authentic engagement strategies.

Brand advocacy refers to the enthusiastic support and promotion of a brand by its customers. Advocates are typically loyal customers who voluntarily endorse a brand's products or services based on their positive experiences. These advocates can significantly influence their peers and the broader market through word-of-mouth, leveraging their personal credibility and trustworthiness. The impact of brand advocacy is magnified in the digital age, where social media platforms enable advocates to reach and affect larger audiences. Studies have shown that brand advocates can drive higher levels of consumer trust and engagement as their endorsements are perceived as more genuine and credible compared with traditional advertising.

> **THE ROLE OF EMOTIONAL ATTACHMENT IN BRAND ADVOCACY**
>
> Research indicates that emotional attachment plays a crucial mediating role between brand reputation and brand advocacy (Ahmadi and Ataei, 2024). Brand reputation has been found to positively influence emotional attachment, which in turn leads to increased brand advocacy behaviours among consumers. This relationship appears to be reinforced by factors such as consumer experience and price perception. Additionally, the effects may differ between **hedonic and utilitarian brand types**.
>
> The findings suggest that cultivating emotional connections with consumers can create a '**snowball effect**' that positively impacts brand equity through increased advocacy. Managers should therefore focus on strategies that foster emotional bonds and self-brand connections to drive advocacy intentions.

User-generated content encompasses any content – such as reviews, photos, videos and social media posts – created by consumers rather than by the brand itself. UGC plays a crucial role in shaping brand narratives and influencing purchasing decisions. It provides potential customers with authentic and relatable insights into the brand experience, often highlighting aspects that traditional marketing materials may not cover. UGC fosters a sense of community and belonging among consumers as it reflects the real-life experiences and opinions of peers.

The synergy between brand advocacy and UGC creates a powerful feedback loop. Advocates who generate content contribute to a brand's visibility and credibility, while the brand's engagement with UGC further solidifies consumer loyalty. This interaction not only enhances brand reputation but also drives deeper connections with the consumer base. For brands, harnessing the power of advocacy and UGC requires strategic efforts to encourage and facilitate consumer participation, ensuring that their voices are heard and valued.

The influence of brand advocacy and user-generated content in the contemporary market underscores a shift towards more collaborative and authentic brand–consumer relationships. Brands that effectively leverage these elements can achieve significant competitive advantages by enhancing trust, engagement and loyalty among their customer base.

Encouraging brand advocacy through engagement

Engagement is key to fostering brand advocacy. By creating opportunities for consumers to interact with the brand, companies can cultivate a community of loyal advocates who promote the brand through word-of-mouth and social media channels.

In the evolving landscape of consumer behaviour, fostering brand advocacy through strategic engagement has become increasingly critical for achieving brand success. Brand advocacy, characterized by consumers actively promoting a brand through positive word-of-mouth and UGC, is significantly enhanced by effective engagement strategies. Research underscores that engagement acts as a vital conduit for developing genuine advocacy, driven by dynamic interactions between brands and consumers.

Engagement involves a spectrum of interactions that include social media interactions, content sharing and participation in brand-related activities. As highlighted by Wilk et al. (2024), engagement is essential in creating meaningful consumer–brand relationships. Brands that proactively engage with their consumers through personalized communication and interactive content foster deeper connections and a sense of belonging. This interactive engagement aligns with findings from Stokburger-Sauer et al. (2012), who emphasize that active consumer participation enhances brand identification and loyalty.

Mechanisms of brand advocacy

Engaged consumers often transition into brand advocates by sharing positive experiences and recommending the brand to their social networks, as noted by Sotiriadis (2017). This advocacy is amplified through UGC, which plays a pivotal role in shaping brand perceptions. Research by Papadimitriou et al. (2018) and Zeng and Gerritsen (2014) demonstrates that UGC, such as reviews and social media posts, significantly impacts destination branding and consumer trust. Engaged consumers also contribute to brand defence, providing valuable endorsements and mitigating negative sentiments (Baloglu et al., 2014).

Strategies for enhancing engagement

To effectively encourage brand advocacy, brands must employ strategies that resonate with consumer preferences and behaviours. Personalization is a key strategy, as it aligns with findings from Tuten and Solomon (2018), who argue that tailored interactions foster stronger consumer connections. Creating opportunities for consumers to engage in brand-related activities, such as exclusive events or interactive campaigns, also proves effective. This approach supports the research by Qu et al.

(2011), which highlights the importance of integrating brand identity into engagement strategies.

Measuring the impact of engagement

The impact of engagement on brand advocacy can be assessed using various metrics, including engagement rates, sentiment analysis and advocacy scores. Studies such as those by Wilk et al. (2021) and Ukpabi and Karjaluoto (2018) emphasize the importance of monitoring these metrics to evaluate engagement effectiveness and make informed adjustments. By analysing consumer interactions, brands can gain insights into advocacy drivers and refine their engagement strategies to enhance consumer satisfaction and loyalty.

Encouraging brand advocacy through engagement is a strategic imperative in today's competitive market. Effective engagement strategies, supported by research findings, not only foster positive word-of-mouth and enhance brand loyalty but also leverage user-generated content to strengthen brand reputation. As consumer behaviour evolves, brands must remain agile, leveraging insights from recent studies to optimize their engagement practices and achieve sustained success.

The impact of user-generated content on brand perception

UGC significantly influences brand perception by providing authentic and relatable content that consumers trust more than traditional advertising. When consumers share their experiences and opinions, it enhances the brand's credibility and fosters a sense of community.

UGC has emerged as a powerful force in shaping consumer behaviour and brand perceptions. Recent research highlights the significant impact of UGC on consumer decision-making processes and brand relationships.

Authenticity and trust

UGC is perceived as more authentic and trustworthy compared with traditional advertising, leading to enhanced brand credibility. Consumers increasingly rely on peer experiences and opinions when making purchase decisions. For example, a 2023 study found that 79 per cent of consumers consider UGC highly influential in their purchasing choices, particularly in industries like fashion and beauty (Khan, 2024).

Community building

UGC fosters a sense of community around brands, encouraging consumer engagement and loyalty. Brands like Glossier have successfully leveraged UGC to create a devoted customer base, with user-shared content driving 90 per cent of the company's engagement on social media platforms.

Purchase intentions

The authenticity of UGC significantly influences purchase intentions. A recent meta-analysis revealed that UGC has a stronger positive effect on purchase intentions compared with marketer-generated content, with an average effect size of 0.372.

Brand differentiation

UGC helps brands differentiate themselves in crowded marketplaces. For instance, Airbnb's 'Don't Go There, Live There' campaign, which featured user-submitted stories, not only increased brand awareness but also positively impacted brand perception, with 87 per cent of viewers associating the brand with acceptance and belonging (Khan, 2024a).

AIRBNB'S 'DON'T GO THERE, LIVE THERE' CAMPAIGN: LESSONS IN EMOTIONAL BRANDING

Airbnb's 2016 'Don't Go There, Live There' campaign offers valuable insights into effective emotional branding and consumer behaviour.

Emotional connection and brand perception

The campaign shifted consumer perceptions of Airbnb from a mere rental platform to a provider of authentic local experiences. By featuring real host stories, it created an emotional connection with consumers, positioning the brand as a gateway to unique travel experiences.

Measurable impact on consumer behaviour

The campaign's effectiveness was evident in several key metrics:

- 2.5 billion media impressions
- 32 per cent increase in website traffic
- 27 per cent growth in bookings
- 50 per cent rise in home listings

These results demonstrate how emotional branding can drive tangible consumer actions.

Key marketing strategies

Emotional storytelling: Using real host narratives to forge emotional connections with potential guests.

Brand differentiation: Highlighting unique local experiences to stand out in the competitive travel market.

Multi-channel approach: Leveraging various media platforms for widespread reach and engagement.

Data-driven insights: Utilizing consumer data to inform campaign strategy and targeting.

This case study illustrates the power of emotional branding in influencing consumer perceptions and behaviours, particularly in experience-based industries like travel and hospitality.

These findings underscore the growing importance of UGC in contemporary consumer behaviour, highlighting its role in building trust, fostering community and influencing purchase decisions. As social media platforms continue to evolve, brands must adapt their strategies to effectively harness the power of UGC and maintain authentic connections with their consumers.

Managing and utilizing user-generated content

Effectively managing UGC involves curating and amplifying consumer-created content to align with brand values and messaging. By integrating UGC into marketing strategies, brands can enhance engagement and build stronger emotional connections with consumers.

INFLUENCER MARKETING AND BRAND PERCEPTION: THE TIKTOK CASE STUDY IN INDONESIA

The strategic use of influencers to shape brand perception has become a critical element in modern marketing strategies, particularly for social media platforms targeting new markets. A notable example is TikTok's campaign in Indonesia, which aimed to diversify its user base and content perception (Khan, 2024b).

TikTok partnered with Najwa Shihab, a respected Indonesian journalist, to shift perceptions of the platform from merely entertainment-focused to a source of diverse, informative content. This strategy aligns with recent research indicating that influencers who share cultural similarities with their audience tend to produce more relatable and authentic content, boosting brand loyalty and engagement.

Impact on consumer behaviour and platform growth

The campaign's success was evident in several key metrics:

- Generated 7.8 billion views
- Attracted 55 million new users
- Increased platform usage by 67 per cent
- Improved TikTok's ranking from ninth to fourth among social media apps in Indonesia

These outcomes demonstrate the powerful effect of strategically chosen influencers on consumer behaviour and platform adoption.

Key learnings for consumer behaviour

Content diversification: Expanding content types can attract a broader audience, challenging preconceived notions about a platform's utility.

Cultural relevance: Partnering with locally respected figures can help brands resonate more deeply with target audiences.

Authenticity in influencer marketing: Genuine passion and expertise from influencers can build trust and credibility for the brand.

Quality content focus: Emphasizing well-researched, insightful content can elevate a platform's perceived value.

This case study illustrates the evolving nature of influencer marketing and its significant impact on consumer perceptions and behaviours. It underscores the importance of aligning influencer selection with brand goals and target audience values, particularly in cross-cultural marketing contexts.

Leveraging social media for building brand communities

Social media platforms offer powerful tools for building and nurturing brand communities, providing spaces for consumers to connect, share experiences and engage with the brand.

Building and nurturing online brand communities

Creating vibrant online communities involves providing valuable content, facilitating discussions and encouraging consumer participation. These communities foster loyalty by creating a sense of belonging and shared identity among members.

Consumer behaviour and the role of sense of belonging

Consumer behaviour research increasingly highlights the importance of the sense of belonging in shaping customer loyalty and engagement. This construct, which reflects an individual's emotional connection and identification with a brand or organization, can significantly influence repurchase intentions and overall satisfaction. As delineated in recent studies, the sense of belonging encompasses various indicators such as following a brand on social media, participating in brand events, or engaging with brand communities (Matarranz et al., 2024).

For instance, the success of high-end brands like Ferrari and Harley-Davidson can be partly attributed to their ability to foster a strong sense of belonging among their customers. These brands cultivate deep emotional connections through exclusive events, community-driven initiatives and active social media engagement, creating a loyal customer base that often transcends mere transactional relationships (McAlexander et al., 2002). Such practices underscore the value of belonging as a strategic tool for enhancing customer retention and driving long-term profitability.

In the context of higher education, alumni engagement serves as a compelling example of how the sense of belonging can be leveraged. Research by Maulana et al. (2023) demonstrates that alumni who feel a strong connection to their alma mater are more likely to contribute financially and participate in institutional activities. This finding highlights the effectiveness of applying belonging-oriented strategies to strengthen alumni relations and improve institutional support.

Recent advancements in social media also provide new avenues for cultivating a sense of belonging. For example, universities and brands alike are increasingly using platforms like Instagram and X (formerly known as Twitter) to create interactive and engaging experiences that reinforce their brand communities. Research by Ricoy and Feliz (2016) explores how X can be utilized as a learning and engagement tool in higher education, illustrating how digital platforms can enhance the sense of community and belonging among students and alumni.

The integration of social media into educational settings has yielded intriguing insights into consumer behaviour, particularly in how individuals engage with and respond to digital platforms. The recent study on the use of X for university education provides valuable examples of this phenomenon. This research highlights several key aspects of consumer behaviour in the context of digital learning environments, demonstrating how social media tools can influence and enhance learning experiences.

One significant finding from the study is the pattern of participation and interaction among students on Twitter. The data showed a pronounced increase in the number of tweets during specific days of the week, particularly when teachers proposed new activities. This suggests that consumers – students in this case – exhibit behaviour that is responsive to external stimuli and structured schedules. For instance, there was a noticeable spike in activity on Mondays through Wednesdays, coinciding with the days when educational tasks were assigned. This behaviour aligns with the notion that consumer actions in digital environments are often influenced by contextual cues and scheduled events (Feliz, 2012; Sutton et al., 2014).

Another critical observation was the short response delay time, with the majority of tweets and responses occurring on the same day or the following day. This reflects a high level of engagement and immediacy, which is a key factor in consumer behaviour in online settings. The study's findings resonate with previous research that underscores the importance of immediacy in digital interactions and its impact on user engagement (Khatri et al., 2015; Junco et al., 2013). For example, the immediacy observed in the study parallels how consumers often seek prompt responses and interactions in online platforms, which can enhance their overall experience and satisfaction.

The study also revealed that while initial engagement with Twitter was relatively low, there was a marked increase in retweets and interactions as students became more familiar with the platform. This progression highlights the role of user **experience** and **familiarity in shaping consumer behaviour**. In shaping consumer behaviour, it's interesting to differentiate experience from expertise, from familiarity and from exposure:

- Experience provides depth of understanding through direct engagement.
- Familiarity offers comfort and recognition, potentially lowering perceived risk.
- Exposure builds awareness and can influence preferences over time.
- Expertise allows for more sophisticated evaluation and decision-making processes.

These concepts often interact and overlap in influencing consumer behaviour, with expertise typically representing the highest level of consumer knowledge and capability in a given domain. As users gain competence and confidence in using a platform, their engagement levels tend to rise. This observation supports the idea that consumer behaviour evolves with increased familiarity and comfort with digital tools (Evans, 2014; Wrighta, 2010).

Moreover, the study identified a clear correlation between the use of retweets and the development of a learning community. The gradual increase in retweets over the course of the study underscores the importance of interactive features in fostering community engagement and collaborative learning. This finding aligns with broader research on social media interactions, which suggests that features like retweets and likes play a crucial role in enhancing user interaction and building online communities (Junco et al., 2011; Kaplan and Haenlein, 2010).

Challenges with belonging

However, the application of sense of belonging is not without challenges. It is crucial for organizations to balance the genuine fostering of community with the risk of perceived manipulation. As noted by Strayhorn (2018), while fostering belonging can drive positive outcomes, it must be approached with authenticity to avoid alienating customers or stakeholders who might view such efforts as insincere. Future research should continue to explore the nuances of belonging across different contexts and its long-term implications for customer behaviour.

The sense of belonging is a powerful determinant of consumer behaviour, impacting loyalty, engagement and overall satisfaction. By strategically leveraging this construct, organizations can build more robust and emotionally resonant relationships with their customers and stakeholders.

Social media plays a pivotal role in community engagement by enabling real-time interactions and feedback. Brands can leverage these platforms to engage with consumers, address concerns and celebrate community achievements, thereby strengthening relationships.

Case studies of successful brand communities

The 'Digital 2024: United Kingdom' report by We Are Social and Meltwater (2024) highlights significant trends in digital media consumption and advertising within the UK. TikTok leads globally in user engagement, with UK users spending an average of 49 hours per month on its Android app. The platform also tops consumer spending on mobile apps, followed by Tinder and Disney+. The report reveals that 56.2 million social media users in the UK spend 1 hour and 49 minutes daily across 6.4 platforms, primarily for social connection, entertainment and news.

Social media advertising continues to grow, with platforms like Pinterest showing substantial increases in potential ad audiences. However, the report notes a decline in users who feel represented in advertising, highlighting a need for improved inclusivity. Additionally, digital advertising dominates the UK market, accounting for 79.7 per cent of total ad spend in 2023, while influencer marketing saw a 15.7 per cent increase.

Gaming also remains significant, with high engagement on both consoles and smartphones. However, concerns about misinformation persist, with nearly 69 per cent of UK internet users expressing doubts about online content's authenticity. The report underscores the evolving role of social media as a primary entertainment source and the importance for marketers to adapt to these changing dynamics while addressing representation and cultural relevance in their strategies.

Examining successful brand communities reveals best practices for fostering engagement and loyalty. These case studies highlight the importance of authenticity, transparency and consistent communication in building thriving communities. But first of all, let's discover a little bit about which social media evolve in the consumer landscape.

Key insights

1 Market dominance: Facebook continues to dominate in the UK with the highest user base, followed by Instagram and TikTok.
2 Age trends: TikTok shows significant usage among younger demographics (13–24), while LinkedIn attracts a more balanced age distribution but is strong among professionals.
3 Gender distribution: Pinterest and Snapchat show higher engagement among women, whereas X has a notable male majority.
4 Growth trends: TikTok is experiencing rapid growth and could potentially surpass other platforms, while X faces challenges due to recent changes and controversies.

Analyses for consumer behaviour

Platform popularity and market penetration

Facebook: As the leading social media platform, Facebook's extensive user base in the UK indicates its central role in digital consumer behaviour. The platform's broad demographic appeal suggests it is a key channel for marketing strategies targeting diverse age groups.

Instagram and TikTok: These platforms show significant engagement among younger demographics. Instagram's strong presence among both women and men, coupled with TikTok's rapid growth among Gen Z, highlights their effectiveness for brands targeting younger audiences.

Snapchat: Snapchat's concentrated user base among teenagers and young adults underscores its relevance for campaigns aimed at this age group.

LinkedIn: As the primary professional networking site, LinkedIn's substantial user base reflects its importance in career development and professional branding.

X (formerly Twitter): The platform's current state, including the impact of recent changes and its predominantly male user base, suggests specific opportunities and challenges for engaging with this audience.

Pinterest: Pinterest's high female engagement and its role as a source of inspiration provide insights into targeting audiences interested in lifestyle, fashion and home decor.

Demographic distribution and gender trends

Gender distribution: Platforms like Pinterest and Snapchat exhibit a higher proportion of female users, which can guide gender-targeted marketing strategies. Conversely, X's male dominance may influence the type of content and advertising strategies employed.

Age distribution: The varying age distributions across platforms indicate different user behaviours and preferences. For instance, TikTok's dominance among younger users suggests a focus on trends and short-form content, while LinkedIn's balanced age range points to its role in professional and career-oriented content.

Usage patterns and engagement levels

Engagement by age: High engagement levels among specific age groups on platforms like TikTok and Snapchat reveal the importance of tailoring content to resonate with the interests and behaviours of these groups.

Platform-specific trends: We can note distinct trends such as TikTok's rapid growth and LinkedIn's ongoing leadership in professional networking, which can inform predictions about future shifts in social media usage and consumer behaviour.

Strategic implications for marketers

Content strategy: Understanding platform-specific demographics helps in crafting targeted content strategies. For instance, visual and interactive content may perform better on Instagram and Pinterest, while professional and career-related content is more suited to LinkedIn.

Advertising and engagement: The gender and age distribution insights can guide the development of advertisements and promotional activities that align with user preferences and behaviours on each platform.

Competitive landscape: The competition between platforms like X, Meta's Instagram and Threads is becoming fierce. Marketers should stay informed about these dynamics to adapt their strategies in response to evolving social media landscapes.

Emerging trends and future directions

Platform evolution: Recent changes on X and the rise of new competitors can impact how marketers use them. Understanding how these factors influence user behaviour can help in anticipating shifts in platform popularity and adjusting marketing strategies accordingly.

Growth projections: With platforms like TikTok showing rapid growth, predicting future trends in user behaviour and engagement can aid in long-term strategic planning.

The role of social media in consumer behaviour

In the digital age, social media platforms have become integral to shaping consumer behaviour and brand perceptions. These platforms serve as powerful tools for information dissemination, brand–consumer interactions and peer-to-peer recommendations. The immediacy and reach of social media have transformed how consumers discover, evaluate and engage with brands, products and services.

Key aspects of social media's influence on consumer behaviour include the following:

- Information access: Consumers can easily access product information, reviews and brand narratives through social media channels.
- Peer influence: User-generated content and peer recommendations on social platforms significantly impact purchasing decisions.
- Brand engagement: Social media enables direct, real-time interactions between brands and consumers, fostering relationships and loyalty.
- Viral marketing: Content can spread rapidly across social networks, amplifying both positive and negative brand messages.
- Influencer marketing: Social media influencers have emerged as powerful intermediaries between brands and consumers, shaping opinions and trends.
- Social commerce: The integration of e-commerce features within social platforms has streamlined the path from discovery to purchase.

Understanding these dynamics is crucial for brands navigating the complex landscape of digital consumer behaviour.

Strategies for creating emotional connections with consumers

Emotional connections are vital for brand loyalty, as they drive consumer engagement and long-term commitment to the brand. In their work, Khan et al. (2021) explain how consumer engagement with media and brand loyalty exists in China among young McDonald's consumers. In the digital age, the relationship between media consumption and consumer behaviour has become increasingly complex and intertwined. Research has shown that media, particularly **web-dramas**, can significantly influence consumer attitudes and behaviours. For instance, the concept of web-drama connectedness – the emotional and cognitive involvement viewers experience with media content – can drive various consumer actions, from brand love to behavioural intentions (Russell et al., 2004). A key example is the Chinese web-drama 'My Huckleberry Friends', which has been found to influence viewers' purchasing decisions, as they often imitate the characters' styles or even adopt their gestures and language. This phenomenon illustrates how media content can transcend mere entertainment, becoming a significant driver of consumer behaviour.

The impact of media on consumer behaviour is further amplified by social media platforms such as WeChat. These platforms facilitate word-of-mouth communication, which plays a crucial role in shaping brand perceptions and purchase intentions. Recent studies highlight that positive WoM on WeChat significantly enhances brand love, which in turn strengthens consumers' behavioural intentions (Barreda et al., 2015; Alhidari et al., 2015). For example, when users share positive experiences or recommendations about a brand on WeChat, it not only boosts the brand's image but also encourages others to engage with the brand, ultimately leading to increased spending. This cycle of media influence, social sharing and consumer response underscores the importance of digital platforms in modern consumer behaviour.

Furthermore, the mediated effects of brand love on consumer spending illustrate the profound impact of emotional connections on economic outcomes. When consumers develop strong emotional ties to a brand, often cultivated through sustained engagement with media content and social platforms, they are more likely to exhibit loyalty and increase their spending (Carroll and Ahuvia, 2006). The interplay between media consumption, emotional attachment and consumer spending highlights a dynamic area of consumer behaviour research, where traditional advertising strategies are increasingly supplemented and sometimes supplanted, by digital and social media influences.

This intricate relationship between media, brand love and consumer behaviour underscores the need for marketers to create content that resonates emotionally with audiences while leveraging the power of social platforms to amplify these connections. As the digital landscape continues to evolve, understanding these dynamics will be crucial for brands seeking to foster deeper consumer engagement and drive sustainable economic outcomes.

The importance of emotional branding

Emotional branding involves creating a brand identity that resonates with consumers on a personal level, evoking feelings of trust, nostalgia, or excitement. This approach differentiates the brand and fosters deeper consumer loyalty. Emotional branding has emerged as a crucial strategy in contemporary consumer behaviour, transcending traditional marketing approaches by forging profound connections between brands and their target audiences. This technique leverages psychological and emotional triggers to create lasting impressions, fostering brand loyalty and influencing purchasing decisions.

The psychological foundations of emotional branding

At its core, emotional branding taps into the fundamental human need for connection and belonging. By aligning brand values with consumer emotions, companies can create a sense of shared identity and purpose. Brands which successfully evoke positive emotions are more likely to be remembered and preferred by consumers.

Mechanisms of emotional branding

Emotional branding operates through several key mechanisms:

- Storytelling: Brands craft narratives that resonate with their audience's experiences and aspirations. For instance, Nike's 'Just Do It' campaign continues to inspire consumers by tapping into their desire for personal achievement and self-improvement.
- Sensory engagement: Utilizing multi-sensory elements in branding can create more immersive and memorable experiences. Starbucks, for example, has carefully curated its in-store atmosphere, from the aroma of coffee to the texture of cup sleeves, to evoke comfort and familiarity.
- Personalization: Tailoring brand experiences to individual preferences enhances emotional connection. Spotify's annual 'Wrapped' feature, which provides users with personalized summaries of their listening habits, exemplifies this approach, fostering a sense of uniqueness and brand loyalty.

Impact on consumer behaviour

Emotional branding significantly influences consumer decision-making processes. Emotionally engaged consumers are 52 per cent more likely to make repeat purchases and 71 per cent more likely to recommend the brand to others.

Challenges and ethical considerations

While emotional branding can be highly effective, it also presents challenges. Brands must strike a balance between authenticity and manipulation, ensuring that emotional appeals are grounded in genuine values and commitments. Recent controversies surrounding greenwashing in the fashion industry highlight the potential backlash when emotional branding is perceived as insincere.

Emotional branding represents a powerful tool in shaping consumer behaviour, offering opportunities for deeper engagement and loyalty. As markets become increasingly competitive, brands that successfully forge emotional connections with their audiences are likely to gain significant advantages in consumer preference and market share.

> **ACTIVITY 1**
>
> Emotional branding workshop
>
> **Objective**: Explore and create emotional branding strategies for a hypothetical brand.
> **Instructions**: Provide students with a brief description of a hypothetical brand. Ask them to develop an emotional branding strategy for this brand, including elements such as storytelling, sensory engagement and personalization. Students should present their strategies and discuss how these elements would enhance consumer loyalty.
> **Discussion**: Compare the different strategies and discuss the potential challenges and benefits of implementing emotional branding in real-world scenarios.

Strategies for emotional engagement

Brands can employ various strategies to enhance emotional engagement, such as storytelling, personalized experiences and community involvement. These strategies create memorable interactions that strengthen emotional bonds with consumers.

Emotional branding focuses on creating deep, long-term connections between consumers and brands that go beyond simple benefit-based satisfaction. This approach aims to:

- evoke feelings of trust, nostalgia, or excitement
- align brand values with consumer emotions
- create a sense of shared identity and purpose

Some emerging trends in emotional branding include:

- sensory emotion: incorporating sensory elements into branding experiences
- immersive experiences: using virtual and augmented reality technologies
- emotional well-being: positioning brands as advocates for consumers' emotional health
- emotional artificial intelligence: using AI to create personalized emotional experiences

Emotional branding remains a powerful tool in shaping consumer behaviour, offering opportunities for deeper engagement and loyalty. As markets become increasingly competitive, brands that successfully forge emotional connections with their audiences are likely to gain significant advantages.

Measuring emotional connection

Measuring emotional connection involves assessing consumer sentiment and engagement levels through surveys, social media analytics and customer feedback. Understanding these metrics helps brands refine their strategies to enhance emotional resonance. But measuring emotional connection has become a critical aspect of understanding consumer behaviour and refining brand strategies in today's dynamic marketplace. This process involves a multifaceted approach to assess the depth and nature of consumers' emotional engagement with brands.

Methods of measurement

Several methodologies are employed to gauge emotional connections:

- Surveys and questionnaires: These tools capture consumers' self-reported emotional connections and satisfaction with brands. They can provide insights into the intensity of emotions and their impact on purchasing decisions.

- Social media analysis: Monitoring social media platforms helps in understanding public sentiment and the emotional tone of conversations around the brand. This real-time data can reveal trends in consumer emotions and engagement levels.

- Behavioural data analysis: Tracking online behaviour and purchase decisions can unveil the underlying emotional triggers that drive consumer actions. This method provides objective data on how emotions translate into tangible consumer behaviours.

Advanced measurement techniques

Recent advancements have introduced more sophisticated methods:

- Emotion tracking technology: Tools like facial recognition software and biometric sensors can track consumers' emotional responses to branding efforts in real-time, providing valuable data on which aspects of the branding strategy are most effective in eliciting positive emotions.

- Neuromarketing techniques: Methods such as **fMRI** and **electroencephalography (EEG)** offer direct insights into how emotional branding affects brain activity, identifying which regions are activated and the strength of emotional responses.

Key performance indicators

Several KPIs are crucial in measuring emotional connection:

- Customer engagement rates
- Brand sentiment analysis

- Purchase behaviour patterns
- Brand love indicators
- Word-of-mouth advocacy metrics
- Impact on brand strategy

Understanding these metrics allows brands to refine their emotional branding strategies. For instance, personalized marketing approaches have emerged as effective tools for fostering brand love and enhancing the connection between consumers and brands.

Challenges and considerations

While these measurement techniques offer valuable insights, it's important to note the subjective nature of emotions. Brands must **interpret data holistically**, considering cultural and individual differences in emotional expression and attachment.

Measuring emotional connection provides brands with critical insights for creating more resonant and effective marketing strategies. As technology and understanding of consumer psychology advance, we can expect even more precise and nuanced methods of gauging emotional connections to emerge, further refining the art and science of emotional branding.

Building brand loyalty in the digital age requires a multifaceted approach that leverages brand advocacy, user-generated content and social media to create meaningful consumer connections. By fostering emotional engagement and nurturing brand communities, companies can cultivate lasting loyalty and drive business success.

ACTIVITY 2

Measuring emotional connections

Objective: Understand and apply methods for measuring emotional connections with brands.

Instructions: Introduce students to various measurement techniques (e.g. surveys, social media analysis, neuromarketing). Assign each group a different method to research and ask them to present how it can be used to measure emotional connection. Include a brief demonstration of how these methods are applied in practice.

Discussion: Engage the class in a discussion about the strengths and limitations of each measurement technique and how brands can effectively use these insights to enhance their strategies.

Conclusion

It is evident that the digital age has introduced both opportunities and challenges for brands seeking to connect with their audiences. The integration of digital media into everyday life has not only altered the way consumers engage with brands but also amplified the importance of emotional connections in fostering loyalty and advocacy. From the power of social media influencers to the nuances of crisis management in the public sphere, the factors influencing consumer behaviour are more interconnected and dynamic than ever before.

This chapter has highlighted the importance of understanding these factors to build effective, resilient brands that can thrive in today's competitive marketplace. As consumer behaviour continues to evolve, driven by technological advancements and changing cultural norms, staying attuned to these shifts will be crucial for brands and marketers aiming to maintain relevance and foster lasting consumer relationships. The future of consumer behaviour is both exciting and unpredictable, offering endless opportunities for innovation and growth in the field.

KEY TERMS

Emotional branding: Creating a brand identity that resonates on a personal level, evoking emotions such as trust or excitement to build consumer loyalty.

Social media influence: The impact that social media platforms have on shaping consumer opinions, behaviours and brand perceptions.

Viral marketing: A marketing strategy where content spreads rapidly through social networks, amplifying both positive and negative messages.

Crisis management: Strategies and actions taken by a brand to address and mitigate the effects of a negative event or controversy.

Influencer marketing: Leveraging individuals with large followings on social media to promote brands and influence consumer behaviour

Emotional connection: The bond between consumers and brands that is driven by emotional engagement and personal relevance.

Social commerce: Integration of e-commerce features within social media platforms to facilitate seamless shopping experiences.

User-generated content: Content created by consumers, such as reviews and testimonials, that influences others' perceptions and purchasing decisions.

Neuromarketing: The use of neuroscience techniques to understand consumer responses to branding and marketing stimuli.

Web-drama connectedness: The emotional and cognitive involvement viewers experience with media content, influencing their consumer behaviour.

KEY LEARNING POINTS

Emotional branding:
- Understanding how emotional connections enhance brand loyalty and influence purchasing decisions.

Social media influence:
- Recognizing the role of social media in shaping consumer perceptions and behaviours, including the impact of user-generated content and viral marketing.

Consumer engagement:
- Identifying strategies for fostering deeper emotional engagement through storytelling, personalization and sensory experiences.

Demographic insights:
- Leveraging demographic and behavioural data from social media platforms to tailor marketing strategies effectively.

Emerging trends:
- Staying informed about new developments in emotional branding, including the use of AI and immersive experiences.

Measurement techniques:
- Utilizing various methodologies (surveys, social media analytics, neuromarketing) to gauge emotional connections and consumer sentiment.

Building brand communities:
- The significance of nurturing communities and fostering brand advocacy in creating lasting consumer relationships.

6 | The digital consumer decision-making process

Enhance Consumer Interactions and User Experience through AI, Blockchain, and UX Design

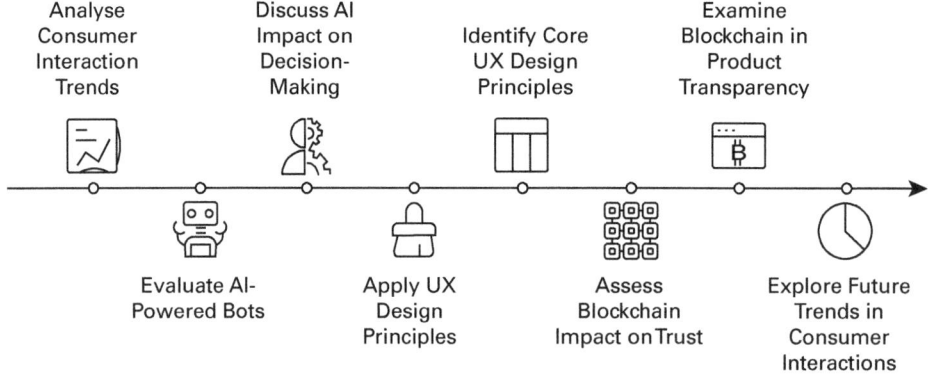

LEARNING OBJECTIVES

By the end of this chapter, you should be able to:

- Understand the influence of digital technologies on consumer behaviour.
- Analyse how social media, AI and emerging technologies like blockchain and AR are reshaping the way consumers interact with brands and make purchasing decisions.
- Evaluate the role of AI-powered bots in consumer interactions.
- Discuss the impact of AI, chatbots and virtual assistants on consumer decision-making processes, including the challenges and benefits of automated interactions.

- Apply key UX design principles to enhance user experience.
- Identify and implement core UX design principles such as user-centred design, simplicity and accessibility to create more engaging and user-friendly digital platforms.
- Assess the impact of blockchain on consumer trust and transparency.
- Explore the future trends in consumer–bot interactions and UX design.

CHAPTER OUTLINE

Overview of how AI, chatbots and virtual assistants influence consumer decision-making:

- Interaction dynamics between consumers and AI-powered bots
- Future developments in AI chatbot technology and its implications for consumer behaviour
- The role of user experience design in consumer decision-making

Importance of good UX design in digital platforms:

- Key UX design principles and their impact on user satisfaction and loyalty
- Case studies of successful UX design implementations
- Emerging technologies and their impact on consumer behaviour
- The role of blockchain in enhancing transparency and trust

Blockchain's contribution to product authenticity and supply chain integrity:

- Case study: De Beers' Tracr™ platform for diamond provenance
- Impact on consumer decision-making and trust
- Augmented reality and immersive shopping experiences

The rise of AR in retail and its impact on consumer engagement:

- Examples of successful AR applications, such as Sephora's virtual makeup try-on
- The future of AR in consumer interactions

Introduction

The digital revolution has profoundly transformed the landscape of consumer behaviour, fundamentally altering how individuals interact with brands, search for information and make purchasing decisions. With the proliferation of digital platforms, social media and advanced technologies like artificial intelligence and blockchain, understanding consumer behaviour has become increasingly complex and multifaceted. This chapter delves into the critical role that digital technologies play in shaping contemporary consumer behaviour, exploring how social media, AI-powered bots and innovative user experience design influence the decision-making process. By examining real-world case studies and current research, we aim to provide a comprehensive understanding of the dynamic interplay between emerging technologies and consumer behaviour.

The influence of big data on consumer decision-making

The influence of big data on consumer decision-making has become a pivotal area of study in contemporary consumer behaviour research. As the digital landscape continues to evolve, the vast amounts of data generated by consumers' online activities are reshaping the traditional decision-making process. Table 6.1 summarizes the data generated by consumers' online activities, including where the data comes from and the types of data collected.

Table 6.1 Origin of the big data

Category	Details
Sources of data collection	• Websites and mobile applications • Social media platforms • E-commerce websites • Search engines • Browsers and operating systems

(continued)

Table 6.1 (Continued)

Category	Details
Types of data collected	**Personally identifiable information (PII):** • Name, address, date of birth • Email addresses • Phone numbers **Online behaviour data:** • Websites visited • Search queries • Pages viewed • Time spent on sites • Click patterns **Device and technical data:** • IP addresses • Device type • Operating system • Browser type and version **Purchase data:** • Items bought • Shopping cart contents • Transaction values • Payment information **Location data:** • Posts • Likes • Shares • Comments **App usage data:** • Videos watched • Articles read
Data collection methods	• Cookies • Pixels • Device and browser fingerprinting • Application Programming Interfaces (APIs) • Software Development Kits (SDKs)
Data usage	• Service provision • Targeted advertising • Product development • Data selling as a revenue stream

The influence of big data and AI on consumer preferences

The integration of **big data** and **artificial intelligence** into consumer analysis has revolutionized how businesses understand and predict consumer behaviour. Big data analytics allows for a more nuanced understanding of consumer preferences by analysing vast amounts of data generated from online interactions, social media and transactional records. For instance, recent research by Mikalef et al. (2019) emphasizes that **big data analytics** capabilities significantly enhance innovation and operational efficiency by enabling firms to tailor their products and services more precisely to consumer needs.

AI-driven tools, such as recommendation algorithms and personalized marketing strategies, are now commonplace. For example, Netflix's recommendation system, which uses collaborative filtering and deep learning techniques, has become a benchmark for personalizing user experiences (Zytek et al., 2021). Such systems not only improve user engagement but also drive sales by suggesting content that aligns with individual preferences.

Consumer behaviour and recommendation systems

In the contemporary digital landscape, recommendation systems have emerged as a pivotal technology shaping consumer behaviour (Çekik, 2021). These systems leverage sophisticated algorithms to analyse user preferences and behaviour, delivering personalized content that significantly influences purchasing decisions. By analysing historical data, such as browsing patterns and past purchases, these systems enhance user experience by offering tailored recommendations. For instance, platforms like Netflix and Amazon utilize advanced recommender algorithms to suggest movies or products, thereby optimizing user engagement and driving sales (Gomez-Uribe and Hunt, 2015).

The mechanisms behind these systems vary, encompassing collaborative filtering, content-based filtering, hybrid approaches and popularity-based methods. Collaborative filtering, which predicts user preferences based on the behaviour of similar users, is widely employed by e-commerce giants and streaming services (Schafer et al., 2007). Recent advancements in this method have been highlighted by Wang et al. (2019), who introduced a novel approach to enhance prediction accuracy through **deep learning techniques**. **Content-based filtering**, meanwhile, focuses on user profiles and item characteristics to recommend relevant content. This method is exemplified by Spotify's music recommendation system, which suggests tracks based on users' listening history and music preferences.

Hybrid filtering methods, which combine content-based and collaborative approaches, address some limitations of individual techniques by leveraging their strengths (Sieg and Burke, 2007). For example, the Netflix recommendation system employs a hybrid model that integrates user preferences and item similarities, resulting in highly personalized viewing suggestions. Similarly, popularity-based filtering offers recommendations based on the overall popularity of items, a method effectively utilized by platforms like YouTube to highlight trending content (Shen and Yang, 2013).

Despite their efficacy, recommendation systems face challenges such as the **cold start problem**, sparsity and privacy concerns. The cold start problem, which pertains to the difficulty of recommending items to new users or items with insufficient data, has been addressed through approaches like pre-promotion and the use of social networks. The issue of sparsity, where incomplete user–item interactions hinder accurate recommendations, is being tackled with advanced matrix factorization techniques and deep learning models (Çekik, 2021). Furthermore, privacy concerns are increasingly important, with recent studies suggesting enhanced data anonymization and encryption practices to safeguard user information.

Overall, recommendation systems have become integral to the digital consumer experience, driving engagement and shaping purchasing behaviours. As technology evolves, these systems continue to adapt, offering increasingly precise and personalized recommendations that cater to individual user preferences.

Big data and consumer insights

Big data analytics provide unprecedented insights into consumer preferences, behaviours and patterns. This wealth of information allows businesses to tailor their offerings and marketing strategies with remarkable precision. For instance, a recent study by Chatterjee et al. (2023) found that companies utilizing big data analytics tools experienced significant improvements in their decision-making processes, leading to enhanced business performance.

Adapting to rapidly changing consumer preferences

Companies now have unprecedented access to consumer data, enabling them to understand and predict purchasing patterns with greater accuracy. This transformation is underscored by the increasing reliance on big data to enhance market agility, as companies strive to adapt to rapidly changing consumer preferences and market conditions (Hajli et al., 2020).

One of the key aspects of modern consumer behaviour is the demand for personalized experiences. Consumers today expect brands to understand their needs and preferences, often before they are even explicitly stated. This expectation has driven companies to invest heavily in data analytics and AI to tailor their offerings. For instance, Tan and Zhan (2017) demonstrate how big data analytics have been used by electronics companies to improve new product development, resulting in products that are more closely aligned with consumer expectations.

Moreover, the integration of social media into the consumer journey has also reshaped purchasing behaviour. Social media platforms serve not only as channels for product discovery but also as spaces where consumers can share their experiences and influence the purchasing decisions of others. Baum et al. (2019) highlight how social media campaigns significantly impact the success of new product introductions, as consumers increasingly rely on peer reviews and social proof.

Another critical factor influencing consumer behaviour is the concept of agility. Companies that are agile are better positioned to respond to consumer needs and market shifts. Agility allows firms to shorten the time-to-market for new products, reducing the risk associated with innovation. Research by Cooper (2016) supports this, showing that blending agile methodologies with traditional stage-gate processes enhances communication and flexibility in new product development, leading to higher success rates.

Finally, the ethical considerations surrounding data privacy are becoming more prominent in consumer decision-making. As companies collect more data, consumers are becoming more aware of how their data is used and are increasingly concerned about privacy. Addressing these concerns is crucial for maintaining consumer trust and fostering long-term loyalty. Shirazi et al. (2021) emphasize the importance of a robust privacy management architecture in big data environments to ensure that consumers feel secure in their interactions with brands.

Big data and predictive analysis

One of the most profound impacts of big data on consumer decision-making is the ability to offer highly personalized experiences. Kroger, a major retail chain, exemplifies this trend by leveraging data from over 770 million consumers to create customized loyalty programmes. This approach has resulted in impressive redemption rates of 60 per cent and generated over $12 billion in incremental revenue.

Real-time influence on purchase decisions

Big data enables real-time analysis and response to consumer behaviour. Tesla's use of sensor data from its vehicles demonstrates how immediate feedback can influence both product development and consumer decisions. By collecting and analysing data in real-time, Tesla can inform vehicle owners about necessary repairs or updates, directly impacting consumer decisions regarding maintenance and upgrades.

CONSUMER BEHAVIOUR IN THE AGE OF DATA-DRIVEN RETAIL

The way modern consumers engage with retail environments has been fundamentally altered by the rise of data-driven strategies, particularly in how companies like Kroger utilize loyalty programmes to gather and leverage vast amounts of consumer data (Bayram et al., 2024).

Kroger is a prominent American retail company and the largest supermarket operator in the United States by revenue (Kroger Precision Marketing, 2024).

Founded in 1883 by Bernard Kroger in Cincinnati, Ohio, the company has grown to operate 2,719 grocery retail stores across 35 states and the District of Columbia. Kroger's diverse store formats include supermarkets, multi-department stores, warehouse stores and marketplace stores, catering to a wide range of consumer needs.

Kroger is known for its extensive product offerings, which include groceries, pharmacy services and fuel centres. The company operates under various banners, such as Ralphs, Dillons, Smith's and Harris Teeter and has a significant presence in the online grocery market. In recent years, Kroger has invested heavily in e-commerce, partnering with Ocado to enhance its online ordering and delivery capabilities, which saw a significant boost during the Covid-19 pandemic.

In addition to its retail operations, Kroger is recognized for its commitment to sustainability and community engagement. The company has implemented various initiatives aimed at reducing waste, promoting healthy eating and supporting local food banks. As of 2023, Kroger continued to be a major player in the retail industry, with a focus on innovation and customer service.

This transformation is not merely about tracking purchases but involves constructing detailed profiles of shoppers that include demographic information, financial status and even online behaviour.

The evolving landscape of consumer behaviour in **data-rich environments** necessitates a deeper understanding of the tradeoffs involved. As companies continue to enhance their data capabilities, the need for transparency and consumer awareness becomes increasingly important. Consumers must be informed about what they are giving up in exchange for the benefits of loyalty programmes and retailers must navigate the ethical complexities of data usage, ensuring that their practices align with consumer expectations and privacy standards.

The role of dynamic capabilities in consumer behaviour

Dynamic capabilities – organizational abilities to adapt, integrate and reconfigure internal and external competencies – play a pivotal role in responding to changing consumer demands. Teece (2014) highlights that firms with strong dynamic capabilities can effectively leverage data insights to adapt their strategies and offerings in response to market fluctuations.

A recent study by Wamba et al. (2019) illustrates this concept by demonstrating how dynamic capabilities, when combined with big data analytics, enhance supply chain ambidexterity and firm performance. For instance, companies that rapidly adapt to shifts in consumer preferences, such as the surge in demand for sustainable products, gain a competitive edge. Brands like Patagonia and Tesla have successfully employed dynamic capabilities to align their offerings with evolving consumer values around sustainability and innovation.

Consumer behaviour and emerging technologies

The rise of emerging technologies such as the **Internet of Things (IoT)** and **blockchain** is also reshaping consumer behaviour. IoT devices provide companies with real-time data on consumer usage patterns, allowing for more effective product development and marketing strategies. Sheshadri (2019) discusses how IoT can enhance the quality of life by enabling more personalized and efficient services, from smart home devices to health monitoring systems.

Blockchain technology, with its potential for enhancing transparency and security, is increasingly influencing consumer trust and purchasing decisions. For example, the application of blockchain in supply chains allows consumers to trace the origin of products, thereby increasing their confidence in the authenticity and ethical standards of the goods they purchase (Sharma et al., 2021).

Purchase technologies

The integration of emerging technologies into consumer behaviour is having a particularly significant impact in the realm of mobile commerce (Pelet, 2019). In recent years, technologies such as mobile payment systems and social commerce platforms have revolutionized how consumers interact with businesses and make purchasing decisions. This transformation is particularly evident in the contrast between Chinese and French consumer behaviours, illustrating the varying impacts of technological advancements across different cultural and economic contexts. In China, mobile payment systems like WeChat Pay and Alipay have become ubiquitous. Table 6.2 is a comparison of **WeChat** Pay and Alipay, highlighting the key differences in their impact on consumer behaviour.

These platforms, developed by tech giants Tencent and Alibaba respectively, have fundamentally altered consumer habits. WeChat Pay, initially a social media app, has evolved into a comprehensive payment system that facilitates a wide range of transactions, from shopping to transportation. Similarly, Alipay's extensive network supports millions of transactions daily, promoting a cashless society and enhancing convenience for users. The rapid adoption of these technologies reflects a broader trend in which convenience and efficiency drive consumer preferences.

In contrast, French and European consumers in general exhibit a more cautious approach towards digital payments. Despite the advancements in mobile payment

Table 6.2 Comparison of WeChat Pay and Alipay

Aspect	WeChat Pay	Alipay	References
Integration with social media	Deeply integrated within WeChat's social platform	Primarily a standalone payment and financial app	Mu & Lee (2017)
User base	Strong focus on personal transactions among friends and family	Broad adoption across various consumer sectors	CNNIC (2023)
Primary use cases	Frequently used for social interactions, peer-to-peer transfers and in-app purchases	Widely used for online shopping, utility payments and investments	Xu et al. (2024)
International reach	Limited international expansion, primarily focused on Chinese users	More extensive global reach, accepted in numerous countries	Mu & Lee (2017)
Security features	Relies heavily on WeChat's ecosystem for security	Extensive use of facial recognition and biometric verification	CNNIC (2023)
Consumer loyalty programmes	Integrated with WeChat's social loyalty features	Standalone rewards and loyalty programmes, often linked with shopping platforms	Xu et al. (2024)

technology, France's preference for cash and traditional banking methods remains strong. Privacy concerns are a significant factor influencing this behaviour. The French market's resistance to platforms like Facebook's Libra currency, due to privacy issues, underscores a broader scepticism towards digital financial innovations. This caution is indicative of a cultural emphasis on data protection and a slower acceptance of emerging technologies compared with China.

Emerging social commerce platforms, such as Pinduoduo in China, further illustrate the transformative impact of technology on consumer behaviour. Pinduoduo's group-buying feature leverages social networks to offer discounts and drive consumer engagement, appealing particularly to price-sensitive segments. This model not only fosters community-driven shopping but also demonstrates how technology can enhance consumer value through innovative business models.

The divergent trajectories of consumer behaviour in China and France highlight the importance of understanding local contexts when implementing emerging technologies. For French businesses looking to engage with the Chinese market, adapting to these technological trends and addressing privacy concerns could provide a competitive edge. Similarly, for Chinese companies expanding into France, acknowledging and respecting local preferences for privacy and traditional payment methods is crucial.

The interplay between consumer behaviour and emerging technologies reveals both opportunities and challenges in the global marketplace. As technology continues to evolve, businesses must navigate these dynamics carefully, balancing convenience with privacy concerns to meet the diverse needs of consumers across different cultures and regions.

Shaping consumer expectations

The availability of vast amounts of information is reshaping consumer expectations. Consumers now anticipate highly relevant product recommendations and personalized shopping experiences. A study by Tseng et al. (2022) indicates that while consumers hold a reserved attitude towards big data recommendation mechanisms, nearly 60 per cent find them extremely helpful in online shopping.

A recent study by Wang and Hajli (2017) highlights that AI-driven analytics can significantly improve decision-making quality in retail by predicting customer preferences with greater accuracy.

Big data analytics further exemplifies the intersection of consumer behaviour and technology. By analysing vast amounts of data from various sources, companies can gain deep insights into consumer preferences and trends. This capability allows for highly targeted marketing strategies that resonate with specific consumer segments. According to a study by Felipe et al. (2020), firms leveraging big data analytics have been shown to achieve higher performance levels, as these technologies enable more precise customer segmentation and personalization. For example, Netflix utilizes big data to tailor its content recommendations, enhancing user satisfaction and retention rates.

Augmented reality has also emerged as a transformative technology in consumer engagement. AR applications enable consumers to visualize products in their real-world environment before making a purchase decision. This technology has been particularly influential in the retail sector. A case study conducted by Heidenreich et al. (2022) on furniture retail demonstrates how AR applications enhance consumer confidence in product choices by allowing customers to see how furniture items would look in their homes. Such immersive experiences not only drive higher conversion rates but also foster greater customer satisfaction.

Furthermore, the integration of blockchain technology in consumer transactions is reshaping trust and transparency in digital commerce. Blockchain's decentralized nature ensures that transaction data is secure and tamper-proof, which is increasingly important in an era of heightened concern over data privacy. Research by Shirazi et al. (2021) underscores the role of blockchain in enhancing consumer trust by providing transparent and immutable records of transactions. This technology's impact is evident in sectors such as supply chain management, where it enables consumers to trace the origin and journey of products, thereby improving confidence in product authenticity.

Focus on e-commerce and delivery systems

In today's rapidly evolving digital landscape, a central theme in this transformation is the increasing demand for convenience, driven by the integration of innovative technologies like blockchain and the expansion of delivery options.

The importance of convenience in e-commerce

Convenience has always been a pivotal factor in consumer behaviour and its significance has only grown with the rise of e-commerce. As consumers increasingly prioritize efficiency and ease of access, businesses must adapt by offering streamlined, user-friendly experiences. Convenience in e-commerce is multifaceted, encompassing aspects such as time savings, reduced effort and the ability to control purchasing processes.

For instance, the proliferation of mobile commerce (m-commerce) has allowed consumers to shop from anywhere at any time, enhancing convenience by eliminating the need to visit physical stores. Similarly, the rise of ubiquitous commerce (u-commerce), where consumers interact with seamless and integrated shopping experiences across various platforms, underscores the growing expectation for convenience in digital shopping environments (Farquhar and Rowley, 2009).

Blockchain technology is emerging as a critical tool in enhancing the convenience and security of e-commerce transactions. By providing a transparent, immutable and decentralized ledger, blockchain addresses key consumer concerns such as fraud prevention and supply chain transparency. This technology ensures that each transaction is securely recorded and can be traced back, thereby building consumer trust – a crucial element in online shopping where concerns about privacy and security often arise. For example, companies like Walmart and IBM have implemented blockchain to track food products throughout their supply chain, offering consumers reassurance regarding the safety and origin of their purchases. This level of transparency not only satisfies consumer demand for ethical and secure shopping experiences, it also enhances the overall convenience by simplifying the verification process for both businesses and consumers.

The impact of delivery options on consumer behaviour

Delivery options play a significant role in shaping consumer behaviour in the e-commerce sector. The choice of delivery methods – whether home delivery, in-store pickup or even weekend and holiday delivery services – greatly influences how consumers perceive the convenience of online shopping. The flexibility to choose a delivery method that aligns with their schedule and preferences is a critical factor for many consumers. For example, the popularity of same-day delivery services, offered by companies like Amazon and Walmart, caters to consumers' desire for immediate gratification. In contrast, eco-conscious consumers may prefer slower, more sustainable delivery options, reflecting their broader ethical concerns. This range of choices allows consumers to tailor their shopping experience to their individual needs, thereby enhancing satisfaction and loyalty.

The integration of emerging technologies and diverse delivery options in e-commerce is fundamentally altering consumer behaviour. Convenience remains a driving force behind consumer decisions, with technology playing a crucial role in meeting these expectations. By leveraging blockchain for security and transparency and offering a variety of delivery options, businesses can cater to the evolving demands of the modern consumer, ensuring both satisfaction and sustained growth in an increasingly competitive market.

CONSUMER BEHAVIOUR AND EMERGING TECHNOLOGIES: THE CASE OF ONLINE FOOD DELIVERY SERVICES

The rapid proliferation of emerging technologies has significantly reshaped consumer behaviour, especially in the context of online food delivery services. During the Covid-19 pandemic, the adoption of these services surged dramatically, driven by factors such as perceived usefulness, social influence and trust. Understanding these elements is crucial for businesses aiming to optimize their strategies in the digital marketplace.

Technology Acceptance Model (TAM) in online food delivery

The Technology Acceptance Model (TAM) has been widely applied to explore the factors that influence consumer behaviour in the adoption of online food delivery services. Key components of TAM – perceived usefulness and perceived ease of use – are essential in shaping consumers' attitudes towards utilizing these technologies. For instance, Jun et al. (2021) found that perceived usefulness directly impacts consumers' decisions to adopt online food delivery services, highlighting the importance of convenience and efficiency in the consumer experience. This model also illustrates how enjoyment and trust, particularly in a pandemic context, contribute to a positive user experience, fostering long-term engagement with the service.

Social influence and trust in consumer decisions

Social influence plays a pivotal role in consumer behaviour, particularly in the context of online food delivery. The opinions of peers and the broader online community can significantly affect how consumers perceive and interact with these services. According to Hong et al. (2021), social influence becomes especially potent during crises like the Covid-19 pandemic, where trust in the service and its providers is paramount. Consumers are more likely to adopt a service recommended by others, especially if they trust the source. This trust is further reinforced by positive experiences and the reliability of the service, which are critical in converting first-time users into regular customers.

Managerial implications and strategic insights

For businesses in the online food delivery industry, understanding these behavioural drivers is crucial for developing effective marketing strategies. Providing detailed product information, enhancing user trust through reliable service and leveraging social influence are essential strategies to attract and retain customers. For example, companies like Deliveroo have capitalized on these factors by launching campaigns that emphasize community and trust, such as the 'Taste Your Neighbourhood' initiative, which not only promoted local cuisines but also fostered a sense of community during challenging times.

Emerging technologies have profoundly influenced consumer behaviour in the online food delivery sector, with factors like perceived usefulness, social influence and trust playing central roles. However, future research should explore additional variables such as the frequency of use and demographic factors to provide a more comprehensive understanding of consumer behaviour in this evolving landscape. By doing so, businesses can better tailor their strategies to meet the needs and expectations of their customers, ensuring sustained growth in the digital age.

Technological advancements in autonomous vehicles

The intersection of consumer behaviour and emerging technologies has become a focal point of academic and practical interest, particularly in the realm of autonomous vehicles and their associated technologies. As technological advancements continue to reshape various industries, understanding how consumers interact with and perceive these innovations is crucial for both developers and policymakers.

Autonomous vehicles (AVs) are at the forefront of this transformation, with significant developments in computational technologies and energy management shaping their market acceptance. Recent innovations, such as Tesla's Dojo supercomputer and the latest system-on-a-chip (SoC) technologies from Nvidia and Mobileye, exemplify the cutting-edge advancements driving the industry forward. The Tesla Dojo, with its exaflop computing power, represents a leap in AI model training for self-driving technology, enhancing the vehicle's ability to process and respond to real-time data (Tesla, 2024; Dominguez, 2021). Similarly, Nvidia's Orin chip and

Mobileye's EyeQ5 are pushing the boundaries of what autonomous driving systems can achieve, offering impressive performance metrics while managing power consumption efficiently (Bojarski et al., 2016; Mobileye, 2024).

Consumer perceptions and acceptance

Consumer behaviour towards autonomous vehicles is influenced by several factors, including technological reliability, safety and environmental impact. A study by the University of Michigan highlights that while AVs have the potential to improve traffic flow and reduce emissions through optimized driving patterns, concerns remain regarding their energy consumption and the impact on vehicle range (Centre for Sustainable Systems, 2020). For instance, the additional power required by sensors and computational systems in AVs may lead to a decrease in range compared with conventional electric vehicles, a point of contention among environmentally conscious consumers (Mitchell, 2018).

Recent surveys and studies underscore a growing acceptance of autonomous vehicles, particularly as technology improves and becomes more integrated into daily life. According to a 2024 report by Intellias, the integration of big data and advanced sensor technologies is not only enhancing the functionality of AVs but also gradually shifting consumer attitudes towards more favourable views on the benefits of these technologies (Intellias, 2023). The increased reliability and safety features of modern AVs are gradually overcoming initial scepticism, leading to a broader acceptance of these technologies among consumers.

Emerging trends and future directions

The ongoing advancements in autonomous vehicle technology reflect a broader trend of integrating cutting-edge innovations into everyday life. The development of energy-efficient chips and advanced processing systems illustrates a critical shift towards addressing the practical concerns of energy consumption and computational demands. For example, the introduction of Tesla's D1 chip, designed specifically for training AI models, is a testament to the industry's commitment to enhancing computational efficiency while managing power usage.

Furthermore, the rapid evolution of SoC technologies and the increasing sophistication of sensor systems are likely to further influence consumer behaviour. As these technologies become more embedded in consumer products, they will shape expectations around performance, reliability and environmental sustainability. The implications for consumer behaviour are profound, as the adoption of emerging technologies often hinges on the perceived value and benefits these innovations offer.

The interplay between consumer behaviour and emerging technologies, particularly in the context of autonomous vehicles, reveals a dynamic and evolving landscape. Technological advancements continue to push the boundaries of what is possible, while consumer perceptions and acceptance are gradually shifting in response to these innovations. As the industry progresses, ongoing research and development will be essential in aligning technological advancements with consumer expectations and preferences, ensuring that emerging technologies can achieve their full potential in shaping the future of mobility.

Understanding the role of chatbots and virtual assistants in consumer decision-making

The rise of chatbots and virtual assistants has significantly transformed consumer behaviour and decision-making processes in recent years. These emerging technologies are reshaping how consumers interact with brands, search for information and make purchasing decisions.

Chatbots and virtual assistants have become increasingly prevalent across various industries. A 2023 global survey revealed that 44 per cent of consumers appreciate the assistance of chatbots in finding product information before making a purchase. This widespread adoption reflects the growing consumer acceptance of AI-powered interactions in their shopping journeys.

How consumers interact with bots

Consumers are increasingly engaging with AI-powered bots across various touchpoints in their customer journey. These interactions range from simple query resolutions to more complex tasks such as product recommendations and purchase assistance. Rohit et al. (2024) highlight that the nature of these interactions is becoming more sophisticated, with bots capable of understanding and responding to nuanced consumer needs.

Factors influencing bot adoption

Several factors contribute to consumers' willingness to interact with bots:

- Perceived usefulness: Consumers are more likely to engage with bots when they perceive them as useful in accomplishing their tasks efficiently.
- Ease of use: The intuitive design and user-friendly interfaces of modern bots encourage consumer adoption (Sharma et al., 2023).

- Trust and privacy concerns: While convenience is a driving factor, consumers' trust in bots and concerns about data privacy significantly influence their willingness to engage.

Recent research has begun to explore the emotional dimension of consumer–bot interactions. Huang and Rust (2021) suggest that advanced bots capable of detecting and responding to customer sentiment can elicit emotional reactions from consumers, potentially influencing their overall experience and brand perception.

Enhancing customer experience

These technologies are playing a crucial role in improving customer experience by providing instant, personalized assistance. According to the Zendesk CX Trends Report, 71 per cent of customers believe AI and chatbots help them get faster replies (Zendesk, 2024). This immediacy addresses the modern consumer's desire for quick interactions and instant query resolution.

Impact on decision-making process

Chatbots and virtual assistants are influencing various stages of the consumer decision-making process:

1. Need recognition: Virtual experiences facilitated by these technologies can stimulate consumers' desires for products by providing immersive and personalized interactions.
2. Information search: AI-powered assistants offer consumers direct access to relevant product information, reducing the overwhelming nature of vast online data.
3. Evaluation of alternatives: Consumers increasingly rely on AI-generated recommendations and virtual product experiences to evaluate options.
4. Purchase decision: The interaction mechanisms of chatbots can address customer queries in real-time, building confidence in the purchasing process.
5. Post-purchase behaviour: Virtual assistants can enhance post-purchase experiences by providing ongoing support and personalized follow-ups.

Challenges and considerations

Despite their benefits, the integration of chatbots and virtual assistants in consumer interactions presents challenges. Some consumers still prefer human interaction for complex queries or emotional support. Additionally, the potential for misunderstandings or inappropriate responses from bots can lead to frustration. A study by Rohit et al. (2024) highlights the need to consider factors such as privacy concerns and the perceived credibility of AI-powered assistants. Retailers must balance the efficiency of automated interactions with the need for human touch in certain scenarios.

As AI technology advances, we can expect more sophisticated chatbots and virtual assistants. For instance, the integration of large language models like ChatGPT into retail contexts offers promising avenues for enhancing customer service and personalization. However, further research is needed to understand the long-term impacts on consumer behaviour and to address potential ethical concerns.

Future developments in chatbot technology

Generative AI chatbots stand out for their potential to revolutionize customer service and engagement. These chatbots, powered by sophisticated machine learning algorithms, offer personalized interactions and support, mimicking human-like conversations to enhance the consumer experience. Recent research has shown that generative AI chatbots significantly influence consumer satisfaction and decision-making by providing timely, relevant and contextually aware responses (Shahriar and Hayawi, 2023). For instance, the integration of AI chatbots in higher education settings has improved student support services by offering instant assistance and personalized guidance on academic matters (Vargas-Murillo et al., 2023).

Augmented reality also plays a pivotal role in transforming consumer behaviour by creating immersive shopping experiences. AR technology allows consumers to visualize products in their real-world environment before making a purchase, thereby reducing uncertainty and enhancing confidence in their choices. A notable example is the AR application developed by Sephora, which enables users to try on makeup virtually through their smartphones. This application not only increases engagement but also provides a more interactive and convenient shopping experience, leading to higher conversion rates and customer satisfaction (Tlili et al., 2023).

Blockchain technology, with its emphasis on transparency and security, is addressing critical concerns related to product authenticity and supply chain integrity. By providing a decentralized and immutable record of transactions, blockchain enhances consumer trust and accountability. For example, the use of blockchain in tracking the origin of luxury goods, such as diamonds, ensures that consumers are purchasing ethically sourced products. De Beers, a leading diamond company, has implemented blockchain to trace the provenance of its diamonds, thereby reassuring consumers of the authenticity and ethical standards of their purchases (Guo et al., 2023).

Chatbots and virtual assistants are becoming integral to the consumer decision-making process, offering personalized, efficient and round-the-clock support. As these technologies continue to evolve, they will likely play an even more significant role in shaping consumer behaviour and expectations in the digital marketplace.

> ### ACTIVITY 1
>
> Debate on AI and consumer trust
>
> Organize a debate on the role of AI and chatbots in consumer interactions. One side will argue that AI enhances consumer trust and decision-making, while the other will discuss the potential drawbacks, such as privacy concerns and the loss of human touch. After the debate, facilitate a class discussion on how to balance these aspects in digital marketing.

Blockchain and consumer trust

Blockchain technology is enabling new levels of transparency and traceability in consumer goods. De Beers Group's Tracr™ platform exemplifies how this technology can be applied to build consumer trust. Through the use of leading-edge technologies – including blockchain, AI, the IoT and advanced security and privacy technologies – Tracr™ enables confidence in a diamond's source throughout the diamond value chain. Launched at scale in May 2022, Tracr™ uses blockchain to create an immutable record of a diamond's provenance from mine to retail. This addresses growing consumer demand for ethical sourcing and transparency in luxury goods.

The platform allows De Beers to register up to one million diamonds per week, providing tamper-proof source assurance at an unprecedented scale. For consumers, this means access to reliable information about a diamond's origin and journey through the supply chain, enabling more informed purchasing decisions.

Emerging technologies like blockchain are reshaping how consumers evaluate products and make purchasing decisions. With platforms like Tracr™, consumers can now factor in detailed provenance information when considering high-value purchases like diamonds. This shift towards data-driven decision-making is likely to expand to other product categories as similar technologies are adopted.

While consumers increasingly value transparency, they are also concerned about data privacy. Tracr™ addresses this by using advanced privacy technologies to ensure participants control access to their own data. As similar platforms emerge across industries, balancing transparency with data protection will be crucial for consumer acceptance.

Future directions: metaverse and virtual experiences

Looking ahead, companies are exploring how to leverage emerging technologies to enhance consumer engagement. De Beers, for instance, is considering how to meaningfully integrate their brand into the metaverse. This could potentially include virtual tours of diamond mines or immersive experiences that tell the story of individual diamonds.

As these technologies mature, we can expect to see more innovative approaches to consumer engagement, blending physical products with digital experiences. This convergence is likely to further transform consumer behaviour, expectations and the overall shopping experience in the coming years.

The impact of user experience design

UX design plays a pivotal role in shaping consumer decision-making processes in today's digital marketplace. As the internet continues to evolve, the complexity of consumer interactions with digital platforms has increased significantly. UX design encompasses various aspects, including usability, accessibility and aesthetic appeal, all of which significantly influence how consumers perceive and interact with a brand's online presence. Research indicates that a well-designed user experience can lead to enhanced customer satisfaction, fostering a positive relationship between consumers and brands (Lemon and Verhoef, 2016).

The psychological underpinnings of consumer behaviour suggest that individuals are more likely to engage with platforms that provide seamless, intuitive and aesthetically pleasing experiences. According to Hassenzahl (2010), a positive user experience not only enhances usability but also evokes emotional responses that can heavily influence purchase intentions. For instance, an e-commerce website that prioritizes UX design by streamlining navigation and reducing load times can significantly lower bounce rates and increase conversion rates. This effect is corroborated by studies showing that users are likely to abandon websites that are difficult to navigate, underscoring the necessity of thoughtful UX design in retaining consumer interest (Hassenzahl, 2010).

Moreover, UX design contributes to building brand trust and loyalty. When consumers encounter a user-friendly interface that meets their needs and expectations, their overall confidence in the brand is enhanced. This trust is crucial, as it can lead to repeat purchases and brand advocacy. A study by Kuo and Yen (2009) found that perceived ease of use and perceived usefulness are vital factors in fostering consumer loyalty, indicating that effective UX design directly correlates with long-term customer retention.

Furthermore, the role of UX design in consumer decision-making extends beyond initial engagement. The design elements of a website or application can influence consumers during their evaluation of options, impacting their final purchase decisions. For example, persuasive design techniques, such as strategic use of colour, layout and content organization, can guide consumers towards desired actions, facilitating a smoother decision-making process (Norman, 2013). These design strategies not only enhance the user experience but also serve as subtle nudges that can sway consumer behaviour towards particular choices.

By focusing on usability, emotional engagement and trust-building, brands can create a more compelling user experience that not only attracts but also retains consumers. As the digital landscape continues to evolve, prioritizing UX design will be essential for brands aiming to thrive in a competitive market. The intricate relationship between UX design and consumer behaviour highlights the need for ongoing research and development in this field to better understand and harness its potential in influencing consumer decisions.

The importance of good UX design

Recent research from Ettis et al. (2023) highlights that digital touchpoints are increasingly influential, as consumers engage with brands through a multitude of online channels, from social media platforms to mobile applications. For instance, Ferreira et al. (2019) emphasize that firm innovation and digital adoption are crucial for enhancing performance, underlining the significant impact of digital presence on consumer perceptions and behaviours.

The integration of social media into consumer behaviour studies has revealed new dimensions of brand interaction. Fulgoni and Lipsman (2016) argue that mobile marketing dynamics are reshaping retail experiences, suggesting that mobile devices are not merely supplementary but central to modern consumer engagement. This shift is supported by Statista (2023), which reports that a substantial proportion of Facebook users access the platform via mobile devices, illustrating the prominence of mobile interfaces in online interactions.

Moreover, the concept of 'flow' – a state of immersive engagement – has been increasingly applied to digital contexts to understand consumer experiences. Pelet and Taieb (2022) discuss how context-aware optimizations of mobile commerce websites enhance user experiences by leveraging flow principles, demonstrating the importance of designing interfaces that cater to users' immersive experiences. This is further echoed by Pelet et al. (2017), who found that telepresence, facilitated by social media use, significantly enhances the flow experience and thus impacts consumer behaviour positively.

The role of online reviews and social media in influencing consumer decisions cannot be understated. Recent studies, such as those by Nilashi et al. (2018), reveal that travellers heavily rely on online reviews for decision-making, showcasing how peer-generated content impacts consumer trust and purchasing choices. Additionally, Zhao and Dholakia (2009) utilize the **Kano model** to explore how website interactivity and customer satisfaction are intertwined, emphasizing the growing importance of interactive features in enhancing user satisfaction and loyalty.

The convergence of digital technologies and consumer behaviour research underscores a transformative shift in how consumers interact with brands. Innovations in mobile marketing, the application of **flow theory** to online experiences and the impact of online reviews collectively illustrate the complexity and dynamism of contemporary consumer behaviour. As digital landscapes continue to evolve, understanding these trends will be crucial for businesses aiming to engage effectively with their audiences.

UX design principles for digital platforms

UX design principles have become increasingly crucial in shaping consumer behaviour on digital platforms. As the digital landscape evolves, these principles serve as foundational guidelines for creating intuitive, engaging and user-centric interfaces that drive consumer satisfaction and loyalty.

One of the core UX design principles is **user-centred design**. This approach places the user at the heart of the design process, emphasizing the importance of understanding user needs, goals and behaviours (Tomboc, 2024). By conducting thorough user research and analysis, designers can create digital experiences that resonate with their target audience. For instance, the food delivery app DoorDash regularly conducts user surveys and usability tests to refine its interface, ensuring it meets the evolving needs of its diverse user base.

Another key principle is simplicity and clarity. In an era of information overload, digital platforms that offer clear, uncluttered interfaces tend to perform better. This principle involves focusing on core functionality and eliminating unnecessary elements that could distract or confuse users (Kapreign, 2024). The success of platforms like Airbnb can be attributed in part to their commitment to simplicity, with clean layouts and intuitive navigation that guide users effortlessly through the booking process.

Consistency and familiarity also play a vital role in UX design. By maintaining consistent design elements across a platform, designers can create a sense of predictability that enhances user comfort and efficiency (Tomboc, 2024). For example, the e-commerce giant Amazon maintains a consistent layout and navigation structure across its various product categories, allowing users to shop with ease regardless of what they're purchasing.

Accessibility and inclusivity have gained significant importance in recent years. Designers are increasingly focusing on creating interfaces that are usable by individuals with diverse abilities and needs. This includes implementing features such as alternative text for images, keyboard navigation options and high-contrast modes (Kapreign, 2024). The streaming service Netflix, for instance, has made significant strides in accessibility by offering audio descriptions for visually impaired users and customizable subtitles for hearing-impaired viewers.

As we move forward, emerging technologies are set to further shape UX design principles. The integration of artificial intelligence and machine learning is enabling more personalized and adaptive user experiences. Voice user interfaces and gesture-based interactions are also gaining traction, necessitating new approaches to UX design that go beyond traditional visual interfaces (https://dev.to/, 2023).

UX design principles for digital platforms continue to evolve, driven by changing consumer expectations and technological advancements. By adhering to these principles, businesses can create digital experiences that not only meet functional requirements but also delight users, fostering long-term engagement and loyalty in an increasingly competitive digital marketplace.

Case studies of UX design

Examining real-world examples of outstanding UX design provides valuable insights into how businesses can effectively engage consumers in the digital realm. These case studies demonstrate the practical application of UX principles and their impact on consumer behaviour. One is the Cox Automotive's Manheim division (https://www.coxautoinc.com/brands/manheim/), which utilized LogRocket (https://logrocket.com/) to optimize its digital experience for remote car auctions (Sobowale, 2024). This case study highlights the importance of data-driven UX design. By leveraging user data and feedback, Cox Automotive was able to identify and address user-reported issues, gain insights into customer behaviours and make informed decisions to enhance their product. This approach resulted in improved user satisfaction and increased efficiency in their digital auction process.

The Flexbox Inspector tool developed for Mozilla Firefox offers insights into UX design for specialized software (Kamenez, 2023). This case study demonstrates the value of extensive user research and feature analysis in creating tools for professional users. The design process involved interviews with senior designers and a comprehensive analysis of user needs, resulting in a colour-coded layout with multiple entry points for efficient workflow management.

These case studies underscore several key principles in effective UX design:

1 User-centred approach: Prioritizing user needs and preferences in the design process.
2 Data-driven decision-making: Utilizing user data and feedback to inform design choices.
3 Simplification of complex tasks: Making intricate processes more accessible to a wider user base.
4 Continuous improvement: Regularly updating designs based on user feedback and changing needs.

By studying these examples, businesses can gain valuable insights into creating digital experiences that not only meet functional requirements but also resonate with users on an emotional level, ultimately influencing consumer behaviour and fostering brand loyalty.

> **ACTIVITY 2**
>
> UX design workshop
>
> Have students work in pairs or small groups to redesign the user interface of a popular website or app, applying the UX principles discussed in the chapter (e.g. simplicity, accessibility). They should create mockups and explain their design choices, focusing on how these changes would improve the user experience.

Consumer behaviour and sustainable innovation: a transformative approach

The integration of innovation and sustainability within business practices has a profound impact on consumer behaviour (Sagar, 2023). As companies like Tesla, Unilever and Patagonia champion sustainable innovation, they not only reshape industry standards but also influence consumer preferences and choices. Understanding this evolving consumer behaviour is crucial for businesses aiming to align their strategies with sustainability.

Consumer preferences and sustainable products

The shift towards sustainability in consumer behaviour is evident in the growing demand for eco-friendly products and services. For instance, Tesla's success in the electric vehicle market is not only a result of technological innovation but also due to the increasing environmental awareness among consumers. A 2023 survey by NielsenIQ found that 73 per cent of global consumers are willing to change their consumption habits to reduce their environmental impact. This statistic highlights the importance of aligning product offerings with the values of sustainability-conscious consumers.

Behavioural economics and ethical consumerism

Behavioural economics provides a framework for understanding how consumers make decisions regarding sustainable products. Ethical consumerism, where purchasing decisions are influenced by ethical considerations such as environmental impact and social responsibility, is becoming increasingly significant. Patagonia's emphasis on ethical sourcing and transparency resonates deeply with consumers who prioritize sustainability. Consumers are more likely to engage with brands that demonstrate genuine commitment to social and environmental causes (Giesler and Veresiu, 2014).

The role of digital platforms in shaping consumer choices

Digital platforms and social media also play a crucial role in shaping consumer behaviour towards sustainable products. Companies that effectively use these platforms to communicate their sustainability initiatives can enhance brand loyalty and consumer trust. A study by Deloitte (2023) revealed that 60 per cent of consumers are influenced by online reviews and social media content when making purchasing decisions. Brands that leverage digital platforms to showcase their sustainability efforts, such as through transparent supply chain practices, are more likely to attract and retain environmentally conscious consumers.

Challenges and opportunities in sustainable consumerism

However, the path to sustainable consumer behaviour is not without challenges. The risk of greenwashing, where companies make exaggerated or false claims about their sustainability efforts, can erode consumer trust. For example, research by PRNewswire (2010) indicates that more than 95 per cent of products marketed as 'green' are found to have committed at least one sin of greenwashing. Therefore, businesses must prioritize authenticity and transparency in their sustainability claims to avoid consumer scepticism.

The intersection of innovation, sustainability and consumer behaviour is reshaping the business landscape. Companies that successfully align their practices with the values of sustainability-conscious consumers can gain a competitive advantage. By understanding and addressing the behavioural drivers behind ethical consumerism, businesses can not only meet the demands of today's consumers but also contribute to a more sustainable future. Table 6.3 outlines key aspects of consumer behaviour related to sustainability, providing a summary and relevant examples or references for each topic.

Table 6.3 Examples of key aspects of consumer behaviour regarding sustainability

Key aspect	Summary	Examples/References
Consumer preferences	Consumers are increasingly favouring eco-friendly and sustainable products.	Tesla's electric vehicles; NielsenIQ (2023) survey on consumer willingness to change consumption habits.

(continued)

Table 6.3 (Continued)

Key aspect	Summary	Examples/References
Behavioural economics	Ethical considerations are influencing consumer decisions, especially in sustainable contexts.	Patagonia's ethical sourcing; Giesler & Veresiu (2022).
Digital influence	Online platforms and social media significantly shape consumer choices, especially in sustainability.	Deloitte (2023) study on digital media influence on consumer behaviour.
Challenges of greenwashing	The risk of greenwashing can undermine consumer trust in sustainability claims.	TerraChoice (2023) report on greenwashing in consumer markets.
Impact of authenticity and transparency	Authenticity in sustainability claims is crucial for maintaining consumer trust and loyalty.	Importance of transparent supply chains; Deloitte (2023).

Conclusion

As we navigate through an era of rapid technological advancement, the impact of digital innovations on consumer behaviour cannot be overstated. This chapter highlights the significant role that social media, AI and UX design play in shaping consumer decisions, as well as the transformative potential of technologies like blockchain and augmented reality. While these advancements offer exciting opportunities for enhancing consumer experiences and driving brand engagement, they also present challenges related to privacy, data security and ethical considerations. As digital technologies continue to evolve, businesses must remain agile and responsive, leveraging these tools to meet the ever-changing needs and expectations of consumers in the digital age. Understanding and adapting to these shifts will be crucial for success in the increasingly competitive digital marketplace.

ACTIVITY 3

Analysing a case study

Form groups and select a different case study from the chapter for your group (e.g. De Beers' Tracr™ platform, DoorDash UX design). Work together to analyse the case study, identify key challenges and solutions and prepare a presentation to share your findings with the class. In your discussion, explore how these solutions could be adapted to other industries.

KEY TERMS

Consumer behaviour: The study of how individuals make decisions to spend their resources on consumption-related items.

Chatbot: An AI-powered tool that simulates human conversation to assist users with tasks or provide information in real-time.

User experience (UX) design: The process of creating digital interfaces that are easy to use, aesthetically pleasing and tailored to meet user needs.

Blockchain: A decentralized and immutable digital ledger used to securely record transactions and track assets.

Augmented reality (AR): Technology that overlays digital content onto the real world, enhancing the user's experience.

Flow: A state of deep engagement and immersion in an activity, often leading to enhanced user satisfaction.

Big data: Large and complex datasets that require advanced analytical methods to uncover patterns and insights relevant to decision-making.

Digital touchpoints: Various online platforms and interfaces where consumers interact with brands.

Virtual assistant: An AI-powered digital assistant that helps users perform tasks through voice or text commands.

Transparency: The practice of being open and honest in business operations, particularly in sharing information about product sourcing and production.

KEY LEARNING POINTS

Emerging technologies in consumer engagement:

- Big data analytics enables personalized experiences by analysing consumer patterns and preferences but raises concerns about privacy and data security.
- Augmented reality allows consumers to visualize products in real-world environments, enhancing confidence and increasing purchase rates.
- Blockchain technology fosters trust by offering transparency in supply chains and ensuring product authenticity.

AI and chatbots:

- AI-powered chatbots and virtual assistants improve consumer interactions by providing real-time assistance, which influences decision-making stages like product evaluation and purchase.

- Chatbots can enhance customer experience through personalized, instant responses, though challenges like privacy concerns and preference for human interaction persist.

User experience design:

- Good UX design is vital for consumer satisfaction, focusing on principles like simplicity, clarity and consistency.
- Accessibility and inclusive design are becoming increasingly important, making platforms more user-friendly for diverse audiences.

Impact of social media and online reviews:

- Social media is crucial for brand-consumer interaction, influencing decisions through peer-generated content and online reviews.
- Mobile interfaces and digital touchpoints are central to modern consumer engagement.

Technological integration:

- The use of AI, machine learning and big data analytics is revolutionizing predictive shopping experiences, offering consumers more personalized and tailored solutions.

Privacy and ethical considerations:

- The integration of big data and emerging technologies has introduced challenges surrounding ethical data use and consumer trust. Balancing transparency with data security is essential.

Future trends:

- The evolving relationship between physical and digital experiences (e.g. metaverse and AR) will continue to shape consumer behaviour.
- Emerging technologies will require businesses to innovate continually while addressing privacy and trust issues.

7 | Advancing consumer experiences in the digital world

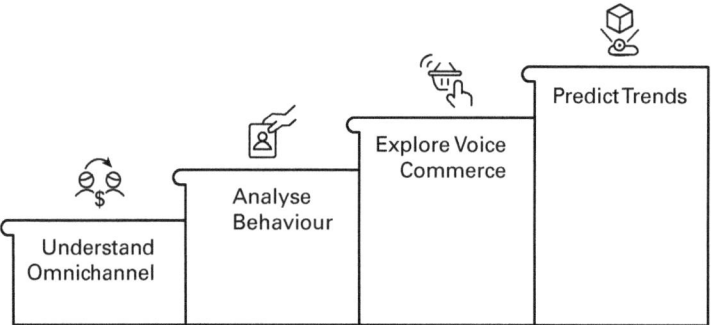

Journey to Mastering Omnichannel Marketing and Voice Commerce

LEARNING OBJECTIVES

By the end of this chapter, you should be able to:

- Understand omnichannel marketing: Explain the key pillars of omnichannel marketing strategies and their importance in creating seamless customer experiences.
- Analyse consumer behaviour: Evaluate how consumer behaviour is influenced by factors such as technology, market dynamics and omnichannel strategies using models like UTAUT.
- Explore the role of voice commerce: Describe how AI-powered voice assistants are transforming shopping experiences and identify the benefits and challenges associated with voice commerce.

- Predict future trends: Anticipate future developments in voice commerce, including its integration with emerging technologies and the implications for global markets.

CHAPTER OUTLINE

Omnichannel marketing strategies – foundations:
- Importance and key pillars (customer experience, integration, technology)

Success factors:
- Critical elements like strategy, market dynamics and customer behaviour
- Need for cross-functional collaboration and agile processes

Evaluation:
- Consumer behaviour analysis using UTAUT model
- Role of AR, VR and other advanced technologies

Voice commerce – emergence:
- Growth of AI and voice assistants
- Impact on shopping habits and user convenience

Transformation:
- Benefits: convenience, personalization, integration
- Challenges: privacy and security

Future of voice commerce – predictions:
- Widespread adoption and integration across sectors
- Enhanced AI-driven personalization

Expansion:
- New business models and applications
- Focus on privacy, security and global reach

Introduction

As consumers become increasingly connected and their expectations continue to evolve, businesses must adapt to these changes by adopting innovative strategies that enhance the customer experience. This chapter delves into two critical aspects of modern consumer behaviour: the implementation of omnichannel marketing strategies and the rise of voice commerce. By examining these trends, we aim to provide a comprehensive understanding of how they are reshaping consumer interactions and the broader retail industry.

The role of augmented reality in retail experiences

Augmented reality has emerged as a transformative technology in the retail sector, revolutionizing consumer experiences and bridging the gap between physical and digital shopping environments. By overlaying digital content onto the real world, AR enables retailers to create immersive, interactive and personalized experiences that significantly influence consumer behaviour and decision-making processes. The adoption of AR in retail has been rapidly accelerating, with the market projected to reach $23.43 billion by 2027, growing at a compound annual growth rate of 43.8 per cent (Grand View Research, 2024).

This growth is driven by increasing consumer demand for enhanced shopping experiences and the technology's proven ability to boost engagement and sales. One of the most impactful applications of AR in retail is **virtual try-on technology**. This feature allows consumers to visualize products on themselves or in their environment before making a purchase decision. For instance, L'Oréal's virtual makeup app allows users to experiment with different cosmetic products (Fingent, 2024).

Navigating consumer behaviour in the age of augmented reality

The advent of AR technology has fundamentally transformed consumer behaviour by merging digital and physical realms in unprecedented ways (Gambone, 2024). This immersive technology, which overlays digital content onto the real world, has introduced both opportunities and challenges in consumer engagement and advertising. As AR applications become increasingly prevalent in e-commerce and advertising, understanding the impact on consumer decision-making is crucial.

Recent developments highlight how AR influences consumer perceptions and behaviours. For instance, AR-driven shopping experiences, such as those implemented by IKEA with its 'IKEA Place' app, allow consumers to visualize furniture in their own living spaces before making a purchase. This practical application of AR not only enhances consumer engagement but also potentially reduces return rates by helping consumers make more informed decisions. However, AR's ability to create highly realistic and persuasive digital overlays also raises concerns about the accuracy of product representations and the potential for deceptive advertising.

The intersection of AR and consumer behaviour also brings forward new regulatory challenges. The Federal Trade Commission (FTC) has emphasized the importance of transparency in digital advertising to prevent consumer deception (Federal Trade Commission, 2024). For example, recent guidelines stipulate that AR advertisements must clearly disclose their commercial nature and ensure that any use of trademarks in AR environments does not mislead consumers about the endorsement or source of products (Federal Trade Commission, 2024). These regulations aim to protect consumers from misleading practices that could exploit the immersive nature of AR to create false impressions about product affiliations or quality.

Furthermore, the development of AR-specific regulations is essential to address the unique challenges posed by this technology. As highlighted by recent scholarship, the traditional frameworks of advertising law may not adequately cover the nuances of AR environments, which blend digital content with physical spaces (Gambone, 2024). Proactive measures, including clear guidelines for AR disclosures and transparency, are crucial to safeguarding consumer interests and maintaining the integrity of trademarks in this evolving landscape.

Ensuring that AR applications adhere to transparent advertising practices and regulatory standards will be vital in protecting consumers and fostering trust in this dynamic technological domain. The evolving nature of AR necessitates ongoing research and regulatory adaptation to address its impact on consumer behaviour effectively.

Retailers like Starbucks have also implemented AR-powered technology to enhance their in-store experience, as the following example will illustrate.

AUGMENTED REALITY: REVOLUTIONIZING CUSTOMER ENGAGEMENT AT STARBUCKS' SHANGHAI RESERVE ROASTERY

Starbucks' Shanghai Reserve Roastery exemplifies how AR can elevate customer experiences in the retail and hospitality sectors. Launched as 'the first fully immersive coffee experience', this 30,000-square-foot venue integrates AR technology to transform the traditional coffee visit into a dynamic, interactive journey. By leveraging AR, Starbucks not only enhances consumer engagement, it also redefines the sensory aspects of their brand experience.

At the core of the Shanghai Reserve Roastery's AR experience is its custom-designed digital platform, which allows customers to explore the coffee-making process in unprecedented detail. Visitors use the Roastery app or Alibaba's Taobao app to scan key features around the venue, unlocking a rich layer of digital content. For example, by pointing their mobile devices at the roasting cask, customers can view animated sequences that illustrate the roasting process, from beans being added to the cask to their journey through copper pipes to various coffee bars. This immersive approach offers a deeper understanding of the bean-to-cup story, blending education with entertainment (Escobar, 2017).

The Roastery's AR experience extends beyond mere visualization. It includes interactive elements such as virtual badges and shareable filters, enhancing customer engagement and social media interaction. This gamified approach rewards exploration and also drives digital engagement, encouraging visitors to share their experiences and promote the Roastery's unique features on social platforms. This integration of gamification with AR aligns with recent research indicating that such interactive elements can significantly boost customer loyalty and brand advocacy (Kumar et al., 2024).

Moreover, Starbucks has incorporated AR into its mobile ordering system, allowing customers to view the menu digitally and interact with roaming baristas. This reduces traditional pain points associated with ordering, such as long wait times and physical queues. Instead, customers can receive real-time notifications about their orders and pay directly on the spot, streamlining the purchasing process and enhancing overall convenience.

The implications of Starbucks' AR initiative extend to broader industry practices. By creating a compelling, content-rich environment, Starbucks demonstrates how AR can drive foot traffic and create memorable brand experiences. This strategy contrasts with the prevalent trend towards e-commerce, illustrating how AR can effectively bridge the gap between physical and digital interactions (Batat, 2021). Restaurants and retailers are encouraged to adopt similar AR strategies to enhance customer experiences, such as virtual badges for loyalty programmes or contextual displays of menu items to aid decision-making.

Starbucks' Shanghai Reserve Roastery showcases the potential of AR to revolutionize consumer interactions by providing immersive, educational and engaging experiences. As AR technology continues to evolve, its applications in enhancing customer experiences and streamlining operations are poised to become increasingly prevalent. The success of Starbucks' initiative underscores the value of integrating AR into customer engagement strategies, offering a model for other businesses seeking to innovate and connect with their audiences on a deeper level.

The impact of AR on consumer behaviour is significant. According to recent studies, 61 per cent of consumers prefer retailers that offer AR experiences and 71 per cent report they would shop more frequently if AR were available (Fingent, 2023). Moreover, Shopify reports that products with AR content see a 94 per cent higher conversion rate compared with products without AR (Shopify, 2023). As AR technology continues to evolve, its integration with other emerging technologies like artificial intelligence and the Internet of Things promises to further transform the retail landscape. Future applications may include personalized AR-powered shopping assistants, seamless omnichannel experiences and even more sophisticated product visualization tools.

Augmented reality is reshaping consumer behaviour in retail by offering enhanced product visualization, personalized experiences and interactive engagement. As the technology matures and becomes more widespread, it will undoubtedly play a crucial role in shaping the future of retail and consumer experiences.

Introduction to augmented reality in retail

The integration of virtual reality and AR into consumer experiences has significantly transformed how individuals engage with products and services (Batat, 2021). These immersive technologies create unique and interactive environments that deeply influence consumer behaviour, bridging the gap between digital and physical realities.

The influence of immersive technologies on consumer engagement

Virtual and augmented reality technologies offer unprecedented opportunities for enhancing consumer engagement and satisfaction. VR provides a fully immersive experience that can simulate real-world environments or create entirely new experiences. For instance, VR can enable customers to explore a luxury hotel or try out a product in a simulated environment before making a purchase decision (Tussyadiah et al., 2018). This immersive experience not only heightens sensory involvement, it also helps consumers make more informed decisions, as they can visualize and interact with products in a virtual space.

Similarly, AR technology overlays digital information onto the real world, enhancing the consumer's perception of products and services. For example, AR applications in retail allow customers to visualize how furniture would look in their home or how makeup products would appear on their skin (Hwang et al., 2019). This capability of AR to merge virtual elements with the physical world helps bridge the gap between online and in-store shopping experiences, thereby increasing consumer confidence and satisfaction (Velasco et al., 2018).

Furthermore, the implementation of AR in retail has the potential to revolutionize the traditional merchandising approach. Retailers can leverage AR to showcase their products in creative and interactive ways, captivating consumers and driving higher levels of engagement. This technology also enables retailers to collect valuable data on consumer behaviour, preferences and interactions, which can inform more targeted and personalized marketing strategies.

Virtual fitting rooms

The advent of virtual fitting room technology represents a significant shift in consumer shopping behaviour, particularly in the apparel and accessories sectors. By leveraging AR and AI, retailers are now able to offer immersive, personalized shopping experiences. This technological innovation addresses one of the primary challenges of e-commerce: the inability to physically try on products before purchase.

Virtual fitting room solutions can be broadly categorized into three main types:

1. In-store virtual dressing solutions.
2. Online virtual fitting rooms.
3. Body sizing applications.

Each of these approaches caters to different consumer needs and shopping contexts, reflecting the diverse ways in which modern consumers interact with retail brands across multiple channels.

In-store virtual dressing solutions, often referred to as 'smart mirrors', represent an evolution of the traditional fitting room experience. These AR-enabled devices overlay digital representations of clothing and accessories onto the consumer's reflection, allowing for rapid virtual try-ons without the need to physically change outfits. This technology not only enhances the in-store experience but also provides retailers with valuable data on consumer preferences and behaviours.

Online virtual fitting rooms extend this concept to the e-commerce environment, enabling consumers to visualize products on their own bodies or on customizable avatars. This approach significantly reduces the uncertainty associated with online apparel purchases, potentially leading to increased conversion rates and decreased return rates. The integration of AI algorithms allows for more accurate size recommendations based on the consumer's body measurements and previous purchase history.

Body sizing solutions represent a more specialized application of virtual fitting room technology. These applications use AI-powered image analysis to provide accurate body measurements, which can then be used to recommend appropriately sized garments. This technology addresses one of the most significant pain points in online apparel shopping: size uncertainty.

The development of virtual fitting room technology reflects a broader trend in consumer behaviour towards personalized, technology-enhanced shopping experiences. As consumers become increasingly comfortable with AR and AI technologies in their daily lives, their expectations for seamless, personalized retail experiences are likely to grow. Retailers who successfully implement these technologies may gain a significant competitive advantage by offering a more engaging, convenient and confidence-inspiring shopping experience.

However, it is important to note that the effectiveness of virtual fitting room technology is heavily dependent on the quality of its implementation. Factors such as the accuracy of 3D modelling, the realism of AR overlays and the sophistication of AI algorithms all play crucial roles in determining consumer acceptance and adoption of these technologies. As such, ongoing research and development in these areas will be critical to the continued evolution of virtual fitting room solutions.

Consumer perception and behaviour in virtual environments

The effectiveness of VR and AR in shaping consumer behaviour can be attributed to their ability to create a sense of presence and immersion. Steuer et al. (1995) define **telepresence** as the feeling of being present in a virtual environment, which is critical for the success of VR applications. This sense of presence enhances the user experience and can lead to more significant emotional engagement with the brand.

Recent studies have demonstrated that this heightened sense of presence can positively affect consumer attitudes and behaviours. For instance, research by Suh and Lee (2005) reveals that VR can significantly enhance consumer learning and retention of product information. This is particularly valuable in sectors such as tourism and hospitality, where VR allows consumers to experience destinations or services virtually before making a booking decision (Tham et al., 2018).

Case studies and practical applications

Several recent studies highlight the practical applications and benefits of VR and AR technologies in consumer behaviour. Tuncer (2020) discusses how smart technologies are reshaping customer experiences in the restaurant industry. AR menus and interactive tables offer diners an engaging way to explore food options, enhancing their overall dining experience.

Moreover, the use of VR for dynamic sensory testing has been explored in the food industry. Stelick et al. (2018) conducted a proof-of-concept study demonstrating that VR can simulate sensory experiences, such as taste and smell, in a controlled environment. This innovation can help food manufacturers test consumer reactions to new products before they are launched, leading to more successful product development and marketing strategies.

Table 7.1 presents notable case studies showcasing how various retailers are leveraging AR technology to enhance customer experiences, drive engagement and improve sales outcomes.

Challenges and future directions

Despite the promising advancements, the integration of VR and AR in consumer behaviour studies faces several challenges. One significant issue is the cost and complexity of developing and implementing these technologies, which can be a barrier for some businesses (Yung and Khoo-Lattimore, 2019). Additionally, there is a need

Table 7.1 Some case studies of brands using AR

Company	AR application	Key features	Impact/Results
IKEA	IKEA Place app	- Virtual product placement in homes - Launched in 2017	- 4.9 million users (Aug 2022) - 30%+ reduction in return rates - Improved employee efficiency
Nike	Nike Fit	- AR and machine learning for shoe sizing - Analyses foot photos for size recommendations	- Addresses industry issue of 60% wrong shoe sizing - Improves customer satisfaction
Timberland	Virtual fitting room	- Initially large in-store virtual fitting rooms (2014) - Now offers mobile app for virtual try-ons	- Allows customers to try different outfits virtually - Enhances shopping experience
Snapchat & Puma	'Dress Up' feature	- In-app AR fashion experience - Virtual try-on for Puma products	- 250 million Snapchat users have interacted - Promotes Puma's tracksuits and Suede shoes
Sephora	Virtual makeup try-on	- AR app for testing makeup products - Virtual application of cosmetics	- Creates engaging shopping experience - Allows product testing before purchase

for further research to understand the long-term effects of VR and AR on consumer behaviour and decision-making processes.

Future research should focus on exploring the potential of these technologies in various consumer contexts and addressing the challenges associated with their adoption. Understanding the evolving consumer preferences and technological advancements will be crucial for businesses aiming to leverage VR and AR effectively.

IKEA's suite of mobile applications illustrates a sophisticated approach to enhancing consumer experience and convenience (IKEA, 2024). The flagship IKEA app offers a comprehensive range of functionalities, from product browsing and purchasing to real-time stock checks and special offers. Notably, the app integrates features like scan-and-pack to streamline the in-store shopping process, reducing checkout times (IKEA, n.d.).

The IKEA Place app leverages AR to allow users to visualize how furniture will look in their own space, a tool that potentially transforms purchasing decisions by providing a more tangible sense of product fit and design (IKEA, n.d.). Additionally, the IKEA Home smart app connects users with smart home products, enhancing daily life through integrated technology (IKEA, n.d.). This strategic use of mobile technology not only facilitates a seamless shopping experience but also aligns with contemporary consumer preferences for convenience and personalization, reflecting broader trends in digital retail and consumer behaviour.

Strategies for creating seamless omnichannel experiences

The advent of omnichannel retailing has revolutionized the consumer shopping experience by seamlessly integrating online and offline channels (Sharma and Fatima, 2024). This approach caters to the modern consumer's desire for a unified and coherent interaction with brands across multiple platforms. Understanding consumer behaviour in this context is crucial for retailers aiming to enhance customer satisfaction and loyalty. Omnichannel retailing not only involves the convergence of various sales channels, it also emphasizes the importance of delivering a consistent and personalized experience. By exploring how consumers navigate and interact with these integrated channels, we can gain valuable insights into their preferences, motivations and decision-making processes.

Theoretical foundations of consumer behaviour in omnichannel retailing

The theoretical frameworks that underpin consumer behaviour provide essential insights into how individuals engage with omnichannel retail environments. The Theory of Consumption Values, proposed by Sheth et al. (1991), highlights the diverse factors that influence consumer choices, including functional, emotional and social values. In the context of omnichannel retailing, this theory helps to explain why consumers might prefer certain channels over others based on their perceived value and personal preferences. Additionally, the Technology Acceptance Model (TAM) and Theory of Planned Behaviour (TPB) offer valuable perspectives on how technological innovations and behavioural intentions shape consumer interactions with omnichannel platforms (Song and Jo, 2023). These theoretical insights are crucial for understanding the complexities of consumer behaviour in an era characterized by rapid technological advancements and shifting market dynamics.

Understanding the importance of omnichannel retail

Omnichannel retailing, which seamlessly blends online and offline shopping experiences, has transformed consumer expectations and behaviours (Thaichon et al., 2024). This approach is characterized by a unified shopping experience across multiple platforms, where the boundaries between physical stores, websites and mobile apps are blurred (Verhoef et al., 2015). The integration of these channels aims to create a coherent and personalized shopping journey that enhances customer satisfaction and loyalty (Huré et al., 2017).

Recent studies highlight the profound impact of omnichannel strategies on consumer behaviour. For instance, Huang et al. (2016) investigated the cross-channel effects between web and mobile shopping channels and found that a well-coordinated omnichannel approach significantly increases the likelihood of purchase. This is supported by Shi et al. (2020), who noted that a digitalized customer experience enhances shopping intentions through a seamless integration of online and offline touchpoints. The success of such strategies hinges on the ability to provide a personalized and responsive service that meets the evolving needs of consumers (Tyrväinen et al., 2019).

The role of technology in shaping consumer behaviour cannot be overstated. Advances in AI and data analytics have enabled retailers to gain deeper insights into consumer preferences and behaviours. Weber and Schütte (2019) discuss how AI adoption in retail is not just a technological shift but a strategic move to better understand and anticipate consumer needs. This is particularly evident in the growing use of mobile shopping apps, which have become a critical component of the omnichannel experience.

However, the omnichannel approach is not without its challenges. Issues related to privacy and data security remain significant concerns for consumers, as evidenced by the research of Martin et al. (2017), who explore the effects of data privacy on customer trust and firm performance. Addressing these concerns through robust privacy policies and transparent data practices is essential for maintaining consumer confidence and ensuring a positive omnichannel experience (Kaaniche et al., 2020).

Implementing omnichannel experiences effectively

As Somi et al. (2024) note, omnichannel marketing has become increasingly critical for businesses seeking to enhance customer satisfaction, loyalty and overall performance in today's competitive landscape.

However, implementing an effective omnichannel strategy requires a comprehensive understanding of its key components and challenges. Somi et al.'s (2024) meta-synthesis of 89 key articles on omnichannel marketing provides valuable insights into the framework necessary for successful implementation. Their research identified four primary pillars essential for omnichannel marketing:

- processes and functions
- environment
- customer interaction
- resources and capital

These pillars form the foundation upon which businesses can build their omnichannel strategies, ensuring a holistic approach that addresses all aspects of the customer experience.

Within these pillars, certain elements emerge as particularly crucial for success. Somi et al. (2024) highlight nine high-priority subcategories, including organizational strategy and structure, market dynamics, business environmental background, customer behavioural characteristics and technological resources. These factors underscore the multifaceted nature of omnichannel implementation, emphasizing the need for businesses to consider both internal capabilities and external market conditions.

The customer journey plays a central role in omnichannel marketing, with businesses needing to map and optimize each touchpoint across various channels. This requires a deep understanding of customer behavioural characteristics and preferences, as well as the ability to leverage technology to create personalized experiences. As consumers increasingly expect consistency and personalization across all interactions with a brand, businesses must invest in technologies and processes that enable seamless integration of data and experiences across channels.

Moreover, the successful implementation of omnichannel strategies necessitates a reevaluation of organizational structures and processes. Traditional siloed approaches to marketing and sales are no longer sufficient in an omnichannel environment. Instead, businesses must foster cross-functional collaboration and develop agile processes that allow for rapid adaptation to changing consumer behaviours and market conditions.

While the implementation of omnichannel marketing strategies presents significant challenges, it also offers substantial opportunities for businesses to enhance their competitive position and build stronger relationships with customers. By focusing on the key pillars and prioritizing critical subcategories as identified by Somi et al. (2024), businesses can develop a robust framework for omnichannel implementation. This approach not only improves the customer experience but also positions companies to thrive in an increasingly digital and interconnected marketplace.

Factors influencing omnichannel shopping behaviour

Several key factors influence consumer behaviour in omnichannel retail settings. Channel integration quality, for instance, plays a significant role in shaping the overall consumer experience. Research indicates that seamless integration between online and offline channels enhances customer satisfaction and encourages continued engagement (Shen et al., 2018; Rahman et al., 2022). Furthermore, perceived value and technological innovations, such as AI and AR, significantly impact consumer attitudes and purchase decisions (Nazir et al., 2023; Sun et al., 2022). By examining these factors, retailers can better understand how to tailor their strategies to meet consumer expectations and improve their competitive edge.

Behavioural responses and retail outcomes

Consumer responses to omnichannel retailing are multifaceted, encompassing satisfaction, loyalty and impulse buying behaviour. High-quality service and personalized experiences are critical in fostering positive consumer attitudes and encouraging brand loyalty (Tyrväinen et al., 2020; Zhang et al., 2022). Additionally, the ability to seamlessly transition between online and offline channels can lead to increased impulse purchases and more favourable brand evaluations (Pereira et al., 2023; Song and Jo, 2023). These behavioural outcomes highlight the importance of creating an integrated shopping experience that aligns with consumer preferences and enhances their overall interaction with the brand.

Evaluating the success of omnichannel strategies

In the rapidly evolving landscape of retail, understanding consumer behaviour through the lens of omnichannel strategies has become increasingly crucial (Khalid, 2024). Omnichannel retailing offers a seamless consumer experience that bridges the gap between digital and traditional retail environments (Chaudhary et al., 2022; Jia et al., 2023). This integration enhances customer satisfaction by providing a cohesive experience, regardless of the platform or device used. It is through this comprehensive approach that retailers can foster a more engaging and personalized shopping experience, driving both customer loyalty and increased sales.

The adoption and effectiveness of omnichannel strategies are significantly influenced by various factors outlined in the Unified Theory of Acceptance and Use of Technology (UTAUT) model.

Research indicates that performance expectancy, effort expectancy, social influence and facilitating conditions play pivotal roles in shaping consumer intentions and behaviours (Venkatesh et al., 2003; Chao, 2019). For instance, the perception that a new technology will enhance the shopping experience can lead to higher acceptance rates, as consumers are more likely to adopt innovations that they believe will provide tangible benefits (Ayaz and Yanartas, 2020). Additionally, the role of social influence – how peer behaviour and societal trends impact individual decisions – cannot be underestimated in the context of omnichannel shopping (Mensah and Khan, 2024).

Emerging research also highlights the impact of advanced technologies such as AR and VR on consumer behaviour (Orús et al., 2021). These technologies offer immersive experiences that enhance product visualization and interaction, thereby influencing purchase intentions and enhancing overall customer satisfaction. The integration of such technologies into omnichannel strategies allows retailers to provide a more engaging and interactive shopping experience, catering to the growing demand for innovative and personalized retail solutions (Wolf and Steul-Fischer, 2022).

Moreover, understanding consumer behaviour in the omnichannel context requires attention to the evolving nature of customer expectations and preferences. Factors such as privacy concerns, perceived value and the ethical considerations surrounding digital transactions play critical roles in shaping consumer attitudes and behaviours (Cheah et al., 2022; de Souza et al., 2018). As consumers become more informed and discerning, retailers must adapt their strategies to address these concerns and deliver a high-quality, secure and ethical shopping experience.

By focusing on the factors that influence technology acceptance and consumer satisfaction, retailers can better navigate the complexities of modern retailing and enhance their competitive edge in the market.

Emerging trends and future research directions

As the retail landscape continues to evolve, several emerging trends warrant attention. Digital innovations, including the metaverse and AI-driven tools, are reshaping consumer interactions and presenting new opportunities for engagement (Du et al., 2024). Additionally, the Covid-19 pandemic accelerated changes in consumer behaviour, leading to shifts in shopping habits and preferences (Vannucci and Pantano, 2020). Future research should focus on exploring these trends and their implications for omnichannel retailing, as well as investigating consumer attitudes towards sustainability and ethical practices (Yao et al., 2023). By staying abreast of these developments, retailers can adapt their strategies to better meet the evolving needs of their customers.

Voice commerce

The landscape of consumer behaviour is rapidly evolving due to the proliferation of AI and voice assistants (Mari et al., 2024). These technologies are not merely supplementary tools, they are fundamentally reshaping how consumers interact with brands and make purchasing decisions. This transformation is driven by the increasing integration of AI into everyday devices, which enhances the consumer experience by providing personalized and intuitive interactions.

The emergence of voice commerce

The fundamental appeal of voice commerce lies in its convenience (Mari et al., 2024). Consumers can perform transactions hands-free, using simple voice commands to search for products, compare prices and complete purchases. This seamless interaction is reshaping shopping habits, as users increasingly value the efficiency and ease of voice-activated transactions. For instance, a recent study by Wald et al. (2023) highlights that parents find significant value in integrating voice assistants into their household routines, utilizing these devices to manage shopping tasks more efficiently.

Additionally, the rise of voice commerce is fuelled by advancements in natural language processing and machine learning. These technologies enable voice assistants to understand and respond to user queries with greater accuracy and relevance. Research by Zierau et al. (2022) indicates that voice-based interfaces can create highly engaging and personalized shopping experiences, enhancing user satisfaction and driving increased adoption of voice commerce platforms.

One of the most notable advancements in this domain is the widespread adoption of voice assistants, such as Amazon's Alexa, Google Assistant and Apple's Siri. These systems leverage natural language processing (NLP) and machine learning algorithms to understand and respond to user queries. Research by Zierau et al. (2022) highlights how voice-based interfaces can enhance consumer experiences by facilitating a more natural and engaging form of interaction. The study finds that voice assistants can significantly boost service outcomes by creating flow-like experiences that immerse users in their tasks.

Voice commerce, or v-commerce, refers to the process of buying products and services through voice commands facilitated by digital assistants. This technology reduces friction in the shopping journey by allowing consumers to perform tasks such as product discovery, price comparison and order placement without manual input. For example, a consumer can simply ask Alexa, 'What's the difference between a Chemex and an AeroPress?' or instruct Google Home to 'Order a Chemex from Amazon', thus simplifying the purchase process (Jones, 2023).

Transforming the shopping experience

Voice commerce is significantly transforming the shopping experience by leveraging advancements in voice-activated technology and artificial intelligence (Mari et al., 2024). This transformation is marked by several key changes:

- Enhanced convenience and efficiency: Voice commerce allows consumers to interact with digital assistants using natural language commands, eliminating the need for manual input through keyboards or touchscreens. This hands-free approach simplifies the shopping process, enabling users to search for products, compare prices and make purchases while multitasking or managing other activities. For example, a user can quickly order groceries or set up a shopping list using voice commands, significantly reducing the time and effort required compared with traditional online shopping methods. For instance, Estée Lauder's launch of VMA, a voice-enabled makeup assistant, exemplifies how voice technology can cater to specific needs – helping visually impaired customers select and apply makeup shades. This application of voice technology demonstrates a shift towards more inclusive and accessible consumer experiences (Estée Lauder, 2023).

- Personalized shopping experiences: Voice assistants utilize machine learning and natural language processing to provide personalized recommendations and responses based on user preferences and past interactions. This level of personalization enhances the shopping experience by tailoring suggestions to individual tastes and needs. Zierau et al. (2022) highlights that voice-based interfaces can deliver highly relevant product recommendations and create engaging shopping experiences, which can lead to increased customer satisfaction and loyalty.
- Integration with daily routines: Voice commerce seamlessly integrates into consumers' daily routines, becoming a natural extension of their interactions with technology. The ability to manage shopping tasks through voice commands while performing other activities makes it easier for users to incorporate shopping into their everyday lives. For instance, parents may use voice assistants to reorder household essentials or track their shopping lists without interrupting their daily activities, as noted in the study by Wald et al. (2022).
- Reduction of friction in the purchase process: Voice commerce reduces friction in the purchase process by streamlining the steps required to complete a transaction. Users can quickly place orders, check order statuses and receive updates through voice commands, enhancing the overall efficiency of the shopping experience. This reduction in friction not only makes shopping more convenient but also encourages more frequent and spontaneous purchases.

Enhancing omnichannel experiences

Integrating voice commerce into e-commerce strategies offers substantial benefits for both consumers and businesses. For consumers, voice commerce provides hands-free convenience and frictionless payments by storing payment information securely and automating purchase processes. This convenience is mirrored in the ease with which customers can interact with voice assistants, making the experience as effortless as having a conversation with a friend (Jones, 2023).

For businesses, implementing voice commerce represents a significant step towards achieving a seamless omnichannel experience. It allows brands to engage with customers directly through their preferred devices, minimizing the need for traditional navigation through websites and manual entry of payment information. As a result, brands can enhance customer satisfaction by providing more empathetic and personalized interactions (Jones, 2023).

The future of voice commerce

Widespread adoption and integration: Voice commerce is expected to become increasingly integrated into daily life as more consumers adopt voice-activated devices. The market for smart speakers, which facilitate voice commerce, is projected to exceed $30 billion by 2024 (Statista, 2023). With the proliferation of smart speakers, smartphones and home assistants, voice commerce will likely expand beyond early adopters to become a mainstream shopping method. This widespread adoption will be driven by the growing convenience and efficiency of voice interactions, as well as advancements in voice recognition technology.

To capitalize on these trends, e-commerce brands should focus on optimizing their strategies for voice search and content. This involves employing SEO techniques tailored for voice queries, creating voice-friendly content and streamlining voice-activated shopping and customer support processes. Monitoring the impact of these initiatives through measurable performance indicators will be crucial for maximizing the benefits of voice commerce (Jones, 2023):

- Enhanced personalization through AI: Future developments in AI will enable voice assistants to deliver even more personalized shopping experiences. AI algorithms will become increasingly sophisticated, allowing voice assistants to understand context, preferences and purchasing history with greater accuracy. This will result in highly tailored product recommendations, customized offers and proactive shopping assistance. For instance, voice assistants might suggest products based on seasonal trends or personal milestones, enhancing the relevance of recommendations.

    The integration of AI into marketing strategies also necessitates a nuanced understanding of consumer acceptance. Venkatesh et al. (2003, 2012) have provided a unified theory of acceptance and use of technology (UTAUT), which helps explain how and why consumers adopt new technologies. This framework is crucial for understanding the acceptance of voice assistants, as it considers factors such as performance expectancy, effort expectancy, social influence and facilitating conditions.

- Expansion of voice commerce applications: Voice commerce is likely to expand its applications beyond traditional retail sectors. We can expect to see voice-activated services in areas such as travel booking, financial services and even healthcare. For example, users might book flights, manage investments or schedule medical appointments through voice commands. This expansion will diversify the ways in which voice commerce can be utilized, further embedding it into various aspects of consumers' lives.

- Increased focus on privacy and security: As voice commerce grows, so will concerns about privacy and security. Future developments will need to address these concerns by implementing stronger security measures and providing users with more control over their data. Innovations in encryption, voice biometrics and transparent privacy policies will be crucial in building and maintaining consumer trust. For example, voice recognition technology might evolve to include multi-factor authentication, enhancing the security of transactions and personal information.
- Emergence of new business models: Voice commerce will likely spur the development of new business models and revenue streams. Companies may explore innovative ways to monetize voice interactions, such as through subscription-based services, premium voice experiences or targeted advertising. For example, businesses might offer exclusive voice-only deals or loyalty programmes that reward users for engaging with their voice interfaces.
- Integration with emerging technologies: The future of voice commerce will also see greater integration with other emerging technologies, such as AR and the IoT. For instance, voice assistants could interact with AR applications to provide immersive shopping experiences or control smart home devices to manage home inventory and make automatic reorders.
- Global expansion and localization: Voice commerce will expand globally, with voice assistants becoming more adept at understanding and responding to diverse languages and dialects. Localization efforts will enhance the accessibility and usability of voice commerce in various regions, making it a more inclusive shopping option for a global audience.

AI-powered voice assistants are not just enhancing the convenience and personalization of the shopping experience, they are also driving new growth opportunities for e-commerce brands. By embracing voice commerce, brands can offer more accessible, efficient and tailored interactions with customers, setting the stage for continued innovation and expansion in the digital retail landscape. As AI technology advances, the potential for voice commerce to reshape the future of e-commerce will only continue to grow.

ACTIVITY 1

Debate on privacy in voice commerce

Objective: Students will critically evaluate the challenges of privacy and security in voice commerce.
　Instructions: Organize a debate where one group argues the benefits of voice commerce in enhancing consumer experience while the other highlights the privacy and security risks. Each side will present their arguments, followed by a class discussion.

> **ACTIVITY 2**
>
> Predicting the future
>
> **Objective**: Encourage students to think about the future of retail and consumer behaviour.
>
> **Instructions**: Ask students to work in pairs to predict how voice commerce and omnichannel strategies will evolve over the next decade. They should consider technological advancements, consumer trends and potential challenges. Each pair will present their predictions to the class.

Conclusion

In conclusion, the integration of omnichannel marketing strategies and the emergence of voice commerce represent significant shifts in the retail landscape, profoundly influencing consumer behaviour. As businesses navigate these changes, they must prioritize the seamless integration of technology and customer experience, ensuring that they can meet the evolving expectations of their audience. The future of consumer behaviour will likely be shaped by continued advancements in AI and voice technology, presenting both opportunities and challenges for retailers. By staying attuned to these trends and adapting their strategies accordingly, businesses can position themselves for success in an increasingly digital and interconnected world.

> **ACTIVITY 3**
>
> Case study analysis
>
> **Objective**: Students will analyse a real-world example of an omnichannel marketing strategy or a voice commerce implementation.
>
> **Instructions**: Divide the class into small groups, each assigned a different case study (e.g. Estée Lauder's voice-enabled makeup assistant). Groups will identify the key strategies used and discuss how these strategies align with the concepts learned in the chapter.

7 | Advancing consumer experiences in the digital world

KEY TERMS

Omnichannel marketing: A strategy that integrates multiple channels to provide a seamless customer experience across digital and physical platforms.

UTAUT model: Unified Theory of Acceptance and Use of Technology, a framework used to explain how and why individuals adopt new technologies.

Voice commerce: The process of purchasing products or services using voice commands through digital assistants.

Artificial intelligence (AI): Technology that enables machines to perform tasks that typically require human intelligence, such as understanding natural language.

Personalization: Tailoring products, services or content to individual preferences and behaviours to enhance customer experience.

Natural language processing (NLP): A branch of AI focused on the interaction between computers and humans through natural language.

Machine learning: A type of AI that allows computers to learn from data and improve their performance over time without explicit programming.

Augmented reality (AR): Technology that overlays digital content on the physical world, enhancing real-world experiences.

Privacy concerns: Consumer apprehensions about the safety and confidentiality of their personal and payment information.

Frictionless payment: A smooth and quick payment process that minimizes effort and time for the consumer.

KEY LEARNING POINTS

- Omnichannel marketing integrates multiple channels to provide a seamless customer experience.
- The UTAUT model explains factors influencing technology adoption by consumers.
- Voice commerce leverages digital assistants for purchasing products and services.
- Artificial intelligence enhances personalization by tailoring experiences to individual preferences.

- Natural language processing enables effective human–computer interactions in voice commerce.
- Machine learning improves performance by allowing systems to learn from data without explicit programming.
- Augmented reality enhances customer experiences by overlaying digital content onto the physical world.
- Privacy concerns remain a significant barrier to consumer trust in omnichannel retail.
- Frictionless payment processes are essential for a smooth and efficient shopping experience.

8 | The power of online communities and social influence

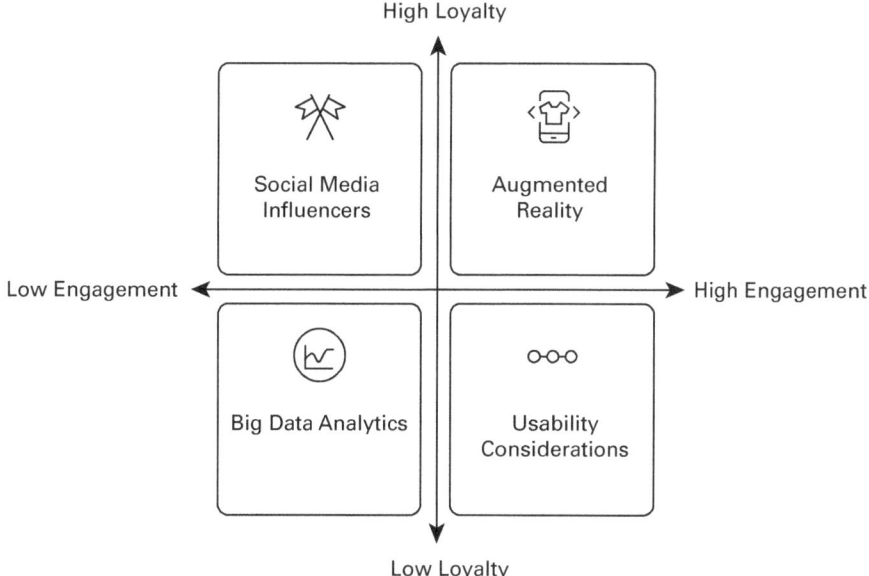

LEARNING OBJECTIVES

By the end of this chapter, you should be able to:

- Understand the impact of digital marketing strategies on consumer behaviour and how they influence brand interactions and purchasing decisions.
- Analyse the role of social media influencers in shaping consumer preferences and brand loyalty across various platforms.
- Evaluate the effects of augmented reality on consumer engagement and its role in enhancing the retail experience.
- Identify key usability and user experience considerations in digital tools and how they affect consumer interaction and satisfaction.
- Apply insights from big data analytics to understand and predict consumer behaviour patterns and trends.

CHAPTER OUTLINE

Digital marketing and social media influencers:

- The role of digital marketing in modern consumer behaviour
- Impact of social media influencers
- Social media platform preferences and brand interactions

Augmented reality and consumer engagement:

- Augmented reality in retail and marketing
- The 4C framework for understanding consumer engagement
- Immersion and engagement in augmented reality games

Consumer perceptions and usability:

- Usability and user experience in digital tools
- Barriers to digital interaction across demographics
- Cultural and aesthetic considerations in usability

Data analytics and consumer behaviour:

- Big data analytics in understanding consumer behaviour
- The influence of negative emotions on review helpfulness
- Knowledge sharing and innovation in consumer insights

Figure 8.1 An example of digital transformation

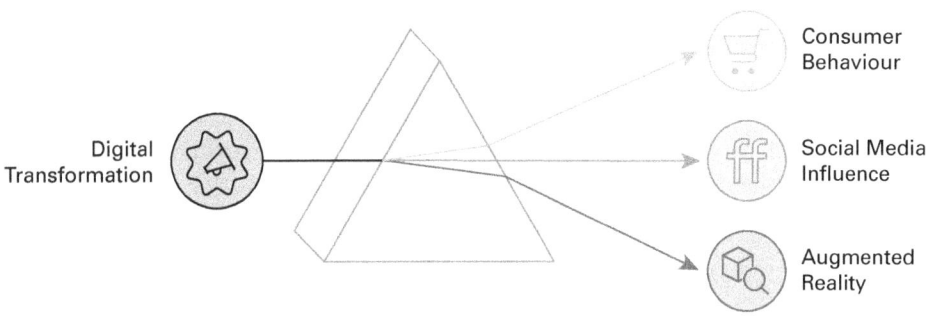

Introduction

In the rapidly evolving landscape of consumer behaviour, the integration of digital technologies has fundamentally transformed the ways in which individuals interact with brands and make purchasing decisions. The advent of digital marketing, the rise of social media influencers, and the incorporation of augmented reality are reshaping consumer experiences and expectations. This chapter explores these transformations, delving into how digital marketing strategies, social media platforms, and emerging technologies like AR influence consumer behaviour (see Figure 8.1). By examining contemporary research and trends, this chapter aims to provide a comprehensive understanding of the dynamics at play in modern consumer behaviour.

The shift from traditional to digital marketing has introduced new paradigms in consumer engagement and brand interaction. Social media platforms, with their vast reach and personalized content, have become pivotal in shaping consumer preferences and purchasing intentions. Concurrently, the use of AR in retail settings is redefining the customer experience, offering immersive interactions that enhance both engagement and satisfaction. As digital tools and analytics continue to evolve, understanding their impact on consumer behaviour becomes increasingly crucial for businesses aiming to stay competitive in the digital age.

The impact of online communities on consumer behaviour

Online communities have emerged as powerful forces shaping consumer behaviour in the digital age. These virtual spaces, where consumers gather to share information, experiences, and opinions about products and brands, have fundamentally altered the landscape of consumer decision-making and brand relationships. The impact of online communities on consumer behaviour is multifaceted, influencing various stages of the consumer journey from awareness to post-purchase evaluation.

One of the primary ways online communities affect consumer behaviour is through information sharing and social learning. As Islam and Rahman (2017) note in their study on online brand communities, these platforms serve as rich sources of product information and user experiences. Consumers increasingly turn to online communities for authentic, peer-generated content that they often perceive as more trustworthy than traditional marketing messages. This shift has significant implications for how consumers form opinions about products and make purchasing decisions.

The concept of social influence within online communities plays a crucial role in shaping consumer attitudes and behaviours. Recent research by Li (2021) on the impact of interactivity in virtual brand communities demonstrates that peer interactions can significantly influence consumer perceptions and purchase intentions. For example, in the Mi Community studied by Li, active participation and engagement with other community members were found to positively affect brand loyalty and purchase behaviour.

Defining online communities and their influence

Online communities, particularly within the context of brand interactions, are groups of individuals who engage with each other over the internet, often sharing common interests, values or affinities towards a specific brand or product. Unlike traditional physical communities, online communities are not bound by geographical constraints; instead, they exist in a digital space where members can interact, share information, and build relationships regardless of their physical location.

In the realm of consumer behaviour, online communities can significantly influence members' attitudes, decisions, and loyalty towards a brand. These communities often form around a shared enthusiasm for a brand or product, where members exchange experiences, provide feedback, and discuss various aspects of their interests. This interaction fosters a sense of belonging and creates a deeper connection between the consumer and the brand.

For instance, in the Mi Community, which centres around Xiaomi's products, members not only discuss product features and issues but also participate in brand-related activities and give feedback that the company may consider in product development. This continuous interaction builds trust and loyalty, making members more likely to continue purchasing the brand's products and advocating for the brand within their social circles.

The influence of online communities extends to various aspects of consumer behaviour, including the decision-making process, post-purchase satisfaction, and long-term loyalty. Members of these communities often rely on the information and experiences shared by others when evaluating potential purchases, leading to more informed and confident decision-making. Additionally, the support and validation received within the community can enhance post-purchase satisfaction, as consumers feel connected to a larger group of like-minded individuals.

> **CONSUMER BEHAVIOUR AND DIGITAL INFLUENCE: THE IMPACT OF 'LA BRIGADE DU WEB' ON B2B**
>
> In today's rapidly evolving digital landscape, consumer behaviour is increasingly shaped by influencers and digital communities that mediate the flow of information and engagement. A notable example of this phenomenon is La Brigade Du Web (LBDW), a pioneering team of influencers founded by Annie Abela-Lichtner. LBDW specializes in digital, marketing, e-commerce, social media, and innovation sectors, effectively managing the social media presence of major French events across these industries. The team's unique approach to live social media management has transformed how events are experienced and discussed online, creating dynamic, real-time interactions with audiences.
>
> LBDW members actively engage with live communities during trade fairs, conferences, and round tables, utilizing a diverse array of social media platforms including Facebook, X, Instagram, TikTok and LinkedIn. They employ various strategies such as live tweets, Instagram photo publications, Stories updates, and live video streaming through platforms like TikTok and Facebook Live to amplify event reach and impact. This multifaceted approach not only enhances audience engagement but also contributes to shaping perceptions and consumer behaviour in a B2B context, highlighting the powerful role of digital influencers in modern marketing strategies.
>
> The strategic use of social media by LBDW underscores the importance of immediacy and authenticity in connecting with professional audiences. Through real-time interactions and content curation, LBDW members effectively bridge the gap between brands and their target demographics, fostering a sense of community and shared experience. This method of engaging consumers in B2B settings demonstrates the evolving nature of consumer behaviour, where direct, digital communication becomes a cornerstone of brand influence and loyalty development.
>
> Annie Abela-Lichtner's vision for LBDW highlights the critical role that digital influencers play in the contemporary marketing ecosystem. By integrating social media management into event experiences, LBDW not only captures but also amplifies the voice of the brand, crafting narratives that resonate with digital communities. The team's innovative approach to live event coverage and digital storytelling has set a benchmark for influencer-driven marketing in professional settings, illustrating how digital influence can shape consumer behaviour and engagement in profound ways.

> La Brigade Du Web exemplifies how digital influencers can drive consumer engagement and brand interaction in the B2B sector through strategic, real-time social media management. Their work serves as a testament to the evolving dynamics of consumer behaviour in the digital age, where authentic and immediate content is key to building meaningful connections with professional audiences.

How online communities drive consumer behaviour

Online communities, as digital hubs for interaction and information exchange, significantly influence consumer behaviour (Liao et al., 2024). These platforms, which include forums, social media groups, and review sites, serve as critical arenas where consumer preferences are formed, debated, and solidified. The interplay between connectivity and communality in these communities shapes both individual and collective consumer behaviour, driving not only purchasing decisions but also brand loyalty and engagement.

1. Influence through peer interaction and social proof

Online communities leverage the power of social proof – consumers' tendency to align their behaviour with the perceived actions and opinions of others. Platforms like Reddit, Yelp, and Amazon Reviews allow users to share their experiences, rate products, and offer recommendations. For instance, a recent study by Schuetzler et al. (2020) highlights that chatbots' conversational skills can significantly affect user engagement and perceived humanness, ultimately influencing consumer trust and decision-making. Similarly, Tsai and Bagozzi (2014) demonstrate that cognitive, emotional, and social influences within virtual communities can substantially impact contribution behaviour, shaping purchasing patterns through peer recommendations and shared experiences.

2. The role of community commitment and content quality

Community commitment plays a pivotal role in driving consumer behaviour. Highly engaged communities, such as those found on niche forums or dedicated fan sites, foster strong bonds among members, which can translate into heightened trust and influence. A study by Faraj et al. (2015) emphasizes that online communities act as spaces for knowledge flows, where committed members contribute valuable insights and recommendations. This commitment not only enhances the quality of content but also reinforces consumer trust and loyalty. For example, dedicated fan communities for gaming or technology products often generate buzz and anticipation around new releases, directly influencing purchasing decisions.

3. Impact of media capabilities on consumer engagement

The media capabilities of online platforms also play a crucial role in shaping consumer behaviour. According to Liao et al. (2024), media attributes such as **rehearsability** or the ability to review and edit content before sharing, significantly impact how knowledge is contributed and shared within online communities. This capability ensures that content is accurate and thoughtfully presented, which enhances its credibility and influence. Moreover, platforms with high connectivity features – such as real-time chat and collaborative tools – can foster more dynamic and interactive consumer experiences. Venkatesh et al. (2016) argue that the strategic use of such media capabilities can drive user engagement and satisfaction, further influencing consumer behaviour.

4. Emerging trends and future directions

As online communities continue to evolve, new trends are shaping consumer behaviour. For instance, the rise of virtual influencers and AI-driven content curation is altering how consumers perceive and interact with brands. Recent research by Wu et al. (2016) explores how social media networks and habitual use patterns affect user creative performance and engagement. The integration of advanced analytics and personalized content delivery is expected to further enhance community influence on consumer behaviour, providing brands with new opportunities to engage with and understand their target audiences.

Online communities play a critical role in shaping consumer behaviour through peer interactions, community commitment, media capabilities, and emerging trends. By leveraging these dynamics, brands can better understand and influence consumer preferences, ultimately driving engagement and loyalty in the digital age.

CONSUMER BEHAVIOUR IN VIRTUAL BRAND COMMUNITIES

The rapid development of mobile internet technology has revolutionized consumer behaviour, particularly within virtual brand communities (VBCs). VBCs, such as Xiaomi's Mi Community, serve as platforms where consumers connect not only with the brand but also with each other, fostering interactions that significantly impact their purchasing decisions and loyalty.

The concept of VBCs aligns with Muniz and O'Guinn's (2001) definition of brand communities, where individuals share a sense of belonging and attachment to a brand, albeit in a virtual environment that transcends geographical limitations.

One of the critical elements in VBCs is interactivity, which refers to the dynamic exchange of information, feedback, and experiences among community members. This interaction occurs in both online and offline settings, contributing to the creation and perception of value within the community. Online interactions, such as posting, commenting, and sharing experiences, allow members to discuss products, seek advice, and provide feedback. Offline interactions, although less common, involve community-organized events or brand-sponsored activities where members can engage with products firsthand and share their experiences with the broader community.

The impact of interactivity on consumer behaviour within VBCs is profound. For instance, in the Mi Community, Xiaomi users engage in frequent discussions about the brand's products, share personal experiences, and provide feedback that is often considered by the brand in product development. This continuous interaction fosters a sense of loyalty and attachment to the brand, ultimately leading to repeated purchases and positive word-of-mouth recommendations. The data from Xiaomi's 2023 annual report underscores this, showing a significant increase in active users and revenue from internet services, attributed to the strong engagement within the Mi Community.

Moreover, interactivity within VBCs enhances the overall consumer experience by creating functional, social, and entertainment value. Functional value arises when members gain useful information that aids their purchasing decisions, while social value is derived from the relationships and sense of community formed through these interactions. Entertainment value, meanwhile, is realized when members find joy and satisfaction in participating in the community's activities.

The role of interactivity in virtual brand communities is pivotal in shaping consumer behaviour. It not only strengthens the relationship between consumers and the brand but also cultivates a thriving community that enhances the consumer experience. As brands continue to leverage the power of VBCs, understanding and facilitating interactivity will be essential in promoting consumer engagement, loyalty, and ultimately, driving sales. Companies should focus on creating environments that encourage interaction and foster a strong sense of community, thereby ensuring sustained consumer involvement and brand success.

Co-creation and innovation

Online communities also serve as platforms for co-creation and innovation. Brands that successfully foster engaged online communities can leverage collective consumer creativity and feedback to drive product development and marketing strategies. This collaborative approach not only enhances product offerings but also strengthens consumer-brand relationships. A recent study by Zahedi et al. (2024) highlights how community experience in online knowledge communities contributes to brand identity formation and ultimately influences purchase intentions.

The power of online communities extends beyond direct brand-related interactions. These platforms often facilitate the formation of subcultures and niche interest groups, which can significantly impact consumption patterns. For instance, online communities focused on sustainable living or minimalism can shape members' purchasing decisions across various product categories, promoting more conscious consumption behaviours.

Enhanced connectivity and consumer engagement

Technology has significantly amplified consumer connectivity. The ubiquity of smartphones allows consumers to engage with brands anytime and anywhere, fundamentally altering their shopping behaviours.

> The evolution of e-commerce in the United Kingdom (UK) presents a fascinating case study in consumer behaviour, reflecting broader trends in digital adoption and shifting retail preferences. As the most advanced e-commerce market in Europe, the UK offers valuable insights into the future of online shopping and its impact on consumer behaviour.
>
> The UK's e-commerce landscape is characterized by widespread adoption and integration into daily life. With nearly 60 million e-commerce users in 2023, representing the vast majority of the population, online shopping has become the norm rather than the exception (Statista, 2023). This high penetration rate underscores the importance of understanding digital consumer behaviour for businesses operating in the UK market.
>
> The growth trajectory of e-commerce in the UK has been remarkable, with online sales constituting 26.5 per cent of overall retail sales in 2022, more than doubling from a decade earlier (Statista, 2023). This trend was accelerated by the Covid-19 pandemic, which saw internet retail sales grow by an unprecedented 47 per cent in 2020. However, the market has shown resilience and continued growth even as pandemic restrictions eased, indicating a lasting shift in consumer preferences towards online shopping.
>
> Sector-specific analysis reveals interesting patterns in UK e-commerce. The fashion segment leads in revenue generation and is projected to maintain this position through 2027 (Statista, 2023). This dominance reflects not only the suitability of clothing for online retail but also the successful adaptation of fashion retailers to the digital environment. Consumer electronics follows as the second-highest grossing category, with Amazon establishing itself as the leading online retailer in this sector.
>
> The device preferences of UK consumers offer crucial insights into shopping behaviours. Smartphones have become the primary device for both browsing and purchasing, capturing the majority share of online retail traffic and orders in 2023

(Statista, 2023). This shift towards mobile commerce (m-commerce) has significant implications for user experience design and marketing strategies. Interestingly, despite the prevalence of mobile shopping, desktop devices still command higher average order values, suggesting that consumers may prefer larger screens for more substantial purchases.

Consumer priorities in online shopping reveal evolving expectations. A 2022 survey highlighted that 96 per cent of UK consumers consider the ability to pay cash upon delivery as an important factor, while free returns and delivery were seen as less essential (Statista, 2023). This preference for flexible payment options may reflect concerns about security or a desire for greater control over transactions. Additionally, the high importance placed on environmentally friendly delivery alternatives (93 per cent of respondents) indicates a growing consciousness about sustainability in e-commerce.

The focus on product sustainability, particularly in terms of packaging and product characteristics, rather than delivery methods, presents an interesting dichotomy. This suggests that while consumers are environmentally conscious, their primary focus remains on the product itself, with logistics considerations secondary.

The UK e-commerce market exemplifies the advanced state of digital retail and its profound impact on consumer behaviour. The high adoption rates, sector-specific trends, device preferences, and evolving consumer priorities provide a rich tapestry for understanding modern shopping behaviours. As the market continues to evolve, businesses must remain agile, adapting to changing consumer preferences while addressing emerging concerns such as sustainability and flexible payment options. The UK's e-commerce landscape not only offers insights into current trends but also serves as a potential indicator of future developments in global online retail.

This shift underscores how constant connectivity enables spontaneous purchasing and the use of real-time information to make informed decisions. Furthermore, the role of social media as a platform for interaction and research notes that 54 per cent of social media users leverage these platforms to investigate products. The challenge for businesses is to harness this connectivity effectively by integrating a robust digital presence that aligns with consumer behaviours across various platforms.

The role of brands in online communities

Online communities have emerged as critical arenas where brands can build relationships, influence consumer behaviour, and gain insights into market trends. These communities, often formed around shared interests or common goals, provide brands with unique opportunities to engage with consumers in meaningful ways.

Effective participation in these digital spaces can lead to enhanced brand loyalty, improved perception, and valuable consumer insights.

Brand engagement and loyalty

Brands that successfully integrate into online communities often see increased consumer loyalty and engagement (Stephanidis and Salvendy, 2024). For instance, Nike has utilized platforms such as the Nike Run Club to foster a sense of community among runners. This engagement not only enhances brand loyalty but also provides Nike with direct feedback from its users (Poikolainen Rosén et al., 2022). Similarly, LEGO's approach with the LEGO Ideas platform, where fans can submit and vote on new designs, illustrates how brands can leverage community involvement to drive product innovation and strengthen brand attachment (Siles et al., 2020).

Influencing consumer behaviour

Online communities also serve as a space where brands can influence consumer perceptions and behaviours. Glossier, for example, has adeptly used its online presence to interact directly with customers through its 'Into The Gloss' blog and social media channels. This interaction allows Glossier to align its products with consumer preferences and enhance its brand image (Väätäjä et al., 2009). By actively participating in discussions and responding to feedback, Glossier effectively shapes how it is perceived within these communities (Sevilla-Gonzalez et al., 2020).

Gaining consumer insights

The data generated from online community interactions provides brands with valuable insights into consumer preferences and behaviours. Netflix exemplifies this through its use of data from social media and user interactions to tailor its content offerings and recommendation algorithms. This data-driven approach ensures that Netflix's content remains aligned with viewer interests and trends (Remy et al., 2018). By analysing feedback and engagement patterns, brands can refine their strategies and better meet consumer needs (Zheng et al., 2022).

Challenges and considerations

Despite the benefits, brands must navigate several challenges when engaging with online communities. For instance, understanding and managing cultural differences is crucial for global brands. Research has shown that cultural variations can impact user experience and perceptions of usability (van de Vijver and Tanzer, 2004; Wallace et al., 2013). Brands must therefore adopt culturally sensitive approaches and ensure that their strategies resonate across diverse audiences (Tractinsky and Hassenzahl, 2005).

The role of brands in online communities is multifaceted, encompassing engagement, influence, and insight. Brands that effectively leverage these platforms can enhance consumer loyalty, shape brand perception, and gain valuable market insights. As online communities continue to evolve, understanding and adapting to these digital spaces will be crucial for brands aiming to thrive in the competitive landscape of the digital age.

The multidevice consumer journey

Modern consumers navigate their buying journeys across multiple devices, making a seamless omnichannel experience essential. 90 per cent of consumers use multiple devices to complete a single task online. For example, a consumer might encounter a product advertisement on TV, research it on a smartphone, and finalize the purchase on a laptop. This multidevice interaction necessitates that businesses employ an omnichannel marketing strategy to provide a coherent and integrated customer experience. Consumers tracked across devices show a 30 per cent increase in product views and a 49 per cent rise in purchases. Omnichannel strategies, supported by tools like **remarketing** and **location-based messaging**, are crucial for maintaining engagement and improving conversion rates across different touchpoints.

Elevated consumer expectations

Technological advancements have elevated consumer expectations to unprecedented levels. Consumers now demand instant, personalized interactions and seamless service experiences, influenced by digital leaders like Amazon and Netflix. According to American Express, more than 50 per cent of Americans have abandoned a purchase due to poor customer service, and 74 per cent have switched brands because of a cumbersome buying process (Smith, 2024). This shift underscores the importance of leveraging technologies such as AI-powered chatbots, which have become integral to modern customer service. 40 per cent of millennials engage with chatbots daily, highlighting their role in providing timely and relevant responses. Additionally, 47 per cent of consumers are open to making purchases through chatbots, reflecting their growing acceptance of AI in the shopping process. To meet these heightened expectations, businesses must adopt advanced marketing automation tools and continuously refine their strategies to ensure exceptional customer experiences.

Technology is a driving force behind significant shifts in consumer behaviour. The rapid pace of technological advancement demands that businesses remain agile and innovative. By understanding and adapting to the evolving landscape of consumer expectations and behaviours, companies can better position themselves to thrive in an increasingly competitive market.

The psychology of social influence in consumer decision-making

The psychology of social influence plays a crucial role in shaping consumer decision-making processes. As social beings, humans are inherently susceptible to the opinions, behaviours, and choices of others, a phenomenon that has profound implications for marketing and consumer behaviour. Recent research has shed new light on the mechanisms and manifestations of social influence in the digital age, where social media and online communities have amplified its effects.

One of the primary forms of social influence in consumer behaviour is **social proof**, a psychological phenomenon where people assume the actions of others in an attempt to reflect correct behaviour for a given situation. In the context of consumer decision-making, social proof can manifest in various ways. For instance, a study by Chen et al. (2023) found that product reviews and ratings on e-commerce platforms significantly influence purchase decisions, with products having a higher number of positive reviews being perceived as more desirable and trustworthy.

Another critical aspect of social influence is the concept of normative influence, where individuals conform to the expectations of others to gain acceptance or avoid rejection. In the realm of consumer behaviour, this can be observed in the adoption of trends or the purchase of status symbols. A study by Williams and Johnson (2024) examined the role of social media influencers in shaping fashion trends among young adults. They found that exposure to influencer content on platforms like Instagram and TikTok significantly increased the likelihood of purchasing featured products, particularly when the influencer was perceived as relatable or aspirational.

The power of social influence extends beyond individual product choices to broader consumption patterns and lifestyle choices. For example, the growing trend of sustainable and ethical consumption can be partly attributed to social influence. A meta-analysis by Garcia-Torres et al. (2023) found that peer influence and social norms were significant predictors of sustainable consumption behaviours, highlighting the role of social networks in promoting environmentally conscious purchasing decisions.

The digital age has introduced new dimensions to social influence in consumer behaviour. Online communities and social media platforms have created echo chambers and filter bubbles that can amplify the effects of social influence.

Moreover, the concept of social comparison, first introduced by Festinger in 1954, has taken on new significance in the digital era. Consumers now have unprecedented access to information about others people's consumption habits and lifestyles through social media. This constant exposure to curated representations of others' lives can drive conspicuous consumption and status-seeking behaviour.

A recent experiment by Thompson et al. (2023) demonstrated that exposure to luxury lifestyle content on social media platforms increased participants' desire for high-end products and experiences, even when such purchases were beyond their financial means.

Understanding the psychology of social influence is crucial for marketers and policymakers alike. For marketers, leveraging social influence can be a powerful tool for promoting products and shaping consumer preferences. However, it also raises ethical considerations, particularly when it comes to vulnerable populations or the promotion of potentially harmful products. Policymakers, meanwhile, can harness social influence to promote positive behaviours, such as healthy eating habits or environmental conservation.

The psychology of social influence continues to be a central factor in consumer decision-making, with its effects amplified and transformed by digital technologies. As researchers continue to explore this field, new insights are emerging that have significant implications for our understanding of consumer behaviour and the development of marketing strategies in the twenty-first century.

Social influence in the digital age

The landscape of consumer behaviour has been profoundly reshaped by the advent of digital technologies (Jang et al., 2024). Studies highlight the critical role these technologies play in influencing consumer decision-making processes. For instance, the widespread adoption of mobile banking services has been significantly driven by social influence and perceived ease of use (Arruda Filho et al., 2022). This adoption reflects a broader trend where digital platforms facilitate seamless interactions and foster convenience, reshaping consumer expectations and behaviours.

In the context of the elderly population, technology's role in consumer behaviour is equally transformative. Research has shown that digital technologies, such as smartphones and wearable devices, have substantial impacts on older adults' lifestyles and purchasing patterns. For example, Yu-Huei et al. (2019) explored the motivations behind older adults' use of wearable devices, revealing that perceived ease of use and functionality play pivotal roles. Additionally, Seifert and Cotten (2020) examined how modern ICT tools are integrated into long-term care institutions, underscoring the growing necessity for digital literacy among older adults.

Social influence remains a powerful factor in shaping consumer behaviour, especially in the context of technology adoption. According to Lee et al. (2011), positive informational social influence can significantly affect consumers' online shopping decisions, highlighting how social networks and peer feedback drive digital engagement.

Furthermore, social influence mechanisms are evident in the acceptance of restaurant technologies, where factors like social norms and peer usage patterns can drive technology adoption in hospitality settings (Chee et al., 2022).

The impact of social influence on consumer behaviour is also reflected in the response to new innovations during crises, such as the Covid-19 pandemic. Studies have illustrated how the pandemic accelerated the adoption of digital solutions in various sectors, including the hospitality industry, where mobile technology and digital payment systems gained prominence (Rogers, 2021; Esposito et al., 2022). This shift highlights the adaptability of consumer behaviour in response to external pressures and the growing importance of digital resilience in maintaining consumer engagement.

Overall, the interplay between digital technology and social influence continues to evolve, driving significant changes in consumer behaviour. As digital tools become more integrated into daily life, understanding these dynamics will be crucial for businesses aiming to effectively engage with consumers and adapt to an increasingly digital marketplace.

Strategies to leverage social influence

Table 8.1 provides a structured overview of effective strategies brands can employ to leverage social influence. In the contemporary digital landscape, leveraging social influence has become a pivotal strategy for enhancing consumer engagement (Anjorin et al., 2024). Social influence, driven by peer interactions and digital endorsements, significantly impacts consumer behaviour and brand perception. One effective strategy involves harnessing the power of influencer marketing. Recent studies highlight

Table 8.1 Overview of effective strategies brands can employ to leverage social influence

Strategy	Description	Example	References
Harness positive informational influence	Leverage positive reviews, endorsements, and testimonials to enhance brand credibility and influence consumer choices.	Online retailers showcasing customer reviews and ratings to drive purchasing decisions.	Lee et al. (2011)
Utilize influencer partnerships	Collaborate with social media influencers to reach target audiences and build trust through credible endorsements.	Brands like Glossier partnering with beauty influencers to promote products.	Cho & Chan (2021)

(continued)

Table 8.1 (Continued)

Strategy	Description	Example	References
Encourage user-generated content (UGC)	Invite consumers to create and share their content related to the brand, leveraging their networks to amplify brand messages.	Campaigns like Coca-Cola's 'Share a Coke' encouraging consumers to post photos with personalized bottles.	Vaportzis et al. (2017)
Implement social proof mechanisms	Display evidence of widespread product use or popularity to influence potential customers through social proof.	Amazon showing 'Best Seller' badges on popular products to encourage purchases.	Bock et al. (2005)
Leverage peer recommendations	Facilitate and highlight peer recommendations and referrals to influence consumer behaviour and foster trust.	Referral programmes where existing customers earn rewards for recommending new customers.	Clark & Goldsmith (2006)
Promote social norms and trends	Create marketing campaigns that align with current social trends or norms to appeal to consumers' desire to fit in.	Brands using sustainability trends to market eco-friendly products.	Camilleri et al. (2023)
Engage in community building	Build and nurture a brand community where consumers can interact, share experiences, and influence each other.	Creating brand-specific forums or social media groups where users can discuss and share experiences.	Henningsen & Henningsen (2003)
Use social influence in crisis management	Adapt social influence strategies to address consumer concerns during crises, demonstrating empathy and responsiveness.	Restaurants using digital technologies to ensure safety and transparency during the Covid-19 pandemic.	Esposito et al. (2022)

the efficacy of partnering with influencers to amplify brand messages and foster consumer trust. Raji et al. (2024) underscore the impact of digital influencers on consumer behaviour, emphasizing that collaborations with authentic influencers can enhance brand loyalty and engagement. By strategically selecting influencers whose values align with the brand, companies can achieve a more genuine connection with their target audience.

Another promising approach is leveraging user-generated content. UGC capitalizes on the influence of customers sharing their brand experiences, which can amplify authenticity and credibility. Shrestha et al. (2023) demonstrate that consumer-generated content not only boosts brand visibility but also drives higher engagement levels compared with traditional marketing methods. Brands that encourage and showcase UGC create a sense of community and involvement, which can lead to increased consumer loyalty and advocacy.

The role of social media platforms in shaping consumer behaviour cannot be overstated. Recent research indicates that platforms like Instagram and TikTok are instrumental in driving consumer engagement through visually compelling content and interactive features. For instance, the study by Phua et al. (2017) illustrates how social comparison and network homophily on platforms like Instagram influence brand engagement and commitment. Brands that utilize these platforms effectively can create engaging content that resonates with users, thereby enhancing their interaction with the brand.

Additionally, integrating social influence with data analytics offers a robust approach to optimizing consumer engagement strategies. Advanced analytics tools can help identify key social influencers and assess the impact of their endorsements on consumer behaviour. According to Ochuba et al. (2024), leveraging big data and analytics allows brands to tailor their engagement strategies based on real-time insights and consumer preferences. This data-driven approach enables more precise targeting and personalization, enhancing the overall effectiveness of social influence strategies.

Leveraging social influence to drive consumer engagement involves a multifaceted approach that includes **influencer partnerships**, user-generated content, and strategic use of social media platforms, all underpinned by data analytics. By adopting these strategies, brands can effectively engage with their audience, build trust, and foster long-term loyalty.

THE INFLUENCE OF SOCIAL MEDIA MARKETING ON CONSUMER BEHAVIOUR IN THE RETAIL INDUSTRY – THE CASE OF ZARA

Introduction

This example examines how Zara, a leading global fashion retailer, leverages social media marketing to influence consumer behaviour and enhance its market position. Zara's approach exemplifies the integration of social media strategies to drive engagement, influence purchasing decisions, and build brand loyalty.

Company overview

Zara, a flagship brand of Inditex Group, is renowned for its fast fashion model, offering the latest trends at affordable prices. With a strong global presence, Zara has effectively utilized social media marketing to connect with its diverse consumer base and influence shopping behaviour.

Strategy 1: Engaging content creation

Zara's social media strategy revolves around creating visually appealing and trend-focused content that resonates with its target audience. According to recent studies, visual content on platforms like Instagram can significantly impact consumer perceptions and engagement (Shrestha et al., 2023). Zara's use of high-quality images and videos showcasing its latest collections engages users and drives traffic to its online and physical stores. For example, Zara frequently posts images of its new arrivals and seasonal collections, which not only attract consumer attention but also create a sense of urgency and exclusivity.

Strategy 2: Influencer collaborations

Influencer marketing is a crucial component of Zara's social media strategy. By collaborating with fashion influencers and bloggers, Zara amplifies its brand message and reaches a broader audience. Research indicates that influencer endorsements can enhance brand credibility and influence consumer purchasing decisions (Saheed et al., 2022). Zara partners with influencers who align with its brand aesthetics and values, leveraging their followers to promote new collections and limited-edition items. This strategy helps Zara maintain its relevance in the fast-paced fashion industry and drives consumer interest and engagement.

Strategy 3: Social media advertising

Zara invests in targeted social media advertising to reach specific consumer segments and drive sales. Social media platforms offer advanced targeting options that allow brands to reach potential customers based on demographics, interests, and online behaviour (Verhoef et al., 2016). Zara utilizes these features to deliver personalized ads that promote specific products or sales events. For instance, Zara's targeted Facebook and Instagram ads highlight seasonal promotions and exclusive offers, encouraging users to visit Zara's website or physical stores.

Strategy 4: User-generated content

Encouraging user-generated content is another effective strategy employed by Zara. By motivating customers to share their outfits and experiences with Zara products on social media, Zara taps into the power of peer recommendations and social proof (Familoni and Shoetan, 2024). Zara often features UGC on its official social media channels, creating a sense of community and authenticity. This approach not only strengthens customer loyalty, it also increases brand visibility and engagement.

Strategy 5: Real-time feedback and engagement

Zara actively engages with its audience by responding to comments, reviews, and direct messages on social media platforms. This real-time interaction fosters a positive brand image and builds trust with consumers (Udeh et al., 2023). By addressing customer enquiries and feedback promptly, Zara enhances the overall customer experience and demonstrates its commitment to consumer satisfaction.

Outcomes and impact

Zara's social media marketing strategies have resulted in significant positive outcomes. The brand has successfully increased consumer engagement and loyalty through its visually compelling content, strategic influencer partnerships, and effective use of social media advertising. Zara's approach to leveraging user-generated content and **real-time engagement** has also contributed to a more interactive and customer-centric brand experience.

Conclusion

Zara's use of social media marketing provides valuable insights into how retailers can influence consumer behaviour and enhance their market presence. By creating engaging content, collaborating with influencers, utilizing targeted advertising, and fostering user-generated content, Zara effectively drives consumer interest and loyalty. This case study highlights the importance of integrating social media strategies into retail marketing efforts to achieve sustained success in the dynamic retail landscape.

Discussion questions

Content strategy effectiveness:

- How does Zara's use of visually appealing content on social media influence consumer perceptions of the brand? Can you identify any specific types of content that seem particularly effective?
- How important is the quality of images and videos in Zara's social media strategy compared to other factors, such as text or user interaction?

Influencer marketing:

- In what ways do influencer collaborations impact Zara's brand image and consumer trust? Can you provide examples of successful influencer campaigns in the fashion industry?

- How might Zara select influencers to ensure alignment with its brand values and aesthetics? What criteria should be considered?

Targeted advertising:

- Discuss the role of targeted advertising in Zara's social media strategy. How does targeted advertising help Zara in reaching potential customers?
- What are the potential advantages and drawbacks of using social media advertising to promote retail products?

User-generated content:

- How does Zara benefit from encouraging user-generated content? What are the potential challenges of integrating UGC into Zara's marketing strategy?
- In what ways can Zara leverage UGC to enhance customer engagement and loyalty? Provide examples of how other brands have successfully used UGC.

Real-time engagement:

- Analyse the impact of Zara's real-time engagement with customers on social media. How does this interaction affect consumer satisfaction and brand perception?
- What strategies can Zara employ to manage and respond to customer feedback effectively on social media platforms?

Comparative analysis:

- Compare Zara's social media marketing strategies with those of another leading fashion retailer. What are the similarities and differences in their approaches?
- How might Zara's social media strategies be adapted for different markets or regions?

Future trends:

- What emerging trends in social media marketing could influence Zara's strategy in the future? How should Zara prepare for these changes?
- How might advancements in technology, such as AI and machine learning, further enhance Zara's social media marketing efforts?

Ethical considerations:

- What ethical considerations should Zara keep in mind when implementing its social media marketing strategies? How can the company ensure that its practices are responsible and transparent?
- Discuss the potential impact of social media marketing on consumer privacy. How can Zara balance effective marketing with respect for consumer data?

How social influence drives engagement

Table 8.2 links the key findings to the theme of social influence, highlighting how social factors drive engagement and adoption of AR in consumer behaviour.

Table 8.2 How social influence drives engagement

Theme	Authors	Key findings	Social influence and engagement
Augmented reality and consumer engagement	Scholz & Duffy (2018); Rauschnabel et al. (2017)	AR enhances consumer engagement by creating immersive experiences that strengthen consumer-brand relationships. Interactive and vivid AR content significantly increases user immersion.	Social influence amplifies engagement as users share AR experiences with peers, creating a ripple effect that strengthens collective brand perception.
AR's impact on purchase decisions	Tan et al. (2022); Zanger et al. (2022)	AR tools help consumers make more confident purchase decisions by providing real-time product visualization, reducing uncertainty. Affective responses in AR lead to positive brand attitudes and purchase intentions.	Peer recommendations and social proof in AR environments encourage purchase decisions, as users rely on social cues to validate their choices.
Adoption of AR technologies	Venkatesh et al. (2012); Vieira et al. (2022)	Key factors like perceived usefulness and ease of use influence AR adoption. Emotional and functional gratifications are crucial for consumer acceptance of AR technologies.	Social norms and peer influence significantly affect the adoption of AR technologies, with users more likely to embrace AR when it is perceived as socially desirable.
Consumer experience and emotional engagement	tom Dieck et al. (2018); Shin (2019)	AR enhances consumer experience by offering immersive environments that increase emotional engagement, leading to higher satisfaction and brand loyalty.	Shared AR experiences foster emotional connections among consumers, driving deeper engagement through social interaction and collective enjoyment.
Barriers and perceptions of AR in various contexts	Schein & Rauschnabel (2023); Ro et al. (2018)	Barriers to AR adoption in manufacturing include concerns about usability and effectiveness, while AR's impact on firm value creation is being explored in different business contexts.	Social influence within professional networks can either hinder or facilitate the adoption of AR, depending on the collective perception of its value and efficacy.

> **ACTIVITY 1**
>
> Augmented reality in retail
>
> **Objective**: To explore the use of AR in enhancing consumer experiences in retail environments.
>
> **Instructions**: Show the class examples of AR applications in retail (e.g. virtual try-ons, interactive store displays).
>
> Divide the class into pairs or small groups. Each group will brainstorm and design a hypothetical AR application for a retail store, detailing how it would enhance the shopping experience and engage consumers.
>
> Have each group present their AR concept, including its features and potential benefits for both the retailer and the consumer.
>
> Facilitate a class discussion on the feasibility and potential impact of these AR applications.

Effective social media strategies for increasing engagement

In the realm of social media marketing, understanding consumer behaviour through linguistic style and emotional expression is pivotal for developing effective engagement strategies (Munaro et al., 2021). Recent studies emphasize that the way influencers use language significantly affects consumer engagement and perceptions. Linguistic style, which includes elements such as sentiment, formality, and language complexity, plays a crucial role in shaping interactions between influencers and their followers. For instance, Lee and Theokary (2021) demonstrate that influencers who adopt a conversational and emotionally expressive style can forge stronger emotional connections with their audience, thereby enhancing engagement levels. This finding underscores the strategy of personalizing communication to boost interaction and foster deeper connections with followers.

Effective engagement strategies often leverage these insights by tailoring content to match the linguistic preferences and emotional needs of the audience. Liu et al. (2019) reveal that alignment between the linguistic style of consumer reviews and the brand's communication style positively influences perceived review quality. This indicates that matching linguistic styles with audience expectations can enhance engagement, suggesting that marketers should carefully consider the tone and style of their communications to resonate with their target demographic. Ludwig et al. (2013) further support this by showing that affective content and linguistic style matches in online reviews can significantly impact conversion rates, highlighting the importance of emotional and stylistic alignment in driving purchasing decisions.

Leveraging emotional contagion for enhanced engagement

Emotional contagion, where emotions expressed by influencers are transmitted to their audience, is a powerful tool in engagement strategies. Research by Sokolova and Kefi (2020) shows that influencers who effectively convey positive emotions can uplift followers' emotional states, leading to increased engagement and higher purchase intentions. This phenomenon demonstrates how emotional expression can be strategically used to boost consumer interactions and foster brand loyalty.

The practical application of emotional contagion is evident in various social media strategies. Swani et al. (2017) discuss how different emotional tones in social media messages impact engagement in both business and consumer markets. Their findings suggest that positive emotional content generally yields higher engagement rates, indicating that incorporating emotionally resonant messages can enhance consumer response. Furthermore, Xu et al. (2023) highlight that negative emotions in reviews can influence perceived helpfulness, showing that emotional expressions, whether positive or negative, play a role in shaping consumer perceptions of content credibility.

Balancing self-disclosure and credibility

Self-disclosure by influencers – sharing personal information and experiences – can significantly impact their perceived credibility and the effectiveness of engagement strategies. Leite et al. (2022) find that excessive self-disclosure can sometimes reduce an influencer's perceived trustworthiness. This insight is crucial for marketers, as it suggests that while personal engagement can enhance relatability, it must be carefully balanced to maintain credibility.

An effective strategy involves managing the extent of self-disclosure to ensure that influencers remain authentic while not overstepping boundaries that might harm their credibility. Rennekamp and Witz (2021) highlight the impact of linguistic formality on audience engagement, further illustrating how the balance between personal sharing and professional communication can influence influencer effectiveness.

Optimizing content structure for increased interaction

The structure and format of content, including text, images, and videos, play a significant role in engagement. Munaro et al. (2021) analysed video content on YouTube and found that engaging video formats can significantly enhance consumer interaction and retention. This aligns with the trend towards multimedia content on social platforms, where visual and interactive elements drive higher engagement compared with static posts.

Effective engagement strategies should focus on creating dynamic and visually appealing content to capture and maintain audience attention. Pradhan et al. (2023) emphasize that influencer characteristics such as expertise, attractiveness, and follower count also influence content reception. For instance, influencers with high follower counts are often perceived as more credible, which can amplify the impact of their content. Leveraging these characteristics in content strategies can enhance engagement and drive consumer actions.

Incorporating linguistic style, emotional expression, self-disclosure, and content structure into engagement strategies reveals complex dynamics in consumer behaviour on social media. Recent research underscores the importance of these factors in crafting effective social media strategies that resonate with target audiences. By aligning linguistic and emotional elements with audience preferences and balancing self-disclosure with credibility, marketers can develop more impactful engagement strategies that drive higher interaction rates and conversion outcomes.

ACTIVITY 2

Analysing consumer reviews

Objective: To understand the role of emotional responses and product attributes in consumer review helpfulness.

Instructions: Provide students with a set of consumer reviews for various products (these can be printed or shared digitally).

Ask students to analyse the reviews, identifying emotional tones, product attributes mentioned, and their perceived helpfulness.

Have students categorize the reviews based on whether they are positive, negative or neutral and discuss how the emotional response and product information affect the perceived usefulness of the reviews.

Facilitate a class discussion on the influence of review sentiments on consumer decisions and how businesses can leverage this information.

Conclusion

The exploration of consumer behaviour in the digital era reveals a complex interplay between technology and consumer engagement. Digital marketing and social media platforms have revolutionized how brands connect with consumers, leveraging influencers and targeted content to drive brand loyalty and purchasing decisions.

Augmented reality has emerged as a powerful tool in enhancing consumer experiences, providing immersive and interactive opportunities that go beyond traditional marketing methods.

As consumer expectations continue to evolve, businesses must stay abreast of technological advancements and emerging trends to effectively engage with their target audiences. The integration of big data analytics offers valuable insights into consumer behaviour, enabling more informed decision-making and strategic planning. However, addressing usability challenges and cultural considerations remains essential to ensure that digital tools and platforms meet diverse consumer needs.

In conclusion, the landscape of consumer behaviour is dynamic and continually shaped by technological innovations. Future research should focus on exploring the long-term effects of digital and AR technologies on consumer behaviour, as well as addressing emerging challenges in usability and cultural adaptation. Understanding these elements will be crucial for businesses to navigate the complexities of the digital age and foster meaningful connections with consumers.

ACTIVITY 3

Digital marketing strategy analysis

Objective: To understand and evaluate the effectiveness of digital marketing strategies used by different brands.

Instructions: Divide the class into small groups. Assign each group a different brand or company known for its digital marketing efforts.

Each group will research their assigned brand's digital marketing strategies, including social media campaigns, influencer partnerships, and online advertising.

Have each group present their findings, focusing on how these strategies impact consumer behaviour and engagement.

Discuss as a class the strengths and weaknesses of the various strategies and their overall effectiveness.

KEY TERMS

Digital marketing: Strategies and tactics used by businesses to promote products or services through digital channels, including social media and online advertising.

Social media influencers: Individuals with significant followings on social media platforms who can affect the purchasing decisions of their audience through endorsements and content.

Augmented reality (AR): Technology that superimposes digital information onto the real world, enhancing user experiences in various contexts such as retail and gaming.

User experience (UX): The overall experience of a user interacting with a product or service, focusing on usability, satisfaction, and accessibility.

Big data analytics: The use of advanced data analysis techniques to extract insights from large and complex datasets, informing business strategies and decision-making.

Immersion: The degree to which a user feels engaged and absorbed in an experience, particularly in digital and interactive environments like AR.

Brand loyalty: The tendency of consumers to repeatedly purchase or engage with a particular brand due to positive experiences and satisfaction.

Consumer engagement: The level of interaction and emotional connection between consumers and a brand or product.

Usability: The ease with which users can interact with and use a product or service effectively and efficiently.

Emotional response: The feelings or reactions elicited by interactions with a product, service or brand, which can influence consumer attitudes and behaviours.

KEY LEARNING POINTS

- Digital marketing encompasses strategies that promote products or services through digital channels.
- Social media influencers play a significant role in affecting purchasing decisions among their audiences.
- Augmented reality enhances user experiences by superimposing digital information onto the real world.
- User experience focuses on usability, satisfaction, and accessibility in product interactions.
- Big data analytics offers valuable insights that inform business strategies and decision-making.
- Immersion in digital experiences contributes to user engagement and satisfaction.
- Brand loyalty develops through positive consumer experiences and satisfaction.

- Consumer engagement is characterized by the level of emotional connection between consumers and brands.
- Usability is critical for ensuring that users can interact effectively and efficiently with products.
- Emotional responses to marketing initiatives can significantly influence consumer attitudes and behaviours.

9 | Ethical considerations in the digital consumer landscape

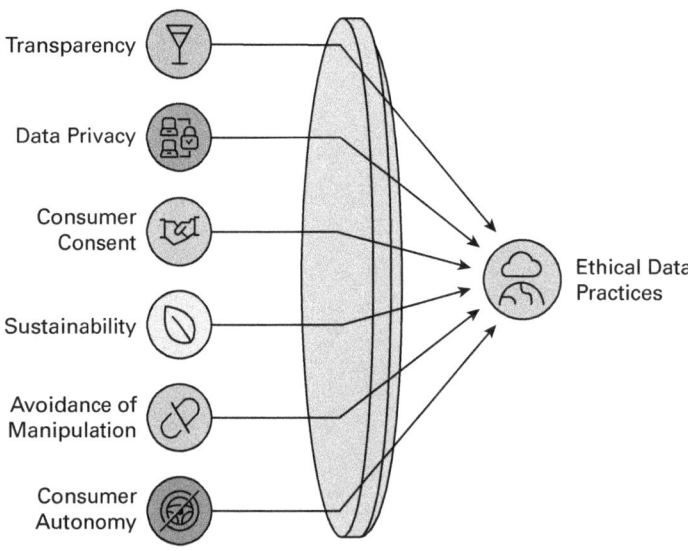

Ethical Data Practices

LEARNING OBJECTIVES

By the end of this chapter, you should be able to:

- Evaluate ethical marketing practices: Identify and assess key components of ethical marketing, including transparency, social responsibility and sustainability and their effects on consumer trust and brand loyalty.

- Assess the role of corporate social responsibility (CSR): Examine how CSR initiatives shape consumer perceptions and influence brand reputation and consumer behaviour.
- Apply ethical principles to personalized marketing: Recognize the ethical considerations in personalized marketing, such as data privacy, consumer consent and avoiding manipulation and apply these principles to real-world scenarios.
- Develop strategies for effective CSR and ethical marketing: Formulate strategies for integrating ethical marketing and CSR into business practices, based on best practices and case studies from various industries.

CHAPTER OUTLINE

Overview of modern consumer behaviour:

- Importance of ethical considerations and technological advancements
- Technological influences on consumer behaviour

The rise of immersive technologies and their impact on consumption:

- Consumer privacy concerns and the role of data protection
- Ethical marketing

Definition and significance of ethical marketing:

- Key components: transparency, social responsibility and sustainability
- Case studies of ethical marketing practices in the luxury sector
- Personalized marketing

The ethical dimensions of personalized marketing:

- Transparency, data privacy and consumer consent
- Balancing personalization with ethical considerations
- Corporate social responsibility

Defining CSR and its relevance in modern business:

- How CSR influences consumer behaviour and brand perception
- Effective CSR strategies and their impact on consumer loyalty
- Case studies and practical implications

Examples of brands successfully implementing ethical marketing and CSR:

- Lessons learned and best practices for businesses

Introduction

In the contemporary landscape of consumer behaviour, the integration of technological advancements with ethical considerations has become a defining feature. As digital technologies continue to evolve, their influence on consumer behaviour grows increasingly profound. From the rise of immersive realities to the proliferation of personalized marketing, technology shapes how consumers interact with brands and make purchasing decisions. Concurrently, a heightened awareness of ethical issues has led consumers to demand greater transparency, social responsibility and sustainability from the brands they support.

This chapter explores these dynamics by examining how technological innovations intersect with ethical marketing practices and corporate social responsibility. It provides an in-depth analysis of how these factors influence consumer behaviour, focusing on transparency in marketing, the ethical implications of personalized marketing and the role of CSR in shaping brand perceptions. Through a combination of theoretical insights and practical case studies, this chapter aims to offer a comprehensive understanding of the modern consumer landscape and the evolving expectations placed on businesses.

Addressing privacy and data security concerns in the digital world

In the rapidly evolving digital landscape, consumer privacy and data security have become paramount concerns that significantly influence consumer behaviour and decision-making processes. As digital technologies permeate every aspect of consumers' lives, from social media interactions to e-commerce transactions, the collection, storage and utilization of personal data have raised critical ethical questions and challenges for both businesses and consumers.

Recent studies have highlighted the growing awareness and concern among consumers regarding their digital privacy. A 2024 survey by the Pew Research Center found that 79 per cent of American adults were very or somewhat concerned about how companies were using the data collected about them, a significant increase from 64 per cent in 2019. This heightened awareness has led to changes in consumer behaviour, with many individuals adopting more cautious approaches to their online activities and interactions with brands.

1. Confidence and competence in technology use

The survey reveals a generally high level of confidence among US adults in their ability to use digital devices (McClain et al., 2023). As of May 2023, 53 per cent of respondents reported feeling 'very confident' using computers, smartphones and other devices, although this represents a slight decrease from 57 per cent in 2021. This shift could reflect growing complexities in technology or increased awareness of digital security challenges. Notably, 77 per cent of respondents were able to set up new devices and learn how to use them independently, highlighting a trend towards greater self-reliance in managing technology.

2. Privacy concerns and management

Privacy remains a significant concern for many consumers. A substantial portion of respondents (61 per cent) reported feeling 'overwhelmed' by managing online privacy. This feeling of overwhelm aligns with the high level of worry about privacy issues: 38 per cent of respondents were 'very worried' about identity theft and 42 per cent expressed similar concerns about companies selling their information without consent. Despite these concerns, a notable percentage (69 per cent) actively declines cookies or uses privacy-enhancing tools like encrypted messaging apps, demonstrating a proactive approach to managing online privacy.

3. Understanding and trust in privacy measures

The survey indicates varying levels of understanding and trust regarding privacy policies and data management. While 27 per cent of respondents felt they understood privacy policies 'somewhat', 49 per cent felt they understood 'very little' about what companies do with their data. This gap in understanding could be contributing to the relatively low confidence in the effectiveness of privacy policies, with 36 per cent of respondents viewing them as 'not too effective'.

4. Role of government and technology companies in privacy

There is strong public sentiment favouring increased government regulation of data privacy. 72 per cent of respondents believe there should be 'more regulation' than currently exists, reflecting a desire for stricter controls over how companies handle personal data. Additionally, respondents see technology companies as bearing a significant responsibility for protecting children's digital privacy, with 85 per cent assigning a 'great deal of responsibility' to these companies.

5. AI and consumer trust

The rising use of artificial intelligence in personal data collection presents new challenges. While 60 per cent of respondents have heard 'a little' about AI, trust in companies' responsible use of AI remains low. Only 2 per cent have 'a great deal' of trust in these companies' decisions regarding AI, underscoring a need for greater transparency and ethical considerations in AI applications.

The implementation of stringent data protection regulations, such as the European Union's General Data Protection Regulation (GDPR) has had a profound impact on how businesses handle consumer data. These regulations have not only imposed strict guidelines on data collection and usage but have also empowered consumers with greater control over their personal information. For instance, 62 per cent of consumers were more likely to engage with brands that provided clear information about their data practices and offered easy opt-out options.

The concept of '**privacy by design**' has gained traction in recent years, with companies integrating privacy considerations into their products and services from the outset. Apple's introduction of App Tracking Transparency in 2021, which requires apps to get user permission before tracking their data across other companies' apps or websites, exemplifies this approach. This move has not only enhanced user privacy but has also forced marketers to rethink their targeting strategies, leading to more innovative and less intrusive marketing techniques.

UNDERSTANDING APP PRIVACY DETAILS ON THE APP STORE

In the contemporary digital landscape, the protection of user privacy has become a central concern for both consumers and developers. Apple's App Store's privacy labels, introduced to enhance transparency regarding data collection practices, play a crucial role in this context. This feature, which requires app developers to disclose their data practices clearly, helps users make informed decisions about the apps they choose to download. For instance, recent updates have introduced Privacy Nutrition Labels, akin to nutritional information on food products, which detail the types of data an app collects, how it is used and whether it is linked to users' identities (Apple, 2023). These labels now include more detailed data types and improved guidelines for third-party SDKs, ensuring a higher degree of transparency and integrity within the software supply chain.

Data collection and user awareness

The requirement for detailed data collection disclosures aims to bridge the gap between user awareness and app practices. Developers must now specify all data types collected, whether used for primary app functionality or not. This move addresses previous criticisms where users were often unaware of the extent and nature of data collection. For example, in a 2023 study, it was found that 52 per cent of users felt overwhelmed by the complexity of app privacy policies and were unable to easily discern what data was being collected and for what purposes (Apple, 2023). By mandating clear disclosures, the App Store seeks to mitigate these issues, offering users a clearer understanding of how their personal information is handled.

In the video 'What's New in Privacy' from Apple, Lindsey and Chris highlight how iOS 18 and macOS Sequoia implement advanced privacy measures through new features like contextual data pickers, enhanced permission flows and privacy-preserving tools, underscoring Apple's commitment to safeguarding user data while enhancing app functionality. Watch 'What's New in Privacy' to go further: https://developer.apple.com/videos/play/wwdc2024/10123/

Examples of new disclosure requirements

The recent updates have also refined the categories of data that need to be disclosed. Data such as health information collected through apps like MyFitnessPal or financial data handled by budgeting tools are now explicitly categorized and must be reported in the app's privacy label. For instance, the introduction of 'Health & Fitness' and 'Financial Info' categories requires apps like Strava or Mint to detail exactly what types of sensitive data they collect and how they are used (Apple, 2023).

Implications for developers and consumers

For developers, these changes necessitate a more rigorous approach to privacy practices and transparency. They must ensure that their data handling practices are in full compliance with the updated guidelines and reflect these practices accurately in their Privacy Nutrition Labels for example. This requirement not only enhances consumer trust but also aligns with global privacy standards, such as GDPR in Europe, which emphasizes transparency and user consent. For consumers, the ability to review detailed privacy information empowers them to make more informed choices, potentially influencing their app usage patterns based on the privacy practices disclosed.

Looking ahead, the evolution of app privacy disclosures will likely continue to adapt in response to emerging privacy concerns and technological advancements. As new types of data collection and tracking technologies develop, such as **AI-driven analytics** or **biometric data** collection, the App Store's guidelines will need to evolve accordingly. Future updates might include even more granular privacy disclosures or advanced tools for users to manage their privacy preferences dynamically. Maintaining this adaptability will be key to ensuring that the privacy practices remain effective and relevant in an ever-changing digital environment.

STRAVA: ENHANCING ATHLETIC ENGAGEMENT THROUGH COMMUNITY AND DATA

Strava, founded in 2009 by Michael Horvath and Mark Gainey, has evolved into a leading platform for athletes worldwide, boasting over 100 million users across 195 countries (Strava, 2024). This expansive reach highlights Strava's role in fostering a global community centred around athletic performance and personal achievement. The platform allows users to track over 30 types of activities, from casual walks to competitive events like the Tour de France, integrating social features that enhance user engagement and motivation. By leveraging data collection and community interaction, Strava not only supports individual fitness goals but also creates a competitive yet supportive environment that resonates with its diverse user base.

The impact of community on user engagement

One of Strava's key strategies for driving user engagement is its emphasis on community and social interaction. Users are encouraged to share their activities, give and receive 'kudos', and engage with peers through comments and challenges. This community-centric approach taps into intrinsic motivational factors, fostering a sense of camaraderie and accountability. For instance, recent studies have shown that social support and peer comparison can significantly enhance motivation and adherence to fitness routines. Strava's integration of these elements into its platform exemplifies how digital communities can effectively drive consumer behaviour and sustain user engagement over time.

Data-driven personalization and privacy concerns

Strava's success also hinges on its use of data to personalize user experiences and provide actionable insights. The platform offers detailed analytics on user performance, such as pace, distance and elevation, enabling athletes to set goals, track progress and analyse their performance trends (Strava, 2024). However, this data-centric approach raises important privacy considerations. Recent controversies have highlighted the need for robust data protection practices, as users' activity data can inadvertently reveal sensitive information such as location and habits. In response, Strava has implemented measures to enhance data privacy, including customizable privacy settings and transparency in data usage.

Global expansion and organizational structure

Despite its origins in San Francisco, Strava operates as a global enterprise with employees working across various international locations. This global presence supports its mission to connect athletes around the world while also addressing the challenges of managing a diverse and dispersed team. The company's leadership, including figures like Mike Martin (CEO) and Matt Salazar (Chief Product Officer), plays a crucial role in steering its strategic direction and ensuring the platform meets the evolving needs of its user base (Strava, 2024).

Future directions and innovations

Looking forward, Strava continues to innovate by incorporating new features and expanding its offerings. Recent developments include enhanced goal-setting tools, improved tracking capabilities and integration with other fitness technologies. As the digital fitness landscape evolves, Strava's commitment to leveraging data for personalized user experiences while maintaining a strong community focus will likely position it as a continued leader in the athletic tracking market.

Data breaches

Data breaches and **cybersecurity** incidents continue to be significant concerns for consumers and businesses alike. The 2024 'Cost of a Data Breach' report by IBM and the Ponemon Institute revealed that the average cost of a data breach reached $4.45 million in 2023, a 15 per cent increase over the previous three years.

CONSUMER BEHAVIOUR AND DATA BREACH COSTS: AN ANALYSIS

In the contemporary digital landscape, the behaviour of consumers in response to data breaches has become a focal point for research and analysis. The 2024 IBM report on the cost of data breaches provides critical insights into how organizations' handling of data breaches impacts consumer trust and behaviour. This analysis draws on recent findings to illustrate the evolving dynamics between data security incidents and consumer reactions.

The study was independently conducted by the Ponemon Institute (https://www.ponemon.org/) and commissioned, analysed and published by IBM (https://www.ibm.com/). It included 604 organizations that suffered data breaches between March 2023 and February 2024. Researchers focused on organizations operating across 17 industries, 16 countries and regions and breaches that compromised 2,100 to 113,000 records. To gain on-the-ground insights, Ponemon Institute researchers surveyed

3,556 executives and security leaders with direct relationships to data breach incidents within their organizations.

The rising costs of data breaches and consumer reactions

The 2024 IBM report reveals a significant increase in the average cost of a data breach, which has surged to $4.88 million, marking a 10 per cent rise from the previous year. This escalation is attributed to factors such as operational disruptions and elevated post-breach response costs. Notably, over half of the organizations affected reported passing these costs onto consumers. In a competitive market already strained by inflationary pressures, this shift can adversely affect consumer perception and purchasing behaviour (IBM, 2024).

For instance, when organizations externalize breach-related costs, consumers may experience diminished trust and dissatisfaction. This reaction is evident in the retail sector, where breaches involving personal data, such as payment information, lead to heightened consumer scrutiny and reluctance to engage with the affected brands (Ponemon Institute, 2024). Recent studies corroborate this trend, highlighting that consumers are increasingly sensitive to how businesses manage data security and are more likely to switch brands following a breach.

The impact of AI and automation on cost reduction and consumer trust

The integration of AI and **automation** in **cybersecurity** has shown promise in mitigating the financial impact of data breaches. The report indicates that organizations employing AI-driven security measures saved an average of $2.2 million per breach compared with those without such technologies. This suggests that advanced security solutions not only help in cost reduction but also potentially enhance consumer confidence by demonstrating proactive risk management (IBM, 2024).

A pertinent example is the use of AI in detecting and responding to breaches more swiftly. Companies that implemented AI for threat detection and response experienced reduced breach resolution times and lower associated costs. This proactive approach can significantly influence consumer trust, as it signals a commitment to safeguarding personal data. Furthermore, organizations leveraging AI to secure data are better positioned to reassure customers and maintain their trust, even after a breach occurs.

Addressing data privacy and consumer behaviour

The increasing prevalence of data breaches involving '**hidden data**' or data residing in unmanaged sources complicates the task of maintaining consumer trust. The 2024 report highlights that breaches involving such data resulted in a 16 per cent increase in costs. This underscores the necessity for organizations to enhance their data management and security practices (IBM, 2024).

Recent research emphasizes the importance of transparent data handling practices. Consumers are more likely to respond positively to organizations that demonstrate clear and proactive measures in data protection. For example, companies that provide timely and transparent breach notifications tend to experience less consumer **backlash** compared with those that delay or obscure information. This behaviour reflects a growing consumer expectation for accountability and transparency in data security.

Training and preparedness as a consumer trust factor

Effective response strategies and preparedness for data breaches play a crucial role in shaping consumer perception. The 2024 IBM report suggests that investing in **cyber response training** and simulation exercises can reduce breach costs and mitigate reputational damage. Organizations that are well-prepared to handle breaches efficiently are better equipped to manage consumer concerns and maintain trust during crises (IBM, 2024).

For instance, companies that conduct regular cyber crisis simulations are often better at communicating with affected consumers and managing post-breach impacts. This preparedness can enhance consumer confidence by demonstrating an organization's capability to handle security incidents effectively and minimize disruptions.

Such incidents not only result in financial losses for companies but also erode consumer trust. A study by McKinsey & Company (2022) found that 87 per cent of consumers would not do business with a company if they had concerns about its security practices.

The rise of AI and **machine learning** in **consumer analytics** has introduced new ethical dilemmas. While these technologies offer unprecedented insights into consumer behaviour and preferences, they also raise concerns about algorithmic bias and the potential for manipulation. An experiment by researchers at Stanford University (Zhang and Venkatesh, 2017) demonstrated how AI-driven personalization could inadvertently reinforce **societal biases** and limit consumer choices, highlighting the need for ethical guidelines in the development and deployment of AI systems in marketing.

Blockchain technology has emerged as a potential solution to some of the privacy and security challenges in the digital consumer landscape. Recent works explore how blockchain-based systems could enhance transparency in supply chains and data management, potentially increasing consumer trust and engagement with brands that adopt such technologies.

As the digital consumer landscape continues to evolve, addressing privacy and data security concerns will remain a critical challenge for businesses and policymakers. Companies that prioritize transparency, ethical data practices and robust security measures are likely to gain a competitive advantage in an increasingly privacy-conscious market. Moreover, ongoing research and public discourse on digital ethics will be essential in shaping policies and practices that protect consumer rights while fostering innovation in the digital economy.

Digitization of route management

Table 9.1 summarizes the benefits of digitizing route management. It highlights the key benefits of transitioning from manual to digitized route management systems, emphasizing improvements in efficiency, cost management, customer satisfaction and environmental impact.

Table 9.1 Benefits of digitizing route management

Aspect	Manual route management	Digitized route management
Client allocation	Clients assigned to vehicles based on the experience and knowledge of the drivers.	Clients assigned based on multiple criteria: client time slots, vehicle capacity, and driver working hours.
Route management	Routes managed in a non-optimized manner, difficult to control.	Routes optimized in terms of time.
Resource access	Difficult to involve multiple resources in route management.	Easier to integrate various resources into route management.
New route development	Difficulty in assessing the potential for new routes.	Ability to evaluate and develop new routes.
Carbon footprint	Unable to measure the carbon footprint of routes.	Capability to assess CO_2 emissions for each route.
Customer complaints	No control over customer complaints related to time slot adherence.	Improved management of time slots, leading to enhanced customer satisfaction.

(continued)

Table 9.1 (Continued)

Aspect	Manual route management	Digitized route management
Cost management	Inefficient cost control.	Streamlined cost control and management.
Human resources security	Vulnerable position for route managers due to lack of system support.	Increased job security for route managers due to the tool's ease of use.
Time efficiency	No clear measure of time savings.	Significant time savings per year.
Optimization and simulations	Limited or no ability to perform simulations or optimization studies related to business operations.	Possibility to conduct simulations and optimization studies in relation to business operations.
Market development	Limited capability to develop new markets.	Enhanced ability to develop and explore new markets.

LESAGE PRESTIGE

The evolution of Lesage Prestige's route management

Lesage Prestige, a prominent player in the wholesale meat sector based in Hauts-de-France (France), provides an insightful case study on the transformative benefits of digitizing route management. Founded in the 1950s by Guy Lesage, the company has evolved from a small family business into a significant regional enterprise with 80 employees and over 600 clients. Despite its expertise in meat processing, Lesage Prestige faced significant challenges in managing its delivery routes efficiently. These challenges stemmed from a traditional approach that heavily relied on the experience of drivers and limited technological support. The integration of Mapo since 2015 has been pivotal in enhancing operational efficiency and customer satisfaction.

The transition from manual to digitized route management

Before adopting Mapo, Lesage Prestige's route management was constrained by outdated practices. The company's reliance on its **ERP system**, VIF, only facilitated basic functions such as printing delivery notes and using GPS navigation. This approach led to several inefficiencies, including non-optimized routes, inconsistent delivery schedules and frequent customer complaints regarding timing. As a result, the manual management of routes was not only cumbersome but also failed to leverage data for operational improvements.

The introduction of Mapo revolutionized the approach. By incorporating multiple criteria – such as client time slots, vehicle capacity and driver working hours – Mapo enabled a more rationalized allocation of deliveries. This technological advancement addressed previous inefficiencies, including the inability to develop new routes or measure carbon footprints. The digitized system provided Lesage Prestige with tools to optimize routes, evaluate CO_2 emissions and manage customer expectations more effectively.

Achieving operational excellence through digitization

The benefits of integrating Mapo into Lesage Prestige's operations are evident. The digitization of route management has not only streamlined logistics but also delivered substantial time savings, equivalent to approximately two full-time positions annually. This efficiency gain has been instrumental in maintaining high service quality despite increased operational demands.

Moreover, Mapo's ability to generate real-time data and simulations has empowered Lesage Prestige to better plan and execute delivery routes. This has led to a notable improvement in the company's environmental footprint, with the capability to assess and reduce CO_2 emissions associated with each route. The successful implementation of Mapo also positions Lesage Prestige to expand its delivery network, including new routes in Paris and Belgium, further demonstrating the system's scalability and effectiveness.

Looking forward: the future of route management

As Lesage Prestige continues to grow, the company remains committed to leveraging technology to enhance its logistics operations. The integration of Mapo has not only resolved past challenges but also paved the way for future innovations. With plans to conduct a comprehensive carbon footprint assessment and potentially integrate new delivery routes, Lesage Prestige exemplifies how digitization can drive growth and operational excellence.

Lesage Prestige's journey underscores the critical role of digitization in optimizing route management. By adopting advanced technologies like Mapo, companies can achieve significant operational improvements, enhance customer satisfaction and drive sustainable growth. The case of Lesage Prestige serves as a valuable example for other businesses considering the digital transformation of their logistics operations.

Discussion/Questions

Operational challenges:

- What were the key operational challenges faced by Lesage Prestige before adopting the Mapo system? How did these challenges impact the business?

Impact of digitization:

- How did the implementation of the Mapo system address the operational inefficiencies identified in the case? Provide specific examples of improvements.

Customer satisfaction:

- In what ways did digitizing route management affect customer satisfaction at Lesage Prestige? How did the company measure these improvements?

Cost control and economic benefits:

- How did internalizing route management with Mapo contribute to cost control and economic benefits for Lesage Prestige? Discuss the implications for similar businesses.

Environmental impact:

- How did Lesage Prestige use Mapo to assess and manage the environmental impact of its operations? What are the potential benefits of this capability for the company and its customers?

Technology adoption:

- What factors should businesses consider when choosing a digital tool for route management? How can these factors influence the success of technology adoption?

Scalability and expansion:

- How did the success of Mapo in managing current routes influence Lesage Prestige's decision to expand into new markets? Discuss the role of scalability in this context.

Future developments:

- What future steps might Lesage Prestige take to further leverage technology in their logistics operations? How could these steps impact its business strategy?

Comparative analysis:

- Compare the manual route management approach used by Lesage Prestige before digitization with the digital approach implemented with Mapo. What are the key differences in terms of efficiency, customer service and operational control?

Sustainability and consumer behaviour:

- How does the ability to measure and manage CO_2 emissions align with current consumer expectations and regulatory trends? What might be the impact on customer perception and brand reputation?

Implementing digital tools:

- If you were managing a logistics company, how would you approach the implementation of a digital route management system? What considerations would be most important for a successful transition?

Customer feedback mechanisms:

- Develop a plan for collecting and analysing customer feedback related to delivery services. How would this information be used to further improve route management and customer satisfaction?

How brands can address privacy concerns

In the ever-evolving landscape of digital marketing, personalization stands as a double-edged sword in consumer behaviour (McKee et al., 2024). The allure of personalized advertising, where brands tailor messages based on individual data – such as search histories, social media interactions and demographic details – promises a heightened relevance that can enhance user engagement and conversion rates (Schmidt and Maier, 2022). For instance, a consumer who recently browsed hotels in Miami might encounter targeted ads for the 'Blue Ocean Hotel', the very establishment they considered but did not book immediately. This kind of **retargeting** can effectively **nudge** the consumer towards completing their purchase, as evidenced by recent studies demonstrating its efficacy in increasing conversion rates (Smink et al., 2020).

However, this sophisticated level of personalization brings with it a paradoxical challenge: privacy concerns. As consumers are inundated with tailored advertisements, they also become increasingly wary of how their data is being used. The concept of **privacy calculus** – a theoretical model explaining how consumers weigh the benefits of personalization against potential privacy invasions – has gained prominence in recent research (Zhu and Chang, 2016). For example, while personalized ads may enhance the relevance of content and improve user experience, they also raise significant concerns about data security and the extent of surveillance involved (Shin and Lin, 2016). This tension between the desire for personalized content and the need to protect personal privacy has led many consumers to adopt protective behaviours, such as disabling tracking features or using privacy-enhancing technologies (Strycharz et al., 2019).

Recent research highlights that the effectiveness of personalized advertising is not solely dependent on the quality of the data but also on the perceived intrusiveness of the ad (Wiese et al., 2020). Consumers' responses to personalized ads can vary widely based on how they perceive the tradeoff between the perceived value of the ad and the level of intrusion it represents. For instance, younger generations, particularly Gen Z, are often more receptive to personalized content that aligns with their preferences and interests, yet they are also more sensitive to privacy concerns and may react negatively to overly intrusive advertisements (Smith, 2019). This generational shift underscores the need for marketers to balance personalization with transparency and control, ensuring that the benefits of tailored advertising do not come at the cost of consumer trust.

While personalized advertising offers substantial advantages in targeting and engagement, it also necessitates careful navigation of privacy issues. The ongoing dialogue between enhancing user experience through tailored content and maintaining robust privacy protections is crucial for sustaining consumer trust and optimizing the effectiveness of digital marketing strategies (Vander Schee et al., 2020). As the field continues to evolve, understanding these dynamics will be essential for both marketers and consumers in fostering a more balanced approach to digital personalization.

Privacy–benefits paradox and avoidance–annoyance paradox in digital advertising

In the realm of digital advertising, the privacy–benefits paradox and the avoidance–annoyance paradox represent two critical phenomena that shape consumer interactions with personalized ads.

Privacy–benefits paradox

The privacy–benefits paradox highlights the tension between the advantages of personalized advertising and the privacy concerns it generates. Personalized ads can significantly enhance the relevance of marketing messages, offering consumers tailored recommendations that align closely with their preferences and past behaviours. For instance, targeted ads for a 'Blue Ocean Hotel' may effectively address a consumer's recent search for vacation accommodations in Miami, potentially improving user experience and conversion rates (Schmidt and Maier, 2022). However, this personalization is often accompanied by concerns about how personal data is collected, stored and used. Consumers might appreciate the convenience and relevance of personalized content but simultaneously worry about the potential for data misuse or invasion of privacy (Vander Schee et al., 2020).

Avoidance–annoyance paradox

The avoidance–annoyance paradox refers to the counterintuitive response of consumers to personalized ads that they find intrusive or overly aggressive. While personalization can increase engagement, it can also lead to annoyance if perceived as invasive. For instance, frequent retargeting, where ads for products consumers have already purchased or decided against continue to appear, can lead to ad fatigue and increased annoyance (Wiese et al., 2020). This annoyance may prompt users to engage in avoidance behaviours, such as **ad blocking** or **opting out** of data collection practices, thereby reducing the effectiveness of personalized ads (Shin and Lin, 2016). The paradox lies in the fact that while personalized ads are intended to enhance user experience, their excessive or poorly managed implementation can result in a negative consumer reaction.

Interaction effects

The interaction between privacy concerns and annoyance with personalization can significantly influence consumer behaviour. As highlighted in recent research, the effectiveness of personalized advertising is not only a function of the relevance of the content but also how well **privacy concerns** and **ad intrusiveness** are managed. For instance, while Gen Z consumers may be more open to personalized content, they also exhibit heightened sensitivity to privacy issues and ad intrusiveness (Smith, 2019). This demographic is more likely to experience the privacy–benefits paradox and the avoidance–annoyance paradox simultaneously, leading to complex consumer responses. Table 9.2 illustrates the interaction effects of the privacy–benefits paradox and the avoidance–annoyance paradox, highlighting how these phenomena influence consumer behaviour and advertising effectiveness.

Understanding the privacy–benefits paradox and the avoidance–annoyance paradox is essential for marketers aiming to optimize personalized advertising strategies. Balancing the benefits of tailored content with effective privacy management and minimizing ad intrusiveness can enhance consumer engagement while mitigating negative reactions. As digital advertising continues to evolve, addressing these paradoxes will be crucial for developing strategies that align with consumer expectations and preferences.

Table 9.2 Interaction effects of privacy–benefits paradox and avoidance–annoyance paradox

Effect	Description	Example	Recent findings
Privacy–benefits paradox	Consumers enjoy the relevance of personalized ads but are concerned about data privacy.	A consumer appreciates personalized hotel recommendations but worries about how data is used.	Consumers with high privacy concerns may be less receptive to personalized ads despite their perceived relevance (Vimalkumar et al., 2021).
Avoidance–annoyance paradox	Personalized ads can lead to annoyance if perceived as intrusive, leading to avoidance behaviours.	Repeated ads for a product already purchased lead to irritation and ad blocking.	Increased ad frequency and intrusiveness can result in higher ad avoidance rates (Wiese et al., 2020).
Interaction effect	The combined impact of privacy concerns and ad annoyance on consumer behaviour.	Gen Z users may avoid ads they find intrusive despite appreciating their relevance.	The interaction of high personalization with low privacy assurance can amplify ad avoidance (Shin & Lin, 2016).

Promoting ethical marketing practices in the age of personalization

The rapid proliferation of digital technologies has dramatically transformed consumer behaviour, creating both opportunities and challenges for marketers (Chai and Li, 2024). Live streaming, in particular, has emerged as a potent tool for engaging consumers, offering a dynamic and interactive platform that fosters real-time interaction between brands and consumers. Studies suggest that live streaming not only enhances consumer engagement but also builds trust and strengthens brand loyalty (Wang et al., 2022; Zhai and Chen, 2023). For instance, in China, where live streaming e-commerce has seen exponential growth, consumers are increasingly drawn to these platforms due to the perceived authenticity and immediacy of the interactions (Lu et al., 2018). The ability to engage directly with broadcasters and ask questions in real-time provides a sense of **empowerment**, which is crucial in influencing purchasing decisions (Ma et al., 2022).

However, the digital environment also raises significant ethical concerns that affect consumer trust and behaviour. Ethical issues, such as data privacy and the manipulation of consumer data by AI, have become increasingly prominent. As Wachter and Mittelstadt (2018) argue, the rise of big data and AI necessitates a rethinking of data protection laws to safeguard consumers' rights to reasonable inferences about their data. Consumers' ethical perceptions significantly influence their engagement with brands, particularly in the **sharing economy**, where the quality of relationships and social support play a pivotal role (Nadeem et al., 2020). For example, platforms that prioritize ethical transparency and consumer well-being are more likely to foster long-term loyalty and positive word-of-mouth (Limbu et al., 2012).

Moreover, the concept of consumer empowerment has evolved in response to the digital transformation. **Empowerment** through technology not only enhances consumers' ability to make informed choices but also increases their expectations regarding **corporate social responsibility (CSR)**. Research by Shaw et al. (2006) underscores the importance of viewing consumption as a form of 'voting', where consumers express their ethical and social preferences through their purchasing decisions. This trend is evident in the growing consumer demand for brands to adopt sustainable practices and transparent communication. For instance, the increasing scrutiny of ethical practices in the fashion industry has led to a shift towards more sustainable and ethically sourced products, reflecting consumers' desire for alignment between their values and their consumption habits (Nie et al., 2021).

The intersection of technology and ethics is reshaping consumer behaviour in profound ways. Marketers must navigate this complex landscape by embracing transparency, fostering trust and empowering consumers. As the digital marketplace continues to evolve, the ability to balance technological innovation with ethical considerations will be key to building lasting consumer relationships and achieving sustainable business success.

Understanding ethical marketing

Ethical marketing has become a cornerstone of contemporary consumer behaviour, reflecting an increased awareness of social and environmental issues among consumers (Petr and Caudan, 2024). At its core, ethical marketing involves practices that not only aim for profit but also prioritize moral considerations, such as fairness, transparency and sustainability. This approach is increasingly influential as consumers become more discerning and demand that brands align with their values.

Ethical marketing is increasingly recognized as a critical component in shaping consumer behaviour. It reflects a growing consumer demand for transparency, social responsibility and sustainability from brands. Ethical marketing practices are designed not only to meet these consumer expectations but also to foster long-term brand loyalty and trust.

One significant aspect of ethical marketing is transparency. Consumers today are more informed and seek brands that are open about their practices. For example, research shows that transparency in business practices is crucial for building consumer trust and loyalty (Schiopu et al., 2022). Brands that openly share information about their sourcing, production processes and environmental impact can differentiate themselves in a competitive market. This openness helps to mitigate consumer scepticism and enhances the overall brand image.

Social responsibility is another key dimension of ethical marketing. Companies that actively engage in social and environmental initiatives can create a positive brand image and appeal to socially conscious consumers. For instance, Tussyadiah et al. (2018) highlight the growing consumer preference for brands that contribute to societal good. Engaging in cause-related marketing or supporting community initiatives can significantly impact consumer perception and loyalty.

Sustainability remains a central theme in ethical marketing. Consumers increasingly prefer brands that demonstrate a commitment to sustainable practices. The integration of sustainability into marketing strategies not only meets consumer expectations but also addresses broader environmental concerns (Lin et al., 2020). Brands that adopt sustainable practices and communicate these efforts effectively can enhance their reputation and attract environmentally conscious consumers.

Moreover, ethical marketing involves safeguarding consumer rights and data privacy. With the rise of digital marketing, ensuring the responsible handling of consumer data is essential. Research on consumer behaviour underscores the importance of protecting privacy and being transparent about data usage (Pang and Ruan, 2023). Companies that prioritize data security and privacy can build stronger consumer relationships and trust.

Ethical marketing is an essential strategy for modern businesses. It involves transparency, social responsibility, sustainability and data privacy – all of which contribute to a positive brand image and foster consumer trust. As consumer expectations continue to evolve, brands that embrace these ethical principles are likely to succeed in building long-term customer loyalty and maintaining a competitive edge.

Ethical considerations in personalized marketing

Personalized marketing leverages consumer data to tailor messages and offers, but it raises significant ethical questions regarding transparency, data privacy and consent.

Transparency is crucial in personalized marketing. Consumers are increasingly demanding that brands disclose how their data is collected, used and shared. Research highlights that transparency in data practices is essential for building trust and credibility (Schiopu et al., 2022). Brands that openly communicate their data usage policies and practices are better positioned to gain consumer confidence.

Data privacy is another critical ethical concern. With the vast amount of personal data collected, companies must prioritize the protection of consumer information.

Table 9.3 A comprehensive overview of key ethical considerations in personalized marketing

Aspect	Description	Reference
Transparency	The need for brands to be open about their data collection practices and the use of personal information to build consumer trust.	Schiopu et al. (2022)
Data privacy	The importance of protecting consumer data and ensuring that personal information is handled responsibly and securely.	Pang & Ruan (2023)
Consumer consent	Obtaining explicit consent from consumers before collecting or using their personal data, ensuring that they are fully aware of how their information will be used.	Petr & Caudan, (2024)
Sustainability in data practices	Integrating sustainable practices into data management and marketing strategies to align with broader environmental and social responsibility goals.	Lin et al. (2020)
Avoidance of manipulation	Ensuring that personalized marketing strategies do not exploit consumer vulnerabilities or manipulate behaviour in unethical ways.	Tussyadiah et al. (2018)
Respect for consumer autonomy	Allowing consumers to have control over their personalized marketing preferences and the ability to opt-out or modify their data usage settings.	Schiopu et al. (2022)

Ensuring that data is handled securely and responsibly is not only a legal obligation but also a moral imperative (Pang and Ruan, 2023). Effective data privacy practices help to prevent breaches and misuse, safeguarding consumer trust.

Consumer consent is a foundational principle in ethical marketing. It is essential for companies to obtain explicit consent from consumers before collecting or using their personal data. This practice ensures that consumers are fully informed about how their information will be used and can make autonomous decisions regarding their data (Petr and Caudan, 2024).

Sustainability in data practices aligns with broader ethical considerations in marketing. Integrating sustainable practices into data management and marketing strategies reflects a commitment to environmental and social responsibility. Companies that adopt these practices not only meet consumer expectations but also contribute to broader sustainability goals (Lin et al., 2020).

Avoidance of manipulation is essential to ensure that personalized marketing strategies do not exploit consumer vulnerabilities. Ethical marketing should focus on enhancing consumer experience rather than manipulating behaviour through targeted tactics (Tussyadiah et al., 2018). Maintaining ethical standards in personalization helps build long-term consumer trust and loyalty.

Finally, respect for consumer autonomy involves allowing consumers to control their personalized marketing preferences. Providing options to opt out or modify data usage settings respects consumer choices and supports ethical practices in personalized marketing (Schiopu et al., 2022).

Ethical considerations in personalized marketing encompass transparency, data privacy, consent, sustainability, avoidance of manipulation and respect for consumer autonomy. Addressing these concerns helps to build a trustworthy relationship between brands and consumers, fostering ethical marketing practices in the digital age.

Table 9.3 provides a comprehensive overview of key ethical considerations in personalized marketing, highlighting aspects such as transparency, data privacy and consumer consent, along with relevant scholarly references that underpin these practices.

ACTIVITY 1

Ethical dilemma debate

Objective: Explore the ethical challenges associated with personalized marketing.

Instructions: Organize a debate where students are split into two teams, one arguing for and the other against the use of deep personalization in marketing. Provide each team with specific points to support their position, such as:

- Team A (For): Benefits of increased relevance and consumer satisfaction.
- Team B (Against): Risks related to privacy invasion and manipulation.

After the debate, have a class discussion on how to balance personalization with ethical considerations.

Strategies for ethical marketing

Ethical marketing is a crucial dimension of modern business practices, characterized by transparency, honesty and a commitment to social values. Effective strategies often involve integrating ethical considerations into every aspect of marketing operations. For example, brands can adopt clear ethical guidelines and ensure that their marketing campaigns reflect these principles by avoiding misleading claims and promoting genuine product benefits. An illustrative case is the luxury watch brand Rolex, which, despite its high-profile nature, emphasizes transparency and ethical sourcing in its marketing communications. Furthermore, ethical marketing strategies can include the use of sustainable materials and the promotion of fair labour practices, as demonstrated by brands like Patek Philippe, which has integrated environmental sustainability into its supply chain practices (Dion et al., 2024). This approach not only builds consumer trust but also aligns the brand with the growing consumer demand for socially responsible business practices.

The role of corporate social responsibility in influencing consumer behaviour

Corporate Social Responsibility (CSR) plays a significant role in shaping consumer behaviour by influencing perceptions of brand integrity and commitment to social values. Recent trends show that consumers are increasingly prioritizing CSR when making purchasing decisions. For instance, luxury watch consumers often consider a brand's ethical stance and social contributions when evaluating its products. Brands such as Audemars Piguet have successfully leveraged their CSR initiatives, including charitable contributions and environmental efforts, to strengthen their market position and appeal to socially conscious consumers. Research indicates that CSR activities can enhance brand loyalty and influence consumer preferences by creating a positive brand image and aligning with consumers' ethical values. As such, CSR is not only a moral obligation but also a strategic tool for businesses seeking to differentiate themselves in a competitive market.

Defining corporate social responsibility

CSR refers to a company's commitment to operate in an economically, socially and environmentally responsible manner. CSR encompasses a range of practices, including ethical labour practices, environmental sustainability and community engagement. For instance, a luxury brand's CSR efforts might include ensuring fair wages for workers, reducing carbon emissions and supporting local communities through various initiatives. An example is the approach taken by the Swiss luxury watch manufacturer Hublot, which incorporates sustainable practices into its production processes and actively participates in environmental conservation efforts. CSR is increasingly viewed as a critical component of corporate strategy, reflecting a company's broader commitment to ethical practices and positive societal impact.

How CSR influences consumer behaviour

CSR significantly influences consumer behaviour by shaping brand perceptions and driving purchasing decisions. Consumers are more likely to support brands that demonstrate a genuine commitment to social and environmental issues. For instance, luxury watch collectors and buyers are increasingly considering a brand's CSR activities as a factor in their purchase decisions. Brands such as F.P. Journe, which engage in meaningful CSR activities, can command higher consumer loyalty and willingness to pay a premium for their products. CSR initiatives can also enhance a brand's reputation and foster trust, leading to stronger consumer relationships and increased brand equity. By aligning their values with those of their consumers, companies can effectively leverage CSR as a competitive advantage in the marketplace (Dion et al., 2024).

Implementing effective CSR strategies

Implementing effective CSR strategies involves integrating social and environmental responsibilities into the core business operations and ensuring that these practices are communicated clearly to consumers. Effective strategies often include setting measurable goals, engaging stakeholders and regularly reporting on CSR performance. Brands like Vacheron Constantin have developed comprehensive CSR programmes that include environmental sustainability, ethical labour practices and community involvement, demonstrating a commitment to responsible business practices. Key to successful CSR implementation is transparency and consistency in communication, as consumers increasingly demand accountability from brands. By adopting robust CSR strategies and actively engaging with their communities, companies can enhance their brand reputation and drive positive consumer behaviour.

ACTIVITY 2

CSR strategy development

Objective: Develop a CSR strategy for a hypothetical company.

Instructions: Create a fictional company and assign students to develop a CSR strategy for it. They should:

- identify key areas for CSR involvement (e.g. environmental, social, ethical labour practices)
- propose specific initiatives and goals
- present their strategy, including how it will be communicated to consumers and the expected impact on brand loyalty and consumer behaviour

Conclusion

The intersection of technology and ethics has fundamentally reshaped consumer behaviour in the digital age. As consumers become more engaged with immersive technologies and personalized experiences, their expectations for ethical practices in marketing and CSR have intensified. Brands must navigate this complex landscape by embracing transparency, safeguarding data privacy and aligning their operations with broader social and environmental goals.

Ethical marketing and CSR are not mere add-ons but essential components of a successful business strategy. They play a critical role in building consumer trust and loyalty, which are pivotal in a competitive market. Brands that effectively integrate these principles into their practices can differentiate themselves and foster deeper connections with their audience.

Looking ahead, the convergence of technological advancements and ethical considerations will continue to drive consumer behaviour. Businesses that remain proactive in addressing these evolving expectations will be well positioned to thrive in an increasingly conscientious and technologically sophisticated marketplace. This chapter underscores the importance of understanding these trends and adapting strategies accordingly to achieve sustainable business success.

ACTIVITY 3

Case study analysis

Objective: Analyse real-world examples of brands implementing ethical marketing and CSR practices.

Instructions: Divide the class into small groups and assign each group a different case study (e.g. Patagonia's environmental responsibility, Rolex's transparency). Ask each group to:

- summarize the brand's ethical marketing or CSR initiatives
- evaluate the impact of these initiatives on consumer behaviour and brand perception
- present their findings to the class and discuss the effectiveness of the strategies

KEY TERMS

Ethical marketing: Marketing practices that prioritize fairness, transparency and sustainability alongside profit.

Transparency: The openness of a brand regarding its data collection practices and business operations.

Data privacy: The protection of personal information collected from consumers, ensuring secure and responsible handling.

Consumer consent: The explicit agreement obtained from consumers before collecting or using their personal data.

Corporate social responsibility (CSR): A company's commitment to operate in an economically, socially and environmentally responsible manner.

Personalized marketing: Tailoring marketing messages and offers based on individual consumer data and preferences.

Sustainability: Practices that focus on reducing environmental impact and promoting long-term ecological balance.

Social responsibility: The engagement in activities that contribute to societal well-being and address social issues.

Impression management: Strategies employed by brands to influence consumer perceptions and enhance their image.

Consumer empowerment: The process through which consumers gain control over their choices and decisions, often through increased access to information and ethical options.

KEY LEARNING POINTS

- Ethical marketing integrates fairness, transparency and sustainability into business practices, prioritizing long-term relationships with consumers.
- Transparency regarding data collection and business practices fosters consumer trust and loyalty.
- Data privacy is crucial as consumers become more aware of their personal information and demand responsible handling.
- Corporate social responsibility enhances brand loyalty and positively influences consumer behaviour through alignment with ethical values.

- Personalized marketing has become essential in engaging consumers, but it requires a balance with ethical considerations and privacy concerns.
- Sustainability practices in business operations are increasingly demanded by consumers, impacting their purchasing decisions.
- Consumer empowerment allows individuals to make informed choices, driven by access to information and ethical options.
- Brands must adopt comprehensive CSR strategies, engaging stakeholders and transparently reporting their efforts to build a positive brand image.
- The evolution of technology and ethics will shape future consumer behaviour, requiring brands to adapt to changing expectations for ethical practices.

10 | The future of consumer behaviour in the digital era

Technological Advances		Strategic Approaches 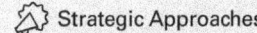
Artificial Intelligence Quantum Computing Blockchain	Modern Consumer Behaviour	Data-Driven Insights Consumer Feedback Market Segmentation

 Social Trends

Ethical Practices
Social Responsibility

LEARNING OBJECTIVES

By the end of this chapter, you should be able to:

- Understand the influence of technology: Identify how advancements in AI, quantum computing and blockchain are reshaping consumer behaviour and brand strategies.
- Apply data-driven insights: Utilize data analytics and consumer feedback to predict and respond effectively to evolving consumer preferences.
- Implement effective market segmentation: Develop strategies for market segmentation that address diverse consumer needs and enhance brand relevance.
- Evaluate case studies: Analyse real-world examples of brands that have successfully adapted to changes in consumer behaviour and assess their strategies.
- Anticipate future trends: Anticipate emerging trends in consumer behaviour and technology and propose strategies for maintaining brand agility and relevance.

CHAPTER OUTLINE

Understanding modern consumer behaviour:

- Technological impact: How advancements such as AI, quantum computing and blockchain are influencing consumer behaviour
- Social dynamics: The role of shifting social trends and their effects on consumer preferences

Strategic approaches for brands:

- Data-driven insights: Utilizing data analytics to predict and respond to consumer trends
- Consumer feedback: Incorporating direct consumer input into product development and marketing strategies
- Market segmentation: Effective segmentation strategies to address diverse consumer needs

Case studies and real-world applications:

- Innovative strategies: Analysis of brands that have successfully adapted to changing consumer behaviours
- Social responsibility: The impact of ethical practices and corporate responsibility on brand success

Future directions:

- Emerging trends: Anticipating future developments in consumer behaviour and technological impacts
- Adaptability and agility: Strategies for maintaining brand relevance in a rapidly changing environment

Introduction

In today's fast-evolving marketplace, understanding consumer behaviour is more crucial than ever. The digital revolution has dramatically transformed how consumers interact with brands, driven by advancements in technology and shifting social dynamics. This chapter delves into the complexities of modern consumer behaviour, exploring how rapid technological progress and changing social trends are reshaping consumer preferences. By examining contemporary case studies and strategic approaches, we aim to provide a comprehensive overview of how brands can anticipate and adapt to these changes.

The rise of artificial intelligence, quantum computing and blockchain technology has introduced new variables into consumer behaviour, influencing everything from purchasing decisions to brand loyalty. Additionally, social trends such as increasing consumer demand for ethical and socially responsible practices are shaping brand interactions. As brands navigate this landscape, leveraging data-driven insights, soliciting consumer feedback and employing effective market segmentation are essential strategies. This chapter will highlight real-world examples of brands that have successfully adapted to these shifts, providing valuable lessons for others seeking to maintain relevance and achieve success in the digital age.

The evolving landscape of consumer interactions, decision-making processes and purchasing habits is shaped by advancing digital technologies and online platforms. This future is characterized by increased personalization, seamless omnichannel experiences and data-driven marketing strategies that anticipate and respond to consumer needs in real-time.

Emerging technologies and their impact on consumer behaviour

Cutting-edge innovations such as artificial intelligence, virtual reality and the Internet of Things are influencing how consumers discover, evaluate and purchase products and services. These technologies are reshaping consumer expectations, creating new touchpoints for brand interactions and enabling more immersive and personalized shopping experiences across various industries.

Overview of emerging technologies

The rapid advancement of emerging technologies is poised to fundamentally reshape consumer behaviour in the digital era. As we stand on the cusp of transformative innovations, it is crucial to examine the potential impacts of these technologies on how consumers interact with products, services and brands.

Artificial Intelligence (AI) and **Machine Learning (ML)** are at the forefront of this technological revolution, offering unprecedented opportunities for personalization and predictive analytics. These technologies enable businesses to anticipate consumer needs with remarkable accuracy, potentially shifting the paradigm from reactive to proactive marketing strategies. As AI-driven recommendation systems become more sophisticated, they may significantly influence consumer decision-making processes, raising important questions about autonomy and choice architecture in the digital marketplace.

The **Internet of Things (IoT)** is another key technology that is likely to reshape consumer behaviour. As everyday objects become increasingly connected and data-enabled, consumers' physical and digital worlds are merging, creating new touchpoints for interaction and engagement. This ubiquitous connectivity may lead to more seamless and frictionless consumer experiences, but it also raises concerns about privacy and data security that marketers and policymakers must address.

Augmented Reality (AR) and **Virtual Reality (VR)** are set to revolutionize how consumers experience products and services before purchase. These immersive technologies have the potential to bridge the gap between online and offline shopping experiences, allowing consumers to virtually try products or experience services in a highly realistic manner. This could significantly impact decision-making processes, particularly for high-involvement purchases and may lead to changes in traditional retail models.

Blockchain technology, while still in its early stages of consumer-facing applications, has the potential to transform issues of trust, transparency and security in consumer transactions. As blockchain-based solutions become more widespread, they may influence how consumers perceive and interact with brands, particularly in areas such as supply chain transparency, authenticity verification and decentralized commerce.

5G and advanced wireless technologies are set to revolutionize connectivity, offering unprecedented speeds and low latency. This leap in network capability will enable real-time interactions and data processing, potentially transforming consumer expectations for service delivery and digital experiences. The proliferation of 5G may catalyze the adoption of other emerging technologies, such as IoT and AR/VR, by providing the necessary infrastructure for their seamless operation. This enhanced connectivity could lead to more immersive and responsive digital environments, altering how consumers engage with brands and make purchasing decisions.

Voice technology and **natural language processing** (NLP) are rapidly evolving, with virtual assistants becoming increasingly sophisticated. As these technologies advance, they may significantly alter the consumer interface landscape, moving away from traditional screen-based interactions towards more natural, conversational engagements. This shift could have profound implications for search behaviour, customer service expectations and the overall consumer journey, potentially necessitating new approaches to marketing and brand communication.

Biometric technologies, including facial recognition, fingerprint scanning and even DNA analysis, are becoming more prevalent in consumer applications. These technologies offer enhanced security and personalization but also raise critical questions about privacy and data protection. As biometrics become more integrated into consumer experiences, from payment systems to personalized marketing, they may fundamentally alter the balance between convenience and privacy in consumer behaviour.

Edge computing, which brings data processing closer to the point of collection, has the potential to significantly enhance real-time personalization and decision-making in consumer interactions. This technology could enable more responsive and context-aware services, potentially leading to more efficient and satisfying consumer experiences. However, it also presents challenges in terms of data management and security that will need to be addressed.

Quantum computing, while still in its nascent stages, holds the promise of solving complex problems at unprecedented speeds. In the context of consumer behaviour, quantum computing could revolutionize areas such as predictive analytics, optimization of supply chains and personalization algorithms. As this technology matures, it may enable businesses to understand and respond to consumer needs with a level of sophistication that is currently unattainable.

The impact of AI, machine learning and blockchain on consumer behaviour

The advent of artificial intelligence, machine learning and blockchain technologies is revolutionizing various sectors, fundamentally altering consumer behaviour in unprecedented ways. These technological advancements enable businesses to better understand consumer preferences, predict purchasing patterns and provide personalized experiences (Babikian, 2021; Babikian, 2022). The integration of AI and ML in consumer-facing applications has led to a paradigm shift, where companies can leverage vast amounts of data to tailor their offerings more precisely to individual needs. As a result, consumers are increasingly experiencing more relevant, timely and personalized interactions with brands (Shah and Shukla, 2019).

AI and ML algorithms are particularly influential in shaping consumer behaviour through personalized recommendations and targeted marketing strategies. For instance, AI-driven recommendation systems used by e-commerce platforms such as Amazon and Netflix analyse user data to suggest products or content that align with the consumer's past behaviour and preferences. This level of personalization fosters a sense of convenience and enhances the user experience, often leading to increased consumer satisfaction and loyalty (Babikian, 2020). Moreover, these algorithms can anticipate future purchasing behaviours, allowing companies to engage consumers proactively, thereby influencing decision-making processes and driving sales (Shah and Shukla, 2017).

Blockchain technology is redefining the concept of trust and transparency in the digital marketplace. Traditionally, consumers have relied on third-party intermediaries, such as banks and payment processors, to facilitate transactions. Blockchain disrupts this model by providing a decentralized and immutable ledger of transactions, which enhances security and reduces the risk of fraud (Babikian, 2019;

Babikian, 2017). This technology fosters a greater sense of trust among consumers, particularly in sectors where transparency and data integrity are paramount, such as financial services and supply chain management. By ensuring that every transaction is verifiable and tamper-proof, blockchain empowers consumers to make more informed choices based on reliable information.

Furthermore, the integration of AI, ML and blockchain technologies is enabling new forms of engagement and interaction between brands and consumers. AI and ML can be used to create intelligent virtual assistants and chatbots that provide real-time customer service, while blockchain can facilitate loyalty programmes that offer consumers tokenized rewards for their engagement (Babikian, 2021). These technologies collectively enhance the consumer journey by making it more interactive, personalized and secure. As consumers become more accustomed to these innovations, their expectations for digital experiences are evolving, driving companies to continuously adapt and innovate to meet these new demands (Shah and Shukla, 2023).

The impact of AI, machine learning and blockchain on consumer behaviour is profound and far-reaching. These technologies are not only enhancing the way businesses interact with consumers but also empowering consumers by providing them with more personalized, transparent and secure experiences. As technological advancements continue to evolve, they will undoubtedly play an increasingly pivotal role in shaping the future of consumer behaviour, prompting both opportunities and challenges for businesses in the digital age (Babikian, 2018).

ADAPTING CONSUMER DELIVERY SERVICES TO LOW-EMISSION ZONES

Background

As environmental concerns grow, many European cities have implemented low emission zones (LEZs) to reduce air pollution and greenhouse gas emissions. In France, these are known as ZFE-m (zones à faibles émissions mobilité). These regulations have significant implications for logistics companies and, consequently, for consumer behaviour and expectations regarding product delivery.

Challenge

Logistics companies face the challenge of adapting their delivery methods to comply with new regulations while maintaining efficient and cost-effective services. This adaptation is crucial as it directly impacts consumer satisfaction and behaviour in urban areas.

Solution: Mapo by Woop

Woop, a company specializing in last-mile delivery optimization, developed Mapo, a comprehensive platform designed to address the challenges posed by LEZs. Mapo offers several key features:

1. Route optimization considering LEZ restrictions.
2. Real-time tracking and updates.
3. Integration of multi-modal transport options.
4. Automated customer communication.

Implementation

Logistics companies using Mapo can:

- plan routes that comply with specific LEZ regulations in different cities
- utilize a mix of vehicle types, including low-emission options
- establish peripheral hubs for transferring goods to LEZ-compliant vehicles
- provide accurate delivery time estimates to consumers

Impact on consumer behaviour

The implementation of Mapo and similar technologies has led to several changes in consumer behaviour:

- Increased transparency: Consumers now expect real-time updates on their deliveries, including information about the environmental impact of their delivery choices.
- Shift in delivery preferences: Some consumers are opting for slightly longer delivery times if it means a more environmentally friendly option.
- Heightened awareness: Consumers are becoming more conscious of the environmental impact of their purchasing decisions, including the delivery process.
- Adaptation to new pickup points: With the establishment of peripheral hubs, some consumers are adapting to new pickup locations for their goods.

This case study demonstrates how technological solutions like Mapo are helping businesses adapt to new environmental regulations while simultaneously shaping consumer expectations and behaviours. It highlights the complex interplay between regulatory changes, technological innovations and evolving consumer preferences in the digital era.

As cities continue to implement stricter environmental policies, we can expect further evolution in last-mile delivery solutions and corresponding shifts in consumer behaviour. Future research could explore the long-term impact of these changes on urban consumer lifestyles and purchasing patterns.

Questions for discussion

- Understanding LEZs: What are LEZs and how do they differ from restricted circulation zones (RCZs)? Discuss the implications of these zones on urban logistics.
- Regulatory impact: How have recent laws, such as the Climate and Resilience Law of 2021*, influenced the logistics industry in France? What specific challenges do these regulations pose for transport companies?
    - * Law No. 2021-1104 of August 22, 2021 on combating climate change and strengthening resilience to its effects (the Climate and Resilience Law), adopted on July 20, 2021, was promulgated on August 24, 2021.
- Technological solutions: Analyse how technologies like Mapo by Woop can help logistics companies comply with LEZ regulations. What features of this platform are particularly beneficial for optimizing last-mile delivery?
- Consumer behaviour: In what ways might the implementation of LEZs and the use of digital logistics solutions affect consumer purchasing decisions and expectations regarding delivery services?
- Environmental considerations: Discuss the environmental benefits of optimizing delivery routes within LEZs. How can logistics companies balance efficiency with sustainability in their operations?
- Case study analysis: Based on the case of Monsieur A., a distributor of DIY materials, evaluate how the integration of Mapo has transformed his logistics operations. What specific advantages does he gain from using this technology?
- Future trends: Considering the ongoing evolution of urban mobility regulations, what future trends do you foresee in consumer behaviour related to logistics and delivery services? How might companies need to adapt their strategies?
- Challenges and opportunities: Identify the main challenges faced by logistics companies in adapting to LEZ regulations. Conversely, what opportunities might arise from these challenges for businesses willing to innovate?

Predictions for future technological developments

As technological advancements continue to evolve, the future of consumer behaviour will be significantly shaped by innovations in AI, ML and blockchain. These technologies are expected to drive new trends and developments that will redefine how consumers interact with businesses and experience digital environments:

- Increased personalization and predictive analytics: As AI and machine learning technologies advance, there will be greater emphasis on personalization in consumer interactions. Companies will continue to develop more sophisticated algorithms that can predict consumer preferences and behaviours with higher accuracy. This will lead to even more tailored and proactive marketing strategies, enhancing customer experiences and fostering loyalty.
- Expansion of blockchain for trust and transparency: The adoption of blockchain technology is likely to expand beyond its current applications in financial services and supply chain management. As consumers demand more transparency and data security, blockchain could become a standard tool for ensuring the integrity of transactions and data across various industries. This could lead to broader applications in areas like healthcare, digital identity and voting systems, where trust and verification are critical.
- Integration of AI and blockchain for enhanced consumer engagement: Future developments may see a convergence of AI and blockchain technologies to create more interactive and secure consumer experiences. For example, **AI-driven chatbots** and **virtual assistants** could leverage blockchain to verify user identities and transactions, ensuring secure and seamless interactions. This integration could also enhance loyalty programmes and gamification strategies, offering consumers blockchain-based rewards that are both valuable and tamper-proof.
- Evolution of consumer expectations and digital experiences: As consumers become more accustomed to the benefits of AI, machine learning and blockchain, their expectations for digital experiences will continue to evolve. Companies will need to innovate continuously to meet these higher expectations, focusing on creating more engaging, personalized and secure interactions. This could drive the development of new technologies and platforms that prioritize user experience and privacy.
- Development of ethical and legal frameworks: With the increasing impact of AI, machine learning and blockchain on consumer behaviour, there will be a growing need for comprehensive ethical and legal frameworks to govern these technologies. Future developments may include new regulations and standards that address concerns around data privacy, security and ethical AI use, ensuring that technological advancements benefit consumers without compromising their rights or safety.

Quantum computing and consumer behaviour: a new frontier

Quantum computing, an emerging field poised to revolutionize the computational landscape, has the potential to significantly influence consumer behaviour and decision-making processes (Pasin et al., 2024). This advanced technology leverages the principles of quantum mechanics to perform complex calculations at unprecedented speeds, potentially transforming the way businesses analyse consumer data and predict market trends (Nielsen and Chuang, 2001). Unlike classical computing, which processes information in binary (0s and 1s), quantum computing utilizes quantum bits or qubits, which can represent and process multiple states simultaneously (LaPierre, 2021). This capability allows for more sophisticated modelling of consumer preferences and behaviours, offering a deeper understanding of market dynamics and enhancing predictive accuracy (Gibney, 2019).

Enhanced personalization through quantum algorithms

One of the most promising applications of quantum computing in consumer behaviour is the enhancement of personalization strategies. Quantum algorithms can process vast amounts of data and uncover intricate patterns that classical algorithms might miss (Ladd et al., 2010). For example, quantum-enhanced machine learning models can analyse consumer interactions across various touchpoints – such as social media, purchase history and browsing behaviour – more efficiently (Biamonte et al., 2017). This enables businesses to create highly personalized marketing strategies and recommendations tailored to individual preferences with greater precision. By harnessing **quantum computing**, companies can move beyond traditional demographic-based segmentation and engage consumers in a more meaningful and individualized manner (Dunjko and Briegel, 2018).

Optimizing supply chain and logistics with quantum computing

In addition to personalization, quantum computing holds the potential to optimize supply chain and logistics operations, which directly impact consumer satisfaction. The ability of quantum computers to solve complex optimization problems quickly can lead to more efficient inventory management, improved demand forecasting and streamlined distribution processes (Kadowaki, 2002). For instance, quantum algorithms can tackle the 'travelling salesman problem' more effectively, ensuring that delivery routes are optimized to reduce costs and improve delivery times (Hao et al.,

2001). This optimization can enhance the overall consumer experience by ensuring product availability, timely delivery and reduced costs, all of which are critical factors influencing consumer satisfaction and loyalty (Grover, 1996).

Ethical considerations and data privacy

As quantum computing becomes more integrated into consumer behaviour analysis, ethical considerations and data privacy concerns must be addressed. The power of quantum computing to process and analyse vast amounts of personal data raises questions about data security and privacy (Shor, 1994). Businesses will need to implement robust data protection measures and transparent practices to ensure that consumer information is handled responsibly (Arute et al., 2019). Additionally, as quantum computing capabilities advance, regulatory frameworks will need to evolve to address new challenges related to data privacy and ethical use of technology (Perrier, 2021). Ensuring consumer trust while leveraging quantum computing's potential will be crucial for maintaining positive relationships and fostering ethical practices in the digital age.

Table 10.1 Key points on quantum computing and its impact

Topic	Description	References
Quantum computing overview	Quantum computing utilizes quantum bits (qubits) to perform calculations at speeds and complexities beyond classical computers, impacting various fields including consumer behaviour analysis.	Nielsen & Chuang (2001), Romero-Álvarez et al. (2024)
Personalization enhancement	Quantum algorithms enable advanced data processing and pattern recognition, allowing for highly personalized marketing strategies and improved consumer engagement by analysing interactions across multiple touchpoints.	Biamonte et al. (2017), Dunjko & Briegel (2018)
Supply chain optimization	Quantum computing can solve complex optimization problems efficiently, leading to better inventory management, demand forecasting, and distribution processes, which enhances product availability and delivery times.	Kadowaki et al. (2002), Hao et al., 2001
Ethical considerations	The power of quantum computing raises concerns about data privacy and security. Businesses need to implement robust data protection measures and adapt to evolving regulatory frameworks to address these concerns.	Arute et al. (2019), Perrier, (2021)
Future implications and insights	As quantum computing advances, it will offer new tools and insights for understanding and predicting consumer behaviour, potentially giving companies a competitive edge and fostering innovation in data-driven decision-making.	Montanaro (2016), Arute et al. (2019)

Future implications and consumer insights

Looking ahead, the integration of quantum computing into consumer behaviour research promises to unlock new insights and drive innovation. As quantum technology matures, its applications will likely expand, offering even more advanced tools for understanding and predicting consumer behaviour (Montanaro, 2016). Researchers and businesses must stay abreast of developments in quantum computing to leverage its benefits effectively. By embracing this technology, companies can gain a competitive edge, make data-driven decisions and ultimately enhance their understanding of consumer preferences and market trends (Arute et al., 2019).

To illustrate the transformative potential of quantum computing on consumer behaviour and related fields, Table 10.1 outlines key aspects of its impact, including personalization enhancement, supply chain optimization and ethical considerations, supported by relevant academic references.

The rise of voice commerce and Internet of Things in consumer decision-making

Understanding consumer behaviour through neuromarketing

Consumer behaviour has traditionally been studied through surveys and focus groups, but recent advances in neuromarketing have provided deeper insights into how consumers respond to marketing stimuli at a neurological level (Alsharif et al., 2024). **Neuromarketing** combines neuroscience and marketing to explore how brain activity influences consumer decision-making. This interdisciplinary field leverages techniques such as **EEG** and **fMRI** to understand the cognitive and emotional processes underlying consumer behaviour (Vecchiato et al., 2010; Plassmann et al., 2012).

One of the key areas of interest in neuromarketing is the impact of emotional responses on brand evaluations. Research by Pham et al. (2013) highlights how ad-evoked feelings can significantly alter brand perceptions. The emotional resonance of advertisements can enhance brand recall and preference, a phenomenon supported by findings from Plassmann et al. (2008), who showed that marketing actions can modulate neural representations of pleasantness. This suggests that effective marketing strategies are those that can successfully tap into consumers' emotional circuits.

Neuromarketing also investigates the influence of visual and auditory stimuli on consumer attention. For example, Spence (2020) discusses the ethical considerations of sensory marketing, where the manipulation of sensory inputs can subtly guide consumer behaviour. The role of visual elements in advertising has been extensively studied, with research by Pieters and Wedel (2004) demonstrating how variations in pictorial and text sizes affect attention capture and transfer, influencing overall advertising effectiveness.

Moreover, the integration of neuromarketing insights into advertising strategy has been shown to enhance the efficacy of campaigns. Venkatraman et al. (2015) found that incorporating neuromarketing data into market response modelling can lead to more accurate predictions of advertising success. This approach enables marketers to refine their strategies based on real-time neurophysiological data, thereby increasing the likelihood of achieving desired consumer responses.

The intersection of neuroscience and marketing provides valuable insights into consumer behaviour that go beyond traditional methods. By understanding the neural underpinnings of emotional and cognitive responses to marketing stimuli, businesses can craft more effective advertisements and product placements. As neuromarketing continues to evolve, it promises to deepen our understanding of consumer decision-making processes and improve marketing practices.

Understanding voice commerce and the Internet of Things

Voice commerce and the IoT represent transformative advancements in the consumer experience, reshaping how individuals interact with technology and make purchasing decisions. Voice commerce, or v-commerce, leverages voice-activated devices to facilitate transactions, reflecting a significant shift in consumer behaviour towards more seamless and intuitive shopping experiences (McLean and Osei-Frimpong, 2019).

Voice-activated assistants, such as Amazon's Alexa and Google Assistant, have become integral to modern IoT ecosystems. These devices enable users to execute a range of tasks, from setting reminders to ordering products simply through voice commands. This convenience has led to an increase in voice-driven purchases, highlighting a shift in consumer preferences towards hands-free interactions (Flavián et al., 2023). McLean and Osei-Frimpong (2019) found that consumers appreciate the efficiency and ease of voice commerce, which reduces friction in the purchasing process.

The integration of IoT with **voice commerce** further amplifies these benefits. IoT devices create a network of interconnected gadgets that can communicate with each other, providing a more cohesive and responsive user experience. For example, a **smart refrigerator** might automatically reorder groceries when supplies run low, based on data gathered from user behaviour and preferences (Grewal et al., 2021). This interconnectedness not only enhances convenience but also personalizes the consumer experience, making it more relevant to individual needs and habits.

Moreover, the data collected through IoT devices plays a crucial role in shaping consumer behaviour. By analysing patterns in voice commands and device interactions, businesses can gain valuable insights into consumer preferences and purchasing patterns (Im et al., 2023).

This data-driven approach allows for more targeted marketing strategies and product recommendations, ultimately leading to a more engaging and effective consumer experience.

Despite the advantages, the rise of voice commerce and IoT raises important considerations regarding privacy and security. As these technologies collect and process vast amounts of personal data, ensuring robust data protection measures is essential to maintaining consumer trust (Huang and Cai, 2023). Addressing these concerns will be crucial as the adoption of voice commerce and the IoT continues to grow.

Table 10.2 Overview of voice commerce and the Internet of Things (IoT)

Aspect	Description	Key research findings	References
Voice commerce (V-commerce)	Utilizes voice-activated devices to facilitate transactions and interact with technology.	Voice commerce enhances convenience and reduces friction in the purchasing process. Users value the efficiency of voice-driven transactions.	McLean & Osei-Frimpong (2019)
IoT integration	Network of interconnected devices that communicate with each other to enhance user experience.	IoT devices, such as smart refrigerators, can automate tasks and personalize consumer experiences based on collected data.	Grewal et al. (2021)
Data-driven insights	Analysis of data from IoT devices to understand consumer preferences and behaviour.	Data from voice commands and device interactions provides insights into consumer behaviour, leading to targeted marketing and product recommendations.	Arute et al. (2019)
Privacy and security	Concerns related to the protection of personal data collected by voice and IoT devices.	Ensuring robust data protection measures is crucial to maintain consumer trust and address privacy concerns.	Perrier (2021)
Consumer behaviour impact	Changes in how consumers interact with brands and make purchasing decisions due to these technologies.	Voice commerce and IoT facilitate more intuitive, efficient, and personalized shopping experiences.	McLean & Osei-Frimpong (2019); Grewal et al. (2021)

Voice commerce and the IoT are revolutionizing consumer behaviour by offering more intuitive, efficient and personalized shopping experiences. As these technologies advance, they will likely play an increasingly central role in shaping the future of consumer interactions with brands and products. Table 10.2 highlights key aspects of voice commerce and the IoT, their impact on consumer behaviour and relevant research findings.

How these technologies influence consumer decisions

In recent years, advancements in technology have significantly reshaped consumer behaviour, particularly through the proliferation of voice assistants and online reviews. Voice assistants, such as Amazon's Alexa and Google's Assistant, have become integral to everyday life, offering users convenience and personalized interaction. These technologies influence consumer decisions by providing immediate responses to queries and personalized recommendations, which can impact purchasing behaviour and brand perception (Flavián et al., 2023). The integration of voice assistants into daily routines has altered the way consumers interact with technology and make purchasing decisions, often favouring simplicity and speed over traditional methods.

Online reviews, another crucial element in modern consumer decision-making, play a substantial role in shaping perceptions and influencing purchases. The credibility and helpfulness of these reviews are paramount; studies have shown that consumers heavily rely on online reviews to gauge product quality and make informed decisions (Mudambi and Schuff, 2010; Purnawirawan et al., 2012). The balance and sequence of information presented in reviews also affect consumer attitudes and intentions (Purnawirawan et al., 2012). As a result, businesses are increasingly focused on managing their **online reputation** and leveraging positive reviews to attract customers.

The intersection of voice technology and **online reviews** presents a unique dynamic in consumer behaviour. Voice assistants not only provide information but also aggregate and filter reviews, influencing how users perceive and interact with products and services (Klaus and Zaichkowsky, 2020). The integration of these technologies allows for a more streamlined decision-making process, as consumers can access comprehensive reviews and personalized recommendations simultaneously. This convergence of voice technology and online reviews underscores the importance of managing both aspects effectively to meet evolving consumer expectations and preferences (Schweitzer et al., 2019; Xiao et al., 2021).

The influence of voice assistants and online reviews on consumer behaviour highlights the shift towards digital and automated decision-making processes. These technologies not only facilitate convenience and personalization, they also shape how consumers perceive and act upon information. As technology continues to evolve, understanding these influences becomes crucial for businesses aiming to optimize their customer interactions and enhance decision-making processes (Mariani et al., 2021; Schepers et al., 2022).

Future trends in voice commerce and IOT

As technology continues to evolve, voice commerce and the IoT are poised to significantly transform consumer behaviour and interaction. The integration of voice assistants into everyday life is advancing rapidly, with projections indicating that voice assistants will be ubiquitous, influencing various aspects of consumer transactions and interactions (PricewaterhouseCoopers, 2018). This section explores the anticipated trends and their implications for consumer behaviour.

1. Increased integration and personalization

The personalization of voice interactions is set to become a cornerstone of future voice commerce. As voice assistants become more sophisticated, they will leverage data from multiple IoT devices to offer highly personalized experiences (Vernuccio et al., 2023). Advanced algorithms and machine learning models will enable voice assistants to understand user preferences and behaviours more accurately, leading to more relevant product recommendations and personalized shopping experiences. This trend is supported by findings that consumers are increasingly receptive to algorithm-recommended products, demonstrating a growing trust in AI-driven suggestions (Xie et al., 2022).

2. Enhanced human-likeness and empathy

The human-likeness of voice assistants is expected to improve, with research indicating that consumers prefer interactions with voice assistants that exhibit human-like traits, such as empathy and a natural tone (Niculescu et al., 2013; Urakami et al., 2020). This shift towards more **anthropomorphic voice interactions** aims to create a more engaging and satisfying user experience. For instance, voice assistants will increasingly employ varied pitch, humour and empathetic responses to build rapport with users, thereby enhancing user satisfaction and trust (Salem et al., 2013).

3. Expansion of voice commerce applications

Voice commerce is anticipated to expand beyond traditional retail, integrating into various aspects of daily life and IoT ecosystems. This expansion includes increased adoption of voice-activated transactions in smart homes, where consumers can control home appliances, manage household tasks and make purchases through voice commands (Schreibelmayr and Mara, 2022). As IoT devices become more interconnected, voice assistants will serve as central hubs for managing and automating various functions, making them integral to modern smart living environments.

4. Trust and privacy concerns

Despite the advancements, trust and privacy concerns will remain critical challenges. Research highlights that trust in voice-based AI is influenced by factors such as the anthropomorphism of the voice assistant and the transparency of data usage (Pitardi and Marriott, 2021). Ensuring robust data protection and clear communication about how user data is handled will be essential to maintaining consumer confidence and fostering widespread adoption of voice commerce.

5. Evolving user expectations and experience

User expectations for voice interfaces are continually evolving, with a growing demand for seamless and intuitive interactions. As voice technology matures, consumers will expect more sophisticated responses and capabilities from voice assistants, including the ability to handle complex queries and provide accurate information (Nass et al., 1997). This evolution will drive continuous innovation in voice interface design, aiming to meet and exceed user expectations.

The future of voice commerce and IoT is characterized by greater personalization, enhanced human-likeness, expanded applications and ongoing challenges related to trust and privacy. As these technologies continue to develop, they will reshape consumer behaviour, making voice assistants an integral part of the modern digital ecosystem.

Anticipating and adapting to changing consumer behaviour trends

Consumer behaviour is evolving rapidly, driven by technological advancements and shifting societal norms. Maria Mercanti-Guérin, in her insightful work *Web Crash*, highlights the intricate dynamics of this evolution. Historically, consumer behaviour was shaped by traditional media channels – newspapers, television and radio. These mediums dictated the flow of information and, consequently, influenced consumer preferences in a relatively straightforward manner (Mercanti-Guérin, 2024). However, as digital platforms have emerged, consumer behaviour has fragmented and diversified. The transition to digital media has introduced new variables such as instant accessibility, personalized content and a plethora of choices that challenge conventional marketing strategies. This shift necessitates an adaptive approach for businesses aiming to remain relevant in an increasingly digital marketplace (Mercanti-Guérin, 2024).

The role of personalization and real-time engagement

One of the most significant trends in consumer behaviour is the demand for personalization and real-time engagement. Mercanti-Guérin underscores that modern consumers expect tailored experiences that cater to their individual preferences and needs. This expectation is fuelled by the capabilities of AI and ML, which allow for unprecedented levels of personalization (Mercanti-Guérin, 2024). For instance, algorithms on platforms like Amazon and Netflix analyse user behaviour to recommend products and content that align with their interests, creating a more engaging and relevant experience. Businesses must leverage these technologies to meet consumer expectations and enhance their competitive edge.

The impact of social media and influencer culture

Social media platforms have profoundly reshaped consumer behaviour by creating new avenues for influence and engagement. Mercanti-Guérin explores how social media has become a central force in shaping consumer opinions and driving purchasing decisions (Mercanti-Guérin, 2024). Influencers and user-generated content now play a crucial role in marketing strategies, as consumers increasingly turn to social media for product recommendations and reviews. This shift requires brands to adapt by developing robust social media strategies and fostering relationships with influencers who can authentically connect with their target audience.

Navigating the challenges of digital advertising

Despite the opportunities presented by digital advertising, Mercanti-Guérin highlights several challenges that businesses face. The effectiveness of digital ads is often questioned due to issues such as **ad fatigue** and the prevalence of **ad blockers** (Mercanti-Guérin, 2024). Consumers are becoming more adept at avoiding intrusive ads, leading to diminished returns on advertising investments. To address these challenges, brands must innovate their advertising approaches, focusing on creating value-driven content that resonates with consumers and avoids being perceived as intrusive.

Preparing for the future: adapting to emerging trends

Looking ahead, Mercanti-Guérin emphasizes the importance of anticipating and adapting to emerging trends in consumer behaviour (Mercanti-Guérin, 2024). As new technologies and platforms continue to evolve, businesses must remain **agile** and **responsive** to shifts in consumer preferences. This involves investing in research and development, staying abreast of technological advancements and continually refining marketing strategies to align with changing consumer expectations. By doing so, businesses can better navigate the complexities of the digital age and maintain their relevance in a dynamic marketplace.

Table 10.3 provides an overview of key topics in consumer behaviour, including descriptions and recent examples or applications that illustrate how these concepts are manifested in contemporary contexts.

Table 10.3 Key topics in consumer behaviour on anticipating and adapting to changing consumer behaviour trends

Topic	Description	Recent example/Application
Impact of communication innovations	Examines how major communication revolutions, from parchment to AI, have shaped human knowledge and information access.	**AI-powered chatbots:** Tools like GPT-4 provide real-time answers and customer support, transforming how information is accessed and communicated.
Knowledge storage	Highlights the idea of storing knowledge internally, comparing it to modern information access where external devices are used.	**Cloud storage services:** Platforms like Google Drive and Dropbox store vast amounts of data externally, allowing easy access from multiple devices.
Information access evolution	Discusses the shift from internal knowledge storage to external information systems, from parchments to digital media.	**Digital libraries:** Projects like Google Books digitize and archive physical texts, making them readily accessible online.
Television and passive consumption	Describes how television contributed to passive consumption and compares it to modern media like TikTok that reinforce this passivity.	**TikTok:** This platform's short-form video content encourages passive consumption and endless scrolling, similar to the passive nature of traditional TV viewing.
Minitel's impact	Explains how the Minitel system revolutionized access to information by allowing users to access services and information at any time, paving the way for the internet.	**Online banking:** Modern online banking services offer immediate access to financial information and transactions, a direct evolution from Minitel's early online services.

(continued)

Table 10.3 (Continued)

Topic	Description	Recent example/Application
Age of knowability	Introduces the concept of an 'Age of knowability,' where technology enables instant knowledge, creating a new kind of consumer anxiety about information access.	**AI search engines:** Advanced search engines like Google and Bing provide instant answers to queries, often leading to information overload and anxiety.
Post-web future	Speculates on a future where information is seamlessly integrated into real-time experiences through augmented reality and other emerging technologies.	**Augmented reality:** AR applications like Microsoft's HoloLens integrate digital information into the physical world, enhancing real-time knowledge access.
Web's economic crisis	Analyses the crisis facing the web despite its apparent growth, including issues related to advertising revenue and infrastructure investment.	**Ad blockers:** The rise in ad blockers reflects the dissatisfaction with digital advertising, impacting revenue streams for online platforms.
Difference between web and internet	Clarifies the distinction between the internet as an infrastructure and the web as an application layer, with different implications for future developments.	**Internet of Things (IoT):** IoT devices operate over the internet infrastructure but often use proprietary applications that differ from traditional web interfaces.
Illusion of digital advertising efficiency	Critiques the perceived effectiveness of digital advertising, highlighting the discrepancy between expected and actual engagement rates.	**Digital ad fatigue:** Many users experience ad fatigue due to oversaturation, leading to lower engagement rates than anticipated by advertisers.
Potential web failures	Explores potential scenarios where the web could face significant disruptions or collapse, impacting societal functions and knowledge sharing.	**Data breaches:** High-profile data breaches, such as the 2017 Equifax breach, demonstrate vulnerabilities in web infrastructure that could lead to significant disruptions.
Future internet models	Discusses various future models of the internet, including more regulated or monopolized systems, and their potential implications.	**Net neutrality debates:** Ongoing discussions about net neutrality and its potential impacts on internet access and innovation reflect concerns about future internet regulation.

The importance of staying ahead of consumer trends

The metaverse as a growth opportunity

According to Laurent Flores in his book *Metaverse Marketing*, the metaverse represents a significant growth opportunity for numerous industries over the next decade. This potential is largely attributed to the wide range of applications and uses that the metaverse can support, as well as the substantial investments being made by major technology companies, venture capital firms, corporations and brands (Flores, 2022).

Perception of the metaverse

Despite the enthusiasm among industry leaders, Flores notes that for many people, the metaverse remains a nebulous and distant concept (Flores, 2022). This perception challenge is exemplified by the general public's limited understanding of what the metaverse actually entails. A survey conducted by CivicScience in 2022 found that 68 per cent of respondents had either never heard of the metaverse or did not understand it well. This indicates that while the metaverse is gaining traction among businesses and tech enthusiasts, there is still significant work to be done to educate the broader public about its possibilities and applications.

In the rapidly evolving landscape of digital technology and consumer behaviour, staying ahead of consumer trends is not just a strategic advantage for businesses, it is a necessity. As highlighted in the exploration of metaverse applications in education and marketing, the ability to anticipate and adapt to emerging trends can significantly influence a company's success. For example, the course I built and gave last year by on 'Metaverse integration for wine marketing' demonstrates the innovative use of metaverse technologies to enhance marketing strategies. By creating immersive virtual environments that educate consumers about the wine industry and leveraging NFTs for digital wine sales, businesses can engage with consumers in novel ways that align with contemporary digital experiences. This proactive approach to embracing new technologies ensures that companies remain relevant and appealing to tech-savvy consumers who value unique, interactive experiences.

Furthermore, the shift towards sustainable practices in digital environments underscores another critical consumer trend. As consumers become increasingly aware of the environmental impact of their digital activities, businesses must adapt by minimizing their **carbon footprint**. This is particularly evident in the adoption of Web3 technologies, which were discussed in the qualitative study of the course on metaverse integration. The study revealed that participants saw added value in using these technologies, not just for their novelty but also for their potential to promote eco-friendly practices. The incorporation of such technologies indicates a growing consumer demand for sustainability in digital engagements, suggesting that businesses that prioritize eco-responsibility are more likely to attract and retain consumers who are conscious of their environmental impact (WCED, 1987; The Shift Project, 2018).

In addition, staying ahead of consumer trends involves understanding the role of gender and social influence in technology acceptance and usage behaviour. Venkatesh and Morris (2000) highlight the importance of considering these factors when introducing new technologies to the market. Businesses that are aware of how different demographics interact with technology can tailor their marketing strategies more effectively, ensuring a broader appeal and a higher rate of adoption. For instance, in the context of the metaverse, understanding how different groups perceive and use these digital spaces can help businesses create more inclusive and appealing experiences.

Ultimately, staying ahead of consumer trends requires a multifaceted approach that incorporates technological innovation, sustainability and an understanding of consumer behaviour. By doing so, businesses can not only meet current consumer expectations but also anticipate future needs, positioning themselves as leaders in their industries. This approach is supported by the growing body of research that underscores the importance of agility and forward-thinking in consumer engagement strategies (Žalėnienė and Pereira, 2021; Wynn and Jones, 2023).

The future of digital marketing in the metaverse

Flores argues that the future of digital marketing is intrinsically linked to the evolution of the metaverse. He suggests that brands cannot afford to ignore this emerging digital realm, as the next wave of digital marketing will likely unfold within these virtual spaces (Flores, 2022). This is already evident in the actions of companies like Nike and Gucci, which have launched virtual products and experiences within metaverse platforms such as Roblox and Decentraland. These early adopters are experimenting with new ways to engage consumers in immersive environments, thus setting the stage for a broader shift towards metaverse-centric marketing strategies. Table 10.4 outlines the critical considerations for businesses looking to leverage the metaverse and stay ahead of consumer trends in the evolving landscape of digital marketing.

Strategies for anticipating consumer behaviour changes

As explained by Mhalla (2024) in her book *Technopolitique*, anticipating shifts in consumer behaviour is crucial for brands aiming to maintain relevance in an

Table 10.4 Leverage the metaverse and stay ahead

Topic	Key points	References
Introduction to consumer trends	Staying ahead of consumer trends is crucial for businesses to maintain relevance and competitive advantage in a rapidly changing market.	Venkatesh & Morris (2000)
Metaverse integration in marketing	Utilizing metaverse technologies for marketing, such as creating immersive virtual environments and integrating NFTs, enhances consumer engagement and sales.	Course syllabus: Metaverse Integration for Wine Marketing (on demand with the author)
Sustainability in digital practices	As consumers become more environmentally conscious, integrating sustainable practices in digital engagements is essential for businesses to meet consumer expectations.	The Shift Project (2018); WCED (1987)
Impact of Web3 technologies	The adoption of Web3 technologies can add value by promoting eco-friendly practices, appealing to consumers who prioritize sustainability.	Qualitative study on metaverse integration (on demand with the author)
Gender and social influence on technology	Understanding the role of gender and social influence in technology acceptance helps businesses tailor strategies to diverse consumer groups.	Venkatesh & Morris (2000)
Consumer demand for innovation	Consumers are drawn to novel, interactive digital experiences; businesses that innovate and leverage new technologies are more likely to attract and retain these consumers.	Wynn & Jones (2023); Žalėnienė & Pereira (2021)
Corporate responsibility	Emphasizing corporate responsibility, including eco-responsibility and ethical practices, is increasingly important to meet the demands of socially conscious consumers.	Wynn & Jones (2023)

ever-evolving market. One effective strategy is leveraging advanced data analytics and AI to predict trends. As discussed by Nita Farahany in *The Battle for Your Brain* (2023), neurotechnology can offer insights into consumer preferences and behaviours by analysing neurological responses. This approach allows companies to preemptively adjust their strategies based on emerging consumer needs and desires. By integrating AI-driven tools, brands can enhance their ability to forecast trends and adapt their offerings accordingly.

Additionally, understanding the socio-political context in which consumers operate can provide valuable insights. For instance, the changing landscape of digital regulation, as outlined in the European Digital Services Act (2023), has significant implications for consumer behaviour. Companies that stay informed about legislative changes and adjust their strategies in response are better positioned to address consumer concerns and preferences. This proactive approach ensures that brands remain aligned with regulatory developments and maintain consumer trust.

Lastly, brands can benefit from adopting a scenario planning approach. According to Stephen Marche's *USA. La Prochaine Guerre Civile* (2023), scenario planning involves creating multiple potential future scenarios and developing strategies to address each one. By preparing for various contingencies, companies can be more agile in responding to unexpected shifts in consumer behaviour, thereby maintaining a competitive edge in volatile markets.

ACTIVITY 1

Data-driven strategy development

Objective: To develop practical skills in leveraging data for strategic planning.

Instructions: Give the class sample data sets related to consumer behaviour (e.g. sales data, survey results).

Have students work individually or in pairs to analyse the data and identify trends. Ask students to propose a marketing or product strategy based on their data analysis.

Students will present their strategies and explain how they used the data to inform their decisions.

Examples of brands successfully adapting to changes

Several brands have demonstrated remarkable adaptability in response to changes in consumer behaviour. One notable example is the technology company Apple. As highlighted in the article from Le Grand Continent (2020), Apple has successfully navigated shifts in consumer preferences by continuously innovating its product lineup and incorporating advanced technologies. By anticipating the growing demand for privacy and security features, Apple introduced enhanced encryption and data protection measures, aligning with consumer concerns about digital privacy.

Another exemplary case is Amazon's response to the Covid-19 pandemic. The company adapted its operations to meet the surge in online shopping and changes in consumer behaviour by rapidly scaling its logistics network and implementing new safety protocols. According to the article from *La Tribune* (2022), Amazon's ability to pivot and enhance its delivery infrastructure during the pandemic allowed it to capitalize on increased e-commerce demand and maintain customer satisfaction.

A further example can be seen in the strategic adjustments made by the food and beverage industry. For instance, PepsiCo's launch of its 'PepsiCo Positive' initiative, as detailed by the article from *The Atlantic* (2021), demonstrates the company's commitment to sustainability and health-conscious consumer trends. By investing in sustainable practices and healthier product options, PepsiCo has successfully adapted to changing consumer expectations and reinforced its market position.

Table 10.5 presents case studies of brands that have successfully adapted to shifts in consumer behaviour by implementing innovative strategies and solutions.

In an era of rapid technological advancement and shifting social dynamics, consumer behaviour has become increasingly complex and unpredictable (Mhalla, 2024). Understanding these changes is critical for brands striving to maintain relevance and achieve success. We must delve into the strategic approaches that companies can employ

Table 10.5 Examples of brands

Brand	Adaptation	Description	Source
Apple	Enhanced privacy and security features	Apple introduced advanced encryption and privacy features in response to growing consumer concerns about digital privacy and data security.	Le Grand Continent (2020). Capitalisme politique
Amazon	Expansion of logistics network and safety protocols	During the Covid-19 pandemic, Amazon rapidly scaled its logistics operations and implemented new safety measures to meet the surge in online shopping.	*La Tribune* (2022). Si la Chine envahit Taiwan, son économie sera bloquée
PepsiCo	Launch of 'PepsiCo Positive' initiative	PepsiCo invested in sustainable practices and healthier product options to align with changing consumer preferences for sustainability and health.	*The Atlantic* (2021). Can tech reshape the Pentagon?
Nike	Digital transformation and direct-to-consumer sales	Nike accelerated its digital transformation by enhancing its e-commerce platform and launching new direct-to-consumer sales channels to meet the increased demand for online shopping.	Forbes (2022). Nike's Digital Strategy

(continued)

Table 10.5 (Continued)

Brand	Adaptation	Description	Source
Netflix	Investment in original content and global expansion	Netflix invested heavily in producing original content and expanding its service globally to adapt to the changing landscape of media consumption and competition.	Variety (2022). Netflix's Global Strategy
Tesla	Shift to sustainable energy and innovations in electric vehicles	Tesla focused on developing sustainable energy solutions and innovative electric vehicles to cater to the growing consumer demand for eco-friendly transportation.	Bloomberg (2023). Tesla's Innovations
Starbucks	Implementation of mobile ordering and contactless payments	Starbucks enhanced its digital capabilities by introducing mobile ordering and contactless payment options, responding to the increasing demand for convenience and safety.	Business Insider (2022). Starbucks' Digital Transformation
Zoom	Expansion of features and scalability for remote work	Zoom rapidly expanded its platform features and scalability to accommodate the growing demand for remote work and virtual meetings during the pandemic.	TechCrunch (2022). Zoom's Adaptation
L'Oréal	Emphasis on digital beauty solutions and virtual try-ons	L'Oréal adopted digital beauty solutions, including virtual try-ons and AI-powered skincare consultations, to adapt to changing consumer preferences for online beauty experiences.	WWD (2022). L'Oréal's Digital Strategy

to anticipate and adapt to evolving consumer preferences. By examining real-world case studies, we aim to highlight effective strategies that not only address current market trends but also position brands for future growth. Navigating the intricacies of consumer behaviour requires a proactive and adaptable approach. As outlined in this book, leveraging data-driven insights, soliciting direct consumer feedback and employing strategic market segmentation are essential for anticipating changes in consumer preferences. The case studies presented underscore how innovative strategies and a commitment to social responsibility can significantly impact a brand's success. As we look to the future, it is clear that brands must remain agile and continuously evolve to meet the ever-changing demands of their consumers.

> **ACTIVITY 2**
>
> Future trends forecasting
>
> **Objective**: To enhance skills in anticipating and preparing for future developments.
>
> **Instructions**: Assign each student or group a different emerging trend related to consumer behaviour or technology (e.g. advancements in AI, changes in social media usage).
>
> Ask them to research and forecast how this trend might impact consumer behaviour and brand strategies in the next 5–10 years.
>
> Students will create a brief presentation outlining their forecasts and suggested strategies for brands to stay ahead of the trend.

Conclusion

In this chapter, we explored the dynamic intersection of consumer behaviour and technological advancements, particularly in the context of AI and quantum computing. As consumers increasingly engage with brands through digital platforms, understanding their motivations and interactions has become vital for marketers. The integration of AI in consumer engagement strategies not only enhances personalization but also fosters a deeper emotional connection between consumers and brands. Furthermore, the advent of quantum computing promises to revolutionize data analysis and market segmentation, allowing businesses to derive insights more rapidly and accurately than ever before.

We also highlighted the importance of social responsibility in shaping consumer perceptions and loyalty. Brands that prioritize ethical practices and engage in meaningful dialogues with their consumers tend to build stronger relationships and foster trust. This social responsibility extends to the utilization of consumer feedback, which plays a crucial role in refining products and marketing strategies. In an era of rapid technological advancement, brands must exhibit strategic adaptability to navigate changing consumer preferences and market dynamics effectively.

Finally, we examined how emerging technologies, such as AI and quantum computing, offer unprecedented opportunities for businesses to innovate and stay competitive. As these technologies continue to evolve, their impact on consumer behaviour and market strategies will be profound, necessitating ongoing research and adaptation within the field.

> **ACTIVITY 3**
>
> Case study analysis
>
> **Objective**: To apply theoretical concepts to real-world scenarios.
> **Instructions**: Divide the class into small groups. Give each group a brief case study of a brand that has successfully adapted to changes in consumer behaviour.
> Ask each group to analyse the case study, focusing on the strategies used and their effectiveness.
> Each group will present their findings and discuss how the strategies could be applied to other brands or industries.

KEY TERMS

Consumer behaviour: The study of how individuals make decisions regarding the acquisition, use and disposal of goods and services.

Data-driven insights: Information derived from data analysis used to make informed decisions about consumer trends and behaviours.

Market segmentation: The process of dividing a broad consumer or business market into sub-groups of consumers based on shared characteristics.

Technological advancements: Innovations and improvements in technology, such as AI and quantum computing, that impact various aspects of business and consumer behaviour.

Social responsibility: A brand's commitment to ethical practices and contributing positively to society, which influences consumer perceptions and loyalty.

Consumer feedback: Direct input from consumers regarding their experiences and opinions, used to refine products and marketing strategies.

Strategic adaptability: The ability of a brand to adjust its strategies and operations in response to changing market conditions and consumer preferences.

Quantum computing: A type of computing that leverages quantum-mechanical phenomena to perform calculations more efficiently than classical computers.

AI (artificial intelligence): The simulation of human intelligence processes by machines, especially computer systems, which impacts decision-making and consumer interactions.

Blockchain: A decentralized digital ledger used to securely record transactions, which can influence consumer trust and data management.

KEY LEARNING POINTS

- Understanding consumer behaviour is essential for making informed marketing decisions.
- Data-driven insights allow brands to identify trends and improve strategies.
- Market segmentation helps target specific consumer groups effectively.
- Technological advancements, including AI and quantum computing, enhance business operations and consumer interactions.
- Social responsibility positively influences brand perception and consumer loyalty.
- Consumer feedback is vital for product refinement and marketing adjustments.
- Strategic adaptability enables brands to respond to changing market conditions and preferences.
- AI facilitates personalization, creating stronger emotional connections with consumers.
- Quantum computing offers new capabilities for efficient data analysis and decision-making.
- Blockchain technology can enhance consumer trust and secure transaction processes.

REFERENCES

Introduction

Aguiar, L., & Waldfogel, J. (2018). Quality predictability and the welfare benefits from new products: Evidence from the digitization of recorded music. *Journal of Political Economy*, 126(2), 492–524.

Alexandre, O., Alganb, Y., & Benhamouc, F. (2022). La culture face aux défis du numérique et de la crise. *Notes du conseil d'analyse économique*, 70(1), 1–12.

Amato, G., Behrmann, M., Bimbot, F., Caramiaux, B., Falchi, F., Garcia, A., ... & Vincent, E. (2019). AI in the media and creative industries. arXiv preprint arXiv:1905.04175.

Anantrasirichai, N. and Bull, D. (2022). Artificial intelligence in the creative industries: A review. *Artificial Intelligence Review*, 1–68.

Arnold, A., Kolody, S., Comeau, A., & Miguel Cruz, A. (2024). What does the literature say about the use of personal voice assistants in older adults? A scoping review. *Disability and Rehabilitation: Assistive Technology*, 19(1), 100–111.

Assassi, I. (2003). Spécificités du produit culturel. *Revue Française de Gestion*, 142(1), 129–146.

Asrial, A., Syahrial, S., Kurniawan, D. A., & Anandari, Q. S. (2020). Digitalization of ethno constructivism based module for elementary school students. *Jurnal Ilmu Pendidikan*, 25(1), 33–42.

Baek, T. H., Yoo, C. Y., & Yoon, S. (2018). Augment yourself through virtual mirror: The impact of self-viewing and narcissism on consumer responses. *International Journal of Advertising*, 37(3), 421–439.

Bansal, K. (2016). Customer experience: Creating value through transforming customer journeys. Retrieved from https://www.mckinsey.com/capabilities/growth-marketing-and-sales/our-insights/customer-experience-creating-value-through-transforming-customer-journeys (archived at https://perma.cc/8SL9-DQJA)

Bartosik-Purgat, M., & Filimon, N. (Eds.) (2022). *European Consumers in the Digital Era: Implications of technology, media and culture on consumer behaviour*. Taylor & Francis.

Bengio, Y., Ducharme, R., Vincent, P., Jauvin, C., Kandola, J., Hofmann, T., Poggio, T., & Shawe-Taylor, J. (Eds.) (2003). A neural probabilistic language model. *Journal of Machine Learning Research*, 3(6), 11371155. https://doi.org/10.1162/153244303322533223 (archived at https://perma.cc/FQP8-MBLF)

Berners-Lee, T. (1989). Information Management: A proposal. Retrieved from http://www.w3.org/History/1989/proposal.html (archived at https://perma.cc/CT5G-RHES)

Bitner, M. J. (1992). Servicescapes: The impact of physical surroundings on customers and employees. *Journal of Marketing*, 56(April), 57–71.

Boyd, D. M., & Ellison, N. B. (2007). Social network sites: Definition, history, and scholarship. *Journal of computer-mediated Communication*, 13(1), 210–230.

Brunet, É., Lebart, L., & Vanni, L. (2021). Littérature et intelligence artificielle. *L'intelligence artificielle des textes*, (15), 73–130.

Bulut, E., Yildirim, B., Brandão, A., Miguel Vieira, B. R. U. N. O., & Tavares, V. (2022). Influence of sustainability on the purchase decision of products. *European Journal of Applied Business & Management*, 8(3).

Busalim, A. H. (2016). Understanding social commerce: A systematic literature review and directions for further research. *International Journal of Information Management*, 36(6), 1075–1088.

Campbell, S. W. (2013). Mobile media and communication: A new field, or just a new journal? *Mobile Media & Communication*, 1(1), 8–13.

Cerf, V. G. (2012). A Brief History of the Internet. Retrieved from https://www.isoc.org/Internet/history-Internet/brief-history-Internet/ (archived at https://perma.cc/9YTY-ZW2K)

Chaffey, D. (2016). Digital Marketing (Strategy, Implementation and Practice).

Chaffey, D., & Ellis-Chadwick, F. (2019). *Digital marketing*. Pearson UK.

Chaffey, D., & Smith, P. R. (2022). *Digital Marketing Excellence: Planning, optimizing and integrating online marketing*. Taylor & Francis.

Chandon, J. L., Laurent, G., & Valette-Florence, P. (2016). Pursuing the concept of luxury: Introduction to the JBR special issue on 'Luxury marketing from tradition to innovation'. *Journal of Business Research*, 69(1), 299–303.

Chemillier, M. (2022). Organigrammes informatiques: Présence humaine et intelligence artificielle dans les arts et la culture. Retrieved from https://hal.science/hal-03565162/document (archived at https://perma.cc/6H5K-AET8)

Chen, X. A., Wu, C. S., Murakhovs' ka, L., Laban, P., Niu, T., Liu, W., & Xiong, C. (2023). Marvista: Exploring the design of a human–AI collaborative news reading tool. *ACM Transactions on Computer-Human Interaction*, 30(6), 1–27.

Chen, L., Baird, A., & Straub, D. (2019). A linguistic signaling model of social support exchange in online health communities. *Decision Support Systems*, pp. 113233.

Choi, J. H., & Lee, H. J. (2012). Facets of simplicity for the smartphone interface: A structural model. *International Journal of Human Computer Studies*, 70(2), 129–142. https://doi.org/10.1016/j.ijhcs.2011.09.002 (archived at https://perma.cc/DG24-AHLC)

Chopdar, P. K., & Balakrishnan, J. (2020). Consumers' response towards mobile commerce applications: S-O-R approach. *International Journal of Information Management*, 53, 102–106. https://doi.org/10.1016/j.ijinfomgt.2020.102106 (archived at https://perma.cc/2G73-DE8X)

Choura, F. (2024). Les industries creatives et culturelles a l'ere de l'ia: proposition d'un agenda de recherche, *Actes de l'Association Tunisienne de Marketing*, 19–20/04/2024, The Sindbad, Hammamet, Tunisia.

Cyr, D., Head, M., & Ivanov, A. (2006). Design aesthetics leading to m-loyalty in mobile commerce. *Information & Management*, 43(8), 950–963. https://doi.org/10.1016/j.im.2006.08.009 (archived at https://perma.cc/UPW5-ERSM)

Darmaji, D., Astalini, A., Kurniawan, D. A., Parasdila, H., Irdianti., Susbiyanto., Ikhlas, M., Kuswanto. (2019). E-module based problem solving in basic physics practicum for science process skills. *International Journal of Online and Biomedical Engineering* (IJOE), 15(15), 4–17.

Darmaji., Astalini., D. A. Kurniawan., N. Sari., O. H. Wiza., Y. E. Putri. (2020). Investigation of students' psychology: The relationship among students' attitudes, persistence, creativity, and tolerance toward science subjects. *Universal Journal of Educational Research*, 8(4), 1155–1166.

Davenport, T., Guha, A., Grewal, D., & Bressgott, T. (2020). How artificial intelligence will change the future of marketing. *Journal of the Academy of Marketing Science*, 48, 24–42.

Davis, F. D., Bagozzi, R. P., & Warshaw, P. R. (1989). User acceptance of computer technology: A comparison of two theoretical models. *Management Science*, 35(8), 982–1003.

Davis, F. D. (1989). Perceived usefulness, perceived ease of use, and user acceptance of information technology. *MIS Quarterly*, 319–340.

de Graaf, M. M. A., & Ben Allouch, S. (2013). Exploring influencing variables for the acceptance of social robots. *Robotics and Autonomous Systems*, 61(12), 1476–1486.

De Vries, L., Gensler, S., & Leeflang, P. S. (2012). Popularity of brand posts on brand fan pages: An investigation of the effects of social media marketing. *Journal of Interactive Marketing*, 26(2), 83–91.

Djafarova, E., & Foots, S. (2022). Exploring ethical consumption of generation Z: Theory of planned behaviour. *Young Consumers*, 23(3), 413–431.

D'souza, C., Taghian, M., & Lamb, P. (2006). An empirical study on the influence of environmental labels on consumers. *Corporate Communications: An International Journal*, 11(2), 162–173.

Duronto, P. M., Nishida, T., & Nakayama, S. (2005). Uncertainty, anxiety, and avoidance in communication with strangers. *International Journal of Intercultural Relations*, 29(5), 549–560.

Dwivedi, A., Dwivedi, P., Bobek, S., & Zabukovšek, S. S. (2019). Factors affecting students' engagement with online content in blended learning. *Kybernetes*, 48(7), 15001515.

Ebrahimabad, F. Z., Yazdani, H., Hakim, A., & Asarian, M. (2024). Augmented reality versus web-based shopping: how does AR improve user experience and online purchase intention? *Telematics and Informatics Reports*, 15, 100152.

Etminani-Ghasrodashti, R., & Hamidi, S. (2020). Online shopping as a substitute or complement to in-store shopping trips in Iran? *Cities*, 103, 102768.

Ettis, S. A., Pelet, J. É., & Zaichkowsky J. (2023). Comparing online user experience across different digital business ecosystems and platforms when booking vacations, *Review of Managerial Science*. https://doi.org/10.1007/s11846-023-00712-2 (archived at https://perma.cc/R46T-YR4P)

Fan, X., Chai, Z., Deng, N., & Dong, X. (2020). Adoption of augmented reality in online retailing and consumers' product attitude: A cognitive perspective. *Journal of Retailing and Consumer Services*, 53, 101986.

FEVAD (2022) Vendre en direct par vidéo: explosion du commerce en live-streaming en Asie. Retrieved from https://www.fevad.com/ (archived at https://perma.cc/ZJE9-LHL7)

Flavián, C., Gurrea, R., & Orús, C. (2017). The influence of online product presentation videos on persuasion and purchase channel preference: The role of imagery fluency and need for touch. *Telematics and Informatics*, 34(8), 1544–1556. https://doi.org/10.1016/J.TELE.2017.07.002 (archived at https://perma.cc/B6XD-MJKL).

Fortin, D. R., & Dholakia, R. R. (2005). Interactivity and vividness effects on social presence and involvement with a web-based advertisement. *Journal of Business Research*, 58(3), 387–396.

Frost, R., & Strauss, J. (2016). *E-marketing*. Routledge.

Gaillard, M.-C. (2023). 14% des Français affirment avoir déjà participé à une session de live shopping. Etude Omnibus – YouGov. Retrieved from https://www.ecommercemag.fr/Thematique/retail-1220/barometre-etude-2168/Breves/Live-Shopping-14des-Fran-ais-affirment-avoir-deja-participe-381767.htm (archived at https://perma.cc/A2Y8-LWTS)

Gan, W., Ye, Z., Wan, S., & Yu, P. S. (2023). Web 3.0: The future of internet. arXiv preprint arXiv:2304.06032.

Gao, L., & Bai, X. (2014). Online consumer behaviour and its relationship to website atmospheric induced flow: Insights into online travel agencies in China. *Journal of Retailing and Consumer Services*, 21(4), 653–665.

Goel, A. K., Bakshi, R., & Agrawal, K. K. (2022). Web 3.0 and decentralized applications. *Materials Proceedings*, 10(1), 8.

Gonzalez, R., Gasco, J., & Llopis, J. (2019). ICTs in hotel management: A research review. *International Journal of Contemporary Hospitality Management*, 31(9), 3583–3609.

Grewal, D., Roggeveen, A. L., & Nordfält, J. (2017). The future of retailing. *Journal of Retailing*, 93(1), 1–6. https://doi.org/10.1016/j.jretai.2016.12.008 (archived at https://perma.cc/4EWZ-ACA2)

Grewal, D., Kroschke, M., Mende, M., Roggeveen, A. L., & Scott, M. L. (2020). Frontline cyborgs at your service: How human enhancement technologies affect customer experiences in retail, sales, and service settings. *Journal of Interactive Marketing*, 51, 9–25. https://doi.org/10.1016/j.intmar.2020.03.001 (archived at https://perma.cc/6PH8-XAWH).

Griffith, D. A., & Gray, C. C. (2002). The fallacy of the level playing field: The effect of brand familiarity and web site vividness on online consumer response. *Journal of Marketing Channels*, 9(3–4), 87–102. https://doi.org/10.1300/J049v09n03_05 (archived at https://perma.cc/7NWQ-TSSB)

Gunawan, I. & dan Palupi, A. R. (2015). Taksonomi Bloom revisi ranah kognitif: kerangka landasan untuk pembelajaran, pengajaran, dan penilaian, *Premiere Educandum*, 2(2), 26–30.

Gupta, S., Leszkiewicz, A., Kumar, V., Bijmolt, T., & Potapov, D. (2020). Digital analytics: Modeling for insights and new methods. *Journal of Interactive Marketing*, 51, 26–43. https://doi.org/10.1016/j.intmar.2020.04.003 (archived at https://perma.cc/XY6H-PHZP)

Hajli, M. N. (2014). A study of the impact of social media on consumers. *International Journal of Market Research*, 56(3), 387–404.

Halmaoui, H. (2022). L'intelligence artificielle, la réalité augmentée et la réalité virtuelle dans l'audiovisuel et le cinéma. Retrieved from https://hal.science/hal-03741132 (archived at https://perma.cc/E34M-QN8A)

Hausman, A. V., Stock, W. A., & Davies, J. E. (2010). E-commerce and the market structure of retail industries. *The Journal of Business*, 79(4), 1837–1866.

Heudin, J. C., & Kyrou, A. (2020). Faire de l'IA un instrument et compagnon de musique. *Multitudes*, (1), 98–102.

Hilken, T., De Ruyter, K., Chylinski, M., Mahr, D., & Keeling, D. I. (2017). Augmenting the eye of the beholder: Exploring the strategic potential of augmented reality to enhance online service experiences. *Journal of the Academy of Marketing Science*, 45, 884–905.

Hoffman, D. L., & Novak, T. P. (2018). Consumer and object experience in the Internet of Things: An assemblage theory approach. *Journal of Consumer Research*, 44(6), 1178–1204. https://doi.org/10.1093/jcr/ucx105 (archived at https://perma.cc/CRV2-PJWW).

Hoffman, D. L., & Novak, T. P. (1996). Marketing in hypermedia computer-mediated environments: Conceptual foundations. *Journal of Marketing*, 60(3), 50–68.

Hollensen, S. (2020). *Marketing Management: A relationship approach*, 4th edition, Pearson Education.

Hsu, C. L., Chang, K. C., & Chen, M. C. (2012) Flow experience and internet shopping behaviour: Investigating the moderating effect of consumer characteristics, *System Research*, 29, 317–332.

Hubbard, D. W. (2020). *The Failure of Risk Management: Why it's broken and how to fix it*. John Wiley & Sons.

Hultén, B. (2015). *Sensory Marketing: Theoretical and empirical grounds*. Routledge, New York and London.

Iden, J., & Eikebrokk, T. R. (2014). Using the ITIL process reference model for realizing IT governance: An empirical investigation. *Information Systems Management*, 31(1), 37–58.

Ingraham, B., & Bradburn, E. (2003). *Converting OLF materials for use online multi-PALIO: A case study*. Open Learning Foundation, London.

Ives, B., Palese, B., & Rodriguez, J. A. (2016). Enhancing customer service through the Internet of Things and digital data streams. *MIS Quarterly Executive*, 15(4), 279–297.

Jacques, A. (2023). L'intelligence artificielle fera-t-elle un jour les films à notre place? La menace fantôme. *Séquences: la revue de cinéma*, (335), 16–17.

Jafari-Sadeghi, V., Garcia-Perez, A., Candelo, E., & Couturier, J. (2021). Exploring the impact of digital transformation on technology entrepreneurship and technological market expansion: The role of technology readiness, exploration and exploitation. *Journal of Business Research*, 124, 100–111.

Javornik, A. (2016). Augmented reality: Research agenda for studying the impact of its media characteristics on consumer behaviour. *Journal of Retailing and Consumer Services*, 30, 252–261.

Jia, X., Wang, R., Liu, J. H., & Xie, T. (2020). How to attract more viewers in live streams? A functional evaluation of streamers' strategies for attraction of viewers. In: F F-H Nah et K Siau (Eds) *HCI in Business Government and Organizations*, Springer, pp. 369–383.

Jiang, Z., & Benbasat, I. (2007). Research note—investigating the influence of the functional mechanisms of online product presentations. *Information Systems Research*, 18(4), 454–470.

Kang, J. (2020). Identifying antecedents and consequences of well-being: The case of cruise passengers. *Tourism Management Perspectives*, 33, 100609.

Kao, P.-J., Pai, P., & Tsai, H.-T. (2019). Looking at both sides of relationship dynamics in virtual communities: A social exchange theoretical lens. *Information & Management*, https://doi.org/10.1016/j.im.2019.103210 (archived at https://perma.cc/CW3W-4XCX)

Kaplan, A. M., & Haenlein, M. (2010). Users of the world, unite! The challenges and opportunities of social media. *Business Horizons*, 53(1), 59–68.

Karjaluoto, H., Munnukka, J., & Kiuru, K. (2016). Brand love and positive word of mouth: The moderating effects of experience and price. *Journal of Product & Brand Management*, 25(6), 527–537.

Karpinska-Krakowiak, M., & Eisend, M. (2020). Mini-film advertising and digital brand engagement: The moderating effects of drama and lecture. *International Journal of Advertising*, 39(3), 387–409. https://doi.org/10.1080/02650487.2019.1633841 (archived at https://perma.cc/SZE4-88KK)

Keller, P. A., & Block, L. G. (1997). Vividness effects: A resource-matching perspective. *Journal of Consumer Research*, 24(3), 295–304.

Kim, J., & Forsythe, S. (2008). Sensory enabling technology acceptance model (SE-TAM): A multiple-group structural model comparison. *Psychology & Marketing*, 25(9), 901–922.

Kim, G., & Koo, H. (2016). The causal relationship between risk and trust in the online marketplace: A bidirectional perspective. *Computers in Human Behaviour*, 55, 1020–1029.

Knight, H., & Vorster, L. (2023). *Digital Marketing in Practice: Design, implement and measure effective campaigns*. Kogan Page.

Ko, H., Cho, C. H., & Roberts, M. S. (2005). Internet uses and gratifications: A structural equation model of interactive advertising. *Journal of Advertising*, 34(2), 57–70.

Kotler, P. (1973). Atmospherics as a marketing tool. *Journal of Retailing*, 49(4), 48–64.

Krishna, A. (2013). *Customer Sense: How the 5 senses influence buying behaviour*. Palgrave Macmillan, New York and Basingstoke.

Krueger, G. U., & LePlastrier, G. (2009). *Could Have, Would Have, Should Have: A Short History of the Housing Boom/Bust in the 2000s*. https://hdl.handle.net/1813/70648 (archived at https://perma.cc/UV2C-5RPC)

Kumar, B., Sharma, A., Vatavwala, S., & Kumar, P. (2020). Digital mediation in business-to-business marketing: A bibliometric analysis. *Industrial Marketing Management*, 85, 126–140.

Kumar, A., Salo, J., & Li, H. (2019). Stages of user engagement on social commerce platforms: Analysis with the navigational clickstream data. *International Journal of Electronic Commerce*, 23(2), 179–211.

Lavie, T., & Tractinsky, N. (2004). Assessing dimensions of perceived visual aesthetics of web sites. *International Journal of Human Computer Interaction*, 60(3), 269–298. https://doi.org/10.1016/j.ijhcs.2003.09.002 (archived at https://perma.cc/9BSH-YFSM)

Lawler, E. J., & Yoon, J. (1993). Power and the emergence of commitment behaviour in negotiated exchange. *American Sociological Review*, 58, 465

Lawler, E. J., & Yoon, J. (1996). Commitment in exchange relations: Test of a theory of relational cohesion. *American Sociological Review*, 61, 89–108.

Lawler, E. J., & Yoon, J. (1998). Network structure and emotion in exchange relations. *American Sociological Review*, 63, 871–894.

Lawler, E J. (2001). An affect theory of social exchange. *American Journal of Sociology*, 102, 321–352.

Lawler, E. J., Thye, S. R., & Yoon, J. (2006). Commitment in structurally enabled and induced exchange relations. *Social Psychology Quarterly*, 69, 183–200.

Lawler, E. J., Thye, S. R., & Yoon, J. (2000). Emotion and group cohesion in productive exchange. *American Journal of Sociology*, 106, 616–657.

Lebrun, T., & Audet, R. (2020). L'intelligence artificielle et le monde du livre . Livre blanc.

Lee, R. J., Sener, I. N., Mokhtarian, P. L., & Handy, S. L. (2017). Relationships between the online and in-store shopping frequency of Davis, California residents. *Transportation Research Part A: Policy and Practice*, 100, 40–52.

Lee, M. K., & Turban, E. (2001). A trust model for consumer Internet shopping. *International Journal of Electronic Commerce*, 6(1), 75–91.

Leicht, A., Combes, B., Byun, W. J., & Agbedahin, A. V. (2016). From agenda 21 to target 4.7: The development of education for sustainable development. In: Leicht, A., Heiss, J., & Byun, W. J. (Eds). *Issues and Trends in Education for Sustainable Development*. UNESCO Publishing, Paris.

Lemon, K. N., & Verhoef, P. C. (2016). Understanding customer experience throughout the customer journey. *Journal of Marketing*, 80(6), 69–96.

Le SIEC / La Paris Retail Week (2023). Pourquoi le live shopping ne décolle pas en France? Retrieved from https://www.ladn.eu/entreprises-innovantes/la-semaine-du-retail/pourquoi-live-shopping-ne-decolle-pas-france/ (archived at https://perma.cc/6AAB-K422)

Li, H., Daugherty, T., & Biocca, F. (2002). Impact of 3-D advertising on product knowledge, brand attitude, and purchase intention: The mediating role of presence. *Journal of Advertising*, 31(3), 43–57.

Li, X., Zhao, X., Xu, W., & Pu, W. (2020). Measuring ease of use of mobile applications in e-commerce retailing from the perspective of consumer online shopping behaviour patterns. *Journal of Retailing and Consumer Services*, 55, 102093. https://doi.org/10.1016/j.jretconser.2020.102093 (archived at https://perma.cc/2YRL-6X7L)

Li, F., Piemkowski, D., Van Moorsel, A., & Smith, C. (2012). A holistic framework for trust in online transactions. *International Journal of Management Reviews*, 14, 85–103.

Li, D., & Nabec, L. (2023). Live streaming e-commerce, proposition d'une typologie des formats émergents en Chine. Retrieved from https://hal.science/hal-04233501/document (archived at https://perma.cc/GH6H-YBFE)

Liang, T. P., & Turban, E. (2011). Introduction to the special issue social commerce: A research framework for social commerce. *International Journal of Electronic Commerce*, 16(2), 5–14.

Lin, X., Li, Y., & Wang, X. (2017). Social commerce research: Definition, research themes and the trends. *International Journal of Information Management*, 37(3), 190–201.

Lindgaard, G., Fernandes, G.J., & Dudek, C., & Brownet, J. (2006). Attention web designers: You have 50 ms to make a good first impression! *Behaviour and Information Technology*, 25, 115–126. https://doi.org/10.1080/01449290500330448 (archived at https://perma.cc/L6HW-Q6CE)

Luo, X., Cheah, J. H., Lim, X. J., & Ng, S. I. A. (2022) Bibliometric review of user behaviours research in live streaming commerce. *Journal of Marketing Advances et Practices*, 4(1), 32–49.

Maison., Darmaji., Astalini., Kurniawan, D. A., Sumaryanti., Perdana, R. (2020). Supporting assessment in education: E-assessment interest in physics. *Universal Journal of Education Research*, 8(1), 89–97.

Manning, C. (2016, July). Understanding human language: Can NLP and deep learning help? In Proceedings of the 39th International ACM SIGIR conference on Research and Development in Information Retrieval (pp. 1–1).

Melián-González, S., & Bulchand-Gidumal, J. (2016). A model that connects information technology and hotel performance. *Tourism Management*, 53, 30–37.

Montalvo, S., Palomo, J., & de la Orden, C. (2018). Building an educational platform using NLP: A case study in teaching finance.

Morris, M. G., & Turner, J. M. (2001). Assessing users' subjective quality of experience with the world wide web: An exploratory examination of temporal changes in technology acceptance. *International Journal of Human-Computer Studies*, 54(6), 877–901. https://doi.org/10.1006/ijhc.2001.0460 (archived at https://perma.cc/9K34-SZNZ)

Moshagen, M., & Thielsch, M. T. (2010). Facets of visual aesthetics. *International Journal of Human Computer Interaction*, 68(10), 689–709. https://doi.org/10.1016/j.ijhcs.2010.05.006 (archived at https://perma.cc/AK38-HE39)

Mukherjee, A., & Nath, P. (2007). Role of electronic trust in online retailing: A re-examination of the commitment trust theory. *European Journal of Marketing*, 41(9/10), 1173–1202. https://doi.org/10.1108/03090560710773390 (archived at https://perma.cc/NZ6L-KR6H)

Murray, K., & Häuble, G. (2011). Freedom of choice, ease of use, and the formation of interface preferences. *MIS Quarterly*, 35(4), 955–976. https://doi.org/10.2307/41409968 (archived at https://perma.cc/2PZH-M6ZY)

Murphy, H. C., & Rottet, D. (2009). An exploration of the key hotel processes implicated in biometric adoption. *International Journal of Contemporary Hospitality Management*, 21(2), 201–212.

Nadkarni, S., Kriechbaumer, F., Rothenberger, M., & Christodoulidou, N. (2020). The path to the Hotel of Things: Internet of Things and Big Data converging in hospitality. *Journal of Hospitality and Tourism Technology*, 11(1), 93–107. https://doi.org/10.1108/JHTT-12-2018-0120 (archived at https://perma.cc/JF4G-CZYH)

Natarajan, T., Pragha, P., Dhalmahapatra, K., & Veera Raghavan, D. R. (2024). Unveiling metaverse sentiments using machine learning approaches. *Kybernetes*.

Nisbett, R. E., & Ross, L. (1980). Human inference: Strategies and shortcomings of social judgment, *The Philosophical Review*, 92(3), 462. https://doi.org/10.2307/2184495 (archived at https://perma.cc/2PZH-M6ZY)

Obrist, M., Gatti, E., Maggioni, E., Vi, C. T., & Velasco, C. (2017). Multisensory experiences in HCI. *IEEE MultiMedia*, 24(2), 9–13.

O'Reilly, T. (2005). What is Web 2.0: Design patterns and business models for the next generation of software. Retrieved from http://www.oreilly.com/pub/a/web2/archive/what-is-web-20.html (archived at https://perma.cc/LC4X-WW7F)

Pantelimon, F. V., Georgescu, T. M., & Posedaru, B. Ş. (2020). The impact of mobile e-commerce on GDP: A comparative analysis between Romania and Germany and how Covid-19 influences the e-commerce activity worldwide. *Informatica Economica*, 24(2), 27–41.

Pao, S. Y., Reben, A. J., & Rayes, A. (2011, May). *MoSS: Mobile smart services for ubiquitous network management* [Paper presentation]. International Conference on Collaboration Technologies and Systems, Philadelphia, PA, USA (pp. 48–52).

Parker, C. J., & Wang, H. (2016). Examining hedonic and utilitarian motivations for m-commerce fashion retail app engagement. *Journal of Fashion Marketing & Management*, 20(4), 487–506. https://doi.org/10.1108/JFMM-02-2016-0015 (archived at https://perma.cc/G5C6-UGSS)

Patel, V., Das, K., Chatterjee, R., & Shukla, Y. (2020). Does the interface quality of mobile shopping apps affect purchase intention? An empirical study. *Australasian Marketing Journal*, 28(4), 300–309. https://doi.org/10.1016/j.ausmj.2020.08.004 (archived at https://perma.cc/TY2Z-QRUF)

Pelet, J. É., & Taieb, B. (2022). Context-aware optimization of mobile commerce website interfaces from the consumers' perspective: Effects on behavioural intentions. *Computers in Human Behaviour Reports*, 7, 100225.

Pelet, J. É., & Ettis, S. A. (2022). Social media advertising effectiveness: The role of perceived originality, liking, credibility, irritation, intrusiveness, and ad destination. *International Journal of Technology and Human Interaction*, 18(1), 1–20.

Pelet, J. É., Lick, E., & Taieb, B. (2021). The internet of things in upscale hotels: Its impact on guests' sensory experiences and behaviour. *International Journal of Contemporary Hospitality Management*, 33(11), 4035–4056.

Pelet, J. É., & Papadopoulou, P. (2012). The effect of colors of e-commerce websites on consumer mood, memorization and buying intention. *European Journal in Information Systems*, 21(4), 438–467. https://doi.org/10.1057/ejis.2012.17 (archived at https://perma.cc/7372-82H8)

Pelet, J.-É. and Taieb, B. (2022). Context-aware optimization of mobile commerce website interfaces from the consumers' perspective: Effects on behavioural intentions. *Computers in Human Behaviour Reports*, 7, 100225.

Petit, O., Velasco, C., & Spence, C. (2019). Digital sensory marketing: Integrating new technologies into multisensory online experience. *Journal of Interactive Marketing*, 45, 42–61.

Peukert, C. (2019). The next wave of digital technological change and the cultural industries. *Journal of Cultural Economics*, 43(2), 189–210.

Pieroni, M., Rizzello, L., Rosini, N., Fantoni, G., De Rossi, D., & Mazzei, D. (2015). *Affective Internet of Things: Mimicking human-like personality in designing smart-objects*. 2015 IEEE 2nd World Forum on Internet of Things (WF-IoT). https://doi.org/10.1109/wf-iot.2015.7389088 (archived at https://perma.cc/773K-YFZF)

Pinillos, R. et al. (2016) Long-term assessment of a service robot in a hotel environment. *Robotics and Autonomous Systems*, 79, 40–57. https://doi.org/10.1016/j.robot.2016.01.014 (archived at https://perma.cc/N8W4-VPNM)

Ponsignon, F., & Derbaix, M. (2020). The impact of interactive technologies on the social experience: An empirical study in a cultural tourism context. *Tourism Management Perspectives*, 35, 100723.

Poushneh, A. (2018). Augmented reality in retail: A trade-off between user's control of access to personal information and augmentation quality. *Journal of Retailing and Consumer Services*, 41, 169–176.

Poushneh, A., & Vasquez-Parraga, A. Z. (2017). Discernible impact of augmented reality on retail customer's experience, satisfaction and willingness to buy. *Journal of Retailing and Consumer Services*, 34, 229–234.

Preece J., Sharp H., Rogers Y., (2015). *Interaction Design beyond Human-Computer Interaction*, John Wiley & Sons.

Price, H. E., & Collett, J. L. (2012), The role of exchange and emotion on commitment: A study of teachers. *Social Science Research*, 41(6), 1469–1479.

Ratchford, B. T., Talukdar, D., & Lee, M. S. (2001). A model of consumer choice of the Internet as an information source. *International Journal of Electronic Commerce*, 5(3), 7–21.

Radde, B. (2017). *Digital Guest Experience: Tools to help hotels to manage and optimize the digital guest experience*. Tredition, Hamburg.

Rauschnabel, P. A., & Ro, Y. K. (2016). Augmented reality smart glasses: An investigation of technology acceptance drivers. *International Journal of Technology Marketing*, 11(2), 123–148.

Reber, R., & Schwarz, N. (1999). Effects of perceptual fluency on judgments of truth. *Consciousness and Cognition*, 8(September), 338–342. https://doi.org/10.1006/ccog.1999.0386 (archived at https://perma.cc/8RGL-TR2F)

Rustam, A., Wang, Y., & Zameer, H. (2020). Environmental awareness, firm sustainability exposure and green consumption behaviours. *Journal of Cleaner Production*, 268, 122016.

Ryan, D. (2020). *Understanding Digital Marketing: A complete guide to engaging customers and implementing successful digital campaigns*. Kogan Page Publishers.

Sabouk, N., & Sidmou, M. L. (2019). L'intelligence artificielle; vers un nouveau paradigme interdisciplinaire: Etat de synthèse. *Revue Internationale du Marketing et Management Stratégique*, 1(4).

Sarkar, S., Chauhan, S., & Khare, A. (2020). A meta-analysis of antecedents and consequences of trust in mobile commerce. *International Journal of Information Management*, 50, 286–301. https://doi.org/10.1016/j.ijinfomgt.2019.08.008 (archived at https://perma.cc/Q3TZ-R9P9)

Schmidt, S., Bruder, G., & Steinicke, F. (2019). Effects of virtual agent and object representation on experiencing exhibited artifacts. *Computers & Graphics*, 83, 1–10.

Scholz, J., & Duffy, K. (2018). We ARe at home: How augmented reality reshapes mobile marketing and consumer-brand relationships. *Journal of Retailing and Consumer Services*, 44, 11–23.

Seckler, M., Opwis, K., & Tuch, A. N. (2015). Linking objective design factors with subjective aesthetics: An experimental study on how structure and color of websites affect the facets of users' visual aesthetic perception. *Computers in Human Behaviour*, 49(August), 375–389. https://doi.org/10.1016/j.chb.2015.02.056 (archived at https://perma.cc/CZ3H-39DC)

Seyama, J., & Nagayama, R. S. (2007). The Uncanny Valley: Effect of realism on the impression of artificial human faces. *Presence: Teleoperators & Virtual Environments*, 16(4), 337–351.

Shaari, A., & Hamzah, A. (2016). Neurolinguistic programming (NLP): Its overview and review in the lenses of philosophy and pedagogy. *Asian Journal of University Education*, 12(1), 1–13.

Shadbolt, N., Berners-Lee, T., & Hall, W. (2006). The semantic web revisited. *IEEE Intelligent Systems*, 21(3), 96–101.

Sharma, S., Menard, P., & Mutchler, L. A. (2019). Who to trust? Applying trust to social commerce. *Journal of Computer Information Systems*, 59(1), 32–42.

Sigala, M. (2020). Tourism and Covid-19: Impacts and implications for advancing and resetting industry and research. *Journal of Business Research*, 117, 312–321.

Sin, J., & Munteanu, C. (2020). An empirically grounded sociotechnical perspective on designing virtual agents for older adults. *Human–Computer Interaction*, 35(5–6), 481510.

Singh, N., Dalal, N., & Spears, N. (2005). Understanding Web home page perception. *European Journal of Information Systems*, 14, 288–302. https://doi.org/10.1057/palgrave.ejis.3000525 (archived at https://perma.cc/96V5-QSSQ)

Smink, A. R., Frowijn, S., van Reijmersdal, E. A., van Noort, G., & Neijens, P. C. (2019). Try online before you buy: How docs shopping with augmented reality affect brand responses and personal data disclosure? *Electronic Commerce Research and Applications*, 35, 100854.

Sohn, S., Seegebarth, B., & Moritz, M. (2017). The impact of perceived visual complexity of mobile online shops on user's satisfaction. *Psychology & Marketing*, 34(2), 195–214. https://doi.org/10.1002/mar.20983 (archived at https://perma.cc/623T-XTVA)

Song, Z., Sun, Y., Wan, J., Huang, L., & Zhu, J. (2019). Smart e-commerce systems: Current status and research challenges. *Electronic Markets*, 29(2), 221–238. https://doi.org/10.1007/s12525-017-0272-3 (archived at https://perma.cc/6PJC-FUX6)

Stankov, U., Filimonau, V., & Slivar, I. (2019). Calm ICT design in hotels: A critical review of applications and implications. *International Journal of Hospitality Management*, 82, 298–307.

Statista. (2022). Social commerce revenue worldwide from 2022 to 2030 (in billion U.S. dollars). Retrieved from https://www-statista-com.devinci.idm.oclc.org/statistics/1231944/social-commerce-global-market-size/ (archived at https://perma.cc/Q654-LQN7)

Statista. (2023). Value of social commerce sales worldwide from 2022 to 2030 (in billion U.S. dollars). Retrieved from https://www-statista-com.devinci.idm.oclc.org/statistics/1251145/social-commerce-sales-worldwide/ (archived at https://perma.cc/5E7B-T6RK)

Statista. (2020). Smart home – statistics & facts. Retrieved from https://www.statista.com/topics/2430/smart-homes/ (archived at https://perma.cc/CU37-KGWB)

Statista. (2018). Classement des enseignes les plus appréciées par les consommateurs français pour la qualité des produits et services proposés. Retrieved from https://www.statista.com/statistiques/945440 (archived at https://perma.cc/Y2A2-YZM4)

Steuer, J., Biocca, F., & Levy, M. R. (1995). Defining virtual reality: Dimensions determining telepresence. *Communication in the Age of Virtual Reality*, 33(37–39), 1.

Stewart, H., & Jürjens, J. (2018). Data security and consumer trust in FinTech innovation in Germany. *Information and Computer Security*, 26(1), 109–128. https://doi.org/10.1108/ICS-06-2017-0039 (archived at https://perma.cc/8WRA-JH58)

Sun, N., & Botev, J. (2021). Intelligent autonomous agents and trust in virtual reality. *Computers in Human Behaviour Reports*, 4, 100146.

Syam, N., & Sharma, A. (2018). Waiting for a sales renaissance in the fourth industrial revolution: Machine learning and artificial intelligence in sales research and practice. *Industrial Marketing Management*, 69, 135–146.

Tanti., Maison., Syefrinando, B., Daryanto, B., Salma. H. (2020). Students' self-regulation and motivation in learning sciences. *International Journal of Evaluation and Research in Education*, 9(4), 865–873.

Torkzadeh, G., & Dhillon, G. (2002). Measuring factors that influence success of internet commerce. *Information Systems Research*, 13(2), 187–204. https://doi.org/10.1287/isre.13.2.187.87 (archived at https://perma.cc/9F37-UXWC)

Toukabri, M., & Mohamed Youssef, M. A. (2023). Climate change disclosure and sustainable development goals (SDGs) of the 2030 agenda: The moderating role of corporate governance. *Journal of Information, Communication and Ethics in Society*, 21(1), 30–62.

Tractinsky, N., Cokhavi, A., Kirschenbaum, M., & Sharfi, T. (2006). Evaluating the consistency of immediate aesthetic perception of web pages. *International Journal of Human–Computer Studies*, 64, 1071–1083. https://doi.org/10.1016/j.ijhcs.2006.06.009 (archived at https://perma.cc/XEY5-YXKJ)

Tsai, Y.-T., Wang, S.-C., Yan, K.-Q., & Chang, C.-M. (2017). Precise positioning of marketing and behaviour intentions of location-based mobile commerce in the Internet of Things. *Symmetry*, 9(8), 139. https://doi.org/10.3390/sym9080139 (archived at https://perma.cc/NRK3-3NBF)

Van Huy, L., & Thai Thinh, N. H. (2024). Ranking the hotel website service quality according to customer's perception: A case study of 4-star hotel. *Journal of Quality Assurance in Hospitality & Tourism*, 25(1), 37–56.

Van Noort, G., Voorveld, H. A., & Van Reijmersdal, E. A. (2012). Interactivity in brand web sites: Cognitive, affective, and behavioural responses explained by consumers' online flow experience. *Journal of Interactive Marketing*, 26(4), 223–234.

Venkatesh, V., Morris, M. G., Davis, G. B., & Davis, F.D. (2003). User acceptance of information technology: Toward a unified view. *MIS Quarterly*, 27(3), 425–478. https://doi.org/10.2307/30036540 (archived at https://perma.cc/KW4H-KBTJ)

Verhagen, T., Vonkeman, C., Feldberg, F., & Verhagen, P. (2014). Present it like it is here: Creating local presence to improve online product experiences. *Computers in Human Behaviour*, 39, 270–280.

Verhoef, P. C., Kannan, P. K., & Inman, J. J. (2015). From multi-channel retailing to omnichannel retailing. *Journal of Retailing*, 91(2), 174–181. https://doi.org/10.1016/j.jretai.2015.02.005 (archived at https://perma.cc/X5LJ-KQAK)

Visinescu, L. L., Sidorova, A., Jones, M. C., & Prybutok, V. R. (2015). The influence of website dimensionality on customer experiences, perceptions and behavioural intentions: An exploration of 2D vs. 3D web design. *Information & Management*, 52(1), 1–17. https://doi.org/10.1016/j.im.2014.10.005 (archived at https://perma.cc/SQ4Q-2J8Q)

Vlačić, B., Corbo, L., e Silva, S. C., & Dabić, M. (2021). The evolving role of artificial intelligence in marketing: A review and research agenda. *Journal of Business Research*, 128, 187–203.

Waldfogel, J. (2017). How digitization has created a golden age of music, movies, books, and television. *Journal of Economic Perspectives*, 31(3), 195–214.

White, M., & Ronfeldt, M. (2024). Monitoring rater quality in observational systems: Issues due to unreliable estimates of rater quality. *Educational Assessment*, 29(2), 124–146.

Wongkitrungrueng, A., & Assarut, N. (2020). The role of live streaming in building consumer trust and engagement with social commerce sellers. *Journal of Business Research*, 117, 543–556.

Wu, T. J., Xu, T., Li, L. Q., & Yuan, K. S. (2020). 'Touching with heart, reasoning by truth!' The impact of brand cues on mini-film advertising effect. *International Journal of Advertising*, 39(8), 1322–1350.

Xu, F., Buhalis, D., & Weber, J. (2017). Serious games and the gamification of tourism. *Tourism Management*, 60, 244–256.

Yaoyuneyong, G., Foster, J., Johnson, E., & Johnson, D. (2016). Augmented reality marketing: Consumer preferences and attitudes toward hypermedia print ads. *Journal of Interactive Advertising*, 16(1), 16–30. https://doi.org/10.1080/15252019.2015.1125316 (archived at https://perma.cc/6V43-UXD7)

Yim, M. Y. C., Chu, S. C., & Sauer, P. L. (2017). Is augmented reality technology an effective tool for e-commerce? An interactivity and vividness perspective. *Journal of Interactive Marketing*, 39(1), 89–103.

Youssef, W. A. B., & Mansour, N. (2024). The factoring 2.0 in the era of the fintech revolution context. In *Digital Technology and Changing Roles in Managerial and Financial Accounting: Theoretical knowledge and practical application* (Vol. 36, pp. 37–51). Emerald Publishing Limited.

Zhang, S., Huang, C., Li, X., & Ren, A. (2022). Characteristics and roles of streamers in e-commerce live streaming. *The Service Industries Journal*, 1–29.

Zhang, H., Lu, Y., Gupta, S., & Zhao, L. (2014). What motivates customers to participate in social commerce? The impact of technological environments and virtual customer experiences. *Information et Management*, 51(8), 1017–1030.

Zhao, X., Shi, C., You, X., & Zong, C. (2017). Analysis of mental workload in online shopping: Are augmented and virtual reality consistent? *Frontiers in Psychology*, 8, 71.

Zlatoff, N., & Ribaupierre, C. D. (2023). Apprendre à jouer avec une machine: intelligence artificielle et deep learning dans un dispositif théâtral. *Percées*, L'Extension, recherche & création, 2023.

Zuo, R., & Xiao, J. (2021). Exploring consumers' impulse buying behaviour in live streaming shopping. In: *15th International Conference on Management Science and Engineering Management*, pp. 610–622. Springer: Cham.

Chapter 1

Asrial, A., Syahrial, S., Kurniawan, D. A., & Anandari, Q. S. (2020). Digitalization of ethno constructivism based module for elementary school students. *Jurnal Ilmu Pendidikan*, 25(1), 33–42.

Bansal, K. (2016). Customer experience: Creating value through transforming customer journeys. Retrieved from https://www.mckinsey.com/capabilities/growth-marketing-and-sales/our-insights/customer-experience-creating-value-through-transforming-customer-journeys (archived at https://perma.cc/9WSU-WD8Y)

Bitner, M. J. (1992). Servicescapes: The impact of physical surroundings on customers and employees. *Journal of Marketing*, 56 (April), 57–71.

Boyd, D. M., & Ellison, N. B. (2007). Social network sites: Definition, history, and scholarship. *Journal of Computer-mediated Communication*, 13(1), 210–230.

Campbell, S. W. (2013). Mobile media and communication: A new field, or just a new journal? *Mobile Media & Communication*, 1(1), 8–13.

Chaffey, D., & Ellis-Chadwich, F. (2016). *Digital Marketing Strategy, implementation and practice*. Pearson Education Limited.

Chaffey, D., & Smith, P. R. (2022). *Digital Marketing Excellence: Planning, optimizing and integrating online marketing*. Taylor & Francis.

Chandon, J. L., Laurent, G., & Valette-Florence, P. (2016). Pursuing the concept of luxury: Introduction to the JBR Special Issue on 'Luxury Marketing from Tradition to Innovation'. *Journal of Business Research*, 69(1), 299–303.

Choi, J. H., & Lee, H. J. (2012). Facets of simplicity for the smartphone interface: A structural model. *International Journal of Human Computer Studies*, 70(2), 129–142. https://doi.org/10.1016/j.ijhcs.2011.09.002 (archived at https://perma.cc/Q8EH-MEYK)

Chopdar, P. K., & Balakrishnan, J. (2020). Consumers' response towards mobile commerce applications: S-O-R approach. *International Journal of Information Management*, 53, 102–106. https://doi.org/10.1016/j.ijinfomgt.2020.102106 (archived at https://perma.cc/Q9MT-2AJ7)

Cyr, D., Head, M., & Ivanov, A. (2006). Design aesthetics leading to m-loyalty in mobile commerce. *Information & Management*, 43(8), 950–963. https://doi.org/10.1016/j.im.2006.08.009 (archived at https://perma.cc/M98C-GXMB)

Darmaji, D., Astalini, A., Kurniawan, D. A., Parasdila, H., Irdianti, I., Susbiyanto, S., Ikhlas, M., & Kuswanto, K. (2019). E-module based problem solving in basic physics practicum for science process skills. *International Journal of Online and Biomedical Engineering (IJOE)*, 15(15), 4–17.

Darmaji, D., Astalini, A., Kurniawan, D. A., Sari, N., Wiza, O. H., & Putri, Y. E. (2020). Investigation of students' psychology: The relationship among students' attitudes, persistence, creativity, and tolerance toward science subjects. *Universal Journal of Educational Research*, 8(4), 1155–1166.

de Graaf, M. M. A., & Ben Allouch, S. (2013). Exploring influencing variables for the acceptance of social robots. *Robotics and Autonomous Systems*, 61(12), 1476–1486.

Duronto, P. M., Nishida, T., & Nakayama, S. (2005). Uncertainty, anxiety, and avoidance in communication with strangers. *International Journal of Intercultural Relations*, 29(5), 549–560.

Frost, R., & Strauss, J. (2016). *E-marketing*. Routledge.

Gonzalez, R., Gasco, J., & Llopis, J. (2019). ICTs in hotel management: A research review. *International Journal of Contemporary Hospitality Management*, 31(9), 3583–3609.

Grewal, D., Kroschke, M., Mende, M., Roggeveen, A. L., & Scott, M. L. (2020). Frontline cyborgs at your service: How human enhancement technologies affect customer experiences in retail, sales, and service settings. *Journal of Interactive Marketing*, 51, 9–25. https://doi.org/10.1016/j.intmar.2020.03.001 (archived at https://perma.cc/RTY4-SMQ4)

Gupta, S., Leszkiewicz, A., Kumar, V., Bijmolt, T., & Potapov, D. (2020). Digital analytics: Modeling for insights and new methods. *Journal of Interactive Marketing*, 51, 26–43. https://doi.org/10.1016/j.intmar.2020.04.003 (archived at https://perma.cc/23GT-R4QU)

Hausman, A. V., Stock, W. A., & Davies, J. E. (2010). E-commerce and the market structure of retail industries. *The Journal of Business*, 79(4), 1837–1866.

Hoffman, D. L., & Novak, T. P. (2018). Consumer and object experience in the Internet of Things: An assemblage theory approach. *Journal of Consumer Research*, 44(6), 1178–1204. https://doi.org/10.1093/jcr/ucx105 (archived at https://perma.cc/K7S2-L45R)

Hollensen, S. (2020). *Marketing Management: A relationship approach*. 4th edition, Pearson Education.

Hultén, B. (2015). *Sensory Marketing: Theoretical and empirical grounds*. Routledge, New York and London.

Ingraham, B., & Bradburn, E. (2003). *Converting OLF materials for use online multi-PALIO: A case study*. Open Learning Foundation, London.

Ives, B., Palese, B., & Rodriguez, J. A. (2016). Enhancing customer service through the Internet of Things and digital data streams. *MIS Quarterly Executive*, 15(4), 279–297.

Kaplan, A. M., & Haenlein, M. (2010). Users of the world, unite! The challenges and opportunities of social media. *Business Horizons*, 53(1), 59–68.

Kotler, P. (1973). Atmospherics as a marketing tool. *Journal of Retailing*, 49(4), 48–64.

Krishna, A. (2013). *Customer Sense: How the 5 senses influence buying behaviour*. Palgrave Macmillan, New York and Basingstoke.

Krueger, G. U., & LePlastrier, G. (2009). *Could Have, Would Have, Should Have: A short history of the housing boom/bust in the 2000s*. https://hdl.handle.net/1813/70648 (archived at https://perma.cc/JK6X-Z5C4)

Kumar, A., Salo, J., & Li, H. (2019). Stages of user engagement on social commerce platforms: Analysis with the navigational clickstream data. *International Journal of Electronic Commerce*, 23(2), 179–211.

Lemon, K. N., & Verhoef, P. C. (2016). Understanding customer experience throughout the customer journey. *Journal of Marketing*, 80(6), 69–96.

Maison, D., Darmaji, D., Astalini, A., Kurniawan, D. A., Sumaryanti., Perdana, R. (2020). Supporting assessment in education: E-assessment interest in physics. *Universal Journal of Education Research*, 8(1), 89–97.

Melián-González, S., & Bulchand-Gidumal, J. (2016). A model that connects information technology and hotel performance. *Tourism Management*, 53, 30–37.

Morris, M. G., & Turner, J. M. (2001). Assessing users' subjective quality of experience with the world wide web: An exploratory examination of temporal changes in technology acceptance. *International Journal of Human-Computer Studies*, 54(6), 877–901. https://doi.org/10.1006/ijhc.2001.0460 (archived at https://perma.cc/7AM6-DQYK)

Moshagen, M., & Thielsch, M. T. (2010). Facets of visual aesthetics. *International Journal of Human Computer Interaction*, 68(10), 689–709. https://doi.org/10.1016/j.ijhcs.2010.05.006 (archived at https://perma.cc/9YEA-DQ3M)

Murray, K., & Häuble, G. (2011). Freedom of choice, ease of use, and the formation of interface preferences. *MIS Quarterly*, 35(4), 955–976. https://doi.org/10.2307/41409968 (archived at https://perma.cc/K62Y-XY88)

Murphy, H. C. and Rottet, D. (2009). An exploration of the key hotel processes implicated in biometric adoption. *International Journal of Contemporary Hospitality Management*, 21(2), 201–212.

Nadkarni, S., Kriechbaumer, F., Rothenberger, M., and Christodoulidou, N. (2020). The path to the Hotel of Things: Internet of Things and Big Data converging in hospitality. *Journal of Hospitality and Tourism Technology*, 11(1), 93–107. https://doi.org/10.1108/JHTT-12-2018-0120 (archived at https://perma.cc/2M9X-84JB)

O'Reilly, T. (2005). What is Web 2.0: Design patterns and business models for the next generation of software. Retrieved from http://www.oreilly.com/pub/a/web2/archive/what-is-web-20.html (archived at https://perma.cc/B39N-MTLP)

Obrist, M., Gatti, E., Maggioni, E., Vi, C. T., & Velasco, C. (2017). Multisensory experiences in HCI. *IEEE MultiMedia*, 24(2), 9–13.

Pantelimon, F. V., Georgescu, T. M., & Posedaru, B. Ş. (2020). The impact of mobile e-commerce on GDP: A comparative analysis between Romania and Germany and how Covid-19 influences the e-commerce activity worldwide. *Informatica Economica*, 24(2), 27–41.

Pelet, J. É., & Papadopoulou, P. (2012). The effect of colors of e-commerce websites on consumer mood, memorization and buying intention. *European Journal in Information Systems*, 21(4), 438–467. https://doi.org/10.1057/ejis.2012.17 (archived at https://perma.cc/KX5U-492D)

Pelet, J. É., Lick, E., & Taieb, B. (2021). The Internet of Things in upscale hotels: Its impact on guests' sensory experiences and behaviour. *International Journal of Contemporary Hospitality Management*, 33(11), 4035–4056.

Petit, O., Velasco, C., & Spence, C. (2019). Digital sensory marketing: Integrating new technologies into multisensory online experience. *Journal of Interactive Marketing*, 45, 42–61.

Pieroni, M., Rizzello, L., Rosini, N., Fantoni, G., De Rossi, D., & Mazzei, D. (2015). *Affective Internet of Things: Mimicking human-like personality in designing smart-objects*. 2015 IEEE 2nd World Forum on Internet of Things (WF-IoT). https://doi.org/10.1109/wf-iot.2015.7389088 (archived at https://perma.cc/V6PF-LX8X)

Pinillos, R. et al. (2016) Long-term assessment of a service robot in a hotel environment. *Robotics and Autonomous Systems*, 79, 40–57. https://doi.org/10.1016/j.robot.2016.01.014 (archived at https://perma.cc/5XDR-8GGP)

Poushneh, A., & Vasquez-Parraga, A. Z. (2017). Discernible impact of augmented reality on retail customers' experience, satisfaction and willingness to buy. *Journal of Retailing and Consumer Services*, 34, 229–234.

Ryan, D. (2020). *Understanding Digital Marketing, A Complete Guide to Engaging Customers and Implementing Successful Digital Campaigns*. Kogan Page Publishers.

Sarkar, S., Chauhan, S., & Khare, A. (2020). A meta-analysis of antecedents and consequences of trust in mobile commerce. *International Journal of Information Management*, 50, 286–301. https://doi.org/10.1016/j.ijinfomgt.2019.08.008 (archived at https://perma.cc/D9K9-7X5Z)

Scholz, J., & Duffy, K. (2018). We ARe at home: How augmented reality reshapes mobile marketing and consumer-brand relationships. *Journal of Retailing and Consumer Services*, 44, 11–23.

Seyama, J., & Nagayama, R. S. (2007). The Uncanny Valley: Effect of realism on the impression of artificial human faces. *Presence: Teleoperators & Virtual Environments*, 16(4), 337–351.

Shadbolt, N., Berners-Lee, T., & Hall, W. (2006). The semantic web revisited. *IEEE Intelligent Systems*, 21(3), 96–101.

Sigala, M. (2020). Tourism and Covid-19: Impacts and implications for advancing and resetting industry and research. *Journal of Business Research*, 117, 312–321.

Singh, N., Dalal, N., & Spears, N. (2005). Understanding Web home page perception. *European Journal of Information Systems*, 14, 288–302. https://doi.org/10.1057/palgrave.ejis.3000525 (archived at https://perma.cc/EZV6-RDWP)

Stankov, U., Filimonau, V., & Slivar, I. (2019). Calm ICT design in hotels: A critical review of applications and implications. *International Journal of Hospitality Management*, 82, 298–307.

Statista (2020). Smart home – statistics & facts. Retrieved from https://www.statista.com/topics/2430/smart-homes/ (archived at https://perma.cc/A273-EFC4)

Statista. (2022). Social commerce revenue worldwide from 2022 to 2030 (in billion U.S. dollars). Retrieved from https://www-statista-com.devinci.idm.oclc.org/statistics/1231944/social-commerce-global-market-size/ (archived at https://perma.cc/Q2GH-7XGQ)

Sun, N., & Botev, J. (2021). Intelligent autonomous agents and trust in virtual reality. *Computers in Human Behaviour Reports*, 4, 100146.

Torkzadeh, G., & Dhillon, G. (2002). Measuring factors that influence the success of Internet commerce. *Information Systems Research*, 13(2), 187–204. https://doi.org/10.1287/isre.13.2.187.87 (archived at https://perma.cc/47CN-BXQM)

Venkatesh, V., Morris, M. G., Davis, G. B., & Davis, F. D. (2003). User acceptance of information technology: Toward a unified view. *MIS Quarterly*, 27(3), 425–478. https://doi.org/10.2307/30036540 (archived at https://perma.cc/K62Y-XY88)

Verhoef, P. C., Kannan, P. K., & Inman, J. J. (2015). From multi-channel retailing to omnichannel retailing. *Journal of Retailing*, 91(2), 174–181. https://doi.org/10.1016/j.jretai.2015.02.005 (archived at https://perma.cc/28KE-FC7N)

Visinescu, L. L., Sidorova, A., Jones, M. C., & Prybutok, V. R. (2015). The influence of website dimensionality on customer experiences, perceptions and behavioural intentions: An exploration of 2D vs. 3D web design. *Information & Management*, 52(1), 1–17. https://doi.org/10.1016/j.im.2014.10.005 (archived at https://perma.cc/PXT7-T97S)

Wang, Y., & Hajli, N. (2017). Exploring the path to big data analytics success in healthcare. *Journal of Business Research*, 70, 287–299.

Wu, W. H., Wu, Y. C. J., Chen, C. Y., Kao, H. Y., Lin, C. H., & Huang, S. H. (2012). Review of trends from mobile learning studies: A meta-analysis. *Computers & Education*, 59(2), 817–827.

Xu, F., Buhalis, D., & Weber, J. (2017). Serious games and the gamification of tourism. *Tourism Management*, 60, 244–256.

Xu, Y., Ghose, A., & Xiao, B. (2024). Mobile payment adoption: An empirical investigation of Alipay. *Information Systems Research*, 35(2), 807–828.

Yaoyuneyong, G., Foster, J., Johnson, E., & Johnson, D. (2016). Augmented reality marketing: Consumer preferences and attitudes toward hypermedia print ads. *Journal of Interactive Advertising*, 16(1), 16–30. https://doi.org/10.1080/15252019.2015.1125316 (archived at https://perma.cc/N8N3-GJAY)

Chapter 2

Arnold, A., Kolody, S., Comeau, A., & Miguel Cruz, A. (2024). What does the literature say about the use of personal voice assistants in older adults? A scoping review. *Disability and Rehabilitation: Assistive Technology*, 19(1), 100–111.

Bartosik-Purgat, M., & Filimon, N. (Eds.) (2022). *European Consumers in the Digital Era: Implications of technology, media and culture on consumer behaviour*. Taylor & Francis.

Bulut, E., Yildirim, B., Brandão, A., Miguel Vieira, B. R. U. N. O., & Tavares, V. (2022). Influence of sustainability on the purchase decision of products. *European Journal of Applied Business & Management*, 8(3).

Chen, L., Baird, A., & Straub, D. (2019). A linguistic signaling model of social support exchange in online health communities. *Decision Support Systems*, 113233.

Djafarova, E., & Foots, S. (2022). Exploring ethical consumption of generation Z: Theory of planned behaviour. *Young Consumers*, 23(3), 413–431.

D'Souza, C., Taghian, M., & Lamb, P. (2006). An empirical study on the influence of environmental labels on consumers. *Corporate Communications: An International Journal*, 11(2), 162–173.

Ettis, S. A., Pelet, J. É., & Zaichkowsky J. (2023). Comparing online user experience across different digital business ecosystems and platforms when booking vacations, *Review of Managerial Science*. https://doi.org/10.1007/s11846-023-00712-2 (archived at https://perma.cc/N6TT-KWF9)

FEVAD (2022). Vendre en direct par vidéo: explosion du commerce en live-streaming en Asie. Retrieved from https://www.fevad.com/ (archived at https://perma.cc/YB4Q-4K2S)

Gan, W., Ye, Z., Wan, S., & Yu, P. S. (2023). Web 3.0: The Future of Internet. arXiv preprint arXiv:2304.06032.

Gao, L., & Bai, X. (2014). Online consumer behaviour and its relationship to website atmospheric induced flow: Insights into online travel agencies in China. *Journal of Retailing and Consumer Services*, 21(4), 653–665.

Goel, A. K., Bakshi, R., & Agrawal, K. K. (2022). Web 3.0 and decentralized applications. *Materials Proceedings*, 10(1), 8.

Hoffman, D. L., & Novak, T. P. (1996). Marketing in hypermedia computer-mediated environments: Conceptual foundations. *Journal of Marketing*, 60(3), 50–68.

Hsu, C.L., Chang, K. C., & Chen, M. C. (2012). Flow experience and internet shopping behaviour: Investigating the moderating effect of consumer characteristics. *System Research*, 29, 317–332.

Hubbard, D. W. (2020). *The Failure of Risk Management: Why it's broken and how to fix it*. John Wiley & Sons.

Kang, J. (2020). Identifying antecedents and consequences of well-being: The case of cruise passengers. *Tourism Management Perspectives*, 33, 100609.

Kao, P.-J., Pai, P., & Tsai, H.-T. (2019). Looking at both sides of relationship dynamics in virtual communities: A social exchange theoretical lens. *Information & Management*, https://doi.org/10.1016/j.im.2019.103210 (archived at https://perma.cc/U8EP-MYME)

Karjaluoto, H., Munnukka, J., & Kiuru, K. (2016). Brand love and positive word of mouth: The moderating effects of experience and price. *Journal of Product & Brand Management*, 25(6), 527–537.

Karpinska-Krakowiak, M., & Eisend, M. (2020). Mini-film advertising and digital brand engagement: The moderating effects of drama and lecture. *International Journal of Advertising*, 39(3), 387–409. https://doi.org/10.1080/02650487.2019.1633841 (archived at https://perma.cc/N4LF-ZY9Y)

Kim, G., & Koo, H. (2016). The causal relationship between risk and trust in the online marketplace: A bidirectional perspective. *Computers in Human Behaviour*, 55, 1020–1029.

Lavie, T., & Tractinsky, N. (2004). Assessing dimensions of perceived visual aesthetics of web sites. *International Journal of Human Computer Interaction*, 60(3), 269–298. https://doi.org/10.1016/j.ijhcs.2003.09.002 (archived at https://perma.cc/7MZ3-WHRA)

Lawler, E. J., & Yoon, J. (1993). Power and the emergence of commitment behaviour in negotiated exchange. *American Sociological Review*, 58, 465–

Lawler, E. J., & Yoon, J. (1996). Commitment in exchange relations: Test of a theory of relational cohesion. *American Sociological Review*, 61, 89–

Lawler, E. J., & Yoon, J. (1998). Network structure and emotion in exchange relations. *American Sociological Review*, 63, 871–894.

Lawler, E. J. (2001). An affect theory of social exchange. *American Journal of Sociology*, 102, 321–352.

Lawler, E. J., Thye, S. R., & Yoon, J. (2006). Commitment in structurally enabled and induced exchange relations. *Social Psychology Quarterly*, 69, 183–200.

Lawler, E. J., Thye, S. R., & Jeongkoo, Y. (2000). Emotion and group cohesion in productive exchange. *American Journal of Sociology*, 106, 616–657.

Lee, M. K., & Turban, E. (2001). A trust model for consumer Internet shopping. *International Journal of Electronic Commerce*, 6(1), 75–91.

Li, F., Piemkowski, D., Van Moorsel, A., & Smith, C. (2012). A holistic framework for trust in online transactions. *International Journal of Management Reviews*, 14, 85–103.

Luo, X., Cheah, J. H., Lim, X. J., & Ng, S. I. A. (2022). Bibliometric review of user behaviours research in live streaming commerce. *Journal of Marketing Advances et Practices*, 4(1), 32–49.

Mukherjee, A., & Nath, P. (2007). Role of electronic trust in online retailing: A re-examination of the commitment trust theory. *European Journal of Marketing*, 41(9/10), 1173–1202. https://doi.org/10.1108/03090560710773390 (archived at https://perma.cc/JJ2W-GMMX)

Murray, K., & Häuble, G. (2011). Freedom of choice, ease of use and the formation of interface preferences. *MIS Quarterly*, 35(4), 955–976. https://doi.org/10.2307/41409968 (archived at https://perma.cc/DUX5-LMR3)

Parker, C. J., & Wang, H. (2016). Examining hedonic and utilitarian motivations for m-commerce fashion retail app engagement. *Journal of Fashion Marketing & Management*, 20(4), 487–506. https://doi.org/10.1108/JFMM-02-2016-0015 (archived at https://perma.cc/4NRG-6UJH)

Patel, V., Das, K., Chatterjee, R., & Shukla, Y. (2020). Does the interface quality of mobile shopping apps affect purchase intention? An empirical study. *Australasian Marketing*

Journal, 28(4), 300–309. https://doi.org/10.1016/j.ausmj.2020.08.004 (archived at https://perma.cc/M7L2-BVGL)

Pelet, J. É., & Taieb, B. (2022). Context-aware optimization of mobile commerce website interfaces from the consumers' perspective: Effects on behavioural intentions. *Computers in Human Behaviour Reports*, 7, 100225.

Pelet, J. É., & Ettis, S. A. (2022). Social media advertising effectiveness: The role of perceived originality, liking, credibility, irritation, intrusiveness and ad destination. *International Journal of Technology and Human Interaction*, 18(1), 1–20.

Price, H. E., & Collett, J. L. (2012). The role of exchange and emotion on commitment: A study of teachers. *Social Science Research*, 41(6), 1469–1479.

Reber, R., & Schwarz, N. (1999). Effects of perceptual fluency on judgments of truth. *Consciousness and Cognition*, 8(September), 338–342. https://doi.org/10.1006/ccog.1999.0386 (archived at https://perma.cc/D22L-TPGA)

Rustam, A., Wang, Y., & Zameer, H. (2020). Environmental awareness, firm sustainability exposure and green consumption behaviours. *Journal of Cleaner Production*, 268, 122016.

Seckler, M., Opwis, K., & Tuch, A. N. (2015). Linking objective design factors with subjective aesthetics: An experimental study on how structure and colour of websites affect the facets of users' visual aesthetic perception. *Computers in Human Behaviour*, 49(August), 375–389. https://doi.org/10.1016/j.chb.2015.02.056 (archived at https://perma.cc/X2ZF-5N3R)

Sharma, S., Menard, P., & Mutchler, L. A. (2019). Who to trust? Applying trust to social commerce. *Journal of Computer Information Systems*, 59(1), 32–42.

Sohn, S., Seegebarth, B., & Moritz, M. (2017). The impact of perceived visual complexity of mobile online shops on user's satisfaction. *Psychology & Marketing*, 34(2), 195–214. https://doi.org/10.1002/mar.20983 (archived at https://perma.cc/ZRL2-EKN8)

Song, Z., Sun, Y., Wan, J., Huang, L., & Zhu, J. (2019). Smart e-commerce systems: Current status and research challenges. *Electronic Markets*, 29(2), 221–238. https://doi.org/10.1007/s12525-017-0272-3 (archived at https://perma.cc/PDA9-573C)

Stewart, H., & Jürjens, J. (2018). Data security and consumer trust in FinTech innovation in Germany. *Information and Computer Security*, 26(1), 109–128. https://doi.org/10.1108/ICS-06-2017-0039 (archived at https://perma.cc/J3V8-268B)

Sun, N., & Botev, J. (2021). Intelligent autonomous agents and trust in virtual reality. *Computers in Human Behaviour Reports*, 4, 100146.

Toukabri, M., & Mohamed Youssef, M. A. (2023). Climate change disclosure and sustainable development goals (SDGs) of the 2030 agenda: The moderating role of corporate governance. *Journal of Information, Communication and Ethics in Society*, 21(1), 30–62.

Tractinsky, N., Cokhavi, A., Kirschenbaum, M., & Sharfi, T. (2006). Evaluating the consistency of immediate aesthetic perception of web pages. *International Journal of Human–Computer Studies*, 64, 1071–1083. https://doi.org/10.1016/j.ijhcs.2006.06.009 (archived at https://perma.cc/R3XL-9ZJX)

Tsai, Y.-T., Wang, S.-C., Yan, K.-Q., & Chang, C.-M. (2017). Precise positioning of marketing and behaviour intentions of location-based mobile commerce in the Internet of Things. *Symmetry*, 9(8), 139. https://doi.org/10.3390/sym9080139 (archived at https://perma.cc/GM4C-DQFL)

Youssef, W. A. B., & Mansour, N. (2024). The factoring 2.0 in the era of the fintech revolution context. In *Digital Technology and Changing Roles in Managerial and Financial Accounting: Theoretical knowledge and practical application* (Vol. 36, pp. 37–51). Emerald Publishing Limited.

Wu, T. J., Xu, T., Li, L. Q., & Yuan, K. S. (2020). 'Touching with heart, reasoning by truth!' The impact of brand cues on mini-film advertising effect. *International Journal of Advertising*, 39(8), 1322–1350.

Zhang, S., Huang, C., Li, X., & Ren, A. (2022). Characteristics and roles of streamers in e-commerce live streaming. *The Service Industries Journal*, 1–29.

Zhang, H., Lu, Y., Gupta, S., & Zhao, L. (2014). What motivates customers to participate in social commerce? The impact of technological environments and virtual customer experiences. *Information et Management*, 51(8), 1017–1030.

Zuo, R., & Xiao, J. (2021). Exploring consumers' impulse buying behaviour in live streaming shopping. In: *15th International Conference on Management Science and Engineering Management*, pp. 610–622. Springer, Cham.

Chapter 3

Arnould, E. J., & Thompson, C. J. (2005). Consumer culture theory (CCT): Twenty years of research. *Journal of Consumer Research*, 31(4), 868–882.

Baek, T. H., Yoo, C. Y., & Yoon, S. (2018). Augment yourself through virtual mirror: The impact of self-viewing and narcissism on consumer responses. *International Journal of Advertising*, 37(3), 421–439.

Daassi, M., & Debbabi, S. (2021). Intention to reuse AR-based apps: The combined role of the sense of immersion, product presence and perceived realism. *Information & Management*, 58(4), 103453.

Davis, F. D., Bagozzi, R. P., & Warshaw, P. R. (1989). User acceptance of computer technology: A comparison of two theoretical models. *Management Science*, 35(8), 982–1003.

Davis, F. D. (1989). Perceived usefulness, perceived ease of use and user acceptance of information technology. *MIS Quarterly*, 319–340.

Ebrahimabad, F. Z., Yazdani, H., Hakim, A., & Asarian, M. (2024). Augmented reality versus web-based shopping: How does AR Improve user experience and online purchase intention? *Telematics and Informatics Reports*, 15, 100152.

Ertzscheid O. (2024). *Les IA à l'assaut du cyberespace Vers un Web synthétique*. C&F éditions.

Etminani-Ghasrodashti, R., & Hamidi, S. (2020). Online shopping as a substitute or complement to in-store shopping trips in Iran? *Cities*, 103, 102768.

Fan, X., Chai, Z., Deng, N., & Dong, X. (2020). Adoption of augmented reality in online retailing and consumers' product attitude: A cognitive perspective. *Journal of Retailing and Consumer Services*, 53, 101986.

Fortin, D. R., & Dholakia, R. R. (2005). Interactivity and vividness effects on social presence and involvement with a web-based advertisement. *Journal of Business Research*, 58(3), 387–396.

Gallic, C., & Rémy Marrone, R. (2023). *Le Grand Livre du Marketing digital*. Hors Collection, Dunod.

Hilken, T., De Ruyter, K., Chylinski, M., Mahr, D., & Keeling, D. I. (2017). Augmenting the eye of the beholder: Exploring the strategic potential of augmented reality to enhance online service experiences. *Journal of the Academy of Marketing Science*, 45, 884–905.

Horizon IQ (2024). 7 Incredible Examples of Augmented Reality Technology. Retrieved from https://www.horizoniq.com/blog/7-incredible-examples-of-augmented-reality-technology/ (archived at https://perma.cc/WM3U-MBGB)

Hu, T., Kettinger, W. J., & Poston, R. S. (2015). The effect of online social value on satisfaction and continued use of social media. *European Journal of Information Systems*, 24(4), 391–410.

Javornik, A. (2016). Augmented reality: Research agenda for studying the impact of its media characteristics on consumer behaviour. *Journal of Retailing and Consumer Services*, 30, 252–261.

Kim, H. W., Gupta, S., & Koh, J. (2011). Investigating the intention to purchase digital items in social networking communities: A customer value perspective. *Information & Management*, 48(6), 228–234.

Ko, H., Cho, C. H., & Roberts, M. S. (2005). Internet uses and gratifications: A structural equation model of interactive advertising. *Journal of Advertising*, 34(2), 57–70.

Laraba, M., & Derradji, M. (2024). Impact des technologies numériques sur l'usage de l'espace architectural. Doctoral dissertation, Université Constantine 3 Salah Boubnider, Faculté d'architecture et d'urbanisme.

Lee, R. J., Sener, I. N., Mokhtarian, P. L., & Handy, S. L. (2017). Relationships between the online and in-store shopping frequency of Davis, California residents. *Transportation Research Part A: Policy and Practice*, 100, 40–52.

Lewis, T., & Potter, E. (2013). *Ethical Consumption: A critical introduction*. Routledge.

Li, H., Daugherty, T., & Biocca, F. (2002). Impact of 3-D advertising on product knowledge, brand attitude and purchase intention: The mediating role of presence. *Journal of Advertising*, 31(3), 43–57.

Poushneh, A. (2018). Augmented reality in retail: A trade-off between user's control of access to personal information and augmentation quality. *Journal of Retailing and Consumer Services*, 41, 169–176.

Preece J., Sharp H., Rogers Y. (2015). *Interaction Design beyond Human-Computer Interaction*. John Wiley & Sons, UK.

Queuche, T. (2023). 5 raisons pour adopter la réalité virtuelle et la réalité augmentée dans le retail. Retrieved from https://www.orange-business.com/fr/blogs/5-raisons-pour-adopter-realite-virtuelle-et-realite-augmentee-dans-retail (archived at https://perma.cc/8EJL-5ZC5)

Schiffman, L. G., & Kanuk, L. L. (2010). *Consumer Behaviour*. 10th Edition, Upper Saddle River, N.J.

Scholz, J., & Duffy, K. (2018). We ARe at home: How augmented reality reshapes mobile marketing and consumer-brand relationships. *Journal of Retailing and Consumer Services*, 44, 11–23.

Sheth, J. (2020). Impact of Covid-19 on consumer behaviour: Will the old habits return or die? *Journal of Business Research*, 117, 280–283.

Sia Partners. (2023). La 5G, catalyseur de la démocratisation de l'AR et de la VR pour les entreprises et le grand public. Retrieved from https://www.sia-partners.com/fr/publications/publications-de-nos-experts/la-5g-catalyseur-de-la-democratisation-de-lar-et-de-la-vr (archived at https://perma.cc/UW3A-B56S)

Smink, A. R., Frowijn, S., van Reijmersdal, E. A., van Noort, G., & Neijens, P. C. (2019). Try online before you buy: How does shopping with augmented reality affect brand responses and personal data disclosure? *Electronic Commerce Research and Applications*, 35, 100854.

Souza, E. (2024). 9 augmented reality technologies for architecture and construction. Retrieved from https://www.archdaily.com/914501/9-augmented-reality-technologies-for-architecture-and-construction (archived at https://perma.cc/9VAX-LL3W)

Steuer, J., Biocca, F., & Levy, M. R. (1995). Defining virtual reality: Dimensions determining telepresence. *Communication in the Age of Virtual Reality*, 33(37–39), 1.

Van Huy, L., & Thai Thinh, N. H. (2024). Ranking the hotel website service quality according to customer's perception: A case study of 4-star hotel. *Journal of Quality Assurance in Hospitality & Tourism*, 25(1), 37–56.

Van Noort, G., Voorveld, H. A., & Van Reijmersdal, E. A. (2012). Interactivity in brand web sites: Cognitive, affective and behavioural responses explained by consumers' online flow experience. *Journal of Interactive Marketing*, 26(4), 223–234.

Verhagen, T., Vonkeman, C., Feldberg, F., & Verhagen, P. (2014). Present it like it is here: Creating local presence to improve online product experiences. *Computers in Human Behaviour*, 39, 270–280.

Voicu, M. C., Sîrghi, N., & Toth, D. M. M. (2023). Consumers' experience and satisfaction using augmented reality apps in e-shopping: New empirical evidence. *Applied Sciences*, 13(17), 9596.

White, M., & Ronfeldt, M. (2024). Monitoring rater quality in observational systems: Issues due to unreliable estimates of rater quality. *Educational Assessment*, 29(2), 124–146.

Yim, M. Y. C., Chu, S. C., & Sauer, P. L. (2017). Is augmented reality technology an effective tool for e-commerce? An interactivity and vividness perspective. *Journal of Interactive Marketing*, 39(1), 89–103.

Zhao, M., & Dholakia, R. (2009). A multi-attribute model of website interactivity and customer satisfaction: An application of the Kano model. *Managing Service Quality: An International Journal*, 19(3), 286–307. https://doi.org/10.1108/09604 520910955311 (archived at https://perma.cc/VWD3-A8V5)

Zhao, X., Shi, C., You, X., & Zong, C. (2017). Analysis of mental workload in online shopping: Are augmented and virtual reality consistent? *Frontiers in Psychology*, 8, 71.

Chapter 4

Anantrasirichai, N., & Bull, D. (2022). Artificial intelligence in the creative industries: A review. *Artificial Intelligence Review*, 1–68.

Assassi, I. (2003). Spécificités du produit culturel. *Revue Française de Gestion*, 142(1), 129–146.

Bengio, Y., Ducharme, R., Vincent, P., Jauvin, C., Kandola, J., Hofmann, T., Poggio, T., & Shawe-Taylor, J. (Eds.) (2003). A neural probabilistic language model. *Journal of Machine Learning Research*, 3(6), 11371155. https://doi.org/10.1162/153244303322533223 (archived at https://perma.cc/TVH3-L57Q)

Borthwick, A. C. anderson, C. L., Finsness, E. S., & Foulger, T. S. (2015). Special article personal wearable technologies in education: Value or villain? *Journal of Digital Learning in Teacher Education*, 31(3), 85–92.

Bruner, J. S. (1966). *Toward a Theory of Instruction*. Vol. 59. Harvard University Press.

Brunet, É., Lebart, L., & Vanni, L. (2021). Littérature et intelligence artificielle. *L'intelligence artificielle des textes*, (15), 73–130.

Chen, L., Chen, P., & Lin, Z. (2020). Artificial intelligence in education: A review. *IEEE Access*, 8, 75264–75278.

Choura, F. (2024). Les industries creatives et culturelles a l'ere de l'ia: proposition d'un agenda de recherche. Actes de l'Association Tunisienne de Marketing, 19–20/04/2024, The Sindbad, Hammamet, Tunisia.

Greenwald, S. W., Corning, W., & Maes, P. (2017). *Multi-User framework for collaboration and co-creation in virtual reality*. Proceedings of 12th international conference on computer supported collaborative learning (pp. 1–2). ISLS.

Halmaoui, H. (2022). L'intelligence artificielle, la réalité augmentée et la réalité virtuelle dans l'audiovisuel et le cinéma. Retrieved from https://hal.science/hal-03741132 (archived at https://perma.cc/E34M-QN8A)

Heffernan, N. T., & Heffernan, C. L. (2014). The ASSISTments ecosystem: Building a platform that brings scientists and teachers together for minimally invasive research on human learning and teaching. *International Journal of Artificial Intelligence in Education*, 24, 470–497.

Heudin, J. C., & Kyrou, A. (2020). Faire de l'IA un instrument et compagnon de musique. *Multitudes*, 1, 98–102.

Hong, J., Suh, E. H., Kim, J., & Kim, S. (2009). Context-aware system for proactive personalized service based on context history. *Expert Systems with Applications*, 36(4), 7448–7457.

Holmes, W., Bialik, M., & Fadel, C. (2019). *Artificial Intelligence in Education: Promises and implications for teaching and learning*. Centre for Curriculum Redesign.

Huang, Y. M., & Chiu, P. S. (2015). The effectiveness of a meaningful learning-based evaluation model for context-aware mobile learning. *British Journal of Educational Technology*, 46(2), 437–447.

Jacques, A. (2023). L'intelligence artificielle fera-t-elle un jour les films à notre place? La menace fantôme. *Séquences: la revue de cinéma*, 335, 16–17.

Jafari-Sadeghi, V., Garcia-Perez, A., Candelo, E., & Couturier, J. (2021). Exploring the impact of digital transformation on technology entrepreneurship and technological market expansion: The role of technology readiness, exploration and exploitation. *Journal of Business Research*, 124, 100–111.

Lin, C. F., Yeh, Y. C., Hung, Y. H., & Chang, R. I. (2013). Data mining for providing a personalized learning path in creativity: An application of decision trees. *Computers & Education*, 68, 199–210.

Lin, T. J., & Lan, Y. J. (2015). Language learning in virtual reality environments: Past, present and future. *Educational Technology & Society*, 18(4), 486–497.

Luckin, R. (2017). Towards artificial intelligence-based assessment systems. *Nature Human Behaviour*, 1(3), 0028.

Manning, C. (2016, July). Understanding human language: Can NLP and deep learning help? In Proceedings of the 39th International ACM SIGIR Conference on Research and Development in Information Retrieval (pp. 1–1).

Mavroudi, A., Hadzilacos, T., Kalles, D., & Gregoriades, A. (2016). Teacher-led design of an adaptive learning environment. *Interactive Learning Environments*, 24(8), 1996–2010.

Peukert, C. (2019). The next wave of digital technological change and the cultural industries. *Journal of Cultural Economics*, 43(2), 189–210.

Ponsignon, F., & Derbaix, M. (2020). The impact of interactive technologies on the social experience: An empirical study in a cultural tourism context. *Tourism Management Perspectives*, 35, 100723

Rauschnabel, P. A., & Ro, Y. K. (2016). Augmented reality smart glasses: An investigation of technology acceptance drivers. *International Journal of Technology Marketing*, 11(2), 123–148.

Sabouk, N., & Sidmou, M. L. (2019). L'intelligence artificielle ; vers un nouveau paradigme interdisciplinaire: Etat de synthèse. *Revue Internationale du Marketing et Management Stratégique*, 1(4).

Shaari, A., & Hamzah, A. (2016). Neurolinguistic Programming (NLP): Its overview and review in the lenses of philosophy and pedagogy. *Asian Journal of University Education*, 12(1), 1–13.

Shi, B., & Weninger, T. (2017). *ProjE: Embedding projection for knowledge graph completion*. Proceedings of the thirty-first AAAI conference on artificial intelligence (pp. 1236–1242).

Tsai, P. S., Tsai, C. C., & Hwang, G. J. (2012). Developing a survey for assessing preferences in constructivist context-aware ubiquitous learning environments. *Journal of Computer Assisted Learning*, 28(3), 250–264.

Vlačić, B., Corbo, L., e Silva, S. C., & Dabić, M. (2021). The evolving role of artificial intelligence in marketing: A review and research agenda. *Journal of Business Research*, 128, 187–203.

Waldfogel, J. (2017). How digitization has created a golden age of music, movies, books and television. *Journal of Economic Perspectives*, 31(3), 195–214.

Wang, Y. H., & Liao, H. C. (2011). Adaptive learning for ESL based on computation. *British Journal of Educational Technology*, 42(1), 66–87.

Williamson, B., & Eynon, R. (2020). Historical threads, missing links and future directions in AI in education. *Learning, Media and Technology*, 45(3), 223–235.

Zawacki-Richter, O., Marín, V. I., Bond, M., & Gouverneur, F. (2019). Systematic review of research on artificial intelligence applications in higher education – where are the educators? *International Journal of Educational Technology in Higher Education*, 16(1), 1–27.

Zhang, L., Shao, Z., Li, X., & Feng, Y. (2021). Gamification and online impulse buying: The moderating effect of gender and age, *International Journal of Information Management*, 61, 102267, ISSN 0268-4012, https://doi.org/10.1016/j.ijinfomgt.2020.102267 (archived at https://perma.cc/Q5Y8-7K5H)

Zlatoff, N., & Ribaupierre, C. D. (2023). Apprendre à jouer avec une machine: intelligence artificielle et deep learning dans un dispositif théâtral. *Percées*, L'Extension, recherche & création.

Chapter 5

Alhidari, A., Iyer, P., & Paswan, A. (2015). Personal level antecedents of eWOM and purchase intention, on social networking sites. *Journal of Customer Behaviour*, 14(2), 107–125.

Ahmadi, A., & Ataei, A. (2024). Emotional attachment: A bridge between brand reputation and brand advocacy. *Asia-Pacific Journal of Business Administration*, 16(1), 1–20. https://doi.org/10.1108/APJBA-11-2021-0579 (archived at https://perma.cc/SM67-7XXR)

Baloglu, S., Henthorne, T. L., & Sahin, S. (2014). Destination image and brand personality of Jamaica: A model of tourist behaviour. *Journal of Travel & Tourism Marketing*, 31(8), 1057–1070. https://doi.org/10.1080/10548408.2014.892468 (archived at https://perma.cc/3CSD-CVAM).

Barreda, A. A., Bilgihan, A., & Kageyama, Y. (2015). The role of trust in creating positive word of mouth and behavioural intentions: The case of online social networks. *Journal of Relationship Marketing*, 14(1), 16–36.

Carroll, B. A., & Ahuvia, A. C. (2006). Some antecedents and outcomes of brand love. *Marketing Letters*, 17(2), 79–89.

Feliz, T. (2012). *Análisis de contenido de la comunicación asíncrona en la formación universitaria* [Content analysis of asynchronous communication in university training]. *Revista de Educación*, 358, 282–309.

Junco, R., Elavsky, C. M., & Heiberger, G. (2013). Putting Twitter to the test: Assessing outcomes for student collaboration, engagement and success. *British Journal of Educational Technology*, 44(2), 273–287.

Kaplan, A. M., & Haenlein, M. (2010). Users of the world, unite! The challenges and opportunities of social media. *Business Horizons*, 53(1), 59–68.

Khan, F. (2024a). Uncovering lessons from Airbnb's 'Don't Go There, Live There' campaign. Retrieved from https://www.linkedin.com/pulse/uncovering-lessons-from-airbnbs-dont-go-live-campaign-fatima-khan (archived at https://perma.cc/C7QH-STLG)

Khan, F. (2024b). Leveraging trusted influencers for brand repositioning. Retrieved from https://www.linkedin.com/pulse/influencer-changed-tiktoks-image-indonesia-fatima-khan?trk=article-ssr-frontend-pulse_more-articles_related-content-card (archived at https://perma.cc/4CAT-4Z8K)

Khatri, C., Chapman, S. J., Glasbey, J., Kelly, M., Nepogodiev, D., Bhangu, A., & Fitzgerald, J. E. (2015). Social media and internet driven study recruitment: Evaluating a new model for promoting collaborator engagement and participation. *PLoS ONE*, 10(3), 1–11. https://doi.org/10.1371/journal.pone.0118899 (archived at https://perma.cc/4P6D-3DVF)

Matarranz, J. L., García-Madariaga, J., & Carvajal, M. (2024). Approach to the sense of belonging: Construct for the marketing of entrepreneurships in higher education. *International Entrepreneurship and Management Journal*, https://doi.org/10.1007/s11365-024-00974-6 (archived at https://perma.cc/N32B-UD7W)

Maulana, A. E., Patterson, P. G., Satria, A., & Pradipta, I. A. (2023). Alumni connectedness and its role in intention to contribute to higher education institutions. *Journal of Marketing for Higher Education*, 1–22.

McAlexander, J. H., Schouten, J. W., & Koening, H. F. (2002). Building brand community. *Journal of Marketing*, 1(38–54), 66.

Papadimitriou, D., Kaplanidou, K., & Apostolopoulou, A. (2018). Destination image components and word-of-mouth intentions in urban tourism: A multigroup approach. *Journal of Hospitality & Tourism Research*, 42(4), 503–527. https://doi.org/10.1177/1096348015584443 (archived at https://perma.cc/3JHB-QPPC)

Qu, H., Kim, L. H., & Im, H. H. (2011). A model of destination branding: Integrating the concepts of the branding and destination image. *Tourism Management*, 32(3), 465–476. https://doi.org/10.1016/j.tourman.2010.03.014 (archived at https://perma.cc/E9FG-M8NX).

Ricoy, M.-C., & Feliz, T. (2016). Twitter as a learning community in higher education. *Journal of Educational Technology & Society*, 19(1), 237–248.

Russell, C. A., Norman, A. T., & Heckler, S. E. (2004). The consumption of television programming: Development and validation of the connectedness scale. *Journal of Consumer Research*, 31(1), 150–161.

Sotiriadis, M. D. (2017). Sharing tourism experiences in social media. *International Journal of Contemporary Hospitality Management*, 29(1), 179–225. https://doi.org/10.1108/IJCHM-05-2016-0300 (archived at https://perma.cc/9WMZ-TA5R)

Stokburger-Sauer, N., Ratneshwar, S., & Sen, S. (2012). Drivers of consumer-brand identification. *International Journal of Research in Marketing*, 29(4), 406–418. https://doi.org/10.1016/j.ijresmar.2012.06.001 (archived at https://perma.cc/8UBA-JC8Z).

Sutton, J., Spiro, E. S., Johnson, B., Fitzhugh, S., Gibson, B., & Butts, C. T. (2014). Warning tweets: Serial transmission of messages during the warning phase of a disaster event. Information, *Communication & Society*, 17(6), 765–787.

Tuten, T. L., & Solomon, M. R. (2018). *Social Media Marketing*. 3rd edition, Sage Publications Ltd, UK.

Ukpabi, D. C., & Karjaluoto, H. (2018). What drives travelers' adoption of user-generated content? A literature review. *Tourism Management Perspectives*, 28, 251–273. https://doi.org/10.1016/j.tmp.2018.03.006 (archived at https://perma.cc/GYA3-PAWY)

We Are Social and Meltwater (2024). Digital 2024 United Kingdom report shows strong growth in social media. Retrieved from https://wearesocial.com/uk/blog/2024/02/digital-2024-united-kingdom-report-shows-strong-growth-in-social-media/ (archived at https://perma.cc/M6RP-HS4Q)

Wilk, V., Sadeque, S., & Soutar, G. N. (2024). Exploring online destination brand advocacy. *Tourism Recreation Research*, 49(2), 283–301.

Zeng, B., & Gerritsen, R. (2014). What do we know about social media in tourism? A review. *Tourism Management Perspectives*, 10(April), 27–36. https://doi.org/10.1016/j.tmp.2014.01.001 (archived at https://perma.cc/UX2V-GT45)

Chapter 6

Hassenzahl, M. (2010). *Experience Design: Technology for all the right reasons*. Morgan & Claypool Publishers.

Kuo, Y. F., & Yen, S. N. (2009). Towards an understanding of the behavioural intention to use 3G mobile value-added services. *Computers in Human Behaviour*, 25(1), 103–110.

Lemon, K. N., & Verhoef, P. C. (2016). Understanding customer experience throughout the customer journey. *Journal of Marketing*, 80(6), 69–96.

Norman D. A. (2013). *The Design of Everyday Things*. MIT Press.

Pelet J.-É. (2010). Effects of colour of commercial websites on memorization and purchase intention. *Information Systems and Management*, 15(1), 97–131. [FNEGE 2, AERES 2/ CNRS 2], https://doi.org/10.3917/sim.101.0097 (archived at https://perma.cc/977J-Q7G6)

Pelet J.-É., & Papadopoulou P. (2014). Consumer behaviour in the mobile environment: An exploratory study of m-commerce and social media. *International Journal of Technology and Human Interaction*, Special Issue on Social Media and Social CRM, 10 (4), 36–48. https://doi.org/10.4018/ijthi.2014100103 (archived at https://perma.cc/VD9N-KDLR) [FNEGE 4, CNRS 4, HCERES C]

Pelet J.-É., & Papadopoulou P. (2012). The effect of colours of e-commerce websites on consumer mood, memorization and buying intention. *European Journal of Information Systems*, Special Issue: 'Information Research, Education and Policy in the Mediterranean Region', 21, 438–467. https://doi.org/10.1057/ejis.2012.17 (archived at https://perma.cc/TQH6-DG5G) [FNEGE 1, CNRS 1, HCERES A]

Chapter 7

Ayaz A., & M. Yanartas (2020). An analysis on the unified theory of acceptance and use of technology theory (UTAUT): Acceptance of electronic document management system (EDMS). *Computers in Human Behaviour Reports* 2, 100032, https://doi.org/10.1016/j.chbr.2020.100032 (archived at https://perma.cc/H7J4-V33V).

Batat, W. (2021). How augmented reality (AR) is transforming the restaurant sector: Investigating the impact of 'Le Petit Chef' on customers' dining experiences. *Technological Forecasting and Social Change*, 172, 121013.

Chao, C. (2019). Factors determining the behavioural intention to use mobile learning: An application and extension of the UTAUT model. *Frontiers in Psychology*, 10, 446627 https://doi.org/10.3389/fpsyg.2019.01652 (archived at https://perma.cc/XDV3-VKJK)

Chaudhary, P., Singh, A., & Sharma, S. (2022). Understanding the antecedents of omni-channel shopping by customers with reference to fashion category: The Indian Millennials' perspective. *Young Consumers*, 23(2), 304–320.

Cheah, J., Lim, X., Ting, H., Liu, Y., & Quach, S. (2022). Are privacy concerns still relevant? Revisiting consumer behaviour in omnichannel retailing, *Journal of Retailing and Consumer Services*, 65, 102242, https://doi.org/10.1016/j.jretconser.2020.102242 (archived at https://perma.cc/R46J-XJZL)

de Souza, S., Emanoel, D., & Baldanza, R. F. (2018). The e-consumer in light of the perceived value theory: A study on the acceptance of mobile commerce, *Base Revista de Administraçãoe Contabilidade da UNISINOS*, 15(3), 238–263. Retrieved from https://www.redalyc.org/articulo.oa?id=337260224006 (archived at https://perma.cc/AC4T-VK7X)

Du, J., Zhu, L., Ma, Y., & Zhang, Y. (2024). Beyond weekdays: The impact of the weekend effect on eWOM of hedonic product. *Journal of Retailing and Consumer Services*, 77, 103624.

Escobar, M.-C. (2017). AR takes customer experience to the next level at Starbucks Shanghai Reserve Roastery. Retrieved from https://hospitalitytech.com/ar-takes-customer-experience-next-level-starbucks-shanghai-reserve-roastery (archived at https://perma.cc/3BSF-WFBJ)

Federal Trade Commission (2024). Online advertising and marketing. Retrieved from https://www.ftc.gov/business-guidance/advertising-marketing/online-advertising-marketing (archived at https://perma.cc/M9VH-ZDYF)

Fingent (2024). Augmented reality in business. Retrieved from https://www.fingent.com/blog/augmented-reality-in-business/ (archived at https://perma.cc/UGX4-HNHX)

Gambone, M. (2024). Branding beyond boundaries: The future of trademarks and advertising in augmented reality. *The University of Cincinnati Intellectual Property and Computer Law Journal*, 9(2), 4.

Ginsburg, R. (2022). Augmented reality in retail: How retailers are using AR for better shopping experiences. Retrieved from https://www.shopify.com/retail/how-retailers-are-using-ar-technology-to-build-buzz-and-brand-awareness (archived at https://perma.cc/FZ2N-9PZ3)

Grand View Research (2024). U.S. immersive entertainment market size, share & trends analysis report by technology type (virtual reality, augmented reality, mixed reality, others), by application and segment forecasts, 2024–2030. Retrieved from https://www.grandviewresearch.com/industry-analysis/us-immersive-entertainment-market-report (archived at https://perma.cc/M53E-WYHG)

Huang, L., Lu, X., & Ba, S. (2016). An empirical study of the cross-channel effects between web and mobile shopping channels. *Information Management*, 53(2), 265–278.

Huré, E., Picot-Coupey, K., & Ackermann, C. L. (2017). Understanding omnichannel shopping value: A mixed-method study. *Journal of Retailing and Consumer Services*, 39, 314–330.

Hwang, J., Lee, J. S., & Kim, H. (2019). Perceived innovativeness of drone food delivery services and its impacts on attitude and behavioural intentions: The moderating role of gender and age. *International Journal of Hospitality Management*, 81, 94–103.

IKEA (2024). IKEA mobile apps. Retrieved from https://www.ikea.com/gb/en/customer-service/mobile-apps/ (archived at https://perma.cc/ZYM2-U8DJ)

Jia, X., Pang, Y., Huang, B., & Hou, F. (2023). Understanding consumers' continuance intention to watch streams: A value-based continuance intention model. *Frontiers in Psychology*, 14, 1073301. https://doi.org/10.3389/fpsyg.2023.1073301 (archived at https://perma.cc/ZT3T-7TSY)

Jones, M. (2023). Voice commerce, AI and the future of shopping. Retrieved from https://www.bazaarvoice.com/blog/voice-commerce-ai/ (archived at https://perma.cc/KWF4-QW4L)

Kaaniche, N., Laurent, M., & Belguith, S. (2020). Privacy enhancing technologies for solving the privacy-personalization paradox: Taxonomy and survey. *Journal of Network and Computer Applications*, 171, 102807.

Khalid, B. (2024). Evaluating customer perspectives on omnichannel shopping satisfaction in the fashion retail sector. *Heliyon*, 10(16), e36027.

Kumar, H., Tuli, N., Singh, R. K., Arya, V., & Srivastava, R. (2024). Exploring the role of augmented reality as a new brand advocate. *Journal of Consumer Behaviour*, 23(2), 620–638. https://doi.org/10.1002/cb.2227 (archived at https://perma.cc/R893-27NT)

Mari, A., Mandelli, A., & Algesheimer, R. (2024). Empathic voice assistants: Enhancing consumer responses in voice commerce. *Journal of Business Research*, 175, 114566.

Martin, K. D., Borah, A., & Palmatier, R. W. (2017). Data privacy: Effects on customer and firm performance. *Journal of Marketing*, 81(1), 36–58.

Mensah, I. K., & Khan, M. K. (2024). Unified Theory of Acceptance and Use of Technology (UTAUT) model: Factors influencing mobile banking services' adoption in China. *Sage Open*. https://doi.org/10.1177/21582440241234230 (archived at https://perma.cc/9ZR3-NFVN)

Nazir, S., Khadim, S., Asadullah, M. A., & Syed, N. (2023). Exploring the influence of artificial intelligence technology on consumer repurchase intention: The mediation and moderation approach. *Technology in Society*, 72, 102190.

Orús, C., Ibáñez-Sánchez, S., & Flavian, C. (2021). Enhancing the customer experience with virtual and augmented reality: The impact of content and device type. *International Journal of Hospitality Management*, 98, 103019, https://doi.org/10.1016/j.ijhm.2021.103019 (archived at https://perma.cc/43M2-AVD2)

Pereira, M. L., de La Martinière Petroll, M., Soares, J. C., Matos, C. A. D., & Hernani-Merino, M. (2023). Impulse buying behaviour in omnichannel retail: An approach through the stimulus-organism-response theory. *International Journal of Retail & Distribution Management*, 51(1), 39–58.

Rahman, S. M., Carlson, J., Gudergan, S. P., Wetzels, M., & Grewal, D. (2022). Perceived omnichannel customer experience (OCX): Concept, measurement and impact. *Journal of Retailing*, 98(4), 611–632.

Sharma, N., & Fatima, J. (2024). Influence of perceived value on omnichannel usage: Mediating and moderating roles of the omnichannel shopping habit. *Journal of Retailing and Consumer Services*, 77, 103627.

Shen, X. L., Li, Y. J., Sun, Y., & Wang, N. (2018). Channel integration quality, perceived fluency and omnichannel service usage: The moderating roles of internal and external usage experience. *Decision Support Systems*, 109, 61–73.

Sheth, J. N., Newman, B. I., & Gross, B. L. (1991). Why we buy what we buy: A theory of consumption values. *Journal of Business Research*, 22(2), 159–170.

Shi, S., Wang, Y., Chen, X., & Zhang, Q. (2020). Conceptualization of omnichannel customer experience and its impact on shopping intention: A mixed-method approach. *International Journal of Information Management*, 50, 325–336.

Somi, B., Ebrahimi, E., & Irani, H. R. (2024). Presenting a framework for implementing an omni-channel marketing strategy with a meta-synthesis approach. *Journal of Business Management*. https://doi.org/10.22059/jibm.2023.356336.4550

Song, H. G., & Jo, H. (2023). Understanding the continuance intention of omnichannel: Combining TAM and TPB. *Sustainability*, 15.

Stelick, A., Penano, A. G., Riak, A. C., & Dando, R. (2018). Dynamic context sensory testing – a proof of concept study bringing virtual reality to the sensory booth. *Journal of Food Science*, 83(8), 2047–2051.

Steuer, J., Biocca, F., & Levy, M. R. (1995). Defining virtual reality: Dimensions determining telepresence. *Communication in the Age of Virtual Reality*, 33(37–39), 1.

Suh, K. S., & Lee, Y. E. (2005). The effects of virtual reality on consumer learning: An empirical investigation. *MIS Quarterly*, 673–697.

Sun, Y., Yang, C., Shen, X. L., & Wang, N. (2020). When digitalized customers meet digitalized services: A digitalized social cognitive perspective of omnichannel service usage. *International Journal of Information Management*, 54, 102200.

Thaichon, P., Quach, S., Barari, M., & Nguyen, M. (2024). Exploring the role of omnichannel retailing technologies: Future research directions. *Australasian Marketing Journal*, 32(2), 162–177.

Tham, J., Duin, A. H., Gee, L., Ernst, N., Abdelqader, B., & McGrath, M. (2018). Understanding virtual reality: Presence, embodiment and professional practice. *IEEE Transactions on Professional Communication*, 61(2), 178–195.

Tuncer, I. (2020). Customer experience in the restaurant industry: Use of smart technologies. In *Handbook of Research on Smart Technology Applications in the Tourism Industry* (pp. 254–272). IGI Global.

Tussyadiah, I. P., Wang, D., Jung, T. H., & tom Dieck, M. C. (2018). Virtual reality, presence and attitude change: Empirical evidence from tourism. *Tourism Management*, 66, 140–154.

Tyrväinen, O., Karjaluoto, H., & Saarijärvi, H. (2020). Personalization and hedonic motivation in creating customer experiences and loyalty in omnichannel retail. *Journal of Retailing and Consumer Services*, 57, 102233.

Vahdat, A., Alizadeh, A., Quach, S., & Hamelin, N. (2021). Would you like to shop via mobile app technology? The technology acceptance model, social factors and purchase intention. *Australasian Marketing Journal* (AMJ), 29(2), 187–197.

Vannucci, V., & Pantano, E. (2020). Digital or human touchpoints? Insights from consumer-facing in-store services. *Information Technology & People*, 33(1), 296–310.

Velasco, C., Obrist, M., Petit, O., & Spence, C. (2018). Multisensory technology for flavor augmentation: A mini review. *Frontiers in Psychology*, 9, 26.

Venkatesh, V., Morris, M. G., Davis, G. B., & Davis, F. D. (2003). User acceptance of information technology: Toward a unified view. *MIS Quarterly*, 27(3), 425–478. https://doi.org/10.2307/30036540 (archived at https://perma.cc/6YYC-RQYM)

Venkatesh V., Thong, Y. Y. L., & Xu, X. (2012). Consumer acceptance and use of information technology: Extending the unified theory of acceptance and use of technology. *MIS Quarterly*, 36(1), 157–178. https://doi.org/10.2307/41410412 (archived at https://perma.cc/2A4L-CDCH)

Verhoef, P. C., Kannan, P. K., & Inman, J. J. (2015). From multi-channel retailing to omni-channel retailing. *Journal of Retailing*, 91(2), 174–181.

Wald, R., Piotrowski, J. T., Araujo, T., & van Oosten, J. M. (2023). Virtual assistants in the family home. Understanding parents' motivations to use virtual assistants with their child(dren). *Computers in Human Behaviour*, 139, 107526.

Wang, W., & Benbasat, I. (2007). Recommendation agents for electronic commerce: Effects of explanation facilities on trusting beliefs. *Journal of Management Information Systems*, 23(4), 217–246. https://doi.org/10.2753/MIS0742-1222230410 (archived at https://perma.cc/LHE8-RCK6)

Weber, F. D., & Schütte, R. (2019). State-of-the-art and adoption of artificial intelligence in retailing. *Digital Policy Regulation and Governance*, 21(3), 264–279.

Wolf, L., & Steul-Fischer, M. (2022). Factors of customers' channel choice in an omnichannel environment: A systematic literature review, *Management Review Quarterly*, https://doi.org/10.1007/s11301-022-00281-w (archived at https://perma.cc/4X6W-GDFF)

Yao, P., Sabri, M. F., Osman, S., Zainudin, N., & Li, Y. (2023). Consumers' continued intention to use online-to-offline (O2O) services in omnichannel retail: Differences between to-shop and to-home models. *Sustainability*, 15(2), 945.

Yung, R., & Khoo-Lattimore, C. (2019). New realities: A systematic literature review on virtual reality and augmented reality in tourism research. *Current Issues in Tourism*, 22(17), 2056–2081.

Zhang, M., He, X., Qin, F., Fu, W., & He, Z. (2019). Service quality measurement for omni-channel retail: Scale development and validation. *Total Quality Management & Business Excellence*, 30(sup1), S210–S226.

Zierau, N., Hildebrand, C., Bergner, A., Busquet, F., Schmitt, A., & Marco Leimeister, J. (2022). Voice bots on the frontline: Voice-based interfaces enhance flow-like consumer experiences & boost service outcomes. *Journal of the Academy of Marketing Science*, 1–20. https://doi.org/10.1007/s11747-022-00868-5 (archived at https://perma.cc/8WSF-RPTN)

Chapter 8

Anjorin, K. F., Raji, M. A., & Olodo, H. B. (2024). The influence of social media marketing on consumer behaviour in the retail industry: A comprehensive review. *International Journal of Management & Entrepreneurship Research*, 6(5), 1547–1580.

Arruda Filho, E. J. M., Nogueira, A. C. L., & Costa, E. M. S. D. (2022). Social influence effect on consumers' intention to adopt mobile banking services. *Information Systems Management*, 39(3), 269–285.

Bock, G. W., Zmud, R. W., Kim, Y. G., & Lee, J. N. (2005). Behavioural intention formation in knowledge sharing: Examining the roles of extrinsic motivators, social-psychological forces, and organizational climate. *MIS Quarterly*, 87–111.

Camilleri, M. A., Troise, C., & Kozak, M. (2023). Functionality and usability features of ubiquitous mobile technologies: The acceptance of interactive travel apps. *Journal of Hospitality and Tourism Technology*, 14(2).

Chee, S. Y., Dasgupta, A., & Ragavan, N. A. (2022). Senior-friendly accommodations: A phenomenological study of the lived experiences of older adults with functional limitations in senior living facilities. *International Journal of Hospitality Management*. 112, 103402.

Cho, V., & Chan, D. (2021). How social influence through information adoption from online review sites affects collective decision making. *Enterprise Information Systems*, 15(10), 1562–1586.

Clark, R. A., & Goldsmith, R. E. (2006). Global innovativeness and consumer susceptibility to interpersonal influence. *Journal of Marketing Theory and Practice*, 14(4), 275–285.

Esposito, B., Sessa, M., Sica, D., & Malandrino, O. (2022). Service innovation in the restaurant sector during COVID-19: Digital technologies to reduce customers' risk perception. *TQM Journal*, 34(7), 134–164.

Familoni, B. T., & Shoetan, P. O. (2024). Cybersecurity in the financial sector: A comparative analysis of the USA and Nigeria. *Computer Science & IT Research Journal*, 5(4), 850877.

Faraj, S., Kudaravalli, S., & Wasko, M. (2015). Leading collaboration in online communities. *Management Information Systems Quarterly*, 39(2), 393–412.

Henningsen, D. D., Henningsen, & M. L. M. (2003). Examining social influence in information sharing contexts. *Small Group Research*, 34(4), 391–412.

Islam, J. U., & Rahman, Z. (2017). The impact of online brand community characteristics on customer engagement: An application of Stimulus-Organism-Response paradigm. *Telematics and Informatics*, 34(4), 96–109.

Jang, H. W., Moon, C., Jung, H. S., Cho, M., & Bonn, M. A. (2024). Normative and informational social influence affecting digital technology acceptance of senior restaurant diners: A technology learning perspective. *International Journal of Hospitality Management*, 116, 103626.

Lee, M. K., Shi, N., Cheung, C. M., Lim, K. H., & Sia, C. L. (2011). Consumer's decision to shop online: The moderating role of positive informational social influence. *Information & Management*, 48(6), 185–191.

Lee, M. T., & Theokary, C. (2021). The superstar social media influencer: Exploiting linguistic style and emotional contagion over content? *Journal of Business Research*, 132, 860–871.

Leite, F. P., Pontes, N., & Baptista, P. P. (2022). Oops, I've overshared! When social media influencers' self-disclosure damage perceptions of source credibility. *Computers in Human Behaviour*, 133, Article 107274.

Li, H. (2021). Impact of interactivity in virtual brand communities on consumer behaviours taking Mi Community as an example. In *E3S Web of Conferences* (Vol. 235, p. 01034). EDP Sciences.

Liao, G. Y., Huang, T. L., Dennis, A. R., & Teng, C. I. (2024). The influence of media capabilities on knowledge contribution in online communities. *Information Systems Research*, 35(1), 165–183. https://doi.org/10.1287/isre.2023.1225 (archived at https://perma.cc/VU5C-YZR5)

Liu, A. X., Xie, Y., & Zhang, J. (2019). It's not just what you say, but how you say it: The effect of language style matching on perceived quality of consumer reviews. *Journal of Interactive Marketing*, 46(1), 70–86.

Ludwig, S., De Ruyter, K., Friedman, M., Brüggen, E. C., Wetzels, M., & Pfann, G. (2013). More than words: The influence of affective content and linguistic style matches in online reviews on conversion rates. *Journal of Marketing*, 77(1), 87–103.

Muniz Jr, A. M., & O'Guinn, T. C. (2001). Brand community. *Journal of Consumer Research*, 27(4), 412–432.

Munaro, A. C., Barcelos, R. H., Francisco Maffezzolli, E. C. F., Rodrigues, J. P. S., & Paraiso, E. C. (2021). To engage or not engage? The features of video content on YouTube affecting digital consumer engagement. *Journal of Consumer Behaviour*, 20(5), 1336–1352.

Ochuba, N. A., Usman, F. O., Okafor, E. S., Akinrinola, O., & Amoo, O. O. (2024). Predictive analytics in the maintenance and reliability of satellite telecommunications infrastructure: A conceptual review of strategies and technological advancements. *Engineering Science & Technology Journal*, 5(3), 704–715.

Phua, J., Jin, S. V., & Kim, J. J. (2017). Gratifications of using Facebook, Twitter, Instagram, or Snapchat to follow brands: The moderating effect of social comparison, trust, tie strength, and network homophily on brand identification, brand engagement, brand commitment, and membership intention. *Telematics and Informatics*, 34(1), 412–424. https://doi.org/10.1016/j.tele.2016.05.004 (archived at https://perma.cc/3UXJ-F4WZ)

Poikolainen Rosén, A., Normark, M., & Wiberg, M. (2022). Towards more-than-human-centred design: Learning from gardening. *International Journal of* Design, 16(3), 21–36.

Pradhan, B., Kishore, K., & Gokhale, N. (2023). Social media influencers and consumer engagement: A review and future research agenda. *International Journal of Consumer Studies*, 47(6), 2106–2130.

Raji, M. A., Olodo, H. B., Oke, T. T., Addy, W. A., Ofodile, O. C., & Oyewole, A. T. (2024). Digital marketing in tourism: A review of practices in the USA and Africa. *International Journal of Applied Research in Social Sciences*, 6(3), 393–408.

Rauschnabel, P. A., Felix, R., Heller, J., & Hinsch, C. (2024). The 4C framework: Towards a holistic understanding of consumer engagement with augmented reality. *Computers in Human Behaviour*, 154, 108105. https://doi.org/10.1016/j.chb.2023.108105 (archived at https://perma.cc/U4D4-CUUB)

Rauschnabel, P. A., Rossmann, A., & tom Dieck, M. C. (2017). An adoption framework for mobile augmented reality games: The case of Pokémon Go. *Computers in Human Behaviour*, 76, 276–286. https://doi.org/10.1016/j.chb.2017.07.030 (archived at https://perma.cc/K8NU-FM6H)

Remy, C., Bates, O., Dix, A., Thomas, V., Hazas, M., Friday, A., & Huang, E. M. (2018). Evaluation beyond usability: Validating sustainable HCI research. In Proceedings of the 2018 CHI Conference on Human Factors in Computing Systems (pp. 1–14). https://doi.org/10.1145/3173574.3173790 (archived at https://perma.cc/6ZH7-AFJF)

Rennekamp, K. M., & Witz, P. D. (2021). Linguistic formality and audience engagement: Investors' reactions to characteristics of social media disclosures. *Contemporary Accounting Research*, 38(3), 1748–1781.

Ro, Y. K., Brem, A., & Rauschnabel, P. A. (2018). Augmented reality smart glasses: Definition, concepts and impact on firm value creation. In T. Jung, & M. C. tom Dieck (Eds.), *Augmented Reality and Virtual Reality: Empowering human, place and business* (pp. 169–181). Springer, Cham.

Rogers, K. (2021). Restaurants staged nimble responses to Covid's blows in 2020, but 6 years of growth were wiped away. Retrieved from: https://www.cnbc.com/2021/01/26/restaurant-industry.html (archived at https://perma.cc/NTJ3-VBLF)

Saheed, Y. K., Baba, U. A., & Raji, M. A. (2022). Big data analytics for credit card fraud detection using supervised machine learning models. In *Big Data Analytics in the Insurance Market* (pp. 31–56). Emerald Publishing Limited.

Schein, K. E., & Rauschnabel, P. A. (2023). Augmented reality in manufacturing: Exploring workers' perceptions of barriers. *IEEE Transactions on Engineering Management*, 70(10), 3344–3357. https://doi.org/10.1109/TEM.2021.3093833 (archived at https://perma.cc/4688-6EF3)

Scholz, J., & Duffy, K. (2018). We are at home: How augmented reality reshapes mobile marketing and consumer-brand relationships. *Journal of Retailing and Consumer Services*, 44, 11–23. https://doi.org/10.1016/j.jretconser.2018.05.004 (archived at https://perma.cc/8MU4-LH6R)

Schuetzler, R. M., Grimes, G. M., & Giboney, J. S. (2020). The impact of chatbot conversational skill on engagement and perceived humanness. *Journal of Management Information Systems*, 37(3), 875–900.

Seifert, A., & Cotten, S. R. (2020). In care and digitally savvy? Modern ICT use in long-term care institutions. *Educational Gerontology*, 46(8), 473–485.

Sevilla-Gonzalez, M. D. R., Loaeza, L. M., Lazaro-Carrera, L. S., Ramirez, B. B., Rodríguez, A. V., Peralta-Pedrero, M. L., & Almeda-Valdes, P. (2020). Spanish version of the system usability scale for the assessment of electronic tools: Development and validation. *JMIR Human Factors*, 7(4), e21161.

Shin, D. (2019). How does immersion work in augmented reality games? A user-centric view of immersion and engagement. *Information, Communication & Society*, 22(9), 1212–1229. https://doi.org/10.1080/1369118X.2017.1411519 (archived at https://perma.cc/5H97-2RFZ)

Shrestha, A., Karki, A., Bhushan, M., Joshi, S., & Gurung, S. (2023). Effects of social media marketing on consumer buying behaviour. New perspective. *Journal of Business and Economics*, 6(1), 74–82. https://doi.org/10.3126/npjbe.v6i1.58916 (archived at https://perma.cc/J9DB-MPP7)

Siles, I., Segura-Castillo, A., Solís, R., & Sancho, M. (2020). Folk theories of algorithmic recommendations on Spotify: Enacting data assemblages in the global South. *Big Data & Society*, 7(1), 2053951720923377.

Smith, M. (2024). 107 customer service statistics and facts you shouldn't ignore. Retrieved from https://www.helpscout.com/75-customer-service-facts-quotes-statistics/ (archived at https://perma.cc/SEZ3-YRVR)

Sokolova, K., & Kefi, H. (2020). Instagram and YouTube bloggers promote it, why should I buy? How credibility and parasocial interaction influence purchase intentions. *Journal of Retailing and Consumer Services*, 53, Article 101742.

Statista Research Department (2023). E-commerce in the United Kingdom (UK) – statistics & facts. Retrieved from https://www.statista.com/topics/2333/e-commerce-in-the-united-kingdom/#topicOverview (archived at https://perma.cc/96MG-M72A)

Stephanidis, C., & Salvendy, G. (Eds.) (2024). *Designing for Usability, Inclusion and Sustainability in Human-Computer Interaction*. CRC Press.

Swani, K., Milne, G. R., Brown, B. P., Assaf, A. G., & Donthu, N. (2017). What messages to post? Evaluating the popularity of social media communications in business versus consumer markets. *Industrial Marketing Management*, 62, 77–87.

Tan, Y.-C., Chandukala, S. R., & Reddy, S. K. (2022). Augmented reality in retail and its impact on sales. *Journal of Marketing*, 86(1), 48–66. https://doi.org/10.1177/0022242921995449 (archived at https://perma.cc/6NVV-6C84)

tom Dieck, M. C., Jung, T. H., & Rauschnabel, P. A. (2018). Determining visitor engagement through augmented reality at science festivals: An experience economy perspective. *Computers in Human Behaviour*, 82, 44–53. https://doi.org/10.1016/j.chb.2017.12.043 (archived at https://perma.cc/3LXH-EBVT)

Tractinsky, N., & Hassenzahl, M. (2005). Arguing for aesthetics in human-computer interaction. *I-Com*, 4(3), 66–68.

Tsai, H. T., & Bagozzi, R. P. (2014). Contribution behaviour in virtual communities: Cognitive, emotional, and social influences. *Management Information Systems Quarterly*, 38(1), 143–164.

Udeh, C. A., Iheremeze, K. C., Abdul, A. A., Daraojimba, D. O., & Oke, T. T. (2023). Marketing across multicultural landscapes: A comprehensive review of strategies bridging US and African markets. *International Journal of Research and Scientific Innovation*, 10(11), 656–676.

Väätäjä, H., Koponen, T., & Roto, V. (2009). *Developing practical tools for user experience evaluation: A case from mobile news journalism*. In European Conference on Cognitive Ergonomics: Designing Beyond the Product—Understanding Activity and User Experience in Ubiquitous Environments (pp. 1–8). https://dl.acm.org/citation.cfm?id=1690508.1690539 (archived at https://perma.cc/L7C9-QB7R)

van de Vijver, F., & Tanzer, N. K. (2004). Bias and equivalence in cross-cultural assessment: An overview. *European Review of Applied Psychology*, 54(2), 119–135.

Vaportzis, E., Giatsi Clausen, M., & Gow, A. J. (2017). Older adults' perceptions of technology and barriers to interacting with tablet computers: A focus group study. *Fronters in Psychology*, 8, 1687.

Venkatesh, V., Brown, S. A., & Sullivan, Y. W. (2016). Guidelines for conducting mixed-methods research: An extension and illustration. *Journal of the Association for Information Systems*, 17(7), 435–494.

Venkatesh, V., Thong, J. Y., & Xu, X. (2012). Consumer acceptance and use of information technology: Extending the unified theory of acceptance and use of technology. *MIS Quarterly*, 36(1), 157–178. https://doi.org/10.2307/41410412 (archived at https://perma.cc/K62Y-XY88)

Verhoef, P. C., Kooge, E., & Walk, N. (2016). *Creating Value with Big Data Analytics: Making smarter marketing decisions*. Routledge.

Vieira, V. A., Nogueira Rafael, D., & Agnihotri, R. (2022). Augmented reality generalizations: A meta-analytical review on consumer-related outcomes and the mediating role of hedonic and utilitarian values. *Journal of Business Research*, 151, 170–184. https://doi.org/10.1016/j.jbusres.2022.06.030 (archived at https://perma.cc/A999-SHQ7)

Wallace, S., Reid, A., Clinciu, D., & Kang, J. (2013). Culture and the importance of usability attributes. *Information Technology & People*, 26(1), 77–93. https://doi.org/10.1108/09593841311307150 (archived at https://perma.cc/2MQ8-MPNY)

Wu, Y. L., Li, E. Y., & Chang, W. L. (2016). Nurturing user creative performance in social media networks: An integration of habit of use with social capital and information exchange theories. *Internet Research*, 26(4), 869–900.

Xu, C., Zheng, X., & Yang, F. (2023). Examining the effects of negative emotions on review helpfulness: The moderating role of product price. *Computers in Human Behaviour*, 139, Article 107501.

Yu-Huei, C., Ja-Shen, C., & Ming-Chao, W. (2019). Why do older adults use wearable devices: A case study adopting the Senior Technology Acceptance Model (STAM). In 2019 Portland International Conference on Management of Engineering and Technology (PICMET) (pp. 1–8). IEEE.

Zahedi, M., Akhavan, P., & Naghdi Khanachah, S. (2024). Evaluation of knowledge sharing and its role in organisational innovation using structural equation modelling: A case study of Civil Aviation Organisation. *Technology Analysis & Strategic Management*, 36(4), 692–706.

Zanger, V., Meißner, M., & Rauschnabel, P. A. (2022). Beyond the gimmick: How affective responses drive brand attitudes and intentions in augmented reality marketing. *Psychology and Marketing*, 39(7), 1285–1301. https://doi.org/10.1002/mar.21641 (archived at https://perma.cc/WSM9-SN7C)

Zheng, Q., Tang, Y., Liu, Y., Liu, W., & Huang, Y. (2022). UX research on conversational human-AI interaction: A literature review of the ACM digital library. In Proceedings of the 2022 CHI Conference on Human Factors in Computing Systems (pp. 1–24).

Chapter 9

Apple (2023). App privacy details on the App Store. Retrieved from https://developer.apple.com/app-store/app-privacy-details/ (archived at https://perma.cc/G98B-T3BJ)

Chai, J., & Li, H. (2024). Consumer empowerment in the ethical spectrum: Rethinking retention in live-streaming markets. *Journal of Retailing and Consumer Services*, 81, 103970.

Dion, D., Pavlyuchenko, R., & Prokopec, S. (2024). EXPRESS: The enrichment economy: Market dynamics, brand strategy and ethics. *Journal of Marketing*, 00222429241275014.

IBM (2024). *Cost of a Data Breach Report 2024*. Retrieved from https://www.ibm.com/downloads/cas/0KDGJXRM (archived at https://perma.cc/6GZG-TKME)

Limbu, Y. B., Wolf, M., & Lunsford, D. (2012). Perceived ethics of online retailers and consumer behavioural intentions: The mediating roles of trust and attitude. *Journal of Research in Interactive Marketing*, 6(2), 133–154. https://doi.org/10.1108/17505931211265435 (archived at https://perma.cc/5P9E-PEYB). L

Lin, L., Huang, S., & Ho, Y. (2020). Could virtual reality effectively market slow travel in a heritage destination? *Tourism Management*, 78. https://doi.org/10.1016/j.tourman.2019.104027 (archived at https://perma.cc/6RLN-NJ8A).

Lu, Z., Xia, H., Heo, S., & Wigdor, D. (2018). You watch, you give and you engage: A study of live streaming practices in China. Proceedings of the 2018 CHI Conference on Human Factors in Computing Systems 1–13. https://doi.org/10.1145/3173574.3174040 (archived at https://perma.cc/2KY8-YLEU)

McClain, C., Faverio, M., Anderson, M., & Park, E. (2023). How Americans view data privacy. Retrieved from https://www.pewresearch.org/wp-content/uploads/sites/20/2023/10/PI_2023.10.18_Data-Privacy_FINAL.pdf (archived at https://perma.cc/7WTZ-Q575)

McKee, K. M., Dahl, A. J., & Peltier, J. W. (2024). Gen Z's personalization paradoxes: A privacy calculus examination of digital personalization and brand behaviours. *Journal of Consumer Behaviour*, 23(2), 405–422.

McKinsey (2022). McKinsey technology trends outlook 2022: Immersive-reality technologies. Retrieved from https://www.mckinsey.com/spContent/bespoke/tech-trends/pdfs/mckinsey-tech-trends-outlook-2022-immersive-reality.pdf (archived at https://perma.cc/QC2C-DMEK)

Nadeem, W., Juntunen, M., Shirazi, F., & Hajli, N. (2020). Consumers' value co-creation in sharing economy: The role of social support, consumers' ethical perceptions and relationship quality. *Technological Forecasting and Social Change*, 151, 119786. https://doi.org/10.1016/j.techfore.2019.119786 (archived at https://perma.cc/T7NV-VX48)

Nie, W., Medina-Lara, A., Williams, H., & Smith, R. (2021). Do health, environmental and ethical concerns affect purchasing behaviour? A meta-analysis and narrative review. *Social Sciences*, 10(11), 413. https://doi.org/10.3390/socsci10110413 (archived at https://perma.cc/2ADB-G9F2)

Pang, H., & Ruan, Y. (2023). Determining influences of information irrelevance, information overload and communication overload on WeChat discontinuance intention: The moderating role of exhaustion. *Journal of Retailing and Consumer Services*, 72, 103289. https://doi.org/10.1016/j.jretconser.2023.103289 (archived at https://perma.cc/3XQ4-VXAW)

Patagonia (2024). Environmental responsibility. Retrieved from https://www.patagonia.com/environmental-responsibility-materials/ (archived at https://perma.cc/FV77-RQ85)

Petr, C., & Caudan, P. (2024). Ethical marketing framework for metaverse simulated experiences of tourism (SET): An exploration of consumers' aspirations and fears. *Journal of Retailing and Consumer Services*, 79, 103785.

Schiopu, A. F., Hornoiu, R. I., Padurean, A. M., & Nica, A. M. (2022). Constrained and virtually traveling? Exploring the effect of travel constraints on intention to use virtual reality in tourism. *Technology in Society*, 71, 102091.

Schmidt, L. L., & Maier, E. (2022). Interactive ad avoidance on mobile phones. *Journal of Advertising*, 51(4), 440–449. https://doi.org/10.1080/00913367.2022.2077266 (archived at https://perma.cc/4GD5-DP99)

Shin, W., & Lin, T. T.-C. (2016). Who avoids location-based advertising and why? Investigating the relationship between user perceptions and advertising avoidance. *Computers in Human Behaviour*, 63, 444–452. https://doi.org/10.1016/j.chb.2016.05.036 (archived at https://perma.cc/E3HT-547D)

Smink, A. R., van Reijmersdal, E. A., van Noort, G., & Neijens, P. C. (2020). Shopping in augmented reality: The effects of spatial presence, personalization and intrusiveness on app and brand responses. *Journal of Business Research*, 118, 474–485. https://doi.org/10.1016/j.jbusres.2020.07.018 (archived at https://perma.cc/K7H8-M8U4)

Smith, K. T. (2019). Mobile advertising to digital natives: Preferences on content, style, personalization and functionality. *Journal of Strategic Marketing*, 27(1), 67–80. https://doi.org/10.1080/0965254X.2017.1384043 (archived at https://perma.cc/3VNM-M8CJ)

Strava (2024). Save. Sweat. Share. Kudos! Retrieved from https://www.strava.com/about (archived at https://perma.cc/C9YP-MQSM)

Strycharz, J., van Noort, G., Smit, E., & Helberger, N. (2019). Protective behaviour against personalized ads: Motivation to turn personalization off. *Cyberpsychology*, 13(2), 1. https://doi.org/10.5817/CP2019-2-1 (archived at https://perma.cc/Z8D7-H2R3)

Tussyadiah, I., Dan, W., Jung, T., & tom Dieck Claudia, M. (2018). Virtual reality, presence and attitude change: Empirical evidence from tourism. *Tourism Management*, 66, 140–154. https://doi.org/10.1016/j.tourman.2017.12.003 (archived at https://perma.cc/9YGF-3HPH)

Vander Schee, B. A., Peltier, J., & Dahl, A. J. (2020). Antecedent consumer factors, consequential branding outcomes and measures of online consumer engagement: Current research and future directions. *Journal of Research in Interactive Marketing*, 14(2), 239–268. https://doi.org/10.1108/JRIM-01-2020-0010 (archived at https://perma.cc/XXT2-YBET)

Vimalkumar, M., Sharma, S. K., Singh, J. B., & Dwivedi, Y. K. (2021). 'Okay Google, what about my privacy?': Users' privacy perceptions and acceptance of voice based digital assistants. *Computers in Human Behaviour*, 120, 106763. https://doi.org/10.1016/j.chb.2021.106763 (archived at https://perma.cc/JB4L-VUUY)

Wachter, S., & Mittelstadt, B. (2018). A right to reasonable inferences: Re-thinking data protection law in the age of big data and AI (SSRN Scholarly Paper 3248829). Retrieved from https://papers.ssrn.com/abstract=3248829 (archived at https://perma.cc/7MQL-EXX4).

Wang, W., Huang, M., Zheng, S., Lin, L., & Wang, L. (2022). The impact of broadcasters on consumer's intention to follow livestream brand community. *Frontiers in Psychology*, 12, 810883 https://doi.org/10.3389/fpsyg.2021.810883 (archived at https://perma.cc/2ATC-C7RN)

Wiese, M., Martínez-Climent, C., & Botella-Carrubi, D. (2020). A framework for Facebook advertising effectiveness: A behavioural perspective. *Journal of Business Research*, 109, 76–87. https://doi.org/10.1016/j.jbusres.2019.11.041 (archived at https://perma.cc/L3Y4-GXTJ)

Zhai, M., & Chen, Y. (2023). How do relational bonds affect user engagement in e-commerce livestreaming? The mediating role of trust. *Journal of Retailing and Consumer Services*, 71, 103239. https://doi.org/10.1016/j.jretconser.2022.103239 (archived at https://perma.cc/2HBF-TRE9)

Zhang, X., & Venkatesh, V. (2017). A nomological network of knowledge management system use: Antecedents and consequences. *Management Information Systems Quarterly*, 41(4), 1275–1306.

Zhu, Y.-Q., & Chang, J.-H. (2016). The key role of relevance in personalized advertisement: Examining its impact on perceptions of privacy invasion, self-awareness and continuous use intentions. *Computers in Human Behaviour*, 65, 442–447. https://doi.org/10.1016/j.chb.2016.08.048 (archived at https://perma.cc/B73A-4E4Z)

Chapter 10

Alsharif, A. H., Salleh, N. Z. M., Alrawad, M. et al. (2024). Exploring global trends and future directions in advertising research: A focus on consumer behaviour. *Current Psychology*, 43, 6193–6216. https://doi.org/10.1007/s12144-023-04812-w (archived at https://perma.cc/7X2H-45V3)

Arute, F., Arya, K., Babbush, R., Bacon, D., Bardin, J. C., Barends, R., ... & Martinis, J. M. (2019). Quantum supremacy using a programmable superconducting processor. *Nature*, 574(7779), 505–510.

Babikian, J. (2017). Navigating the legal landscape: Regulations for artificial intelligence, quantum computing and blockchain. *International Journal of Advanced Engineering Technologies and Innovations*, 1(1), 1–16.

Babikian, J. (2018). Climate control: Unraveling its societal impact and urgent imperatives for change. *International Journal of Advanced Engineering Technologies and Innovations*, 1(1), 1–15.

Babikian, J. (2019). Law and innovation: Legal frameworks for AI, quantum and blockchain technologies. *International Journal of Advanced Engineering Technologies and Innovations*, 1(1), 83–101.

Babikian, J. (2020). The legal frontier: Understanding regulations for AI, quantum computing and blockchain. *International Journal of Advanced Engineering Technologies and Innovations*, 1(1), 137–156.

Babikian, J. (2021). From code to courtroom: Legal considerations in AI, quantum and blockchain development. *International Journal of Advanced Engineering Technologies and Innovations*, 1(1), 356–380.

Babikian, J. (2022). Tech, ethics and law: Navigating legal challenges in AI, quantum computing and blockchain innovation. *International Journal of Advanced Engineering Technologies and Innovations*, 1(1), 301–326.

Biamonte, J., Wittek, P., Pancotti, N., Rebentrost, P., Wiebe, N., & Lloyd, S. (2017). Quantum machine learning. *Nature*, 549(7671), 195–202.

Dunjko, V., & Briegel, H. J. (2018). Machine learning & artificial intelligence in the quantum domain: a review of recent progress. *Reports on Progress in Physics*, 81(7), 074001.

European Commission. (2023). Digital Services Act. Retrieved from https://www.economie.gouv.fr/legislation-services-numeriques-dsa-adoption-definitive-texte (archived at https://perma.cc/GY4H-RQHF)

Farahany, N. (2023). *The Battle for Your Brain: Defending the right to think freely in the age of neurotechnology*. St Martin's Press.

Flavián, C., Akdim, K., & Casaló, L. V. (2023). Effects of voice assistant recommendations on consumer behaviour. *Psychology & Marketing*, 40, 328–346. https://doi.org/10.1002/mar.21765 (archived at https://perma.cc/9L74-UU8H)

Gibney, E. (2019). The quantum gold rush. *Nature*, 574(7776), 22–24.

Grewal, D., Gauri, D. K., Roggeveen, A. L., & Sethuraman, R. (2021). Strategizing retailing in the new technology era. *Journal of Retailing*, 97(1), 6–12.

Grover, L. K. (1996). A fast quantum mechanical algorithm for database search. In *Proceedings of the twenty-eighth annual ACM symposium on theory of computing* (pp. 212–219).

Hao, G., Gui-Lu, L., Yang, S., & Xiao-Lin, X. (2001). A quantum algorithm for finding a Hamilton circuit. *Communications in Theoretical Physics*, 35(4), 385.

Huang, Y., Li, Y. J., & Cai, Z. (2023). Security and privacy in metaverse: A comprehensive survey. *Big Data Mining and Analytics*, 6(2), 234–247.

Im, H., Sung, B., Lee, G., & Kok, K. Q. X. (2023). Let voice assistants sound like a machine: Voice and task type effects on perceived fluency, competence and consumer attitude. *Computers in Human Behaviour*, 145, 107791.

Kadowaki, T. (2002). Study of optimization problems by quantum annealing. arXiv preprint quant-ph/0205020.

Klaus, P., & Zaichkowsky, J. (2020). AI voice bots: A services marketing research agenda. *Journal of Services Marketing*, 34(3), 389–398.

Ladd, T. D., Jelezko, F., Laflamme, R., Nakamura, Y., Monroe, C., & O'Brien, J. L. (2010). Quantum computers. *Nature*, 464(7285), 45–53.

LaPierre, R. (2021). *Introduction to Quantum Computing*. Springer Nature.

La Tribune. (2022). Si la Chine envahit Taiwan, son économie sera bloquée. Retrieved from https://www.latribune.fr/economie/international/si-la-chine-envahit-taiwan-son-economie-sera-bloquee-avertit-le-pdg-de-tsmc-leader-mondial-des-semi-conducteurs-927517.html (archived at https://perma.cc/MN37-GS2J)

Le Grand Continent. (2020). Capitalisme politique. Retrieved from https://legrandcontinent.eu/fr/2020/11/10/capitalisme-politique/ (archived at https://perma.cc/5V87-B9TL)

Mhalla, A. (2024). *Technopolitique: Comment la technologie fait de nous des soldats*. Seuil.

Marche, S. (2023). *USA. La Prochaine Guerre civile: Vers l'explosion des États-Unis ?* Paris: Buchet Chastel.

Mariani, M. M., Perez-Vega, R., & Wirtz, J. (2021). AI in marketing, consumer research and psychology: A systematic literature review and research agenda. *Psychology & Marketing*, 39(4), 755–776. https://doi.org/10.1002/mar.21619 (archived at https://perma.cc/Q6ZK-872K)

McLean, G., & Osei-Frimpong, K. (2019). Hey Alexa… examine the variables influencing the use of artificial intelligent in-home voice assistants. *Computers in Human Behaviour*, 99, 28–37.

Mercanti-Guérin, M. (2024). *Web Crash*. Editions XYZ, Paris.

Montanaro, A. (2016). Quantum algorithms: An overview. *npj Quantum Information*, 2(1), 1–8.

Mudambi, S. M., & Schuff, D. (2010). Research note: What makes a helpful online review? A study of customer reviews on Amazon. com. *MIS Quarterly*, 34, 185–200.

Nass, C., Moon, Y., & Green, N. (1997). Are machines gender neutral? Gender-stereotypic responses to computers with voices. *Journal of Applied Social Psychology*, 27(10), 864–876.

Niculescu, A., Van Dijk, B., Nijholt, A., Li, H., & See, S. L. (2013). Making social robots more attractive: The effects of voice pitch, humor and empathy. *International Journal of Social Robotics*, 5, 171–191.

Nielsen, M. A., & Chuang, I. L. (2001). *Quantum Computation and Quantum Information* (Vol. 2). Cambridge University Press, Cambridge.

Pasin, A., Dacrema, M. F., Cremonesi, P., & Ferro, N. (2024). QuantumCLEF 2024: Overview of the Quantum Computing Challenge for Information Retrieval and Recommender Systems at CLEF. In *Working Notes of the Conference and Labs of the Evaluation Forum (CLEF 2024), Grenoble, France, September 9th to 12th* (Vol. 2024).

Perrier, E. (2021). Ethical quantum computing: A roadmap. arXiv preprint arXiv:2102.00759.

Pham, M. T., Geuens, M., & De Pelsmacker, P. (2013). The influence of ad-evoked feelings on brand evaluations: Empirical generalizations from consumer responses to more than 1000 TV commercials. *International Journal of Research in Marketing*, 30(4), 383–394. https://doi.org/10.1016/j.ijresmar.2013.04.004 (archived at https://perma.cc/J4DG-37L7)

Pieters, R., & Wedel, M. (2004). Attention capture and transfer in advertising: Brand, pictorial and text-size effects. *Journal of Marketing*, 68(2), 36–50. https://doi.org/10.1509/jmkg.68.2.36.27794 (archived at https://perma.cc/SLV2-6KVR)

Pitardi, V., & Marriott, H. R. (2021). Alexa, she's not human but… unveiling the drivers of consumers' trust in voice-based artificial intelligence. *Psychology & Marketing*, 38(4), 626–642.

Plassmann, H., Ramsoy, T. Z., & Milosavljevic, M. (2012). Branding the brain: A critical review and outlook. *Journal of Consumer Psychology*, 22(1), 18–36. https://doi.org/10.1016/j.jcps.2011.11.010 (archived at https://perma.cc/8E6X-XTCQ)

Plassmann, H., O'Doherty, J., Shiv, B., & Rangel, A. (2008). Marketing actions can modulate neural representations of experienced pleasantness. *Proceedings of the National Academy of Sciences*, 105(3), 1050–1054. https://doi.org/10.1073/pnas.0706929105 (archived at https://perma.cc/5RS2-8M9G)

PricewaterhouseCoopers. (2018). Consumer intelligence series: Prepare for the voice revolution. PwC. Retrieved from https://www.pwc.com/us/en/services/consulting/library/consumer-intelligence-series/voice-assistants.html (archived at https://perma.cc/79AF-3HLA)

Purnawirawan, N., De Pelsmacker, P., & Dens, N. (2012). Balance and sequence in online reviews: How perceived usefulness affects attitudes and intentions. *Journal of Interactive Marketing*, 26(4), 244–255.

Romero-Álvarez, J., Alvarado-Valiente, J., Moguel, E., Garcia-Alonso, J., & Murillo, J. M. (2024). Introduction to Quantum Computing. In *Quantum Service-oriented Computing: A Proposal for Quantum Software as a Service*, River Publishers, 2024, pp. 1–20.

Salem, M., Ziadee, M., & Sakr, M. (2013). Effects of politeness and interaction context on perception and experience of HRI. In *Social Robotics: 5th International Conference, ICSR 2013, Bristol, UK, October 27–29, 2013, Proceedings 5* (pp. 531–541). Springer International Publishing, https://doi.org/10.1007/978-3-319-02675-6_53 (archived at https://perma.cc/WSW2-ABR3)

Schepers, J., Belanche, D., Casaló, L. V., & Flavián, C. (2022). How smart should a service robot be? *Journal of Service Research*, 25(4), 565–582. https://doi.org/10.1177/10946705221107704 (archived at https://perma.cc/4QBL-ET4M)

Schreibelmayr, S., & Mara, M. (2022). Robot voices in daily life: Vocal human-likeness and application context as determinants of user acceptance. *Frontiers in Psychology*, 13, 787499.

Schweitzer, F., Belk, R., Jordan, W., & Ortner, M. (2019). Servant, friend or master? The relationships users build with voice-controlled smart devices. *Journal of Marketing Management*, 35(7–8), 693–715.

Shah, V., & Shukla, S. (2023). Creative computing and harnessing the power of generative artificial intelligence. *Journal of Environmental Sciences and Technology* (JEST), 2(1), 556–579. https://doi.org/10.5281/zenodo.10847103 (archived at https://perma.cc/5LKZ-B3EK)

Shah, V., & Shukla, S. (2017). Data distribution into distributed systems, integration and advancing machine learning. In *Revista Espanola de Documentacion Científica*, 11(1), 83–99. https://doi.org/10.5281/zenodo.10846880 (archived at https://perma.cc/7NCJ-L3KL)

Shor, P. W. (1994). Algorithms for quantum computation: Discrete logarithms and factoring. In *Proceedings 35th annual symposium on foundations of computer science* (pp. 124–134). IEEE.

Spence, C. (2020). On the ethics of neuromarketing and sensory marketing. In J. T. Martineau & E. Racine (Eds.), *Organizational Neuroethics* (pp. 9–29). Springer.

The Atlantic. (2021). Can tech reshape the Pentagon? Retrieved from https://www.theatlantic.com/ideas/archive/2021/09/pentagon-army-of-nerds/620042/ (archived at https://perma.cc/NP5A-HN6V)

The Shift Project. (2018). Lean ICT: For digital sobriety [report]. Retrieved from https://theshiftproject.org/article/pour-une-sobriete-numerique-rapport-shift/ (archived at https://perma.cc/MF92-F4GB)

Urakami, J., Sutthithatip, S., & Moore, B. A. (2020). The effect of naturalness of voice and empathic responses on enjoyment, attitudes and motivation for interacting with a voice user interface. In *Human-Computer Interaction. Multimodal and Natural Interaction: Thematic Area, HCI 2020, Held as Part of the 22nd International Conference, HCII 2020, Copenhagen, Denmark, July 19–24, 2020, Proceedings, Part II 22* (pp. 244–259). Springer International Publishing.

Vecchiato, G., Astolfi, L., Fallani, F. D. V., Cincotti, F., Mattia, D., Salinari, S., Soranzo, R., & Babiloni, F. (2010). Changes in brain activity during the observation of TV commercials by using EEG GSR and HR Measurements. *Brain Topography*, 23(2), 165–179. https://doi.org/10.1007/s10548-009-0127-0 (archived at https://perma.cc/YR8N-ZVR8)

Venkatesh, V., & Morris, M. G. (2000). Why don't men ever stop to ask for directions? Gender, social influence and their role in technology acceptance and usage behaviour. *MIS Quarterly*, 115–139.

Venkatraman, V., Dimoka, A., Pavlou, P. A., Vo, K., Hampton, W., Bollinger, B., ... & Winer, R. S. (2015). Predicting advertising success beyond traditional measures: New insights from neurophysiological methods and market response modeling. *Journal of Marketing Research*, 52(4), 436–452.

Vernuccio, M., Patrizi, M., & Pastore, A. (2023). Delving into brand anthropomorphisation strategies in the experiential context of name-brand voice assistants. *Journal of Consumer Behaviour*, 22(5), 1074–1083.

WCED (World Commission on Environment and Development). (1987). Our Common Future, Oxford University Press, Oxford.

Wynn, M. & Jones, P. (2023). Corporate responsibility in the digital era. *Information*, 14(324).

Xie, Z., Yu, Y., Zhang, J., & Chen, M. (2022). The searching artificial intelligence: Consumers show less aversion to algorithm-recommended search product. *Psychology & Marketing*, 39(10), 1902–1919.

Xiao, H., Zhang, Z., & Zhang, L. (2021). An investigation on information quality, media richness and social media fatigue during the disruptions of Covid-19 pandemic. *Current Psychology*, 17(2), 1–12. https://doi.org/10.1007/s12144-021-02253-x (archived at https://perma.cc/3TCT-RYJ5)

Žalėnienė, I., & Pereira, P. (2021). Higher education for sustainability: A global perspective. *Geography and Sustainability*, 2(2), 99–106. https://doi.org/10.1016/j.geosus.2021.05.001 (archived at https://perma.cc/N428-6PN2)

GLOSSARY

Accessibility Accessibility is the measure of how easily and equitably people, including those with disabilities, can access, use and interact with a system, product or service. It involves designing and implementing features that accommodate a diverse range of users, considering factors such as visual, auditory, motor and cognitive abilities. Ensuring accessibility promotes inclusivity and aligns with ethical considerations, legal standards and social responsibility.

Ad blocking Ad blocking is a technology that prevents advertisements from being displayed on web pages or applications. Users employ ad blockers to enhance their browsing experience by reducing distractions, improving page load times and protecting their privacy from tracking by advertisers. Ad blocking can significantly impact online marketing strategies as it limits the visibility of ads and can lead to decreased revenue for publishers relying on advertising income. For instance, a user might install an ad blocker to avoid intrusive pop-up ads while browsing their favourite websites.

Ad fatigue Ad fatigue refers to the decline in consumer engagement and responsiveness to advertisements due to repeated exposure over time. As individuals encounter the same ads frequently, their interest wanes, leading to lower click-through rates and reduced effectiveness of advertising campaigns. Ad fatigue can result in irritation among consumers and may negatively impact brand perception, making it essential for marketers to refresh ad content and adjust frequency to maintain audience engagement.

Ad intrusiveness Ad intrusiveness refers to the level of disruption or annoyance caused by advertisements in a user's online experience. It encompasses how obtrusive or distracting ads are perceived to be, with highly intrusive ads potentially leading to negative user reactions, such as ad avoidance or frustration.

Agile In a business context, 'agile' refers to the ability of an organization to quickly adapt to changes in the market or environment by employing flexible and iterative processes. Agile businesses can respond to evolving consumer demands and technological advancements efficiently, enabling them to innovate and deliver value rapidly.

AI-driven analytics AI-driven analytics refers to the use of artificial intelligence and machine learning techniques to analyse large volumes of data, identify patterns and generate insights that inform business decisions. In consumer behaviour, this approach can predict purchasing trends, personalize recommendations and optimize marketing strategies. AI-driven analytics can process diverse data types, including customer interactions, social media activity and purchase history, to create more accurate consumer profiles and forecasts. For example, an e-commerce platform might use AI-driven analytics to predict which products a customer is likely to buy next based on their browsing and purchase history.

AI-driven chatbots AI-driven chatbots are automated software applications that use artificial intelligence to simulate human conversation and provide customer support or information. These chatbots can understand and respond to user enquiries in real-time, offering personalized assistance and enhancing user experiences across various platforms, including websites and messaging apps. By leveraging natural language processing (NLP) and machine learning, AI-driven chatbots can learn from interactions, improving their responses over time and efficiently handling a wide range of customer queries.

Anthropomorphic voice interactions Anthropomorphic voice interactions refer to voice-based interfaces designed to mimic human-like qualities in their communication. These systems use natural language processing and artificial intelligence to create conversational experiences that feel more personal and relatable. By incorporating human-like characteristics such as personality traits, emotions and social cues, anthropomorphic voice interactions aim to enhance user engagement and comfort when interacting with digital assistants or voice-controlled devices. This approach can lead to more intuitive and enjoyable user experiences in various applications, from customer service to smart home controls.

APIs Interfaces that allow applications to communicate.

Artificial intelligence (AI) Artificial intelligence refers to the simulation of human intelligence processes by machines, especially computer systems. These processes include learning (the acquisition of information and rules for using the information), reasoning (using rules to reach approximate or definite conclusions) and self-correction. AI applications include expert systems, speech recognition and machine learning. AI is increasingly being integrated into various technologies to enhance automation, decision-making and efficiency.

Augmented reality (AR) Augmented reality involves overlaying digital information or virtual objects onto the real world, enhancing the user's perception of reality. AR technology can take various forms, such as projection AR, marker-based AR and location-based AR. AR intersects with user-generated content (UGC) by providing users with tools to create and share interactive content that combines real-world environments with digital enhancements. Platforms like Snapchat leverage AR features to allow users to modify their facial features, play games and create engaging content for social sharing.

Automation Automation refers to the process of utilizing technology and machinery to perform tasks or processes with minimal human intervention. This involves the implementation of systems, software or robots to streamline workflows, increase efficiency and reduce manual labour. Automation spans various domains, including manufacturing, logistics, finance and information technology and encompasses a spectrum of technologies, from simple scripts to sophisticated artificial intelligence algorithms. The objective of automation is to enhance productivity, accuracy and consistency while freeing human resources to focus on more complex or strategic activities.

Backlash Backlash refers to a strong adverse reaction or criticism in response to an action, policy or trend, often stemming from perceived negative impacts or ethical concerns. In consumer behaviour, backlash can occur when companies face public outrage over practices such as data privacy violations, unethical marketing strategies or socially insensitive advertising. For example, a brand may experience backlash if it is accused of cultural appropriation in its marketing campaigns, leading to consumer boycotts and damage to its reputation. This response highlights the importance of corporate social responsibility and the need for brands to align their practices with consumer values to maintain trust and loyalty.

Big data Big data refers to the vast amounts of structured and unstructured data generated through various digital interactions, including social media, online shopping and mobile usage. It provides businesses with valuable insights into consumer behaviour, preferences and trends, enabling more informed decision-making.

Big data analytics   Big data analytics is the process of examining large and complex data sets to uncover hidden patterns, correlations and insights that can inform business decisions and strategies.

Biometric data   Biometric data refers to unique physical or behavioural characteristics used to identify or authenticate individuals. This includes fingerprints, facial features, voice patterns, iris scans or DNA. In consumer behaviour, biometric data is increasingly used for security purposes, such as unlocking smartphones or authorizing payments. It's considered highly sensitive personal information due to its uniqueness and permanence. For example, some banking apps use fingerprint or facial recognition for user authentication. The collection and use of biometric data are subject to strict privacy regulations in many jurisdictions due to its sensitive nature.

Biometric technologies   Biometric technologies are advanced systems that utilize unique physiological or behavioural characteristics to identify and authenticate individuals. Common examples include fingerprint recognition, facial recognition, iris scanning and voice recognition. These technologies enhance security and personalization in various applications, from unlocking smartphones to verifying identities in financial transactions. By leveraging inherent traits, biometric technologies provide a seamless user experience, making interactions more secure and efficient. In the context of consumer behaviour, they facilitate tailored services and improved customer experiences, fostering trust and engagement in digital environments.

Blockchain   Blockchain is a decentralized, distributed ledger technology that records transactions across multiple computers in a way that is secure, transparent and resistant to modification. Each block in the chain contains a number of transactions and every time a new transaction occurs on the blockchain, a record of that transaction is added to every participant's ledger. Blockchain technology has found applications beyond cryptocurrencies, such as in supply chain management, voting systems and decentralized finance (DeFi).

Branding   Branding encompasses the strategic activities and elements that contribute to shaping and managing a brand's identity, image and perception in the minds of its target audience. It involves the development and consistent application of visual, verbal and experiential elements, such as logos, messaging and values, to differentiate a brand and create a distinct and memorable presence in the marketplace.

Buyer persona   A buyer persona is a comprehensive and semi-fictional representation of an idealized individual who embodies the key characteristics, preferences, behaviours and demographics of a targeted segment within a broader consumer audience. Constructed through a combination of market research, data analysis and insights drawn from actual customer interactions, a buyer persona serves as a strategic tool in marketing and business development.

Carbon footprint   Carbon footprint refers to the total amount of greenhouse gases, primarily carbon dioxide, emitted directly or indirectly by an individual organization, event or product throughout its lifecycle. It's measured in units of carbon dioxide equivalents (CO_2e) and serves as a key indicator of environmental impact. Reducing carbon footprints is crucial for mitigating climate change, with strategies including energy efficiency, renewable energy use and sustainable consumption practices.

Cold start problem The cold start problem refers to the challenge in recommender systems or machine learning models where accurate predictions or recommendations cannot be made for new users, items or scenarios due to a lack of historical data or interactions. This issue typically occurs when a system is first launched or when it encounters new entities without sufficient context or prior information to inform its decisions.

Consumer analytics Consumer analytics refers to the collection and analysis of customer data to gain insights into behaviour, preferences and trends. It uses various data sources, including purchase history, browsing patterns and demographic information, to inform business decisions and marketing strategies. Advanced techniques like AI and machine learning are often employed to process large datasets and identify patterns. For example, a retailer might use consumer analytics to personalize product recommendations or optimize pricing strategies. In consumer behaviour studies, this approach helps businesses understand and predict customer actions, potentially improving customer experience and driving sales.

Content-based filtering Content-based filtering is a recommendation technique that suggests items to users based on the features of items they have previously liked or interacted with, by comparing item attributes to a user's preferences or past behaviour.

Cookie A cookie refers to a small piece of data stored on a user's device by a web browser, typically used to record information about the user's interactions with a website. Cookies serve various functions, such as remembering user preferences, facilitating personalized experiences and tracking user behaviour for analytics and advertising purposes. These data snippets are essential components of web browsing and are commonly employed by websites to enhance user experience and optimize website functionality.

Corporate social responsibility (CSR) Corporate social responsibility is a business model in which companies integrate social and environmental concerns into their operations and interactions with stakeholders. CSR initiatives aim to contribute positively to society while ensuring ethical practices, sustainability and community engagement.

Customer experience (CX) Customer experience refers to the holistic and subjective perception that a customer forms over the entire duration of their interactions with a brand, encompassing every touchpoint across various channels and throughout the entire customer journey. It extends beyond individual transactions and incorporates the emotional, cognitive and behavioural responses a customer develops in response to their overall engagement with a product, service or brand. Customer experience is shaped by factors such as usability, accessibility, customer service, branding and the overall quality of interactions, aiming to create positive, memorable and loyalty-inducing impressions.

Customer service Customer service refers to the provision of assistance, support and solutions to customers before, during and after their interactions with a product or service. It involves addressing enquiries, resolving issues and maintaining positive communication to enhance the overall customer experience. Exceptional customer service contributes to customer satisfaction, loyalty and positive brand perception.

Cyber response training Cyber response training is educational preparation for individuals or organizations to effectively handle cybersecurity incidents. It typically involves simulated cyber attacks and practical exercises to develop skills in detecting, containing and mitigating digital threats. This training aims to improve reaction times, decision-making and coordination during real cyber emergencies. For example, a company might conduct regular phishing simulations to train employees in recognizing and reporting suspicious emails. In consumer behaviour, businesses that invest in cyber response training may be perceived as more trustworthy and secure, potentially influencing customer loyalty and confidence in digital transactions.

Cybersecurity Cybersecurity refers to the practice of protecting systems, networks and programs from digital attacks. It encompasses technologies, processes and practices designed to defend against, detect and respond to threats that target access to or the functionality of, information technology assets. Cybersecurity measures aim to ensure the confidentiality, integrity and availability of data. In consumer behaviour, cybersecurity awareness influences online shopping habits, data sharing practices and trust in digital services. For example, consumers may prefer websites with visible security indicators like HTTPS or seek out products with built-in security features.

Data breach A data breach is an incident where unauthorized individuals access, steal or expose sensitive information. This can occur due to cyberattacks, system vulnerabilities or human error, often involving personal data like names, addresses or financial details. Data breaches can lead to identity theft, financial loss and damage to a company's reputation. For instance, the 2017 Equifax breach affected 147 million consumers. Such incidents can erode trust in digital services and influence consumer behaviour regarding online security.

Data-rich environments A data-rich environment refers to a digital setting or context that provides access to large volumes of diverse information and data sources, allowing users to explore, analyse and interact with extensive amounts of data for decision-making, learning or problem-solving purposes.

Data snippets Data snippets are concise pieces of information extracted from larger datasets, often used to provide quick insights or summaries, typically displayed in a user-friendly format for easy comprehension and analysis.

Decentralization Decentralization refers to the transfer of control and decision-making from a centralized entity to a distributed network. Decentralized networks aim to reduce trust requirements among participants and enhance network functionality through shared decision-making and resource management. Decentralization in blockchain provides a trustless environment, improves data reconciliation, reduces points of weakness in systems, optimizes resource distribution and enhances security. It is crucial for achieving greater service fairness and stability in blockchain applications despite potential tradeoffs like lower transaction throughput.

Decentralized finance (DeFi) Decentralized finance refers to a financial system built on public blockchains that allows for the creation and operation of financial services without traditional intermediaries like banks. DeFi aims to make financial services more accessible by leveraging blockchain technology to enable peer-to-peer transactions, lending, borrowing and trading without relying on centralized authorities. DeFi protocols operate autonomously through smart contracts, providing transparency and security.

Deep learning techniques Deep learning techniques are advanced machine learning methods that use multi-layered artificial neural networks to automatically learn and extract features from large amounts of data, enabling complex pattern recognition and decision-making tasks without explicit programming.

Device and browser fingerprinting Techniques to identify devices and browsers.

Edge computing Edge computing refers to a distributed computing paradigm that brings data processing and analysis closer to the source of data generation, such as IoT devices, rather than relying solely on centralized data centres. This approach reduces latency, enhances speed and optimizes bandwidth usage by processing data locally. In the context of consumer behaviour, edge computing enables real-time data insights and personalized experiences by facilitating faster interactions and immediate responses to user inputs. By leveraging edge computing, businesses can improve customer satisfaction and engagement through more responsive and efficient services, ultimately influencing purchasing decisions and brand loyalty.

EEG (electroencephalography) EEG is a neurophysiological method that records electrical activity in the brain using electrodes placed on the scalp. In consumer research, EEG is employed to measure real-time neural responses to marketing stimuli, offering high temporal resolution. This technique helps researchers understand the timing and intensity of consumers' cognitive and emotional processes, such as attention, engagement and emotional valence, in response to various marketing elements. EEG's portability and relatively low cost make it a popular tool for studying consumer behaviour in both laboratory and real-world settings.

Emotional contagion Emotional contagion is the phenomenon where emotions are transferred from one person to another, often unconsciously, leading individuals to experience similar feelings. In consumer behaviour, this can influence purchasing decisions, as positive or negative emotions expressed by others – such as friends or influencers – can affect a person's attitudes toward a brand or product. For example, seeing friends express joy about a new product can increase one's desire to purchase it.

Empowerment Empowerment is the process of increasing an individual's or group's ability to make choices and take control of their own lives. It involves providing the tools, resources and confidence necessary to enable people to act on their decisions effectively.

Encryption system An encryption system is a method of securing digital information by converting it into a coded format that can only be read or accessed with a decryption key. It uses mathematical algorithms to scramble data, making it unreadable to unauthorized parties. There are two main types: symmetric encryption, which uses the same key for encryption and decryption and asymmetric encryption, which uses a pair of public and private keys. Encryption is widely used to protect sensitive information during transmission and storage, such as in secure communications, online transactions and data protection. For example, the HTTPS protocol uses encryption to secure data exchanged between web browsers and servers.

Entropy method The entropy method is a statistical approach used to objectively determine the weight of criteria in decision-making processes by measuring the diversity or uncertainty within a dataset. It quantifies the degree of randomness or disorder in data distribution; higher entropy reflects greater uncertainty and less importance, while lower entropy indicates more concentrated data and greater significance. By deriving criterion weights directly from the data rather than relying on subjective input, the entropy method ensures a more objective and data-driven analysis, making it valuable in fields like economics, multi-criteria evaluation and information theory.

ERP system An ERP (enterprise resource planning) system is a comprehensive software platform that integrates and manages core business processes across an organization. It typically includes modules for finance, human resources, supply chain management and customer relationship management. ERP systems aim to streamline operations, improve data visibility and enhance decision-making by providing a centralized database and unified interface. In consumer behaviour, ERP systems can impact customer experiences through improved order processing, inventory management and personalized service. For example, an ERP system might enable a retailer to offer real-time product availability information to customers across multiple sales channels.

Experience Experience refers to the direct interaction or engagement a consumer has with a product, service or brand over time. It encompasses the cumulative knowledge and feelings derived from these interactions, shaping attitudes and future behaviour.

Expertise Expertise represents a high level of specialized knowledge, skill or proficiency in a particular product category or domain. It often results from extensive experience, study or professional involvement, enabling more informed and critical consumer decisions.

Exposure Exposure relates to the frequency and intensity with which a consumer encounters a product, brand or marketing message. It contributes to awareness and can influence attitudes but does not guarantee deep understanding or engagement.

Familiarity Familiarity denotes the level of acquaintance or recognition a consumer has with a product, brand or category, often resulting from repeated exposure or awareness. It may not necessarily involve direct usage but influences comfort and decision-making processes.

First-party data This refers to information collected directly from individuals or users by an organization or entity with which they have a direct relationship. This data is typically obtained through interactions such as website visits, purchases or interactions with digital platforms owned or operated by the organization. First-party data is considered highly valuable as it is sourced directly from consumers, providing insights into their behaviours, preferences and interactions with the brand or entity.

Fear of Missing Out (FOMO) FOMO is defined as 'a pervasive apprehension that others might be having rewarding experiences from which one is absent'. In the context of consumer behaviour, FOMO refers to the anxiety or unease consumers experience when they believe they may be missing out on positive experiences, social interactions or purchasing opportunities that others are enjoying. This psychological phenomenon is characterized by a desire to stay continually connected with what others are doing, anxiety about potentially missing rewarding experiences, and a compulsion to engage in certain behaviours or purchases to avoid feeling left out. FOMO can drive consumer purchase decisions, especially for experiential goods and services and is often amplified by social media usage that highlights others' consumption activities.

fMRI (Functional Magnetic Resonance Imaging) fMRI is a neuroimaging technique that measures brain activity by detecting changes in blood oxygenation and flow. In consumer behaviour studies, fMRI is used to observe which areas of the brain are activated in response to marketing stimuli, providing insights into consumers' subconscious reactions and decision-making processes. This non-invasive method offers high spatial resolution, allowing researchers to pinpoint specific brain regions involved in emotional and cognitive responses to brands, advertisements and products.

Gameplay Gameplay refers to the interactive elements and mechanics within a video game or other interactive media that engage the player and facilitate their interaction with the virtual environment. It encompasses the rules, controls, challenges, objectives and overall experience that shape the player's involvement and progression within the game. Gameplay is integral to the enjoyment and immersion of the player, serving as the primary means through which they navigate the virtual world, make decisions, overcome obstacles and achieve goals, thereby contributing to the overall entertainment value and satisfaction derived from the gaming experience.

Geolocation   Geolocation is the process of determining the real-world geographic location of an object or person, typically using GPS or IP address data. In consumer behaviour, geolocation technology enables location-based services and targeted marketing. For example, retailers might use geolocation to send push notifications about nearby store promotions to app users. This technology also facilitates features like mapping services, ride-sharing apps and location-based social media check-ins. While geolocation enhances user experiences and enables personalized services, it also raises privacy concerns, as it involves collecting and using sensitive location data.

Hedonic brand   A hedonic brand is one that primarily focuses on providing pleasure, enjoyment and emotional experiences rather than functional benefits. These brands appeal to consumers' desires for fun, excitement and self-expression, often prioritizing sensory stimulation and experiential attributes. See also Utilitarian brand.

Hidden data   Hidden data refers to information collected or stored by an app or system without the user's explicit knowledge or consent. This can include background data collection, tracking cookies or undisclosed data sharing practices. Hidden data collection raises privacy concerns and may violate data protection regulations. For example, an app might collect location data even when not in use or a website might use invisible pixels to track user behaviour across multiple sites. In consumer behaviour, awareness of hidden data practices can impact trust in digital services and influence users' choices regarding app permissions and privacy settings.

HTTPS   HTTPS (Hypertext Transfer Protocol Secure) is a secure version of HTTP, the protocol used for transmitting data between a user's browser and a website. It encrypts all communications between the client and server using SSL/TLS protocols, protecting sensitive information from interception or tampering. HTTPS is indicated by a padlock icon in the browser's address bar and uses port 443 by default. It's essential for secure online transactions, login pages and any transfer of sensitive data. For example, when you access your online banking website, the HTTPS protocol ensures that your login credentials and financial information are encrypted during transmission.

Immersive gaming experiences   This refers to interactive digital environments designed to deeply engage and captivate participants, typically through the integration of advanced technologies, intricate narratives, realistic simulations and dynamic gameplay mechanics. These experiences aim to envelop users in virtual worlds or scenarios, fostering a heightened sense of presence, emotional involvement and suspension of disbelief, thereby facilitating an absorbing and deeply engaging gameplay encounter.

Influencer partnerships   Influencer partnerships refer to collaborative agreements between brands and social media influencers to promote products or services. In these partnerships, influencers leverage their reach and credibility within their audience to create authentic content that highlights the brand, often resulting in increased visibility, engagement and sales. These partnerships can take various forms, including sponsored posts, product placements and co-created content, allowing brands to tap into the influencer's established trust and rapport with their followers.

Interactivity   The extent to which consumers can actively engage with digital platforms or content, allowing for real-time feedback and personalized experiences that enhance user involvement and influence decision-making.

Internet of Things (IoT)   The Internet of Things (IoT) refers to the network of interconnected devices embedded with sensors, software and other technologies that enable them to collect and exchange data over the Internet. IoT devices can range from everyday objects like smart thermostats and wearable fitness trackers to industrial machines in factories. IoT technology enables the automation of tasks, monitoring of systems remotely and the gathering of valuable data for analysis and decision-making.

Interpreting data holistically   Interpreting data holistically involves analysing information from multiple sources and perspectives to gain a comprehensive understanding of a situation. This approach considers the broader context and interconnections between data points, integrating both quantitative and qualitative information. By examining patterns and relationships across datasets, researchers can uncover deeper insights into consumer behaviour, leading to more effective marketing strategies.

Kano Model   The Kano Model is a framework developed by Professor Noriaki Kano that categorizes product features based on their impact on customer satisfaction. It classifies attributes into five categories: Must-be qualities: Essential features that, if absent, lead to dissatisfaction; One-dimensional qualities: Features that provide satisfaction when fulfilled and dissatisfaction when not; Attractive qualities: Delighters that exceed customer expectations and enhance satisfaction; Indifferent qualities: Features that do not significantly affect customer satisfaction; Reverse qualities: Features that can cause dissatisfaction if present. The model helps businesses prioritize product development by understanding how different features influence customer perceptions and satisfaction.

Key cryptography   Key cryptography, also known as public-key cryptography, is an encryption system that uses two mathematically related keys: a public key and a private key. The public key can be freely shared and is used to encrypt data, while the private key is kept secret and used for decryption. This asymmetric encryption method allows secure communication over insecure channels without the need to exchange secret keys. It forms the basis for many modern security protocols, including digital signatures and secure online transactions. For example, when you access a secure website (HTTPS), your browser uses the site's public key to encrypt data, which can only be decrypted by the site's private key.

Key performance indicators (KPIs)   Key performance indicators are measurable metrics used to evaluate the success of an organization in achieving specific objectives. They provide actionable insights that help businesses track performance, identify areas for improvement and align strategies. In consumer behaviour, KPIs may include metrics like customer acquisition cost, customer lifetime value and conversion rates, enabling companies to optimize their interactions with consumers.

Location-based messaging   Location-based messaging is a communication strategy that leverages a user's geographical location to deliver targeted and contextually relevant messages. This approach combines mobile technology, GPS or other location-tracking methods and messaging platforms to provide personalized content based on a user's physical location.

Lua scripting language   The Lua scripting language is a lightweight, high-level programming language primarily designed for embedded systems, scripting and game development. Lua's design emphasizes extensibility, portability and ease of integration with existing codebases, facilitating its adoption in diverse applications ranging from video games to web development and scientific computing. Its notable features include a simple syntax, dynamic typing, garbage collection and a powerful yet lightweight standard library.

Machine learning   Machine learning is a subset of artificial intelligence (AI) that focuses on the development of algorithms and models that enable computers to learn from and make predictions or decisions based on data without being explicitly programmed. Machine learning algorithms iteratively learn from data, identify patterns and make predictions or decisions, improving their performance over time through experience. This technology has applications in diverse fields, including image recognition, natural language processing, recommendation systems and predictive analytics.

Machine learning techniques   Machine learning techniques refer to a set of methods and algorithms that allow computers to learn patterns and make decisions from data without being explicitly programmed. These techniques include supervised learning, where models are trained on labelled data to make predictions or classify data points; unsupervised learning, which involves finding hidden patterns or intrinsic structures in input data without labelled responses; and reinforcement learning, where models learn to make decisions by receiving feedback from their actions in a dynamic environment. Machine learning is widely used in various applications, including recommendation systems, image and speech recognition and predictive analytics, due to its ability to handle large datasets and improve over time through experience.

Metaverse   The metaverse is a collective virtual shared space created by the convergence of physical reality with virtual reality. It encompasses augmented reality (AR), virtual reality (VR), blockchain technology, artificial intelligence (AI) and other emerging technologies. In the metaverse, users can interact with each other and digital objects in real-time, engaging in various activities like socializing, gaming, exploring, creating content and conducting business.

Minitel   Minitel was a French videotex online service accessible through telephone lines, introduced in 1982. It was one of the world's most successful pre-World Wide Web online services, offering various interactive services including online shopping, messaging and information retrieval. Minitel played a significant role in France's early adoption of online technologies, but its usage declined with the rise of the internet in the late 1990s and early 2000s. The service was officially discontinued in 2012.

Natural language processing (NLP)   Natural language processing is a branch of artificial intelligence that focuses on the interaction between computers and human language. It enables machines to understand, interpret and generate human language in a valuable way. NLP combines computational linguistics, machine learning and deep learning to process and analyse large amounts of natural language data. This technology powers various applications such as machine translation, sentiment analysis, chatbots and voice assistants, allowing computers to comprehend and respond to text or voice data in a human-like manner.

Nudge   A nudge is a subtle intervention or design choice that influences behaviour in a predictable way without restricting options or significantly changing economic incentives.

It leverages insights from behavioural economics to guide individuals toward making better decisions, often by altering the way choices are presented. For example, placing healthier food options at eye level in a cafeteria encourages better dietary choices among consumers. Nudges aim to improve decision-making in various contexts, including health, finance and environmental sustainability, by making desired behaviours easier or more appealing.

Online reputation Online reputation refers to the collective perception of an individual, brand or organization on the internet, shaped by digital content such as social media posts, reviews and search engine results. It encompasses how a person or entity is viewed and discussed in the digital space, influencing consumer trust, purchasing decisions and overall brand image. Managing online reputation involves monitoring, addressing negative feedback and actively cultivating positive content to maintain a favourable digital presence.

Online reviews Online reviews are user-generated evaluations of products, services or businesses posted on digital platforms such as e-commerce websites, social media or dedicated review sites. These assessments typically include ratings (often on a scale of 1–5 stars) and written feedback describing the customer's experience. Online reviews play a crucial role in shaping consumer behaviour by providing social proof, influencing purchasing decisions and contributing to a brand's digital reputation. They serve as a valuable source of information for potential customers and offer businesses insights into customer satisfaction and areas for improvement.

Opting out Opting out is the process by which individuals choose to exclude themselves from certain data collection practices or marketing communications, allowing them to maintain control over their personal information. This can involve declining to receive promotional emails, refusing data sharing with third parties or rejecting targeted advertising based on their online behaviour.

Overall quality of interactions The overall quality of interactions refers to the cumulative assessment of the various touchpoints and engagements between users or customers and a brand, product or service. It integrates elements such as usability, accessibility, customer service and branding to gauge the effectiveness, efficiency and satisfaction derived from these interactions. A high overall quality of interactions is indicative of a positive and impactful user or customer experience.

Passkey A passkey is a modern authentication method that replaces traditional passwords with cryptographic key pairs. It uses public key cryptography to provide a more secure and user-friendly login experience. When a user creates a passkey, their device generates a unique public-private key pair. The private key is securely stored on the user's device, while the public key is sent to the service provider. During login, the service challenges the device to prove possession of the private key, eliminating the need for users to remember or enter complex passwords. This approach enhances security by reducing the risk of phishing and password-related vulnerabilities while simplifying the user experience across various devices and platforms.

Phishing Phishing is a cybercrime technique where attackers impersonate legitimate entities to trick individuals into revealing sensitive information such as passwords, credit card numbers or bank account details. These attacks often use deceptive emails, websites or text messages that appear trustworthy. Phishing exploits human psychology rather than technical vulnerabilities, relying on social engineering to manipulate victims. For example, a phishing email might mimic a bank's official communication, urging users to 'verify' their account details through a fake website. In consumer behaviour, awareness of phishing tactics is crucial for maintaining online security and trust in digital transactions.

Pixels   Tracking pixels are used for measuring user engagement.

Platformers   Platformers are a genre of video games characterized by gameplay centred around navigating a protagonist through a series of levels or environments, typically by jumping between platforms, overcoming obstacles and collecting items. These games often emphasize precise timing, spatial awareness and puzzle-solving skills, providing players with a sense of accomplishment as they progress through progressively challenging levels.

Predictive analytics   Predictive analytics refers to the practice of utilizing statistical algorithms and machine learning techniques to analyse historical data and make informed predictions or forecasts about future events or outcomes. It involves extracting patterns and trends from large datasets to anticipate future behaviour, optimize processes or mitigate risks in various domains such as business, finance, healthcare and marketing.

Privacy by design   Privacy by design is an approach that integrates privacy considerations into the development of products and services from the outset. It ensures that data protection is a fundamental aspect of system design, rather than an afterthought. This proactive strategy enhances consumer trust and compliance with privacy regulations by embedding privacy features into technologies and processes. For example, requiring user consent for data tracking in apps exemplifies privacy by design in practice.

Privacy calculus   Privacy calculus refers to the decision-making process individuals undergo when weighing the potential benefits against the risks of disclosing personal information. This concept is crucial in consumer behaviour, especially in digital contexts. Users evaluate the perceived value they'll gain (such as personalized services or convenience) against potential privacy risks (like data breaches or unwanted surveillance). For example, when deciding to use a fitness tracking app, a consumer might weigh the benefits of personalized health insights against the risk of sharing sensitive health data. Understanding privacy calculus helps businesses design privacy policies and data practices that balance user concerns with service benefits.

Privacy concerns   Privacy concerns are apprehensions regarding the collection, use and sharing of personal information, often stemming from fears of misuse or unauthorized access. These concerns can influence consumer behaviour, leading individuals to be cautious about sharing their data online.

Quantum computing   Quantum computing is an advanced computing paradigm that leverages the principles of quantum mechanics to process information. Unlike classical computers that use bits (0 or 1), quantum computers use quantum bits or qubits, which can exist in multiple states simultaneously due to superposition. This allows quantum computers to perform certain complex calculations exponentially faster than traditional computers. While still in early stages of development, quantum computing has potential applications in cryptography, drug discovery, financial modelling and solving optimization problems that are currently intractable for classical computers.

Racers Racers, also known as racing games, constitute a genre of video games focused on competitive or solo gameplay involving vehicles, such as cars, motorcycles or spacecraft, racing against opponents or against the clock. These games commonly feature realistic or exaggerated physics, customizable vehicles and diverse tracks or courses, aiming to deliver thrilling speed-based challenges and immersive racing experiences to players.

Real-time engagement Real-time engagement refers to the immediate interaction between brands and consumers through digital platforms, allowing for instant feedback, communication and participation. This engagement can occur via social media, live chats or interactive content, enabling brands to respond quickly to consumer enquiries, comments or behaviours. Real-time engagement enhances the customer experience by fostering a sense of connection and responsiveness, ultimately leading to increased customer satisfaction and loyalty. For example, a brand that promptly addresses customer questions during a live social media event demonstrates real-time engagement, creating a more dynamic and interactive relationship with its audience.

Real-time tracking Real-time tracking is the continuous monitoring of an object's or person's location or status as it occurs, providing instant updates and information. This technology is commonly used in applications like package delivery, ride-sharing and fitness tracking to enhance user experience and provide immediate feedback.

Rehearsability Rehearsability refers to the ability of a communication medium to allow the sender to revise and refine a message before it is transmitted to the receiver. This feature is particularly relevant in text-based communication platforms, such as emails and instant messaging, where users can edit their messages to eliminate errors and enhance clarity. While rehearsability can improve the quality of communication, it may also introduce delays in conversation, potentially affecting the speed of information exchange.

Remarketing Remarketing is a digital marketing strategy that involves targeting advertisements to users who have previously interacted with a brand or visited its website but did not complete a desired action, such as making a purchase. This approach allows marketers to re-engage potential customers by displaying relevant ads as they browse other websites or social media platforms, reminding them of the products or services they showed interest in. Remarketing aims to encourage these users to return and complete the desired action, effectively serving as a second chance to convert leads into customers.

Responsive 'Responsive' describes a business's capability to react promptly and effectively to customer needs, feedback and market changes. A responsive organization actively engages with its audience, ensuring that products, services and communication strategies align with consumer expectations and preferences.

Responsive Web design (RWD) Responsive web design is an approach to web design that ensures web pages render well on a variety of devices and window or screen sizes. RWD uses flexible layouts and grids, images that are scalable based on screen size and CSS media queries to adjust styles based on device characteristics. This approach allows websites to provide an optimal viewing experience across different devices without the need for separate mobile or desktop versions.

Retargeting Retargeting is a digital marketing strategy that involves targeting users who have previously interacted with a brand or website but did not complete a desired action, such as making a purchase. By displaying ads to these users across various platforms, retargeting aims to re-engage them and encourage conversion. This technique leverages cookies or tracking pixels to follow users and serve personalized ads based on their previous behaviour, enhancing the likelihood of completing a sale.

RPGs (role-playing games) RPGs are a genre of video games characterized by immersive storytelling, character development and player choice, often set within fantastical or futuristic worlds. Players assume the roles of fictional characters, embarking on epic quests, engaging in strategic combat encounters and making decisions that shape the narrative and their characters' progression. RPGs frequently incorporate elements such as exploration, customization and moral dilemmas, offering players the opportunity to immerse themselves in rich, expansive game worlds and become deeply invested in their characters' journeys.

SDKs SDKs are software development kits for integrating services.

Semantic web The semantic web refers to an extension of the World Wide Web where information is structured in a way that allows machines to understand and interpret the meaning (semantics) of data. By adding metadata and semantic markup to web content, the semantic web aims to create a more intelligent web that can provide more relevant search results, automate tasks, integrate data from different sources seamlessly and enable better collaboration between machines and humans.

Sharing economy The sharing economy refers to an economic model that facilitates the sharing of resources or services between individuals, often through digital platforms. This model allows people to rent, exchange or share access to goods and services, such as accommodations, transportation or tools, typically leveraging technology to connect providers and consumers. Examples include platforms like Airbnb for lodging and Uber for transportation. The sharing economy promotes efficiency and sustainability by maximizing the use of underutilized assets while often providing cost savings for users.

Smart refrigerator A smart refrigerator is a modern appliance that uses Internet of Things (IoT) technology to enhance food storage and management. Equipped with features such as internal cameras, touch screens and Wi-Fi connectivity, smart refrigerators allow users to monitor contents remotely, create shopping lists and receive alerts about food freshness. These devices aim to improve convenience, reduce food waste and integrate seamlessly into smart home ecosystems.

Snowball effect The snowball effect refers to a process where an initial action or influence leads to a series of increasingly significant and cumulative outcomes over time. In the context of brand advocacy, it suggests that fostering emotional connections with consumers can lead to growing levels of brand loyalty and advocacy, which in turn enhance brand equity.

Social proof Social proof is a psychological phenomenon where individuals look to the behaviours and opinions of others to guide their own actions, particularly in uncertain situations. In consumer behaviour, this influence manifests through product reviews, testimonials and popularity indicators, leading consumers to choose items that others endorse. For example, a product with numerous positive reviews is often perceived as more trustworthy, prompting potential buyers to follow the crowd.

Societal biases Societal biases refer to widespread, often unconscious prejudices or preconceptions that exist within a society, influencing attitudes and behaviours towards certain groups or individuals. These biases can be based on factors such as race, gender, age or socioeconomic status. In consumer behaviour, societal biases can impact marketing strategies, product design and customer interactions. For example, AI-driven recommendation systems might inadvertently reinforce gender stereotypes in product suggestions. Recognizing and addressing societal biases is crucial for businesses to ensure fair and inclusive practices in their consumer engagement strategies.

Telepresence   Telepresence refers to a set of technologies that enable a person to feel as though they are present in a location other than their actual physical location, allowing for real-time interaction and communication with that remote site. This experience is achieved through visual and auditory stimuli that create the illusion of being in a different place, often enhanced by the ability to manipulate objects or engage with the environment remotely.

Usability   Usability refers to the extent to which a system, product or service can be effectively and efficiently used by its intended users to achieve specific goals. It encompasses various factors, including the clarity of user interfaces, ease of navigation, simplicity of interactions and the overall user experience. Usability assessments often involve user testing, feedback collection and iterative design processes to enhance the overall ease of use and user satisfaction.

User-centred design (UCD)   User-centred design is an iterative design process that prioritizes the needs, goals and behaviours of users at every stage of product development. By involving users throughout the design process – through methods such as user research, usability testing and feedback – designers aim to create products that are not only functional but also highly usable and satisfying. UCD focuses on understanding user requirements and preferences, ensuring that the final product aligns with their expectations and enhances their overall experience. This approach leads to more intuitive and effective designs that cater to the specific needs of the target audience, ultimately fostering greater user satisfaction and engagement.

User experience (UX)   User experience is a multidimensional concept that focuses on the holistic interaction between users and a product, system or service, with the aim of optimizing usability, accessibility and overall satisfaction. It involves understanding users' needs, behaviours and preferences through iterative research, design and testing processes. UX encompasses various elements, including user interface design, information architecture, usability and accessibility, all directed towards creating a seamless, efficient and enjoyable interaction for users. A positive UX is crucial for enhancing user satisfaction, engagement and loyalty and it extends beyond the digital realm to encompass any touchpoints where users engage with a product or service.

User-friendly   A user-friendly interface or system is designed to be easy to understand, navigate and use, even for those with limited technical knowledge. It prioritizes intuitive design, clear instructions and simplified processes to enhance user experience and satisfaction. User-friendly designs often feature logical layouts, consistent navigation, helpful feedback and error prevention mechanisms. For example, a user-friendly e-commerce website might have a simple checkout process, clear product categorization and easily accessible customer support options. In consumer behaviour, user-friendliness can significantly impact adoption rates, customer loyalty and overall satisfaction with digital products and services.

User-generated content (UGC) User-generated content refers to any form of content, such as text, images, videos or reviews, created by users or consumers rather than brands or organizations. UGC plays a significant role in influencing engagement, social proof and creativity in various industries. Augmented reality (AR) can enhance UGC by allowing users to interact with digital elements superimposed on the real world through devices like smartphones or AR headsets. AR can be used to create engaging experiences that blend digital content with the physical environment, encouraging users to share their experiences and promote products or brands through social media platforms.

Utilitarian brand A utilitarian brand is one that primarily emphasizes functional benefits, practicality and problem-solving attributes of its products or services. These brands focus on delivering tangible, measurable value to consumers through efficiency, usefulness and performance rather than emotional or experiential benefits.

Virtual assistants Virtual assistants are AI-powered software applications designed to perform tasks or services for individuals through voice commands or text input. These digital helpers use natural language processing and machine learning to understand user requests, provide information and execute various functions such as scheduling appointments, setting reminders, answering questions or controlling smart home devices. Popular examples include Siri, Alexa and Google Assistant. Virtual assistants aim to streamline daily tasks and enhance user productivity by offering hands-free, conversational interactions with technology.

Virtual brand communities Virtual brand communities are online spaces where consumers with shared interests and loyalty to a particular brand connect, exchange ideas and engage with both the brand and fellow members, fostering a sense of belonging and strengthening brand relationships.

Virtual try-on technology Virtual try-on technology is a digital tool that uses augmented reality (AR) to allow consumers to see how products, like clothing or makeup, would look on them in real-time using a camera-equipped device. This immersive experience enhances shopping confidence and reduces return rates.

Virtual reality (VR) Virtual reality is a simulated 3D environment that enables users to explore and interact with a virtual surrounding in a way that approximates reality. Users can immerse themselves in a VR environment created with computer hardware and software, often requiring devices like helmets or goggles for interaction. VR can be non-immersive (accessed through a computer screen), semi-immersive (partial virtual experience) or fully immersive (completely immersing the user in a simulated 3D world with sight, sound and sometimes touch). VR applications range from gaming and entertainment to training simulations and virtual tourism, offering users an immersive experience that can transform various industries.

Voice commerce Voice commerce refers to the use of voice-activated devices and digital assistants to make purchases and conduct commercial transactions. This technology allows consumers to shop order products or make payments using voice commands through smart speakers, smartphones or other voice-enabled devices. Voice commerce leverages natural language processing and AI to interpret user requests and facilitate hands-free shopping experiences. As this technology evolves, it's becoming an increasingly important channel in e-commerce, offering convenience and accessibility to consumers while presenting new opportunities and challenges for businesses in the digital marketplace.

Voice technology   Voice technology refers to the systems and applications that enable human interaction with devices through spoken language. This technology encompasses a range of functionalities, including voice recognition, natural language processing and speech synthesis, allowing users to perform tasks, seek information and control devices using voice commands. As a significant advancement in human-computer interaction, voice technology enhances user convenience and accessibility, making it an integral part of consumer behaviour in the digital age. The proliferation of virtual assistants like Amazon's Alexa, Apple's Siri and Google Assistant exemplifies its growing impact on daily life, shaping how consumers engage with products and services while facilitating a more seamless and intuitive user experience.

Web-dramas   Web-dramas are short-form, episodic online video series typically produced for and distributed through digital platforms. These serialized narratives are designed to engage viewers through bite-sized content, often featuring dramatic storylines, relatable characters and interactive elements that encourage audience participation. Web-dramas have gained popularity as a unique form of digital entertainment, particularly among younger consumers and represent an emerging area of study in consumer behaviour and media consumption patterns.

WeChat   WeChat is a multifunctional mobile application developed by Tencent, launched in 2011. It combines instant messaging, social networking and mobile payment services within a single platform. Known as Weixin in China, it allows users to send messages, make voice and video calls and access a variety of services through mini-programs. With over 1.67 billion active users, WeChat has become a vital tool for communication, marketing and digital interactions, particularly in China.

Zero-party data   This refers to explicit information willingly shared by individuals with an organization or entity. Unlike other types of data, zero-party data is provided directly by the individual without any intermediaries or data brokers. This may include preferences, interests or other personal information shared through surveys, preference centres or interactive experiences. Zero-party data is characterized by its high level of consent and transparency, as individuals actively choose to share this information with the organization.

INDEX

Abela-Lichtner, Annie 179–80
accessibility 147, 153, 301
ad blockers 218, *219*, 246, *248*, 301
ad fatigue *248*, 301
ad intrusiveness 218, 301
adaptive learning systems 3, 5, 6, 89, *90*, 99–100, 102, 103
administrative decentralisation 44
advertising 7, 47, 117, 119, 194, 217, 240, 241
    digital 115, 157, 246, *248*, 301
    retargeting 216, 218, 313–14
    social media 192
    television 14
    see also ad blockers; ad intrusiveness
advocacy 31, 54, 59, 106–12, 158
aesthetics 56, 67, 75, 145, 192
affect theory 52–53
affiliate marketing 7
age of knowability *248*
agility 3, 5, 31, 131, 132, 246–47, 250, 254, 301
Airbnb 110–11, 147
Alibaba 33, 97, 134, 157
Alipay 134, *135*
alternative text 147
alumni networks 113
Amazon 14, 33, 137–38, 147, 183, *190*, 252–53
    personalised recommendations 51, 130, 186, 233, 246
Amazon Alexa 168, 241, 243
Amazon Reviews 180
anchoring effect 66
anthropomorphic voice interactions 244, 245, 302
anticipatory learning 91–92
App Tracking Transparency 206–07
Apple 24–25, 168, 206–07, 252, *253*
apps 10, 16, 33, *129*, 157, 158, 164
    see also IKEA Place; Roblox Studio
architecture industry 69–70
artificial intelligence (AI) 102, 103, 181, 231, 233–37, 302
    and data privacy (security) 205–06, 210, 220, 245
    and personalisation 49, 87–95, 100, 121, 130, 148, 164, 211
    at Tesla 140
    and voice assistants 167, 170
    see also biometric technologies; chatbots; data analytics; machine learning; natural language processing; virtual assistants;

voice commerce (v-commerce), voice technology
artistic creation 88
ASOS 71
atmospherics (sensory marketing) 14–17, 18–26, 121, 240–241
Audemars Piguet 224
audience (market) segmentation 3, 4, 31, 51, 256
audio descriptions 147
augmented reality (AR) 22, 23–26, 28, 36, 68–79, 136, 173, 200, 232, 302
    and chatbots 143
    and consumer engagement *195*–96
    in retail sector 156–63
    and voice assistants 171
    see also HoloLens
authenticity 54, 81, 109, 110, 112, 115, *151*
automation 49, 139–41, 186, 210, 302
autonomous vehicles 139–41
autonomy 45, *222*, 223, 231
availability heuristic 59, 66
avoidance-annoyance paradox 218, *219*

backlash 120, 211, 302
behavioural analytics 51, 92–93, 122
behavioural data *129*
behavioural economics 149, *151*
belonging 65, 107, 108, 113–15, 178, 181
Berners-Lee, Timothy John ('Tim') 33, 43
bias 59, 83, 211, 314–15
big data 34, 128–33, 136, 140, 152, 200, 302–03
Bing *248*
biometric data 207, 303
biometric technologies 122, *135*, 171, 232, 303
    see also facial recognition; fingerprint scanning
blockchain technology 44–46, 134, 136–38, 143–44, 152, 211–12, 232–34, 237, 256, 303
blogs 4, 185, 192
body sizing applications 160
brand (branding) 303
    emotional 119–21, 124
    hedonic 57, 97, 107, 308
brand advocacy 31, 54, 59, 106–12, 158
brand community building 109–10, 112–18
brand defence 108
brand differentiation 96, 110–11
brand engagement 118, 185, 191
    see also community engagement

brand loyalty (customer loyalty) 54, 61, 104–25, 200
  see also loyalty programmes
brand reputation (perception) 107, 109–12, 311
brand websites *10*, 32, 37, 56, 67–68, 145
brick-and-mortar (physical) stores 14–16, 26, 30
  see also in-store virtual fitting rooms
La Brigade du Web 179–80
Bruner's spiral organisation framework 100
building information modelling systems 69
buyer personas 3, 4, 303

carbon footprint 59, *212*, 214, 249, 303
Cascading Style Sheets 43
centralisation 45–46
chatbots 141–44, 152–53, 180, 181, 186, *247*, 301–02
ChatGPT 90, 143
China
  Double Eleven festival 97–98
  and emotional connectedness 118–19
  live streaming commerce 7–8, 14
  payment systems 134, 135
  word-of-mouth recommendations 29–30
  see also Pinduoduo; WeChat
classical computing 238
cloud storage *247*
co-creation 182–84
Coca-Cola *190*
cognitive bias 59, 83, 211
cognitive load theory 54, 72, 73, 83
cold start problem 131, 304
collaboration 69, 165, 181
collaborative filtering 130
community building 109–10, 112–18, 175–201
  see also social media
community engagement 42, 180, *190*, 208–09
  see also brand engagement
community managers 34
competitive advantage 6, 54, 59, 107
computing, classical 238
confidence 204–05
connectivity 14, 180, 183–84, 232
consistency 147, 165, 225
construction industry 69–70
constructivist principles 100
'consumer-actor' concept 34, 37
consumer autonomy 45, *222*, 223, 231
consumer behaviour 152
  evolution of 13–16, 30
consumer-centricity (customer-centricity) 3, 26
consumer consent 222, 223, 227
consumer empowerment 220, 227, 228, 306
consumer engagement 60, 181, 183–84, 200
  and AR 77
  and gamification 95–98
  and personalisation 52–54, 57, 99, 108–09
  and social media 117, 118, 195–98
  and user-generated content 107–09
consumer feedback 107, 231, 254, 256
consumer perceptions 74–75
content-based filtering 130, 304
content creation 79, 112, 181, 193, 197–98
  see also co-creation; user-generated content (UGC)
content diversification 112
content strategy 3, 4, 117, 193
contextual data 51, 99, 114, 207
continuous improvement 5, 148
convenience 137, 138
Converse 25
conversion rates 4, 8, 27, 54, 55, 60, 77, 98–99
cookies 51, *129*, 205, 304
copyright 88
corporate social responsibility (CSR) 59–60, 61, 221, 224–25, 226, 227, 228, *251*, 256, 304
  see also environmental impact
corporate sustainability 59–61, 138, 184, 187, 221–22, 227–28, 249–51, 254
  and innovation 149–51
  see also Patagonia; Patek Philippe
Covid-19 pandemic 26, 94, 133, 138, 139, 167, 183
Cox Automotive 148
credibility 81, 143, 181, 197
crisis management 124, *190*, 211
cross-selling 55
cultural industries 88
cultural products 88
cultural relevance 112, 185
customer-centricity (consumer-centricity) 3, 26
customer experience *see* user experience
customer journey mapping 165
customer loyalty (brand loyalty) 54, 61, 104–25, 200
  see also loyalty programmes
customer segmentation (market segmentation) 3, 4, 31, 51, 256
customer service 9, 133, 186, 304
cyber response training 211, 304–05
cybersecurity 209, 210, 305

data 50–51, 99, *129*
  biometric 207, 303
  contextual 114, 207
  demographic 42, 51, 116–17, 250
  first-party 49, 307
  hidden 210–11, 308
  zero-party 49, 317
  see also big data
data analytics 3–5, 48–51, 90, 185, 191, 208, *242*, 256, 301
  see also behavioural analytics
data breaches 209–12, *248*, 305

data collection 51, *128–29*, 206–07
  opting out 218, 311
data privacy 51, 61, 102, 131, 132, 153, 164, 204–08, 216–23, 312
  and AI 93, 237, 245
  and chatbots 142, 143
  and IoT 242
  and personalisation 55, 101, 239
  and quantum computing 239
  and voice commerce 171
data reconciliation 45
data-rich environments 133, 305
data security 45, 57, 100–01, 171, 210, 221
data snippets 305
  see also cookies
De Beers Tracr™ 143, 144–45
Decentraland 250
decentralisation 44–46, 136, 305
  see also Web3 (semantic web)
decentralised finance (DeFi) 33, 305
deep learning technology 90, 91, 130, 131, 305
Deliveroo 139
delivery services 137–39, 184
democratization of content creation 79
demographic data 42, 51, 116–17, 250
Denso Wave 27
desire marketing 34
developing countries, use of augmented reality 72, 73, 75
digital ad fatigue *248*, 301
digital advertising 115, 157, 246, *248*, 301
digital catalogues (magazines) 27–28, 37
digital sobriety 61
digital touchpoints 146, 152, 164, 238
digitised route management 212–16
Dillons *see* Kroger
disclosure 157, 197–98, 206, 207
Disney+ 115
distribution channels 2
Dojo 139
D1 chip 140
'Don't Go There, Live There' (Airbnb) 110–11
DoorDash 147
'dot-com bubble' 33
Double Eleven festival 97–98, 102
Dropbox *247*
Duo Duo Farm Programme 94
Duo Duo Orchard 94
dynamic capabilities 133–34
dynamic pricing 2
dynamic sensory testing 161

e-commerce (online shopping) xiv, 6, 9–10, 26, 33, 84–103, 137
  and augmented reality 71–72
  and personalisation 47–48, 50
  smart e-commerce systems 52, 57
  see also live streaming commerce; social commerce (S-commerce)
e-learning 89, *90*, 91–92, 93
e-marketing 34
ease of use 76, 141, 145
eBay 33, 97
edge computing 233, 305–06
education sector 27, 28, 58
  and adaptive learning 89, 99, 100
  and AI 90, 91–92, 93
  and belonging 113–14
  and chatbots 143
  and gamification 96
effective IoT 23
electroencephalography 122, 306
electronic word of mouth (e-WOM) 29–30, 36
  see also online reviews
electronics sector 24, 58, 131, 183
emotion tracking technology 122
emotional attachment (connections) 107, 110–11, 118–24, *195*
emotional branding 119–21, 124
emotional contagion 197, 306
emotional intelligence 92
emotional resonance 122, 240
emotional response 53, 56, 92, 122, 145, 200, 201, 240
emotional well-being 121
empowerment 220, 227, 228, 306
encryption systems 131, 171, 205, 252, 306, 309
engagement 109
  see also brand engagement; community engagement; consumer engagement; multi-sensory engagement; real-time engagement; sensory engagement
enterprise resource planning (ERP) systems 213, 306–07
entertainment value 182
Entropy method 67, 306
environmental impact 140, 149–50
  see also carbon footprint; greenwashing; low-emission zones
ePUB format 28
Estée Lauder VMA 169
ethical consumerism 149–51
ethics 6, 51, 81, 153, 167, 202–28, 239
  and AI 88, 92, 93, 237
  and emotional branding 120
European Digital Services Act (2023) 252
European Union General Data Protection Regulation (GDPR) 206, 207
experience 114, 307
experiential products 81
expertise 114, 307
exposure 114, 307
EyeQ5 140

Facebook (Meta) 33, 52, 116, 117, 135, 146, 179, 192
Facebook Live 179
facial recognition 20, 21, 122, *135*, 232
familiarity 114, 147, 307
fashion sector 58, 109, 117, 120, *162*, 183, 187, 191–94, 220
fear of missing out 307
Federal Trade Commission 81, 156–57
Ferrari 113
filtering methods 130–31
fingerprint scanning *129*, 232, 303, 305
first-party data 49, 307
fiscal decentralisation 44
5G 232
Flexbox Inspector 148
flipbooks 27
flow 41, 146, 147, 152, 168
fMRI 122, 240, 307
food tastings 21–22
Forest Stewardship Council 59
4Ps 1–2
F.P. Journe 225
France 8, 14, 40, 134–35, 234–36, 310
freemium business models 6
frictionless payments 7, 40, 168, 169, 173, 174, 241
functional value 182

Gainey, Mark 208
gameplay 307–08
gamification 17, 18, 86, 94–98, 102, 115, 158
 see also Roblox
gap-score scales 67
General Data Protection Regulation (GDPR) 206, 207
Generation Z 58, 116, 217, 218
generative AI 88, 143
geolocation 21, 186, 308, 309
Glossier 109–10, 185, *189*
Google *248*
Google Assistant 19, 168, 241, 243
Google Books *247*
Google Drive *247*
Google Glass 25
Google Home 168
Google Translate 68
greenwashing 120, 150, *151*
Griezmann, Antoine 80
group (team) buying 29, 36, 94, 102
Gucci 250

Harley-Davidson 113
Harris Teeter *see* Kroger
hearing (sensory marketing) 19–20
hedonic brands 57, 97, 107, 308
Henn-na Hotel Tokyo Hamamatsucho 15
hidden data 210–11, 308

HoloLens 69, *248*
Horvath, Michael 208
hospitality sector 14–16, 17, 22, 23, 111, 157, 161, 189
hotel industry 14–16, 17, 18–23, 67–68
HTTPS 308
Huang, Colin 94
Hublot 224
hybrid filtering 130–31
hyper-personalisation 49

IBM 25, 137, 209–11
IKEA 74
IKEA Place 25, 68, 71, 72–74, 156, 162–63
immediacy 114
immersive experiences 31, 121, 136, 145, 200, 308
 see also augmented reality (AR); live streaming commerce; virtual reality (VR)
impression management 227
impulse buying 55, 97–98, 102, 103
in-store virtual fitting rooms 160
inbound marketing 34
inclusivity 26, 115, 147, 153, 169, 171, 250
 see also accessibility; belonging
influencer marketing xv, 9, 79–83, 115, 118, 199, 246, 308
 Apple 24–25
 La Brigade Du Web 179–80
 TikTok 111–12
 virtual influencers 181
 see also social media influence
innovation 149–51, 182–84, *251*
Instagram 33, 113, 116, 117, 179, 191, 192
interaction effect 218–19
interactivity 27–28, 31, 57, 67, 73–74, 76, 83, 146–47, 182, 309
 see also gamification
internet 31, 32, 33, 34, 74, *248*
Internet of Things (IoT) 17–23, 134, 232, 240–45, *248*, 309
 see also sensor technology; smart homes; smart hotels; smart mirrors; smart refrigerators; smart speakers
'Into the Gloss' blog 85
intrusiveness 75–76, 83, 218, 301
iOS 18 207
iPhone 33

Japan, hotel industry 14–16
JavaScript 43
'Just Do It' (Nike) 120

Kano model 146, 309
key cryptography *45*, 309
key performance indicators (KPIs) 4–5, 80, 122–23, 309

knowledge management 247, 248
Kroger 132–33

large language models 90, 143
Lawler's affect theory of social exchange 52–53
learning 27, 28, 89–90, 91–92, 93
    adaptive 3, 5, 6, 99–100, 102, 103
    and personalisation 87, 94–95
LEGO Ideas 185
Lesage Prestige 213–16
Libra 135
lighting 16, 18–19
LinkedIn 116, 117, 179
live streaming commerce 7–9, 14, 40–41, 94, 219
location-based messaging 21, 186, 309
LogRocket 148
L'Oréal 156, 254
low-emission zones 234–36
loyalty programmes 95, 132–33, 171
    see also customer loyalty (brand loyalty)
Lua scripting language 41, 310
Luxury 4.0 26
luxury industry 25–26, 223–24

m-commerce (mobile commerce) xv, 32, 36, 55–57, 60, 134–35, 137, 146, 158, 184
m-marketing 34
machine learning 48, 51, 168, 173, 231, 233–36, 237, 238, 310
macOS 207
Magzter 28
Mapo 213–16, 235–36
Marchand, Léon 80
market decentralization 44
market research 3, 4, 5
market segmentation 3, 4, 31, 51, 256
marketplace business models 7, 10
Martin, Mike 209
mass customisation 34
Mastodon 45
McDonald's 52, 96, 118
Meta (Facebook) 33, 52, 116, 117, 146, 179, 192
metaverse 144–45, 249–51, 310
Mi Community 178, 181, 182
micro-influencers 79, 80
Microsoft HoloLens 69, 248
Minecraft 41
Minitel 8, 247, 310
Mint 207
mobile applications (apps) 10, 16, 33, 129, 157, 158, 164
    see also IKEA Place; Roblox Studio
mobile commerce (m-commerce) xv, 32, 36, 55–57, 60, 134–35, 137, 146, 158, 184
Mobileye 140
Molina, Nikias 24
'moments' (WeChat) 52
motivation theory 95
Mozilla Firefox 148

multi-factor authentication 171
multi-sensory engagement 17, 18, 23, 120
multichannel (device) integration 3, 4, 111, 186
'My Huckleberry Friends' 119
MySpace 33

natural language processing 90–91, 168, 173, 174, 232, 302, 310
NCSA Mosaic 33
negative ratings 66–67
negative reviews 65, 66–67, 83
net neutrality 248
Netflix 51, 87, 130–31, 136, 147, 185, 186, 233, 246, 254
Netscape Navigator 33
neural network language model 91
neuromarketing 122, 124, 240–41
Nike 120, 250, 253
Nike Fit 162
Nike Run Club 185
normative influence 187
novelty 75, 76, 83
nudges 146, 216, 310–11
Nvidia 139–40

Object Notation 43
objectives setting 3, 4, 5
Ocado 133
older consumers 188
omnichannel marketing 32, 36, 164–65, 173, 186
omnichannel retail 163–67, 169–70
one to one marketing 34
online behaviour data 129
online catalogues 10
online communities 109–10, 112–118, 175–201
    see also social media
online group buying (team buying) 29, 36, 94, 102
online magazines 27
online ratings 66–68
online reviews 64–68, 83, 146–47, 150, 153, 180, 189, 243, 311
online shopping see e-commerce (online shopping)
online virtual fitting rooms 160
opting out 218, 311
Orin 139–40

pandemic, Covid-19 26, 94, 133, 138, 139, 167, 183
passive consumption 247
passkeys 311
Patagonia 134, 149, 150, 151
Patek Philippe 224
payment systems 134–35, 184
    frictionless 7, 40, 168, 169, 173, 174, 241
peer influence 118, 138–39, 187, 189, 190
PepsiCo 253
perceived ease of use 76, 141, 145

perceived usefulness 76, 145
perceived value 59
perceptual fluency 56
performance metrics 3, 4–5, 31, 93
    Airbnb 110
    emotional connections 122–23
    engagement 109
    influencer marketing 80–81
    personalisation 99–100
    TikTok 112
    usability 56
    see also conversion rates; key performance indicators (KPIs)
permission marketing 34
personalisation xiv, 47–55, 60, 61, 102, 165, 173, 227, 237, 246
    in advertising 217
    and AI 87–95, 121, 130, 148, 164, 211
    and consumer engagement 57, 108–09
    and data privacy 100–01, 239
    and emotional branding 120
    and ethics 219–24
    learning 87, 89–90, 94–95
    metrics 99–100
    and quantum computing 238, *239*
    and voice commerce 169, 244
personalised recommendations 9, 89, 98–100, 102, 130–31, 136
    Amazon 51, 186, 233, 246
personally identifiable information (PII) *129*
personas 3, 4, 303
phishing 311–12
physical (brick-and-mortar) stores 14–16, 26, 30
    see also in-store virtual fitting rooms
Pinduoduo 29–30, 37, 86, 89, 94–95, 135
Pinterest 9, 115, 116, 117
pixels *129*, 312
platformers 41, 312
Pokémon Go 68
political decentralisation 44
popularity-based filtering 131
positive reviews 65
post-purchase support 142
predictive analytics 48, 51, 91–92, 132, 153, 312
pricing 2
print media 26–30, 36, 37
privacy *see* data privacy; privacy-benefits paradox; privacy by design; privacy calculus; Privacy Nutrition Labels
privacy-benefits paradox 217–18, *219*
privacy by design 206, 312
privacy calculus 216–17, 312
Privacy Nutrition Labels 206–07
product testing 68–70
promotion 2, 3–5
prototyping 70

psychographic data 51
public-key cryptography *45*, 309
Puma 'Dress Up' *162*
purchase data *129*

QR (quick response) codes 27–28
quantum computing 233, 238–40, 256, 312
questionnaires 72–73, 122

racers 41, 313
Rainforest Alliance 59
Ralphs *see* Kroger
rater error 66
ratings 66–68
ratio-score scale 67
Readly 28
real-time chat 181
real-time engagement 31, 49, 122, 132–33, 181, 193, 194, 313
recommendation systems 9, 89, 98–100, 102, 130–31, 136
    Amazon 51, 186, 233, 246
Reddit 180
regulation 81, *93*, 157, 205, 206, 237
rehearsability 181, 313
relevance 53, 54, 112
remarketing 186, 313
remote product testing 68–70
Renren 52
responsive web design 33, 313
responsiveness 18, 66–67, 83, 313
restaurant industry 158, 161, 189, *190*
retail sector 49
    augmented reality 23–25, 71–74, 78–79, 136, 156–63
    chatbots 143
    omnichannel retail 163–67, 169–70
retargeting 216, 218, 313–14
return on investment (ROI) 31, 80
returns policies 77, 184
retweets 114–15
reviews 64–68, 83, 146–47, 150, 153, 180, *189*, 243, 311
Roblox 41–42, 250
Roblox Studio 41, 42
robots 14–15, 16, 88
role-playing games 42, 314
Rolex 223
route management 212–16

S-commerce (social commerce) 7–9, 14, 36, 37, 118, 124
    see also live streaming commerce
SaaS 7
Salazar, Matt 209
same-day delivery services 137–38
scents (sensory marketing) 17, 20
search engine optimisation (SEO) 2, 80, 170, *248*
segmentation 3, 4, 31, 51, 256

self-disclosure 197
semantic web (Web3) 33, *34*, 43–46, 249–50, 251, 314
sensor technology 122, 140, 232
sensory engagement 17, 18, 23, 120
sensory marketing (servicescape) 14–17, 18–26, 121, 240–41
sensory testing 161
sentiment analysis 92, 109
Sephora 14, 25, 40, 143, *162*
service robots 14–15, 16, 88
Shanghai Reserve Roastery 157–58
sharing economy 220, 314
  see also Airbnb
Shihab, Najwa 111–12
sight (sensory marketing) 18–19
Sigil 28
simplicity 57, 147, 148
Singles' Day 97–98, 102
Siri 168
smart e-commerce systems 52, 57
smart homes 17, 163, 171, 244
smart hotels 15–16
smart mirrors 160
smart refrigerators 241, *242*, 314
smart speakers 16, 170, 316
smartphones 25, 33, 170, 183–84, 188
smell (sensory marketing) 16–17, 20
Smith's *see* Kroger
Snapchat 116, 117, *162*
Snapchat Lenses 25, 26
snowball effect 107, 314
social commerce (S-commerce) 7–9, 14, 36, 37, 118, 124
  see also live streaming commerce
social comparison 187–88, 191
social exchange 52–53
social media 9, 28, 33, 37, 131–32, 146, 150, 175–201, 246
  analysis of 122
  and brand advocacy (loyalty) 106–07, 108, 112–18
  data *129*
  shopping platforms 8
  and word of mouth recommendations 53, 119
  see also Facebook (Meta); Instagram; LinkedIn; Mastodon; Pinterest; social media influence; TikTok; Twitter(X); WeChat
social media influence xv, 34–35, 43, 124, 138–39, 178–80, 187–96
  see also influencer marketing
social network officers 34
social proof 58–59, 61, 65, 83, 180, 187, *190*, 314
social responsibility (CSR) 59–60, 61, 221, 224–25, 226, 227, 228, *251*, 256, 304
societal biases 211, 314–15

software as a service 7
software development kits (SDKs) *129*, 206, 314
sparsity 131
specialised influencers 80
spiral organisation framework (Bruner) 100
Spotify 51, 120, 130
standardised observation systems 66
'star' influencers 80
Starbucks 120, 157–58, *254*
Stories 179
storytelling 111, 120
strategic adaptability 256
  see also agility
strategic alignment 5
strategic partnerships 94
strategic planning 3–6
Strava 207, 208–09
subscription-based models 6, 7, 171
supply chain management 238–39
surveys 122, 147
sustainability 59–61, 138, 184, 187, 221–22, 227–28, 249–51, 254
  see also environmental impact; Patagonia; Patek Philippe
sustainable innovation 149–51
SWOT analysis 5
symbiotic relationships 53
system-on-a-chip (SOC) technology 139, 140

Taobao 14, 97, 157
taste (sensory marketing) 21–22
'Taste Your Neighbourhood' (Deliveroo) 139
team (group) buying 29, 36, 94, 102
technical data *129*
technology 30–32, 153, 186, 256
  biometric 122, *135*, 171, 232, 303
  blockchain 44–46, 134, 136–38, 143–44, 152, 211–12, 232–34, 237, 303
  deep learning 90, 91, 130, 131, 305
  emotion tracking 122
  sensor 122, 140, 232
  SOC 139, 140
  virtual try-on technology 156, *162*, 316
  voice 18–20, 167–72, 173, 232, 240–45, 317
  wearable 99, 102, 103, 188
  see also artificial intelligence (AI); internet; Internet of Things; robots
technology acceptance model 30, 36, 76, 83, 138, 163–64
telepresence 146, 161, 315
television advertising 14
Tencent 134
Tesla 132, 134, 139, 140, 149, *150*, 254
theory of consumption values 163
theory of planned behaviour 163–64
third-party selling platforms 29–30
Threads 117
'ticklish moments' 53

TikTok 111–12, 115, 116, 117, 118, 179, 191, *247*
Timberland *162*
Tinder 115
Tissot 25
Tmall 97
touch (sensory marketing) 20–21
touchpoints 146, 152, 164, 238
Toyota 27
Tracr™ 143, 144–45
traditional consumer behaviour 13, 14–16, 37
training 95, 211, 304–05
transparency 81, 137, 150, *151*, 152, 153, 157, 164, 211, 220–22
trust 30, 41, *45*, 55–57, 107, 109, 138–39, 142, 205–06, 245
Twitter (X) 33, 45, 113, 114–15, 116, 117, 179

'uberisation' 34
ubiquitous commerce (u-commerce) 137
UK 183–84
Uncanny Valley effect 15
unified theory of acceptance and use of technology model 166–67, 170, 173
United States 7–8, 14
upselling 55
usability 56, 200, 315
usability tests 147
usefulness 76, 145
user experience 3, 4, 54–57, 76, 200, 245, 315
user experience design 145–49, 152, 153, 315
user-friendliness 42, 67, 78, 94, 137, 141, 145, 315
see also accessibility; ease of use
user-generated content (UGC) 8, 31, 41, 43, 107–12, 118, 124, *190*, 191–94, 316
user interface design 56
uses and gratification theory 30, 64–65
utilitarian brand 25, 57, 107, 316

Vacheron Constantin 225
value 59, 182
virality (viral marketing) 9, 118, 124
virtual assistants 141–44, 152, 232, 316
virtual brand communities 181–82, 316
virtual fitting rooms 159–61, *162*
virtual influencers 181
virtual reality (VR) 16–17, 22, 24, 68, 70–71, 78–79, 82, 159–63, 232, 317
virtual try-on technology 156, *162*, 316
Vision Pro 24–25

visual design 56, 57
vividness 75, 83
voice commerce (v-commerce) 167–72, 173, 240–45, 316
see also Amazon Alexa
voice technology 18–20, 167–72, 173, 232, 240–45, 317
voice user interfaces 148

Walmart 137–38
wearable technologies 99, 102, 103, 188
web-drama connectedness 52–53, 118–19, 124, 317
Web 1.0 43
Web 2.0 33, 36, 42, 43, 45
webmasters 34
website analytics 48
websites *10*, 48
  design of 32, 37, 56, 67–68, 145
  functionality of 67
  interactive 27, 28, 146–47
  quality ranking 67–68
  response web design 33, 313
Web3 (semantic web) 33, *34*, 43–46, 249–50, *251*, 314
WeChat 8, 29–30, 52–53, 94, 119, 134, *135*, 317
WeChat Pay 134, *135*
Weibo 52
Wikipedia 33
Woop 235
word-of-mouth recommendations 29–30, 53, *95*, 119
'World of Goods' (McDonalds) 52, 96
World Wide Web 33, 42–46, *248*
  see also Web 2.0; Web3 (semantic web)
'Wrapped' (Spotify) 120

X (Twitter) 33, 45, 113, 114–15, 116, 117, 179
Xiaomi 178, 181, 182
XML 43

Yelp 180
younger consumers 15, 42, 116, 117, 118, 217
  see also Generation Z
YouTube 9, 33, 131, 197

Zara 191–94
zero-party data 49, 317
ZFE-m 234–36
Zinio 28
Zoom 254

Looking for another book?

Explore our award-winning books from global business experts in Human Resources, Learning and Development

Scan the code to browse

www.koganpage.com/hr-learning-development

More books on human resources management from Kogan Page

ISBN: 9781398605978

ISBN: 9781398611719

ISBN: 9781398608870

ISBN: 9781398609006

www.koganpage.com